RIVERFLOW

There are many people and places connected to rivers: fishermen whose livelihood depends on river ecosystems, farms that need irrigation, indigenous groups whose cultures rely on fish and flowing waters, cities whose electricity comes from hydroelectric dams, and citizens who seek wild nature. For all of these people, instream flow is vitally important to where and how they live and work. *Riverflow* reveals the diverse and creative ways people are using the law to restore rivers, from the Columbia, Colorado, Klamath, and Sacramento – San Joaquin watersheds in America, to the watersheds of the Tweed in England and Scotland, the Fraser in Canada, the Saru in Japan, the Nile in North Africa, and the Tigris–Euphrates in the Middle East. *Riverflow* documents that we already have the legal tools to preserve the ecological integrity of our waterways; the question is whether we have the political will to deploy these tools effectively.

Paul Stanton Kibel is Professor at Golden Gate University School of Law and Director of its Center on Urban Environmental Law. He has also taught Water Policy in the West at Berkeley's Goldman School of Public Policy, and Water Law at Berkeley Law School. He is Natural Resource Counsel to the Water and Power Law Group, and his previous books include *The Earth on Trial: Environmental Law on the International Stage* (1998) and *Rivertown: Rethinking Urban Rivers* (2007).

Riverflow

THE RIGHT TO KEEP WATER INSTREAM

PAUL STANTON KIBEL

Golden Gate University School of Law

CAMBRIDGE
UNIVERSITY PRESS

CAMBRIDGE
UNIVERSITY PRESS

University Printing House, Cambridge CB2 8BS, United Kingdom

One Liberty Plaza, 20th Floor, New York, NY 10006, USA

477 Williamstown Road, Port Melbourne, VIC 3207, Australia

314-321, 3rd Floor, Plot 3, Splendor Forum, Jasola District Centre, New Delhi - 110025, India

103 Penang Road, #05-06/07, Visioncrest Commercial, Singapore 238467

Cambridge University Press is part of the University of Cambridge.

It furthers the University's mission by disseminating knowledge in the pursuit of
education, learning and research at the highest international levels of excellence.

www.cambridge.org
Information on this title: www.cambridge.org/9781108927765
DOI: 10.1017/9781108933117

© Paul Kibel 2021

First published 2021
First paperback edition 2021

A catalogue record for this publication is available from the British Library

Library of Congress Cataloging in Publication data
NAMES: Kibel, Paul Stanton, author.
TITLE: Riverflow : the right to keep water instream / Paul Stanton Kibel, Golden Gate
University School of Law.
DESCRIPTION: Cambridge, United Kingdom ; New York, NY : Cambridge University
Press, 2021. | Includes bibliographical references and index.
IDENTIFIERS: LCCN 2020051773 | ISBN 9781108832137 (hardback) | 9781108927765
(paperback) | ISBN 9781108933117 (ebook)
SUBJECTS: LCSH: Water rights. | Water trusts.
CLASSIFICATION: LCC K3496 .K53 2021 | DDC 346.04/32–dc23
LC record available at https://lccn.loc.gov/2020051773

ISBN 978-1-108-83213-7 Hardback
ISBN 978-1-108-92776-5 Paperback

I trace these rivers from the cities to the seas to remind me what I already know.

Frank Turner, *Rivers*

Water is wet. Some water we swim in. Water helps fish swim. Water law people know about water. We have some things to tell. Now you know about water.

Malcolm Solomon Kibel, age 5

Contents

Maps

Foreword: Marching Away from Folly
Felicia Marcus

Professor Paul Stanton Kibel has given us a gift with *Riverflow: The Right to Keep Water Instream*. He has given us the gift of removing any excuse that we lack adequate legal tools to protect our rivers and waterways and restore needed instream flows. *Riverflow* is an antidote to the line often attributed (correctly or incorrectly) to Mark Twain that "whiskey is for drinking and water is for fighting." Professor Kibel makes clear, in a readable and unavoidable way, that the law already provides us with the authority, the means, and the obligation to strike a more ecologically sustainable balance between the instream needs of rivers and the diversion and impoundment of rivers.

For decades, the California State Water Resources Control Board (California Water Board) struggled to make good on its mission of balancing all uses of the waters of the state. During that time, the water wars have raged, punctuated by often illusive moments of progress. During my years as Chair of the California Water Board, we put forth a vision for sharing our waters, with some success and many scars to show for it. During the worst drought in modern times for California (mid-2010s), we exercised our public trust and "waste and unreasonable use" powers in a modest way to deal with the emergency, and did so with a rapidity made possible only during an "emergency." Two decades earlier, the California Water Board had increased flows in the Bay Delta under an agreement leveraged by the threat of tougher standards being imposed by the United States Environmental Protection

* Felicia Marcus, a graduate of New York University Law School, served as a member and then Chair of the California State Water Resources Control Board from 2012 to 2019. She also previously served as Region IX Administrator for the United States Environmental Protection Agency, Executive Vice President for the Trust for Public Land, President of the City of Los Angeles Board of Public Works, and Western Director for the Natural Resources Defense Council.

Agency (USEPA) that followed the state's failure to act over many years on the Bay Delta. That pressure from the USEPA came after litigation under the Clean Water Act to force the agency to do its job. Three decades earlier, during the early 1990s, as a result of a resourceful band of activists and lawyers and their allies hundreds of miles away in Los Angeles, the California Water Board stepped up the restore flows to Mono Lake in the Eastern Sierras to help implement the California Supreme Court's 1983 *National Audubon* case, one of the most beautiful and important legal opinions of the century, after a process that took a decade.

But the politics surrounding water, in California and elsewhere, can be fierce, the gains incremental, and progress agonizingly slow. Philanthropy runs out of patience to support the time-consuming efforts to use the law effectively over time to make progress, even though at times those tools have been the only things that have led to that progress. Too often, the tools sometimes feel seemingly absent or out of reach. But they aren't, and they should not be. This is why Professor's Kibel's book *Riverflow* has come none too soon. For *Riverflow* is not an academically remote piece of scholarship but rather an inventory and revelation of how the law has been and can be deployed to preserve the instream values of rivers.

Historically, the duration of treaties and other agreements often has been described in terms such as "as long as the sun shines, the grass grows, and the rivers flow," "as long as the grass grows and the rivers run," or "As long as the moon shall rise, as long as the rivers flow. As long as the sun will shine, as long as the grass shall grow."[1] The beauty, and the tragedy, of this poetic phrasing was that to many people, not just native people, the notion of rivers running permanently dry was incomprehensible. Though droughts have come, they then have gone.[2] The notion that a river could run dry, whether mighty or a nearby life-giving creek, was a thing that only an early science fiction writer could conjure.[3]

And yet, in the nineteenth, twentieth, and twenty-first centuries, many waters have ceased to flow, so much so that those who remember what was lost are in many cases long gone.[4] Some have been lost through intentional

---

[1] Because so many tribal treaties in the United States and Canada were not honored in many ways, let alone duration, the terms have also come to be seen with an ironic eye by many Native Americans. www.enotes.com/homework-help/explain-significance-phrase-long-grass-grows-water-446554; Johnny Cash, 1964 song "As long as the grass shall grow."

[2] John Steinbeck, *East of Eden*. "During the dry years, the people forgot about the rich years, and when the wet years returned, they lost all memory of the dry years. It was always that way."

[3] Intentional use of water as a tool in conflict or a source of conflict excepted. See Peter Gleick and Jason Morrison, Pacific Institute Water Conflict chronology update, http://worldwater.org/wp-content/uploads/2013/07/ww8-red-water-conflict-chronology-2014.pdf.

[4] With apologies to J. R. R. Tolkien.

effort or international conflict.[5] Others disappeared stealthily, through the slow drip of myriad incremental diversions.

The lush and gigantic Aral Sea in Central Asia was diverted in the twentieth-century Soviet Union for agricultural and industrial development. Dust storms have proliferated, fisheries have been eradicated, and local economies have plummeted. The Mekong River that is the lifeblood of China, Vietnam, Cambodia, Laos, Myanmar, and Thailand has seen massive diversions along its banks, topped by massive dam projects in or funded by China that now have huge stretches of the river running dry, or nearly dry, with droughts exacerbated for millions.[6] Ethiopia and Egypt are fighting over the Grand Ethiopian Renaissance Dam project on the Nile in Ethiopia, upstream of Egypt as well as Sudan. The words on both sides of the controversy over the Grand Ethiopian Renaissance read as existential threat, with Ethiopia claiming the project is essential to counter poverty and famine while Egypt has at times threatened to destroy the project with its air force if Ethiopia proceeds for the same reasons. Here at home, the great Colorado River that winds through seven Western States and upon which 40 million people in the United States depend has been dammed and diverted to the point that the river rarely makes it to the Sea of Cortez, despite international agreements, and has left the Colorado River Delta wetlands starving for water.

In California, the giant Tulare Lake that once covered much of the Central Valley disappeared in the 1930s due to upstream diversions. By the middle of the twentieth century, every major watershed in the Sierra had been dammed and its waters diverted for mining, agriculture, and urban water use. In many cases that water was diverted hundreds of miles away through storage and conveyance projects that are among the public works wonders of the world. What was once the mighty Tulare Lake bed is now a sea of some of the most productive farmland in the world with nary an indication of the lake that was once there.

Along the Southern Sierra in California, cumulative diversions and Friant Dam have dried up 60 miles of the San Joaquin River, which historically ran from its headwaters through the San Joaquin Delta and San Francisco Bay to the Pacific Ocean, until recent attempts to reintroduce flow at times that salmon could return home to spawn. In the Eastern Sierras, Los Angeles had diverted so much water from parts of the Owens Valley that the worst dust

---

[5] See note 3.
[6] 'Our River was like a God': How Dams and China's Might Imperil a River, www.nytimes.com/2019/10/12/world/asia/mekong-river-dams-china.html?action=click&module=RelatedLinks&pgtype=Article or China Limited the Mekong's Flow, Other Countries Suffered a Drought, www.nytimes.com/2020/04/13/world/asia/china-mekong-drought.html.

pollution in the nation existed, and Mono Lake was on the verge of disappearing by the 1970s and 1980s.

Less visible are the diversions that fail to dry a river completely but destroy much of its basic ecological functions. Along the rivers that flow into the San Joaquin-San Francisco Bay and Delta (Bay Delta) in California, as much as 80–90 percent of important river tributaries are diverted at times of year that are critical for salmon and other native species of fish. Fish survival has plummeted, as has a once vibrant fishing industry. There are certainly other factors at play than water diversions, like loss of habitat, invasive species, even global warming, but make no mistake, reduction in water flows at critical times of year is the controlling feature of the problem. Overall, half of the waters that once fed the complex Bay Delta ecosystem are diverted for other human uses, and most of that is diverted through pumps in the middle of the Delta ecosystem in such a way that many species of fish are killed either through passage through the pumps themselves or by being waylaid and tossed around by the power of the pumps' artificially reversed flows in that tidal estuary. Depletion of flows combined with the power of the pumps frequently makes it impossible for species to migrate as they had done for millennia or makes them easier prey for invasive predator species. And, as Professor Kibel documents throughout *Riverflow*, depletion of instream flows leads to slower flows and higher temperatures, which stress native fish species like salmon and steelhead trout to the point of vulnerability or death.

These water projects (the Central Valley Project and the State Water Project) are at the same time the sustainers of a miracle of food production and social and economic urban development that defines modern California and upon which the nation and other nations rely. The projects were built prior to modern environmental laws and our broader societal recognition that the preservation of nature is also in our human interest. They were envisioned and built before we knew we could divert so much in a single lifetime that it would doom species like salmon and delta smelt dependent upon flows. But, now we have that knowledge – so what do we do about it?

As Professor Kibel points out eloquently and clearly in the pages that follow, we are not without legal tools to redress these losses, but we do appear to be without the will to adequately use those tools. As Kibel writes in *Riverflow*, "the policy status quo staggers forward and the gap between policy and science widens." In part, the problem can be laid at the feet of "politics," but what are politics but the struggle between opposing views in society? Part of the problem is a bias toward the "win–lose" or "winner-take-all" mindset that politics seems to reward more often than it should. Part of the challenge is that to act requires the courage to balance competing interests transparently and, with clear respect for science, to make a decision that is not simply one of the choices proposed by competing parties. The decision-makers have to construct the "balanced" answer themselves, knowing that balance is in the eye of the beholder and that they will be sued by those who wanted more for their perceived interest. To paraphrase Phil Isenberg, former Chair of both the Delta Vision Blue Ribbon Task Force and the Delta Stewardship Council, everyone is "for" balance; they just perceive what *they* want as the ideal balance.

Professor Kibel offers a way to use these tools, and to narrow the gap between science and policy – not necessarily to restore all waters to their original pristine shape at enormous cost to the communities and industries dependent upon the diversion of those waters, but in ways that share those waters more equitably between people and fish and wildlife. We rely on these waters for food, for our sense of connection to the earth, and for our shared sense of what it means to be human. That is perhaps one of the most interesting things about both the ancient and more recent sources of law detailed in *Riverflow* – whether old or new, these sources of law require us to use our human skills to balance competing uses, rather than demanding that we simply turn back the clock or defer to the status quo.

After my time in the trenches at the United States Environmental Protection Agency in the 1990s working on a series of water agreements dealing with the Bay Delta, including the much-acclaimed Bay Delta Accord, I left the divisive world of California water to join the Trust for Public Land (TPL). The Bay Delta Accord was the first of many attempts to negotiate a comprehensive approach to balancing instream needs and demand for out-of-stream diversions in the Sacramento River–San Joaquin River watersheds. TPL is a national conservation organization that works to bring together landowners, governmental agencies, communities, environmentalists, and philanthropists to protect wilderness, to restore degraded lands, to build urban parks, and to protect working landscapes. There, I saw myriad breakthroughs happen across the nation each year, as people reached across traditional divides to use practical as well as innovative legal, financing, and public outreach tools to save a place; to secure an agricultural, ranching, or forestry lifestyle while also protecting nature; or to create spaces for people to come together in nature in urban areas. It was refreshing; it was inspiring; it was really hard work, really human work. It involved working to try to find shared interests. It was about people from all of those walks of life seeing if they could come together to make something wonderful happen in their communities by sharing rather than fighting (although the will to do so frequently came after successful fights by others against proposed developments).

After returning to the water world some seven or so years later, to serve first as a member of the Delta Stewardship Council and later Chair of the California Board, I was struck by how much had not changed in California water, and how much more elusive restorative agreements were in water, despite some encouraging efforts pointing the way toward some better balance.[7] I saw that our earlier agreements on the Bay Delta, like the Bay Delta Accord, had not saved the species, and that fish stocks had in fact actually plummeted. I saw many of the same people, speaking past many of the same people, years later, sometimes just louder and slower.

It seemed the story had not proceeded along an arc of progress but instead years of stalemate on Bay Delta action, punctuated by agreements that staunch the bleeding or even appear to make some progress, which are then set back by inaction or delay. Task force reports and plans are written, some quite excellent, but implementation is an entirely different story.[8] As administrations change at whatever level of government, the retrenchment happens, and the sabers rattle anew, and things get set back. Philanthropic funders, tired of never-ending battles and eager to work on other issues, move on to other issues and fail to help those who would stay at a table and hold the line, or are prepared to make use of and effectively deploy the legal sources and tools that Professor Kibel lays out for us in *Riverflow*.

The fundamental historic truth is that the only thing that has yielded progress has been the use, or the threat of the full use, of our legal tools, whether the Clean Water Act, the California Porter–Cologne Act, the federal and state endangered species laws, California Fish and Game Code Section 5937, public trust law, or the prohibition of waste and unreasonable use enshrined in the California Constitution at Article X, Section 2. This history, which is in fact the daylighting of legal precedent, is at the core of Professor Kibel's *Riverflow*.

We tried to use those tools judiciously during the administration of California Governor Jerry Brown (2000–2018) whether in protecting the last important undammed salmon habitat on Mill, Deer, and Antelope Creeks, or in stemming the draining of the Russian River by pumping of interconnected groundwater, so that fish could get between puddles to huddle to survive, or in promoting water conservation, or in making truly painful choices about where to let the water flow during our horrendous drought. We didn't get all of those choices right, but we chose to act rather than to shrink from our responsibility. We moved on a serious effort to share the waters of the Bay Delta systems

7 Delta Vision Blue Ribbon Task Force Report (2008).
8 Delta Vision Blue Ribbon Task Force Report (2008).

between the ecosystem and diverters without being forced by lawsuits or the federal government, which had been the background of past California Water Board efforts. We proposed leaving more water instream for fish and wildlife, an amount that science said would help give the ecosystem a chance to function as an ecosystem, or in the words of one reporter, "let the rivers act as rivers," and did so in a way that sought to balance that against also valuable agricultural and urban use.

We also even offered an olive branch to water users that would let them keep diverting more water if they came together to use that water in a collective and intentional way when the fish most needed it, coupled with habitat restoration that could do more for fish and wildlife than water alone could do but which we had no authority to order.

We lived through the outrage on all sides – that we dared to act, or that we didn't dare enough. We acted on our first part of the plan to restore the lower San Joaquin River, as the settlements we had hoped for made some progress, but not nearly enough to substitute for what we had reasonably proposed. In the year plus that has followed, a new administration – that of California Governor Gavin Newsom – has continued the talks, but whether the California Water Board will act on the rest of the Bay Delta Plan (Sacramento River and Delta proper), and whether any agreements reached will truly be adequate for implementation, is still an open question despite enormous effort.

I firmly believe that if the general public understood what has been lost and what is at stake with our rivers, and if they knew that established tools to help protect our shared natural heritage were not being used, they would support their use. They would demand their use. And there would be more political will to act.

People care about water. They may know it because they love to raft, fish, and experience rivers, rapids, delta, bay, or ocean. Some of them feel grateful for the life-giving force that a river just *is* – whether to fish and wildlife, to the communities along the river, or to those who drink and bathe in a river's waters that have been transported and treated through pipelines and treatment plants along the way. We saw urban California step up and save 24 percent of their water during the last drought to the calls of "we're all in this together," and we saw water agencies put out over half a billion dollars for landscape rebates that were almost instantaneously grabbed up as soon as each tranche was offered. Public opinion polls at the time said that urban residents cared about both the environment and agriculture in holding back on their water use, not just about saving their own local agency's supplies. In my experience, rural residents and people in agriculture also care very deeply about the natural world they live close to.

Many people care about water because of the importance of saving ecosystems generally and want to be on the side of humanity that understands that we have a relationship between the earth, its life-giving waters, and ourselves that we can't totally pinpoint but know is real. It is something of a test of who we are. History and future generations will judge us for whether we could turn the tide and figure out how to restore far more of what we have lost, and whether we can figure out how to live in greater harmony with nature and each other.

As a member of the baby boomer generation in the United States, I know we have failed in some ways thus far on climate change, on keeping enough water instream so that rivers function as rivers, on failing to get basic water for life and sanitation to all people, and on other things even as we have pride for establishing our core environmental laws and regulations.

But I have also seen signs of progress and of hope, whether on experimental restoration of the upper San Joaquin River, the inspiring agreements and progress on removing dams along the Klamath River and other large-scale dam removal projects recently done or in process, or the efforts of seven states in the United States and the federal government and Mexico to send pulse flows of the Colorado River delta.[9] The passage of the Human Right to Water as California state policy and follow-on progress to get safe drinking water to underserved Californians over the past six years is inspirational if far from done. Collaborative efforts to restore floodplains in the Bay Delta for flood control and fish survival and to use rice fields for fish sanctuary hold massive promise. At the local level, efforts to restore functional watersheds for flood control, water supply, water quality, and urban greening are in their heyday, as Los Angeles County passed a $300 million per year measure to capture urban stormwater for resilience and urban greening and the City of Los Angeles has pledged to recycle 100 percent of its wastewater by 2035. In the Bay Area, 9 counties and 100 cities came together in an unprecedented way to vote to spend half a billion dollars and organize themselves together for the purpose of restoring wetlands to protect against the ravages of climate change–induced sea level rise rather than each building piecemeal seawalls that may have held the sea at bay for a while, maybe, but wouldn't add shoreline open space or ecosystem function.

The same is true internationally, as committees come together across five countries (Kazakhstan, Uzbekistan, Tajikistan, Kyrgyzstan, and Turkmenistan) to restore at least some part of the Aral Sea,[10] and as Australia struggles with how

9   www.azcentral.com/in-depth/news/local/arizona-environment/2020/04/19/how-mexicos-dry-colorado-river-delta-being-restored-piece-by-piece/5082051002/.
10 Patrick Walters, *Aral Sea Recovery?*, NATIONAL GEOGRAPHIC (April 22, 2010).

to share the waters of the Murray–Darling Basin between humanity and nature.[11] We are at a turning point, a precipice of choice about who we are. We have the tools, but we need the will to use them in a determined and yet still graceful way.

Barbara Tuchman, the eminent historian, in her book *The March of Folly*, chronicles instances of governments or leaders making really bad choices even when they had all of the facts they needed to do otherwise. She has examples of the French and the United States in Vietnam, of King George III losing the colonies in North America, and assorted other choices that were made despite abundant factual evidence that they were leading to predictably disastrous outcomes. In terms of managing and conserving water resources in general, and preserving necessary instream flows in our rivers in particular, the question is whether we can march away from folly, and whether we can adjust policy to face the facts and honor science.

As Professor Kibel recounts in *Riverflow*, and with particular force in his conclusion on "Policy Disconnected from Science," the signs are all around us, from the near collapse of the once teeming Bay Delta ecosystem to overly optimistic reliance on hatcheries, that there is unfortunately still much folly in the water policy sector. But there are examples from *Riverflow* that show, at times, we are starting to march in the right direction. An example that resonated with me was Professor Kibel's account of how the development of the California Water Board's public trust flow criteria (referred to as the Flow Criteria Report) for the Bay Delta in 2010 eventually led to the California Water Board's adoption of base instream flows for the San Joaquin River tributaries in 2018. Here we had an initial informational process grounded in science that described what the ecosystem needed to survive and improve without reference to balancing. The Flow Criteria Report then served as the foundation for a subsequent regulatory process where the balancing occurred that made tangible progress to benefit instream interests like fisheries while still accounting for those reliant on diversions, captured in a final form amenable not only to direct enforcement but also to adjustment over time. This is a template for what the subheading of *Riverflow* – the right to keep water instream – looks like in action, even though far from done and far from sound-bite simple.

Are we going to be the generation that loses salmon and delta smelt? Are we going to be the generation that sucked our rivers dry? Will we look at the tributaries of California's Bay Delta with regret and longing as so many in

---

[11] Margaret Simons, *Cry Me a River: The Tragedy of the Murray-Darling Basin*, 77 QUARTERLY ESSAY (2020).

Central Asia mourn the passing of the Aral Sea? Will we look at fishermen and women whose livelihood is being snuffed out more and more each year, and sigh with sorrow but go on about our days? Or will we be the generation that figures out how to do something about it? And we must do it not by turning our backs on the good men and women who farm or grow communities with the waters of our rivers but by figuring out a way to break through the fighting words and talking points and legitimate fears on all sides and make those hard choices to achieve a more balanced relationship with nature.

At times, I question whether we can change course. We certainly have the capacity for that kind of leadership, but rising to it seems just out of reach. Because of many people in the conservation, agricultural, urban, and government arenas trying mightily to restore or protect some remnant of "what once was before all who remember are gone," I remain hopeful, energized, and optimistic that we can march in the right direction. At this critical turning point, Professor Kibel's book gives us the toolkit to do so with intelligence, grace, and insight, coupled with the powerful inspiration that these are not new concepts and tools. They are tools that enlightened leaders and civilizations have established and used for centuries. We are the inheritors of this heritage. As Professor Kibel remarks in the first chapter of *Riverflow*,

> [t]he 1983 *National Audubon* decision by the California Supreme Court is therefore not so much the starting point for the recognition of a public right to keep water instream, but is rather simply a reaffirmation of a public right to keep water instream that can be traced to the origins of the United States, and before that to the English common law and Roman law.

We just need to summon the will to use this remarkable inheritance, and use these tools with the balance and tenacity they require. That is no easy task, and not for the faint of heart. But it is essential. Because unless we do, it will get way more uncomfortable when we are left only with regrets for not having acted collaboratively, empathetically, and intelligently when we could have.

Take heart, and read along with *Riverflow*. It reveals how we arrived where we are and helps point toward where we need to go.

Felicia Marcus

Emeryville, California

Acknowledgments

Portions of Chapter 1 (Instream Rights and the Public Trust) were based on material previously published in *The Public Trust Navigates California's Bay Delta*, NATURAL RESOURCES JOURNAL (2011).

Portions of Chapter 2 (Instream Rights and Unreasonable Use) were based on material previously published in *In the Field and In the Stream: California Reasonable Use Law Applied to Water for Agriculture*, MCGEORGE LAW REVIEW (2014).

Portions of Chapter 3 (Instream Rights and Dams) were based on material previously published in *Passage and Flows Considered Anew: Wild Salmon Restoration via Hydro Relicensing*, PUBLIC LAND AND RESOURCES LAW REVIEW (2015).

Portions of Chapter 4 (Instream Rights and Watershed Governance) were based on material previously published in *Truly a Watershed Event: California's Water Board Proposes Base Flows for the San Joaquin River Tributaries*, CALIFORNIA WATER LAW JOURNAL (2016).

Portions of Chapter 5 (Instream Rights as Federal Law Recedes) were based on material previously published in *California Rushes In – Keeping Water Instream for Fisheries Without Federal Law*, 42 WILLIAM AND MARY ENVIRONMENTAL LAW & POLICY REVIEW 477 (2018).

Portions of Chapter 6 (Instream Rights as Water Temperatures Rise) were based on material previously published in *A Salmon Eye Lens on Climate Adaptation*, OCEAN & COASTAL LAW JOURNAL (2013).

Portions of Chapter 7 (Instream Rights as Sea Level Rises) were based on material previously published in *Sea Level Rise, Saltwater Intrusion and Endangered Fisheries: Shifting Baselines for the Bay Delta Conservation Plan*, UC DAVIS ENVIRONS LAW JOURNAL (2015).

Portions of Chapter 8 (Instream Rights and Groundwater Extraction) were based on material previously published in an article (co-authored with Julie Gantenbein) in *Fisheries Reliant on Aquifers: When Groundwater Extraction Depletes Surface Water Flows*, UNIVERSITY OF SAN FRANCISCO LAW REVIEW (2020).

Portions of Chapter 9 (Instream Rights and Old Canals) were based on material previously published in A *Man-Made Waterway Absorbed into the Natural Landscape – Adaptive Reuse of England's Manchester Ship Canal*, a chapter in the book titled ROUTLEDGE HANDBOOK OF URBAN ECOLOGY (Routledge 2020).

Portions of Chapter 10 (Instream Rights and Water as an Investment) were based on material previously published in *Grasp on Water: A Natural Resource That Eludes NAFTA's Notion of Investment*, ECOLOGY LAW QUARTERLY (2007) and Two Rivers Meet: At the Confluence of Crossborder Water Law and Foreign Investment Law (co-author Jon Schutz), chapter in book *Sustainable Development in World Investment Law* (Kluwer 2009).

Portions of Chapter 11 (Instream Rights and International Law) were based on material previously published in *Damage to Fisheries by Dams: The Interplay Between International Water Law and International Fisheries Law*, UCLA JOURNAL OF INTERNATIONAL LAW AND FOREIGN AFFAIRS (2017).

Portions of Chapter 12 (Instream Rights and Irrigation Subsidies) were based on material previously published in *WTO Recourse for Reclamation Irrigation Subsidies: Undermarket Water Prices as Foregone Revenue*, VIRGINIA ENVIRONMENTAL LAW JOURNAL (2014).

Portions of Chapter 13 (Instream Rights and Pacific Salmon) were based on material previously published in *Of Hatcheries and Habitat: Old and New Conservation Assumptions in the Pacific Salmon Treaty*, WASHINGTON JOURNAL OF ENVIRONMENTAL LAW AND POLICY (2020).

Portions of Chapter 14 (Instream Rights and Hatchery Fish) were based on material previously published in *Salmon Lessons for the Delta Smelt: Unjustified Reliance on Hatcheries in the October 2019 USFWS Biological Opinion*, ECOLOGY LAW CURRENTS (2020).

Portions of Chapter 15 (Instream Rights as Indigenous Rights) were based on material previously published in A *Human Face to Instream Flow: Indigenous Rights to Water for Salmon and Fisheries*, EMORY INTERNATIONAL LAW REVIEW (2020).

Introduction

Publicum Ius Aquae

Many people around the world are familiar with the concept of a legal right to use water. That is, the right to divert water out of stream for consumptive use, or the right to use water instream to generate hydropower. This concept of a legal right is private in nature, a right held by the party that uses the water to grow crops, to provide water for domestic use, to operate a hydropower facility on a river. For example, in the American West, such private entitlements to water include riparian surface water rights (which derive from the early English common law) and prior appropriation surface water rights (which emerged after the California gold rush).

Alongside these accepted notions of private rights to water, however, there is an equally long tradition in many countries of a public right to keep water instream – for fisheries, for navigation, for flows to preserve water quality. In the Roman Empire, the Latin term was *publicum ius aquae* (public water right) and was closely related to the status of fish and instream flows as *res communis* (things held/owned in common by the public) under Roman law.[1] Two thousand years ago, as parties pressed their private rights to divert the waters of the Tiber River as it coursed through Rome, such parties were confronted with and restrained by countervailing public rights under *publicum ius aquae* and *res communis* principles to keep water instream. As per the late water law Professor Joseph Sax explains:

> These common things had two special qualities as property. One was that they could not be privately owned, but were common to everybody. The second thing was that they were for common use. Everybody had a right to use them. These common things could not be bought and sold in the ordinary way since they were for everybody's use ... What were those things? The sea and the seashore, and navigable rivers and harbors were the most important things in Roman Law that were common property.[2]

In terms of the recognition of flowing water as *res communis* under Roman law, the following passage from the sixth-century Justinian Institutes is often quoted: "These things are by natural law common to all: air, flowing water, the sea, and consequently the shores of the sea."[3] But as Professors J.B. Ruhl and Thomas A.J. McGinn noted in a recent article, the Justinian Institutes "was an attempt to summarize and synthesize Roman law going back many centuries before their publication."[4] According to Ruhl and McGinn, the oft-quoted passage from the sixth-century Justinian Institutes therefore reflects the writings of earlier Roman jurists, such as Marcian and Gaius, from the second and third centuries, leading Ruhl and McGinn to conclude that, in regard to Roman law public trust principles, "Justinian represents at best the end of the story, if not an entirely new beginning."[5]

In 1215, King John of England signed the Magna Carta, which mandated the removal of fishweirs from rivers throughout England, imposing limits on the Crown's ability to convey property rights to waterways.[6] English common law also added the trustee component to *res communis*, holding that certain common resources were held by the Crown for the benefit of the Crown's subjects. Thus, the English Crown held title to such common property in the capacity of a trustee for the public (citizens), which were the true beneficiaries, thereby imposing traditional trustee fiduciary obligations on the Crown in its management of such property. Moreover, if the Crown improperly administered its trust duties in regard to such public or common property, citizens (as trust beneficiaries) had a legal right to bring an action against the Crown as trustee.

When the English Crown conveyed rights to the land encompassing the thirteen original colonies in North America (that later became the United States of America), the Crown conveyed this land subject to the royal obligation to preserve the colonies' public trust resources for the benefit of the people.[7] With the American Revolution, the royal public trust obligations to the colonies were conveyed to the new state legislatures of each of the former thirteen colonies. The Northwest Ordinance of 1787 then declared that new states were to be subsequently admitted to the United States on "equal footing" with the original thirteen colonies, with the same rights to the tidewaters and the lands under them. The Northwest Ordinance of 1787 further provided: "The navigable waters leading into the Mississippi and St. Lawrence and the carrying places between the same, shall be common highways, and forever free, as well to the inhabitants of said territory as to the citizens of the United States ... without any tax, import or duty therefor." In language strikingly similar to that found in the Northwest Ordinance of 1787, the 1850 Act admitting California to the United States of America provided: "All the navigable waters within the State shall be common highways and forever free, as well as to the inhabitants of such State as to citizens of the United States, without any tax, import or duty thereof."

As Professor Joseph Sax recounts:

> [W]e developed the idea that the states would take over the role that the king had played because, just as the king was the sovereign, the states in America are sovereign. The law of England became the law of America. We imported the Trust idea, but switched the role of the king to the state, and the state became the owner and Trustee for the public ... At the moment of independence for the 13 colonies, and for every subsequent state at the moment of statehood, ownership of all the land beneath tidal and navigable waters, up to the ordinary high-water mark, became the property of the state and subject to the Trust.[8]

So the English common law picked up on the *res communis* principle and retranslated it as the public trust, holding that the Crown (as trustee) held title to certain natural resources in trust for the public. These resources include ensuring sufficient instream water for navigation and fisheries. The English common law concept of the public trust has in turn been recognized in the United States, with (pursuant to the 1892 *Illinois Central Railroad* decision by the United States Supreme Court)[9] state governments taking over from the Crown as trustees.

Outside of the United States, many other former British colonies have also retained the public trust doctrine following their independence from Britain. As Professor Michael Blumm noted in the 2012 article he co-authored with Rachel Guthrie, titled *Internationalizing the Public Trust Doctrine: Natural Law and Constitutional and Statutory Approaches to Fulfilling the Saxion Vision*:

> [T]he public trust doctrine has become internationalized and, in the process, has moved to the forefront of environmental protection in several countries. In India, which has given the public trust doctrine the most detailed judicial consideration of any jurisdiction outside the United States, the doctrine has natural law origins and an extremely broad scope. In Pakistan, the public trust is constitutionally entrenched ... In Kenya, the doctrine provided a remedy for the discharge of raw sewage into the Kiserian River ... In South Africa, the doctrine is of constitutional dimension and at the center of the country's statutes concerning water resources.[10]

In regard to India, Blumm and Guthrie report as follows:

> The Indian public trust doctrine originated in the Supreme Court of India's 1997 decision in *M.C. Mehta v. Kamal Nath*, which involved Span Resort's proposal to dredge, blast and reconstruct the riverbed of the Beas River to redirect the river to avoid flooding that threatened its resort.[11]

The Indian Supreme Court ruled that the lease (from the government to the resort) violated the public trust doctrine. The court said the doctrine was part of Indian law because Indian jurisprudence was inherited from English common law, and prevented the "aesthetic use and the pristine glory of the natural resources, the environment, and the ecosystems of our country ... [from being] eroded for private commercial or any other use unless the courts find its necessary, in good faith, for the public good and the in the public interest to encroach upon the said resources." In a sweeping opinion, the court also adopted wholesale the entirety of American public trust jurisprudence citing both the *Illinois Central Railroad* decision and Professor Sax's article, and ultimately declaring the public trust doctrine to be "the law of the land."[12]

In regard to South Africa, Blumm and Guthrie note as follows:

The National Water Act also devotes considerable attention to the public trust doctrine. In its preamble, the Act recognizes that "water is a natural resource that belongs to all people" and acknowledges that "the National Government's overall responsibility for and authority over the nation's water resources and their use, including the equitable allocation of water for beneficial uses, the redistribution of water and international water matters ... " Section 3 of the Water Act, entitled "Public trusteeship of nation's water resources," established "water is protected, used, developed, conserved, managed and controlled in a sustainable and equitable manner, for the benefit of all persons ... while promoting environmental values." This language clearly incorporates the public trust doctrine into water management in South Africa.[13]

In the United States, the recognition of the ways the public trust provisions of law apply to the maintenance of instream flow were noted by leading water law scholars in a series of influential articles published in the decade from 1970 to 1980. In 1970, Professor Sax published his article, *The Public Doctrine in Natural Resources Law: Effective Judicial Intervention*.[14] In 1979, Professor Dan Tarlock published his article, *The Recognition of Instream Flow Rights: New 'Public' Western Water Rights*.[15] In 1980, Professor Harrison Dunning published his article, *The Significance of California's Public Trust Easement for California Water Rights Law*.[16]

Reflecting and building on the work of Professors Sax, Tarlock, and Dunning, in the California Supreme Court's landmark 1983 decision in *National Audubon Society v. Alpine County Superior Court*, the Court held that the public trust is not subsumed within the state water rights system and continues to impose independent and ongoing obligations on the state to protect public trust resources whenever feasible.[17] The *National Audubon* case ultimately resulted in California's State Water Board imposing modifications to the City of Los Angeles' existing appropriative water rights to reduce diversions from tributaries to Mono Lake in the Eastern Sierras.[18]

When viewed in this historical context, the 1983 *National Audubon* decision by the California Supreme Court is therefore not so much the starting point for the recognition of a public right to keep water instream but is rather simply a reaffirmation of a public right to keep water instream that can be traced to the origins of the United States, and before that to the English common law and Roman law.

Beyond the public trust, California's Constitution and Water Code also contain provisions relating to the reasonable use and waste of water. These provisions of California law provide that the unreasonable and wasteful use or diversion of water is unlawful under state law. California Courts and California's State Water Board have relied on the reasonable use provisions in the California Constitution and the California Water Code in a number of instances to restrict rights of diversion and storage (in dams) and to require sufficient instream flows to maintain fisheries and water quality.

Yet, notwithstanding that public trust and reasonable use provisions have been enforced by courts and relied upon by agencies as legal authority to preserve adequate instream flow, it is worth noting that these provisions are still more often than not referred to as the "public trust doctrine" and the "reasonable use doctrine" rather than as "public trust law" and "reasonable use law." The reasonable use provisions of California law are set forth in Article X of the California Constitution, yet the continued use of the "doctrine" qualifier at times seems to suggest that these reasonable use provisions should perhaps somehow be considered a legal "theory" rather than established law. This treatment and characterization of the requirements and prohibitions of Article X of the California Constitution differs from the way other constitutional provisions are often viewed and discussed.

The Fifth Amendment of the United States Constitution forbids the government from taking private property without paying the owner of the property just compensation. However, we don't speak of the "takings doctrine" but rather of "takings law." The Fifth Amendment of the United States Constitution provides that all citizens are entitled to the equal protection of the law regardless of gender or race. However, we don't speak of the "equal protection doctrine" but rather of "equal protection law." The First Amendment of the United States Constitution protects citizens' right to free speech. However, we don't speak of the "free speech doctrine" but rather of "free speech law."

Is it different to speak of a legal *doctrine* rather than to speak of the *law*? Black's Law Dictionary defines a "doctrine" as "a legal principle that is widely adhered to." Black's Law Dictionary defines "law" as "the body of authoritative grounds for judicial and administrative action." These definitions of "doctrine" and "law" are similar in some respects, but they are not the same. Pursuant to Black's Law Dictionary, the term "law" suggests established enforceable rights, while the term "doctrine" suggests legal principles that are sometimes recognized and followed but sometimes are not.

Posing the question of whether the public trust and reasonable use provisions are the law itself or merely legal doctrines is an apt framework to approach this book. For the chapters in *Riverflow* that follow are an exploration of the extent to which the law now recognizes enforceable public rights to keep water flowing instream, and the relationship of such public instream rights to the private right to divert water out of stream or impound water behind dams.

In Chapter 1, *Instream Rights and the Public Trust*, we consider California's Bay Delta, where fresh water from the Sacramento River and the San Joaquin River meets the salt water from San Francisco Bay. California's Bay Delta has been mired in litigation and political controversy for decades. In the 2009 Delta Reform Act, the California State Water Board was ordered to conduct hearings to establish instream flow criteria to protect public trust fisheries in the Bay Delta. This chapter examines how the statutory deployment of the public trust in the 2009 Delta Reform Act built on the California Supreme Court's 1983 *National Audubon* decision, and details the California State Water Board proceedings leading up to the public trust Delta flow criteria adopted in August 2010.

In Chapter 2, *Instream Rights and Unreasonable Use*, we review the application of the reasonable use provisions of the California Constitution and the California Water Code to out-of-stream diversions of water for agriculture. After noting that there are analogous reasonable use provisions in the water law of other states and other nations, this review highlights that in California, there are separate lines of judicial decisions relating to the application of reasonable use requirements to "in the field" impacts and irrigation practices, and to "in the stream" impacts related to effects of reduced instream flow on fisheries, saltwater intrusion/salinity and water quality. This review also identifies the potential for expanded reliance on reasonable use requirements to improve efficiency and reduce waste in terms of agricultural irrigation and to improve instream conditions for fisheries.

In Chapter 3, *Instream Rights and Dams*, we assess the interplay between the dam relicensing provisions of the Federal Power Act in the United States and efforts to maintain and restore wild salmon stocks in the American West. The provisions of the Federal Power Act provide opportunities for federal and state wildlife agencies to insist upon the installation of fish passage and enhanced downstream releases of water as part of the dam relicensing process. Additionally, the water quality certification provisions of the Clean Water Act provide a mechanism for states to insist on changes to dam operations and downstream releases to ensure consistency with state water quality require-ments, including those requirements related to fisheries. Taken together, these provisions of the Federal Power Act and the Clean Water Act provide a legal basis to insist on changes to how existing dams operate so that such operations are more supportive of wild salmon restoration. This relicensing framework may hold lessons for other nations considering how to regulate dams that are designed to operate over an extended period of time.

In Chapter 4, *Instream Rights and Watershed Governance*, we analyze the 2018 decision by California's State Water Board to require base instream flows for the three main tributaries to the San Joaquin River – the Merced River, the Mokelumne River, and the Tuolumne River. These base flows were devel-oped to improve instream conditions for declining salmon and steelhead trout runs. This chapter explains how these base flows (which were proposed pursuant to the federal Clean Water Act and California's Porter-Cologne Water Quality Act) built on the Bay Delta public trust flow criteria adopted by the State Water Board in 2010. This chapter also discusses proposals to require the development and implementation of watershed plans throughout California. It concludes by noting how these tributary base flows are consistent with the concept of "watershed governance" advocated by John Wesley Powell in the late nineteenth century. Efforts to manage water resources at the watershed level are not unique to California, and may hold lessons for other watersheds such as the Colorado River basin.

In Chapter 5, *Instream Rights as Federal Law Recedes*, we confront the outcome of the November 2016 federal elections in the United States, with the election of Donald Trump as President and a Republican-controlled Congress. These election results meant that federal water law and federal agencies involved in managing water began playing a reduced role in ensuring that sufficient water is left instream to support fisheries. Faced with this outcome, stakeholders interested in maintaining such instream flows for fisheries took stock of the provisions of California water law that could be relied upon, independent of federal law and federal agencies, to preserve such flows. This chapter also discusses efforts by Congress to preempt such reliance on California water law, and how such reliance on California water law relates to larger debates about the role of "progressive federalism" following the November 2016 federal elections. It also notes how the problem of upstream diversions in the Tigris River–Euphrates River basin in Iraq, Syria, and Turkey are analogous to the problems in California resulting from upstream diversions.

In Chapter 6, *Instream Rights as Water Temperatures Rise*, we survey the law and policy framework for whether cold-water fisheries, such as salmon and steelhead trout, will be able to adapt to rising instream temperatures that will result from climate change. Salmon and steelhead are best suited to water temperatures at or below 55 degrees (Fahrenheit). In the range of 55–60 degrees (Fahrenheit), these fisheries begin to suffer reduced health and reproductive success, and above 60 degrees (Fahrenheit) they are generally unable to survive. There are recognized policies to assist salmon and steelhead in this transition, from additional releases of cooler water from upstream reservoirs behind dams, to the removal of dams or installation of fish passage features to allow fish to reach cooler waters in the upper reaches of watersheds, to enhanced shading of streams where spawning occurs. There are a number of federal and California laws that are poised to play a more meaningful role in helping cold-water fisheries adapt to climate change by mandating the implementation of such climate adaptation policies – the federal Endangered Species Act, the National Environmental Policy Act, the California Environmental Quality Act (CEQA) – but it remains to be seen whether these laws will be interpreted and deployed to do so. These adaptation efforts in California and the United States may be of interest to other nations with salmon stocks at risk from global warming.

In Chapter 7, *Instream Rights as Sea Levels Rise*, we focus on whether existing environmental impact assessment laws, such as the CEQA, are able to address the ways that climate change will alter the baseline conditions against which proposed projects will operate. The chapter presents a case study of California's proposed Bay Delta Conservation Project (BDCP), which later morphed into what was known as the California WaterFix and (under Governor Newsome of California) is now being referred to as the Delta Conveyance Facility. The BDCP/California WaterFix/Delta Conveyance Facility proposes, among other things, to allow potential increased diversions of fresh water from the Sacramento River–San Joaquin River watershed. CEQA analysis of the project's impacts on fisheries was premised on current saltwater intrusion levels, yet it is expected that climate change-induced sea level rise will significantly increase saltwater intrusion and therefore increase adverse impacts on fisheries during the lifetime of the project. This case study suggests that the use of future baseline conditions in environmental impact assessments may be needed to adequately analyze and mitigate climate-change related effects such as sea level rise. The use of such future baselines could also be used in environmental impact assessment laws outside the United States.

In Chapter 8, *Instream Rights and Groundwater Extraction*, we investigate how the law addresses surface waters that are interconnected to groundwater, and the ways that groundwater extraction can reduce instream surface flows and impact fisheries. In California, the most recent legal effort to deal with this interconnection comes in the form of the 2014 Sustainable Groundwater Management Act (SGMA). The Sustainable Groundwater Management Act calls for the development of basin-specific groundwater plans that are designed to avoid certain specified undesirable results associated with groundwater pumping, including the depletion of surface water flows. This chapter identifies how SGMA's regulatory framework presents an opportunity to better manage groundwater extraction to protect the instream flows needed to maintain healthy fisheries. Other countries, such as Australia, are also addressing the impacts of groundwater pumping on surface flows and fisheries and may benefit from studying SGMA's approach.

In Chapter 9, *Instream Rights and Old Canals*, we take stock of the changing nature of historic man-made shipping waterways such as the Erie Canal in New York and the Manchester Ship Canal in England. Many older canals are too shallow and too narrow to handle today's larger commercial container ships but are being repurposed for recreational boating, as well as a setting for canal-side parks and trails. This transition not only involves man-made navigational structures being absorbed into the natural landscape, and viewed more as rivers, but also citizens reclaiming private space as public environmental amenities. Although some of these canals may be managed and operated by private companies, the waters and adjacent lands of these canals are increasingly perceived and valued as public blue-green open space. The chapter places the experience with the Manchester Ship Canal in the context of other man-made (or altered) watercourse such as the Columbia Slough in Portland, Oregon and the Los Angeles River in California.

In Chapter 10, *Instream Rights and Water as an Investment*, we turn our attention to how the investor protection provisions of the North American Free Trade Agreement (NAFTA) apply to water. Chapter 11 of NAFTA sets forth a mechanism for investors to bring a claim against the nations that are parties to the agreement – Canada, Mexico, and the United States – when they believe the government has taken actions "tantamount to the expropriation" of private property. Irrigation districts from the state of Texas brought a claim against Mexico pursuant to NAFTA Chapter 11 alleging interference with purported rights to divert and use the waters of the Rio Grande. The case involved provisions of the 1944 Waters Treaty between Mexico and the United

States (which allocates the waters of the Rio Grande between the two nations), which raised the question of the relationship between international investment law and international water law. This chapter offers a case study of the claims presented by the Texas irrigation districts, the defenses and responses presented by Mexico to these claims, and the NAFTA dispute panel's ultimate resolution of the controversy. It also notes how similar disputes may arise in North Africa and South America, where the relationship between international water law treaties and international investor protection treaties remains to be clarified.

In Chapter 11, *Instream Rights and International Law*, we look at how damage to fisheries caused by dams is addressed under several sources of international law, including international fisheries law, international water law, and international environmental impact assessment law. Among the issues addressed by these international law sources are the rights involved when fisheries serve "vital human needs" and whether there are ongoing obligations under international law to monitor the impacts on fisheries following construction of dams and (based on such monitoring) to modify the operations of such dams to mitigate documented adverse effects on fisheries.

In Chapter 12, *Instream Rights and Irrigation Subsidies*, we evaluate the extent to which the subsidization of irrigation water by the United States Bureau of Reclamation (Reclamation) implicates international trade rules. When Reclamation subsidizes the costs of providing fresh water for irrigation in agricultural production, such subsidization can result in tiered water pricing. With tiered pricing, farms pay the government less per unit than other water users. This tiered pricing can distort the water marketplace in a manner that encourages wasteful irrigation practices and leaves insufficient water instream for fisheries. The 1994 World Trade Organization Agreement on Subsidies and Countervailing Measures (WTO Subsidies Agreement) provides that one WTO member country may impose countervailing measures against another WTO member country that makes a "financial contribution" that is specific to "certain enterprises." The WTO Subsidies Agreement further provides that "government revenue . . . otherwise due [that] is forgone" can qualify as a "financial contribution" and that governments must be paid "adequate remuneration" for goods provided. Chapter 10 assesses the potential applicability of the WTO Subsidies Agreement's foregone revenue and adequate remuneration provisions to Reclamation irrigation subsidies. This chapter's analysis may also be applicable to other countries, such as Brazil, Japan, and India that help subsidize irrigation for domestic farmers for crops that are then exported.

In Chapter 13, *Instream Rights and Pacific Salmon*, we examine the 1985 Pacific Salmon Treaty between Canada and the United States, which was negotiated to deal with evidence that Pacific salmon stocks originating in Canada and United States were in decline. The Pacific Salmon Treaty sought to establish total annual fishing limits for Canadian and the United States fishing fleets based on forecasts of the total abundance of Pacific salmon. As the Pacific Salmon Treaty has been implemented, however, there has been a reoccurring pattern of annual abundance forecasts overestimating the actual abundance of salmon stocks. The discrepancies between Pacific Salmon Treaty abundance forecasts and actual reported abundance levels appear to be due in part to a conservation model that fails to take proper account of the differences and relationship between wild salmon and salmon artificially propagated in hatcheries. Recent amendments to the Pacific Salmon Treaty, which went into effect in 2019, provide a potential mechanism to bring the conservation of wild salmon stocks and their habitat into the Pacific Salmon Treaty's abundance forecasting model. And improvement in salmon habitat, on a functional level, means ensuring adequate instream flows and improving upstream and downstream passage. These hatchery and habitat issues under the Pacific Salmon Treaty (between Canada and the United States) may be pertinent to other bilateral salmon conservation and management regimes, such as the regime between Japan and Russia.

In Chapter 14, on *Instream Rights and Hatchery Fish*, the topic of fish hatcheries (introduced in Chapter 13) is explored in the context of delta smelt. The delta smelt is a fish species found only in the brackish waters of the Bay Delta in California, and with a limited ability to tolerate waters with high salinity. The species is presently facing potential extinction and is listed under the Endangered Species Act, where for the past decade efforts have focused on increasing instream freshwater flow into the Bay Delta to reduce the salinity levels caused by seawater intrusion. In 2019, the federal government proposed shifting the focus of delta smelt restoration from efforts to reduce salinity through instream flows to developing a new hatchery program to supplement dwindling wild delta smelt stocks. This chapter considers the new hatchery-reliant approach for delta smelt in the context of the previous experience with hatchery-reliant salmon restoration (discussed in more detail in Chapter 13), and in the context of emerging science about the anticipated impacts of introducing hatchery delta smelt into the wild.

In Chapter 15, *Instream Rights as Indigenous Rights*, we venture into the realm of human rights. There are many indigenous communities in the United States whose religion, rituals, and identity are bound up with salmon – such as the Yakima Nation in the Columbia River basin and the Karuk Nation in the Klamath River basin. There are also indigenous communities outside of the United States with deep ties to salmon – including First Nations on Vancouver Island in Canada's British Columbia, the Itelman ethnic group in Russia's Kamchatka Peninsula, and the Ainu people on Japan's Saru River. This chapter looks at sources of domestic and international law, including the 1855 Stevens Treaties between tribes and the United States and declarations and covenants adopted by the United Nations, which indigenous communities have sought to rely on to preserve salmon by preserving the instream flows that sustain salmon. This analysis reveals the ways that indigenous rights can frame how we interpret other sources of law affecting instream flow and fisheries like environmental impact assessment laws and the public trust.

The book's conclusion, *Policy Disconnected from Science*, highlights a persistent and fundamental theme in the preceding chapters' analysis – the frequent nonalignment between science and policy in the water sector. There are many examples where there is now strong scientific consensus as to the severity and cause of water resource degradation, such as the impact of hatcheries on salmon and delta smelt stocks, such as seawater intrusion resulting from excessive upstream diversions of rivers, such as the impacts of reduced instream flow on maintaining cooler water temperatures needed by cold-water fisheries, such as the permanent loss of water to basins due to high evapotranspiration rates for irrigation. In these situations, the strong scientific consensus often points to the necessary policy solutions, yet these necessary policy solutions often present an acute economic threat to certain stakeholders whose interests are aligned with the status quo policy frame- work. So, predictably, such stakeholders work to cast doubt on the scientific consensus regarding the severity and causes of underlying problems in the water sector in an effort to prevent the adoption and implementation of policies that are responsive to these problems. That is, great political and legal effort is put in by certain stakeholders to perpetuate the disconnect between science and policy, often by asserting that additional studies need to be undertaken before policy action is taken. A sharper understanding of this dynamic is an essential starting point to crafting effective remedies to coun- ter it.

As the material in *Riverflow* suggests, the day may soon be near when we can stop referring to the public trust and reasonable use provisions of law as "doctrines" and simply acknowledge them as enforceable public rights to keep flowing water instream, as "authoritative grounds for judicial and admin- istrative action" per Black's Law Dictionary. Alongside the public trust and reasonable use provisions of law, the chapters in *Riverflow* reveal that the right to keep water instream is also grounded in provisions in the Endangered Species Act, Clean Water Act, Federal Power Act, National Environmental Policy Act, 1855 Stevens Treaties with Native American tribes, CEQA, and California Fish and Game Code (in the United States). Beyond the United States, this right is grounded in the National Water Act (in South Africa), Japanese Constitution (in Japan), the World Bank's Environmental Assessment Policy, international water law, international fisheries law, international environmental impact assessment law, WTO subsidy rules, the Canada–United States Pacific Salmon Treaty and United Nations declarations and covenants recognizing indigenous rights. In today's world, these sources of law are the practical means by which we can give substance and effect to *publicum ius aquae*.

Paul Stanton Kibel
North Berkeley, California
May 2020

Notes

1. Joseph Sax, *Introduction to the Public Trust Doctrine*, in proceedings of 1996 Public Trust Workshop (organized by the National Instream Flow Program).
2. Joseph Sax, *Introduction to the Public Trust Doctrine*, in proceedings of 1996 Public Trust Workshop (organized by the National Instream Flow Program).
3. J.B. Ruhl & Thomas A.J. McGinn, *The Roman Public Trust Doctrine: What Was It and Does It Support an Atmospheric Trust?* 47 *Ecology Law Quarterly* 1 (2020) at 14.
4. J.B. Ruhl & Thomas A.J. McGinn, *The Roman Public Trust Doctrine: What Was It and Does It Support an Atmospheric Trust?* 47 *Ecology Law Quarterly* 1 (2020) at 5.
5. J.B. Ruhl & Thomas A.J. McGinn, *The Roman Public Trust Doctrine: What Was It and Does It Support an Atmospheric Trust?* 47 *Ecology Law Quarterly* 1 (2020) at 47.
6. Timothy Mulvaney, *Instream Flows and the Public Trust*, 22 *Tulane Environmental Law Journal* 315, 31 (1999).
7. Timothy Mulvaney, *Instream Flows and the Public Trust*, 22 *Tulane Environmental Law Journal* 315, 346–347 (1999).
8. Joseph Sax, *Introduction to the Public Trust Doctrine*, in proceedings of 1996 Public Trust Workshop (organized by the National Instream Flow Program).
9. 146 U.S. 387 (1892).

10. Michael C. Blumm & Rachel D. Guthrie, *Internationalizing the Public Trust Doctrine: Natural Law and Constitutional and Statutory Approaches to Fulfilling the Saxion Vision*, 45 U.C. Davis Law Review 741 (2012).
11. Michael C. Blumm & Rachel D. Guthrie, *Internationalizing the Public Trust Doctrine: Natural Law and Constitutional and Statutory Approaches to Fulfilling the Saxion Vision*, 45 U.C. Davis Law Review 741 (2012) at 761.
12. Michael C. Blumm & Rachel D. Guthrie, *Internationalizing the Public Trust Doctrine: Natural Law and Constitutional and Statutory Approaches to Fulfilling the Saxion Vision*, 45 U.C. Davis Law Review 741 (2012) at 761.
13. Michael C. Blumm & Rachel D. Guthrie, *Internationalizing the Public Trust Doctrine: Natural Law and Constitutional and Statutory Approaches to Fulfilling the Saxion Vision*, 45 U.C. Davis Law Review 741 (2012) at 790–791.
14. Joseph Sax, *The Public Trust Doctrine in Natural Resource Law: Effective Judicial Intervention*, 68 Michigan Law Review 473 (1970).
15. Dan Tarlock, *The Recognition of Instream Flow Rights; New 'Public' Western Water Rights*, 25 Rocky Mountain Mineral Law Institute 24 (1979).
16. Harrison Dunning, *The Significance of California's Public Trust Easement for California Water Rights Law*, 14 U.C. Davis Law Review 357 (1980).
17. 658 P.2d 709 (Cal. 1983).
18. Paul Stanton Kibel, *The Public Trust Navigates California's Bay Delta*, 51 Natural Resources Journal 35 (2011).

1

Instream Rights and the Public Trust

As legal creatures go, the public trust is an odd duck. Public trust principles are often echoed in constitutional provisions, but constitutions are often not the source of the public trust. Statutory provisions often reference the public trust, but its legal foundation is not found in such statutes. The public trust has been characterized as a property interest, but one that is not held by any particular entity.

The public trust is also now a legal concept that continues to gain broader acceptance internationally. As noted in the Introduction to this book, variations of the public trust have now been recognized in such countries as India, Kenya, and South Africa.[1] Given that the origins of the public trust can be traced back to the English common law, it is perhaps not surprising that it has often been given a positive reception in many of England's former colonies (such as India, Kenya, South Africa, and the United States), which are the inheritors of this tradition.

In California, a comprehensive legal elucidation of the public trust was set forth in the California Supreme Court's 1983 decision in *National Audubon Society* v. *Superior Court* (*National Audubon*).[2] This case centered on whether the California State Water Resources Control Board (State Water Board) was required to consider modification of previously issued water diversion rights granted to the City of Los Angeles in light of evidence of the dire impacts of such diversions on instream public trust resources. The instream public resources involved in the litigation were Mono Lake and its tributary creeks in the Eastern Sierras.

In *National Audubon*, the California Supreme Court held that the public trust imposes a duty of "continuing supervision" on trustee agencies to ensure that public trust resources are protected whenever feasible and that the State Water Board had breached this duty by failing to consider impacts on instream public trust resources both at the time the water diversion rights were granted

MAP 1.1 Map of San Francisco Bay Delta, with the convergence of Sacramento
and San Joaquin Rivers *(source: ResearchGate)*

and subsequent to such issuance. The holding in *National Audubon* eventually resulted in the State Water Board's 1994 modification of the previously
issued water diversion licenses to secure additional instream flows in Mono
Lake's tributaries and to restore elevation levels and reduce salinity levels in
Mono Lake.

As a result of California legislation signed into law in November 2009, the
public trust was again at the center of competing claims to the state's instream
resources. Section 85086 of the 2009 Sacramento–San Joaquin Delta Reform
Act (2009 Delta Reform Act) ordered the State Water Board to conduct
proceedings to "develop new flow criteria for the Delta ecosystem necessary
to protect public trust resources." The Sacramento–San Joaquin Delta (Bay
Delta) is where the fresh water of the Sacramento River and the San Joaquin

River converges and flows down to meet the salt water that enters through San Francisco Bay and the Carquinez Strait. The Bay Delta is the water diversion hub for California's two largest water distribution systems – the federal Central Valley Project and the State Water Project – that collectively provide irrigation to over 4.5 million acres of farmland and drinking water to over 20 million residents. It is also the largest estuary on the West Coast and a critical ecological resource, serving as fisheries habitat for delta smelt, steelhead trout, and salmon.

The California legislature's deployment of the public trust in the 2009 Delta Reform Act is both innovative and controversial, and merits careful study by other states and countries attempting to more effectively address the problem of inadequate freshwater instream flows.

A TWO-STEP METHODOLOGY

Two important early judicial precedents to the 1983 *National Audubon* decision by the California Supreme Court were the 1892 decision in *Illinois Railroad Company* v. *State of Illinois* (*Illinois Central*)[3] and the 1913 decision in *People* v. *California Fish Company* (*California Fish Company*).[4]

In *Illinois Central*, the Illinois state legislature had granted a railroad fee title to nearly the entire Lake Michigan waterfront in the city of Chicago. The United States Supreme Court found that such a conveyance was inconsistent with the state of Illinois' public trust obligations, explaining: "The State can no more abdicate its trust over the property in which the whole people are interested, like navigable waters and the soils under them, than it can abdicate its police powers."[5]

In *California Fish Company*, the California Supreme Court held that government conveyances of interests in public trust resources were "impressed with the public trust." The litigation in *California Fish Company* involved the state's grant of certain lands submerged beneath San Francisco Bay. The California Supreme Court did not void the grant outright but instead clarified that the "title to the soil" is "subject to the public right of navigation" in the waters above such submerged lands.[6]

In terms of the California Supreme Court's *National Audubon* decision on Mono Lake, there are two unique ecological conditions that characterize this water body. First, the waters in Mono Lake are so saline that the only fish and insects that populate it are the Mono Lake brine shrimp and the Mono Lake alkali fly. Second, there were two natural islands in the lake – Negit Island and Paoha Island. These two islands were home to a colony of California gulls representing 85 percent of the California gull breeding population.

In 1940, the California Division of Water Resources, a predecessor agency to the State Water Board, issued appropriative water right permits to the City of Los Angeles Department of Water and Power (LADWP) to divert nearly the entire flow of creeks that are tributary to Mono Lake. As the diversions of the tributary creeks accelerated in the 1970s, the level of Mono Lake dropped steadily. As its level fell, the waters of Mono Lake became increasingly saline so that brine shrimp and alkali fly populations began to decline. The drop in lake level also caused a land bridge to form between Negit Island and the lakeshore, providing coyotes with access to the California gull colonies.

In *National Audubon*, relying on *Illinois Central* and *California Fish Company*, the California Supreme Court issued the following four holdings in connection with the public trust: (1) that the power of state agencies to grant licenses for water diversion is conditioned on the affirmative duty of the state of California to consider the public trust in the allocation of water resources and to protect public trust uses whenever possible; (2) that this affirmative duty imposes a "continuing" obligation of supervision (extending beyond when the appropriative water diversion licenses are initially issued) to ensure that the exercise of such licenses provides proper protection of public trust resources; (3) that the California Division of Water Resources had not initially fulfilled its public trust obligation by approving LADWP's application to divert water from the Mono Lake tributaries without first assessing the impact of such proposed diversion on Mono Lake's public trust resources and uses; and (4) that because the public trust is a "continuing" obligation the State Water Board must now review LADWP's diversion licenses to take proper account of the state's public trust obligations.

In its *National Audubon* decision, the California Supreme Court stopped short of itself determining the specific lake elevation levels for Mono Lake that would comport with public trust requirements, and also stopped short of itself adopting specific instream flow criteria for Mono Lake's tributary creeks. Instead, the California Supreme Court opted to provide the State Water Board with an initial opportunity to craft this more specific instream flow and lake-level criteria. In response to the *National Audubon* decision, in 1994, the State Water Board issued Decision 1631, which established a "two-step" public trust methodology to implement the *National Audubon* holding.[7]

In the first step of its public trust analysis, the State Water Board would determine what levels of instream flow and lake elevation were needed to fully protect the public trust resources at issue. In the second step of its public trust analysis, the State Water Board would evaluate the extent to which the measures required to achieve full protection of public trust resources were "feasible."

Turning to the first step of its two-step public trust analysis, Decision 1631 concluded that a lake level of 6,384 feet would protect the gulls from the coyote access to Negit Island by assuring inundation of the land bridge between Negit Island and the shore, and that a lake level at or near 6,390 feet will restore salinity levels to maintain the aquatic productivity of the lake in good condition.

After completing the first phase of its public trust analysis, the State Water Board then turned to the second "feasibility" step of its two-step public trust methodology. In considering the question of feasibility of reducing LADWP's diversions of Mono Lake's tributary creeks, Decision 1631 evaluated LADWP's water supply system as a whole, taking into account such aspects as opportunities for LADWP to improve water conservation and water reclamation, and reducing the costs of replacing water diversions to protect public trust resources. The State Water Board determined that, during the initial twenty-year period to restore Mono Lake's elevation level, protection of public trust resources would reduce LADWP's Mono Lake tributary export by approximately 32,200 AF per year.

Based on its assessment of LADWP's water supply as a whole, Decision 1631 found that the estimated additional water supply costs to LADWP did not "make it infeasible to protect public trust resources in the Mono Basin in accordance with the terms of this decision."[8]

It should be noted that, in the course of the State Water Board Mono Lake hearings, LADWP resisted the two-phased public trust methodology adopted by the State Water Board in Decision 1631. As California water policy specialist Cynthia Koehler notes:

> Despite the strong wording of *National Audubon*, it was not certain that the Water Board would start from the premise that its first duty was to protect the Mono Basin . . .. Indeed, LADWP argue strenuously that the Board should first determine LADWP's optimal water needs, and then craft the public trust protections so as to avoid harm to water diverters. This proposed interpretation would have stood National Audubon on its head . . .. The Water Board prudently declined this invitation.[9]

As detailed later, the public trust provisions in California's 2009 Delta Reform Act are rooted in the two-step public trust instream flow methodology employed by the State Water Board in Decision 1631 on Mono Lake.

DECADES OF DISPUTE

A full account of the Bay Delta water resource battles in recent decades is beyond the scope of this chapter. However, a general sense of the key themes, stakeholders, and laws involved is needed to understand the frustrations and objectives that led to the inclusion in the California 2009 Delta Reform Act of statutory provisions mandating that the State Water Board conduct public trust proceedings to establish Delta flow criteria.

In terms of the main water diversion infrastructure and water diversion operations pertaining to the Delta, much of this infrastructure and these operations relate to the federal Central Valley Project (operated by the federal Bureau of Reclamation) and California's State Water Project (operated by the California Department of Water Resources).

The federal Central Valley Project was authorized in the 1930s primarily to provide irrigation to farms in California's Central Valley (which stretches north–south from Redding to Bakersfield). The bulk of Central Valley Project infrastructure was constructed in the 1940s and the 1950s, and includes Shasta Dam on the Sacramento River (north of the City of Redding) and Friant Dam on the San Joaquin River (near the City of Fresno) and extensive pumping facilities in the Bay Delta (near the City of Tracy).

California's State Water Project was authorized in the late 1950s primarily to provide water supply for municipal urban use, particularly for growing cities in central and southern California. The bulk of State Water Project infrastructure was constructed in the 1960s and the early 1970s, and includes Oroville Dam (on the Feather River, the largest tributary to the Sacramento River) and extensive pumping facilities in the Bay Delta (near Tracy).

In a 2001 law review article, Patrick Wright, a veteran of Bay Delta water allocation disputes and a former senior California water policy advisor to both the US Environmental Protection Agency and the governor of California, observed:

> For the previous two decades, water planning and politics have been charac-terized by conflict rather than cooperation. Each of the major interest groups have been powerful enough to block each other, in court or at the ballot box, but none have been powerful enough to enact their own agenda. Environmental groups, for example, have been successful in blocking new reservoirs, but unable to stop increased diversions from the Delta that have contributed to listings of several fish species under the federal Endangered Species Act .... [T]he resulting stalemate has prevented progress in either restoring the San Francisco Bay Delta or improving the state's water supply reliability.[10]

During the late 1990s, under the leadership of California's Republican Governor Pete Wilson and President Clinton's Interior Department Secretary, Bruce Babbitt, a comprehensive set of policies and programmatic

priorities were developed pursuant to what became known as the CALFED
Bay Delta Program to help better integrate environmental restoration and water
supply objectives in the Bay Delta. The more cooperative CALFED Bay Delta
process began to fracture and unravel in the mid-2000s, however, and litigation
under the federal Endangered Species Act (ESA) took center stage. In 2004, the
federal National Marine Fisheries Service (NMFS) adopted a biological opinion pursuant to the ESA in connection with a proposed plan for joint operation
of the Bay Delta diversion pumps by the federal Central Valley Project and the
State Water Project. In 2008, a federal district court invalidated NMFS' 2004
ESA Biological Opinion due to the absence of evidence to support the findings
that the proposed diversion pumping adequately protected the endangered
fisheries such as salmon, steelhead trout, and smelt.

In January 2008, Governor Schwarzenegger's Delta Vision Blue Ribbon
Task Force released its report *Our Vision for 'the California Delta'*. This report
sought to articulate a common policy consensus between those interests
pressing for continued water diversions from the Bay Delta and those interests
seeking to curtail such diversions to restore the Bay Delta's fisheries. *Our
Vision for 'the California Delta'* noted:

> Public trust principles, well established in the American legal system with
> roots back to England and parallel principles in other legal systems, provide
> a way to frame decisions about the use of water in the Delta and the Delta
> watershed. In our legal system, water is not owned by any user, but the State of
> California and public retain ownership. Users gain the right to use water in
> various ways (riparian, appropriative, etc.) but those rights are conditional as
> stated both in the term reasonable use and by the underlying public trust for
> protection of the resource. Public trust principles should provide an ethic and
> foundation for public policy making regarding water resources in all of
> California and are especially relevant and important in the Delta."

The Delta Vision Blue Ribbon Task Force's 2008 observations about the
potential role of the public trust in Bay Delta water policy making would
soon find expression in the provisions of California's 2009 Delta
Reform Act.

STATE WATER BOARD PROCEEDINGS

The 2009 Delta Reform Act added section 85086 to the California Water
Code, which provides:

> [T]he board shall, pursuant to its public trust obligations, develop new flow
> criteria for the Delta ecosystem necessary to protect public trust resources. In

carrying out this section, the board shall review existing water quality object-ives and use the best available scientific information. The flow criteria for the Delta ecosystem shall include the volume, quality, and timing of water necessary for the Delta ecosystem under different conditions. The flow criteria shall be developed in a public process by the board within nine months of the enactment of this division.

Significantly, section 85086 also specified that the State Water Board public trust Delta flow criteria proceedings were "informational proceedings" that would not be considered "pre-decisional" in terms of any subsequent board actions. The statutory language in section 85086 therefore makes clear that, unlike State Water Board water right hearings such as the one that resulted in Decision 1631 for Mono Lake and its tributaries, the Delta flow criteria established pursuant to section 85056 would not by themselves result in any direct modification of existing California water diversion rights.

Section 85086's intentional statutory bifurcation of the two-phased public trust analysis for instream water resources makes sense, as the first phase of the public trust analysis is essentially a scientific inquiry while the second phase of the public trust analysis is an inquiry that inherently involves political and economic considerations. Section 85086, by its very design, seeks to preserve the integrity of the State Water Board's science-based findings regarding Delta flow criteria by expressly guaranteeing that water rights holders will have subsequent and separate opportunities to present evidence regarding the economic impacts of reduced diversions before such Delta flow criteria are relied upon to modify existing water rights.

Two main points of contention surfaced in the spring 2010 comments submitted to the State Water Board in connection with section 85086: (1) economic feasibility of potential Delta outflow criteria; and (2) qualitative versus quantitative flow criteria.

On the first point of contention (regarding economic feasibility), many Bay Delta water diverters submitted comments proposing that the State Water Board take into account such diverters' economic reliance on Bay Delta diversions in developing public trust Delta flow criteria. For instance, in a comment letter to the State Water Board, the California Department of Water Resources (DWR) stated:

> The [Delta Reform] Act requires the State Water Board to "develop new flow criteria for the Del ta ecosystem necessary to protect public trust resources" ... DWR believes that if this mandate is to be achieved, the Board must develop the Delta flow criteria thro ugh a process that balances the benefits and costs to other beneficial uses of water and public trust resources.[12]

The California DWR, in a separate comment letter, expanded on this theme:

> The reasonable level of protection for a given use can only be defined in reference to the costs it imposes upon other uses. When a particular level of protection is advocated for a given use, the first question that should be asked is, what are the costs of that level of protection on other uses. Parties and interests will in and recommend various levels of protection for the public trust resources. However, it is only after the Board has considered all of those interests and uses, and after it has balanced them and made a reasonable allocation of water among them, that we can discover the level of protection to which any given use, or resource, is entitled.[13]

The approach recommended by the California DWR, which called for evaluation of second-phase "feasibility" consideration in the context of the section 85085-mandated public trust Delta flow criteria proceedings, was resisted by environmental conservation and fishery stakeholders.

As another example, the comment letter submitted by Environmental Defense Fund placed the section 85056 public trust Delta flow criteria proceedings in the context of the two-phased public trust analysis previously established in State Water Board Decision 1631:

> At this stage the only "balancing" allowed is that between competing trust uses themselves ... This is how the State Board proceeded in the Mono Lake case when the courts handed the matter back to it for application of the court's ruling. The SWRCB's initial analysis addressed the various trust resources of the Mono Basin and the water requirements necessary to ensure the future sustainability of those resources .... The SWRCB's second step is to turn to the question of whether it is "feasible" to provide the water resources necessary to protect the trust values at issue, or whether accepting harm to those resources rises to the level of "practical necessity."[14]

On the second point of contention (regarding qualitative versus quantitative Delta outflow criteria), some water users and water project operators argued that, due to scientific certainty, the public trust Delta flow criteria developed by the State Water Board should be limited to "narrative" flow criteria and should not include quantitative "numeric" flow criteria. This position was advocated in the comment letter submitted jointly by the San Luis and Delta–Mendota Water Authority, State Water Contractors, Westlands Water District, Santa Clara Valley Water District, Kern County Water Agency, and Metropolitan Water District of Southern California, which suggested:

The current state of the science clearly demonstrates numeric flow criteria cannot be properly established until flow is studied in a proper context that analyzes the ecological services it provides, and it is determined that flow is the proper mechanism to provide those services ... [G]iven scientific uncertainties ... the State Water Board cannot, at this time, reach any final quantitative conclusion on flow needs.[15]

Environmental conservation and fishery organizations instead proposed that the State Water Board develop quantitative instream flow criteria pursuant to section 85086 of the 2009 Delta Reform Act. More specifically, detailed and numerically specific proposed Delta flow criteria were included in the State Water Board submissions of the following organizations: American Rivers, Natural Heritage Institute, California Sportfishing Protection Alliance, California Water Impact Network, Environmental Defense Fund, Bay Institute, and Natural Resources Defense Council. In its comments to the State Water Board as to why narrative flow criteria were inadequate, the Environmental Defense Fund asserted:

A policy decision [by the State Water Board] to delay establishment of quantified and clear flow criteria until the science reaches this ideal level of predictability would be tantamount to a policy decision to tolerate the continued decline of the Bay-Delta ecosystem and its fishery resources.[16]

THE YEAR 2010 PUBLIC TRUST DELTA FLOW CRITERIA

On August 3, 2010, the State Water Board adopted its *Delta Flow Criteria Report*. Section 1.1 of the *Delta Flow Criteria Report* was titled "Legislative Directive and State Water Board Approach." Under the subheading "State Water Board's Public Trust Responsibilities in this Proceeding," the *Draft Delta Flow Criteria Report* explained:

Under the public trust doctrine, the State Water Board must take the public trust into account in the planning and allocation of water resources, and to protect public trust uses whenever feasible. (*National Audubon Society v. Superior Court* (1983) 33 Cal. 3d 419, 446). Public trust values include navigation, commerce, fisheries, recreation, scenic and ecological value. "In determining whether it is 'feasible' to protect public trust values like fish and wildlife in a particular instance, the (State Water] Board must determine whether protection of those values, or what level of protection, is 'consistent with the public interest.' (*State Water Resources Control Board Cases* (2006) 136 Cal.App.4th 674, 778). The State Water Board does not make any determination regarding the feasibility of the public trust recommendation and consistency with the public interest in this report.

In this forum, the State Water Board has not considered the allocation of water resources, the application of the public trust to a particular water diversion or use, water supply impacts ... Any such application of the State Water Board's public trust responsibilities, including any balancing of public trust values and water rights, would be conducted through an adjudicative or regulatory proceeding. Instead, the State Water Board's focus here is solely on identifying public trust resources in the Delta ecosystem and determining the flow criteria, as directed by Water Code Section 85086.[17]

Of particular importance was the State Water Board's adoption of "quantitative" (numeric) rather than "qualitative" (narrative) flow criteria. More specifically, in section 1.2 titled "Summary Deteninationst" under a subheading titled "Flow Criteria and Conclusions," the *Delta Flow Criteria Report* provided:

> In order to preserve the attributes of natural variable system to which native fish species are adapted, many of the criteria developed by the State Water Board are crafted as percentages of natural or unimpaired flows. These criteria include: 75 percent of unimpaired Delta outflow from January through June; 75 percent of unimpaired Sacramento River inflow from November through June; and 75 percent of unimpaired San Joaqu in River inflow from February through June.[18]

Before adopting its final *Delta Flow Criteria Report* in August 2010, the State Water Board circulated a draft of its *Delta Flow Criteria Report* in July 2010. The Delta outflow criteria adopted in the final report were identical to those presented in the draft report.

Predictably, water users and water project operators were generally displeased with the State Water Board's ultimate approach to Delta Flow criteria. Commenting on the July 2010 draft report, the California DWR stated:

> DWR understands that [the State Water Board] interpreted its charge in Water Code Section 85086 of the Delta Reform Act to produce recommendations for Delta outflow necessary to protect public trust resources ... without considering the feasibility of implementing the flow recommendations.
>
> [The State Water Board] acknowledges on page 12 of the Draft Report that the public trust doctrine required [the State Water Board] to "preserve, so far as consistent with the public interest, the uses protected by the trust."(*National Audubon Society v. Superior Court* (1983) 33 Cal.3d 4 I 9, 447.) These public interest considerations are critical to [the State Water

Board's] discharge of its public trust obligations. However, in developing the Draft Report, the [State Water Board] takes a much more limited approach. By not considering the public interest in this report, or determining whether the flow criteria are consistent with the public trust, [the State Water Board] fails to appropriately discharge its public trust obligations, as required by the Delta Reform Act.[19]

In contrast, environmental conservation and fishery groups were generally pleased with the State Water Board's end product. As set forth in a comment letter, which was submitted jointly by the Bay Institute, California Coastkeeper Alliance, California Sportfishing Alliance, California Water Impact Network, Defenders of Wildlife, Environmental Defense Fund, Natural Resources Defense Council, Planning and Conservation League, and Sierra Club California:

> Our organizations collectively represent hundreds of thousands of Californians concerned about keeping the Bay-Delta alive and healthy and restoring our dwindling salmon and other aquatic species. We applaud the draft that you have prepared identifying the flow needs of the Estuary's public trust resources, and particularly commend your careful analysis of the over-whelming scientific support that has demonstrated for many years that we are, and have been, extracting too much water from the estuary and its watershed to support those trust resources sustainably.[20]

STRATEGIC DEPLOYMENT OF THE PUBLIC TRUST

Unlike in the case of Mono Lake basin with just one municipal diverter and user of instream water, in the case of the Bay Delta state and federal agencies there operate multiple diversion facilities throughout the Sacramento River and San Joaquin River watersheds, and there are myriad agricultural and municipal interests throughout the state that use water diverted from the Bay Delta specifically and the Sacramento River and San Joaquin River watersheds more broadly.

These circumstances do not suggest that public trust protections are any less applicable or binding in the Bay Delta than they are in the Mono Lake basin, but they do suggest that when it comes to the Bay Delta, the phase-two feasibility component of the two-phased public trust analysis is likely to be a contentious, politicized, and potentially protracted undertaking.

In adopting section 85086 of the 2009 Delta Reform Act, the California legislature took an honest and sober account of the complexities involved in application of the phase-two feasibility component of the public trust analysis to the Bay Delta, and wisely chose an approach that can best be described as "intentional decoupling." That is, instead of waiting to have the State Board (or a court) attempt to address the first phase and second phase of the public trust analysis in the context of a single water right proceeding seeking to modify Bay Delta diversion entitlements, the California legislature strategically used section 85086 to statutorily compel the State Water Board to complete the first phase of its Bay Delta public trust analysis within a specified time frame while reserving for another day and another proceeding the completion (by either the State Water Board or a court) of the second phase of the Bay Delta public trust analysis.

Although no litigation was filed challenging the validity of the State Water Board's final Bay Delta public trust flow criteria, the courts may have an opportunity to put these criteria to use. In September 2010, the nonprofit organizations California Water Impact Network, California Sportfishing Protection Alliance and AquaAlliance filed a petition for writ of administrative mandate in Sacramento County Superior Court against the State Water Board and the California DWR.[21] The first cause of action in this petition was for violations of the California public trust doctrine, and alleged in pertinent part:

> Respondents' actions in increasing annual pumping after 2000, and the Board's failure to enforce its public trust authority after the effects of that pumping became apparent, constitutes a prejudicial abuse of discretion, in that Respondents did not proceed in the manner required by the Public Trust law, and no substantial evidence supports the Board's failure to take action to amend DWR's permit to reduce diversion and protect the Bay-Delta estuary and its species. Defendant Board has an affirmative duty to protect trust resources. Over the years and continuing to the present time, the Defendant Board's permitting process and failure to enforce permit requirements has caused there to be a substantial decline in the food web, in fish numbers, in water quality and in hydrologic changes which have caused injury to the ecosystem and to members of the public, including Plaintiffs. Present ecological conditions in the Bay-Delta have contributed to the closure of the commercial and sport-fishing fishing seasons off the California coast, resulting in the near complete loss of recreational fishing opportunities for anglers.[22]

In their prayer for relief, petitioners seek a declaration that "Defendant SWRCB [State Water Board] has failed to enforce and Defendant DWR's operation have violated the California Public Trust in the Bay Delta," and seek to "enjoin Defendant DWR from diverting water from the Bay-Delta until such time as Defendant DWR's operations conform with law" and to "enjoin Defendant SWRCB [State Water Board] from allowing operation of state water export projects until such time that Defendant DWR comes into compliance with the law."[23] The claims and relief sought in the petition may now require the court to confront the second phase of the two-phased public trust analysis – the "feasibility" component – in the context of the Bay Delta flow requirements. What was outside the scope of section 85086 of California's 2009 Delta Reform Act may be front and center.

As the petitioners in this litigation seek evidentiary support for their public trust claims, it is foreseeable, if not likely, that they will attempt to rely (at least in part) on the findings and recommendations set forth in the final State Water Board Bay Delta public trust flow criteria. The public trust's journey through the Bay Delta therefore appears far from over.

In terms of its implications beyond California and the United States, in countries such as India, Kenya, and South Africa where the public trust is recognized, the bifurcated approach in California's Delta Reform Act highlights that there is both an informational/process-based component and a substantive component to the public trust. The informational/process-based components suggest that, regardless of the ultimate substantive decision made about what level of protection public trust resources are afforded, the public trust can be understood to require the careful and thorough evaluation of what level and type of protection would be needed to fully protect public trust resources. This evaluation can then serve as an objective reference point for the more policy-based decision about whether this full protection can feasibly or should in fact be provided. The California Delta Reform Act's approach to the Bay Delta public trust flow criteria offers an interesting model of how to insulate and safeguard the preliminary informational component of the public trust, so that it is at heart a scientific inquiry rather than a political-balancing act.

Notes

1. Michael C. Blumm & Rachel D. Guthrie, *Internationalizing the Public Trust Doctrine: Natural Law and Constitutional and Statutory Approaches to Fulfilling the Saxion Vision*, 45 UC DAVIS LAW REVIEW 741 (2012).
2. 33 Cal. 3d 41 9 (1983).
3. 146 U.S. 387 (1892).
4. 138 P. 79 (Cal. 1913).
5. 146 U.S. 387, 453 (1892).
6. 138 P. 79, 87 (Cal. 1913).
7. *Mono Lake Basin Water Rights Decision 1631*, State of California Water Resources Control Board (September 28, 1994).

8. *Mono Lake Basin Water Rights Decision 1631*, State of California Water Resources Control Board (September 28, 1994) at p. 177.

9. Cynthia L. Koehler, *Water Rights and the Public Trust Doctrine: Resolution of the Mono Lake Controversy*, 22 ECOLOGY LAW QUARTERLY 541, 5777 (1995).

10. Patrick Wright, *Fixing the Delta: The CALFED Bay Delta Program and Water Policy under the Davis Administration*, GOLDEN GATE UNIVERSITY LAW REVIEW 331, 332 (2001).

11. Governor's Delta Vision Blue Ribbon Task Force, *Our Vision for 'the California Delta'* (January 2008).

12. Memorandum from the State of California Department of Water Resources for the Delta Flow Criteria Proceedings (January 14, 2010) pp. 1–2.

13. *Written Summary of the California Department of Water Resources for the Public Information Proceeding to Develop Flow Criteria for the Delta Ecosystem Necessary to Protect Public Trust Resources* (February 16, 2010).

14. Environmental Defense Fund, *Closing Comments for Informational Proceeding to Develop Flow Criteria for the Delta Ecosystem Necessary to Protect Public Trust Resources* (2010) at pp. 7–8.

15. *Summary of Written Testimony from State and Federal Water Contractors to State Water Resources Control Board Delta Flow Criteria Proceedings* (March 24, 2010) at p. 3.

16. Environmental Defense Fund, *Closing Comments for Informational Proceeding to Develop Flow Criteria for the Delta Ecosystem Necessary to Protect Public Trust Resources* (2010), at pp. 1–2.

17. State Water Resources Control Board, *Development of Flow Criteria for the Sacramento-San Joaquin Delta Ecosystem, Prepared Pursuant to the Sacramento-San Joaquin Delta Reform Act of 2009* (adopted August 3, 2010) at pp. 1–3.

18. State Water Resources Control Board, *Development of Flow Criteria for the Sacramento-San Joaquin Delta Ecosystem, Prepared Pursuant to the Sacramento-San Joaquin Delta Reform Act of 2009* (adopted August 3, 2010) at p. 5.

19. *California Department of Water Resources Comments on Flow Report* (July 29, 2010) at p. 1.

20. *Comment Letter from the Bay Institute, California Coastkeeper Alliance, California Sportfishing Protection Alliance, California Water Impact Network, Defenders of Wildlife, Environmental Defense Fund, Natural Resources Defense Council, Planning and Conservation League and Sierra Club California to State Water Resources Control Board* (July 29, 2010) at p. 1.

21. Verified Petition for Writ of Mandamus and Declaratory and Injunctive Relief, *California Water Impact Network v. California State Water*

Resources Control Board (Sacramento County Superior Court, filed September 2, 2010).

22. Verified Petition for Writ of Mandamus and Declaratory and Injunctive Relief, *California Water Impact Network* v. *California State Water Resources Control Board* (Sacramento County Superior Court, filed September 2, 2010) at pp. 10–11.

23. Verified Petition for Writ of Mandamus and Declaratory and Injunctive Relief, *California Water Impact Network* v. *California State Water Resources Control Board* (Sacramento County Superior Court, filed September 2, 2010) at p. 17.

2

Instream Rights and Unreasonable Use

California is one among many regions around the world dealing with water scarcity pressures, and these scarcity pressures are compounded by the economic importance of California's wine sector. As discussed in this chapter, growing grapes can be economically precarious for many reasons, including the vulnerability of grapes to early season frost episodes. One of the main strategies for wine growers to protect grapes from frost is to continuously mist vineyards with water prior to and during the periods in the growing season when temperatures can temporarily drop below freezing. This frost protection technique is used for vineyards not only in California but also in other wine-growing regions such as New Zealand.

For instance, a 2018 article in *Wine Enthusiast* magazine documented how grape growers in the New Zealand's Central Otago region used sprinklers to combat frost. According to Andrew Donaldson, owner of the Akitu Winery in the New Zealand's Central Otago region, "In spring, our primary defense is water sprinklers." The article reports: "These sprinklers exploit the latent heat developed through freezing. Water is sprayed over the vines, which freezes in a clear film around the newly formed shoots. In the frosty air, this change from liquid to solid releases heat and protects the shoot. Encrusted in ice, the shoot is safe."[1]

The diversion of water for use as frost protection for vineyards, however, can reduce instream flow from nearby rivers and creeks during frost periods with adverse impacts on fisheries and water quality. The reliance on sprinklers for frost protection in California's Russian River watershed, and the impacts on fisheries in the watershed, has recently given rise to controversy, regulation, and litigation over what constitutes the "reasonable use" of water in such circumstances. As discussed in this chapter, this recent situation in the Russian River watershed is merely the latest installment in the evolving legal concept of "reasonable use" under California water law.

DOING MORE WITH LESS IN CALIFORNIA

When it comes to freshwater consumption in California, going forward the state will need to learn to do more with less. There are at least two main reasons why California will need to learn to do more with less water. First, there is a growing population in the state, a population that is increasingly urban, which means there will be greater demand for urban municipal domestic water supplies. Second, there are now increasing demands to leave additional amounts of surface fresh water instream. The demands for additional instream flow relate in part to the declining condition of California's native fisheries (such as salmon, steelhead, and smelt). They also relate to water quality and salinity concerns. With reduced freshwater flows in our coastal rivers, seawater is pushing further upriver, and increasingly saline water cannot be used for drinking water or irrigation. With seawater intrusion, excessive upstream diversion of fresh water threatens the very supply of fresh water. The long-standing debate over water exports from the Sacramento–San Joaquin Delta, and the impact of such Delta exports on salinity, water quality, and native fisheries, is perhaps the most prominent illustration of such demands for additional instream flow.

The latest installment in this debate came in April 2014, when the Ninth Circuit Court of Appeals reversed former federal district court Judge Oliver Wanger's 2010 decision on the Biological Opinion prepared by the United States Fish and Wildlife Service (USFWS) for Delta smelt, a species listed under the federal Endangered Species Act. In its March 2014 ruling, the Ninth Circuit upheld the USFWS imposition of restrictions on Delta exports related to the operation of the Central Valley Project and the State Water Project to ensure additional instream flows to reduce salinity and maintain habitat for the Delta smelt.[2]

As California turns its attention to how to do more with less in terms of freshwater resources, there are two considerations that are likely to be in play. First, presently about 77 percent of the fresh water in California is used by irrigated agriculture.[3] Given this level of usage, it is therefore likely that agricultural irrigation will be the main focus of efforts to improve water efficiency in the state. Second, the California Constitution and the California Water Code contain provisions establishing that all water use in the state must be reasonable and cannot be wasteful. These constitutional and statutory prohibitions on unreasonable use of water may be increasingly relied upon as a legal basis to press for more efficient irrigation practices in California's agricultural sector.

These two considerations converged in January 2011, when Delta Watermaster Craig Wilson (a state official) presented a report to the State Water Resources Control Board titled *The Reasonable Use Doctrine & Agricultural Water Use Efficiency*.[4] The introduction to this publication stated:

> The underlying premise of this report is that the inefficient use of water is an unreasonable use of water. Accordingly, the reasonable use doctrine is available prospectively to prevent general practices of inefficient water use .... Maximizing the efficient use of water by projects that reduce consumptive water use is particularly important for the Sacramento/San Joaquin Delta. More efficient use of water upstream of the Delta can increase water flows into the Delta.

Specific recommendations in the 2011 report on *The Reasonable Use Doctrine & Agricultural Water Use Efficiency* included the following: (i) create a "reasonable water use unit" within the State Water Resources Control Board (State Water Board) Division of Water Rights, whose mission would be "to enforce the prohibition against the waste or unreasonable use of waste"; (ii) require diverters of water for agricultural use to evaluate and implement "appropriate conservation practices," which might include irrigation systems that reduce evapotranspiration; and (iii) "irrigating only when necessary" (reducing irrigation of crops during stress-tolerant growth stages).

Whether implementation of these recommendations is politically feasible or politically advisable are important questions, but questions that are beyond the scope of what this chapter will cover. This chapter will instead focus on the more limited question of the extent to which California reasonable use law provides a legal basis and legal foundation for the types of agricultural irrigation efficiency and water conservation recommendations presented in the 2011 Delta Watermaster report.

1926 *HERMINGHAUS* DECISION AND 1928 CALIFORNIA CONSTITUTIONAL AMENDMENT

In 1928, the California Constitution was amended to provide in pertinent part as follows:

> It is hereby declared that because of the conditions prevailing in this State the general welfare requires that ... the waste or unreasonable use or unreasonable method of use of water be prevented .... The right to water or to the use or flow of water from any natural stream or water resource in this state ... does

not and shall not extend to the waste or unreasonable use or unreasonable method of use or unreasonable method of diversion of water.

The 1928 amendment to the California Constitution, in turn, provided the basis for the adoption of Section 100 of the California Water Code. Section 100 of the California Water Code provides as follows: "The right to water or the use or flow of water in or from any natural watercourse shall be limited to such water as shall be reasonably required ... and such right does not and shall not extend to the waste or unreasonable use or unreasonable method of use or unreasonable method of diversion of water."

As we consider the irrigation-related recommendations in the 2011 Delta Watermaster report, it is important to remember the events that prompted the adoption in 1928 of the California constitutional amendment. The main catalyst for this 1928 constitutional amendment was the California Supreme Court's 1926 decision in the case of *Herminghaus* v. *Southern California Edison Company (Herminghaus)*.[5]

The *Herminghaus* litigation involved a dispute between a downstream riparian water rights user (Herminghaus) and a proposed upstream hydro-electric project under an appropriative right that would reduce downstream flows. The downstream riparian user had a ranch and diverted nearly all of the flow of a river to flood irrigate grasses on her land. She claimed generally that the grasses were used as pasture for ranching, but little or no information was presented at trial about the types or numbers of livestock that grazed on these grasses. In its decision, the California Supreme Court found that the extent to which the grasses were actually used for livestock was not legally relevant, holding that "in a dispute between a riparian and a non-riparian the riparian's water rights are not limited by any measure of reasonableness."

The California Supreme Court's unwillingness in *Herminghaus* to evaluate the potential reasonableness and wastefulness of diverting such quantities of water, without a showing of the extent to which such grasses were actually being used for livestock grazing, prompted the 1928 constitutional amendment, which held that "all" water use and diversion rights in California – whether riparian, appropriative, or based on some other entitlement – must be reasonable and cannot be wasteful.

"IN THE FIELD" AND "IN THE STREAM"

In terms of reviewing California court decisions and State Water Board actions implementing the 'reasonable use/waste' provisions of the California Constitution and California Water Code, it is useful to keep in mind the distinction between concerns about water "in the field" and concerns about water "in the stream." That is, sometimes the focus of California reasonable use law has been on the loss/ usage of water on the agricultural lands being irrigated, and at other times the focus of California reasonable use law has been on the instream impacts of diverting water for use on agricultural lands.

Water in the Field

Tulare and Flood Irrigation

In the 1935 *Tulare Irrigation District* v. *Strathmore Irrigation District* (*Tulare*) case, the California Supreme Court reviewed the practice in California's Central Valley of flood irrigating farmland in the winter (before planting seeds in the spring) to "drown out gophers" that might be living in the fields.[6] In reviewing this practice, the California Supreme Court noted:

> What is a reasonable beneficial use, where water is present in excess of all needs, would not be a reasonable beneficial use in an area of great scarcity and great need. What is a reasonable beneficial use at one time may, because of changed conditions, become a waste of water at a later time.

The *Tulare* Court then found: "It seems quite clear to us that in such an area of need as the Kaweah delta the use of an appreciable quantity for this purpose [gopher drowning] cannot be held to be a reasonable beneficial use."

Erickson and Evaporation Losses

In the 1971 *Erickson* v. *Queen Valley Ranch Company* (*Erickson*) decision, the California Court of Appeal reviewed a trial court decision in which it had been determined that five-sixths of the water diverted into an earthen canal was lost en route to the point of use for agricultural irrigation (due to evaporation to air and absorption by soil). In *Erickson*, the trial court had found these transmission losses "reasonable," but the California Court of Appeal reversed, holding:

> By holding that transmission losses accounting to five-sixths of the flow are reasonable and consistent with local custom, the court effectually placed the seal of judicial approval on what appears to be an inefficient and wasteful means of transmission …. A finding of reasonableness which cloaks a transmission loss amounting to five-sixths of the diverted flow fails to respond to the demand of constitutional policy.[7]

Erickson clarified that while diverting water for agricultural irrigation may constitute a beneficial use of freshwater resources, excessive losses of water to evaporation or soil absorption used in connection with agricultural irrigation may constitute an unconstitutionally unreasonable and wasteful use of such water.

Some of the 2011 Delta Watermaster report recommendations focused specifically on efforts to reduce the amount of water evapotranspiration occurring in agricultural fields, so *Erickson* provides legal support for grounding determinations of unreasonable and wasteful irrigation practices on evaporation-related concerns.

IID, Canal Spills and Excess Tailwater

In its 1986 *Imperial Irrigation District* v. *State Water Resources Control Board* (*IID*) decision, the California Court of Appeal considered the application of California reasonable use law to allegations of water lost due to irrigation canal spills and excess tailwater running from agricultural fields.[8] Tailwater was the water that spilled out of the canal at its terminus because it was not being used for irrigation. After complaints were filed with the California Department of Water Resources (DWR), which delivered water to Imperial Irrigation District (IID) customers, DWR referred the matter to the State Water Board. In 1984 the State Water Board issued Decision 1600, finding that the failure of IID to implement appropriate water conservation measures to address the canal spills and tailwater runoff constituted unreasonable use of water pursuant to the requirements of the California Constitution.[9]

Imperial Irrigation District filed suit challenging the State Water Board's unreasonableness determination, and the trial court found that Decision 1600's conclusion that the canal maintenance and irrigation practices of IID violated the California Constitution's prohibitions on the unreasonable use and waste of water were "without binding effect."[10] In its 1986 decision, the California Court of Appeal then reviewed the extensive body of California reasonable use law and inquired: "In the light of these constitutional, statutory and Supreme Court authorities, which apparently establish all-encompassing adjudicatory authority in the [State Water Board] on matters on water resource management, how could the trial court have found an absence of such authority in the matter of unreasonable water use under article X, section 2?" The California Court of Appeal answered its question by reversing the trial court, finding "[W]e hold that in this case IID's use of water under appropriative rights that the [State Water Board's] authority includes the power to adjudicate the article X, section 2, issue of unreasonable use of water by IID."

IID provides support for the authority of the State Water Board to find that the failure of an agricultural water user to implement appropriate water conservation measures in agricultural fields, such as proper maintenance of irrigation canals and reducing tailwater runoff, may be violative of California reasonable use law.

Water in the Stream

In considering water diverted out of stream for agricultural usage, it should be noted that the 2011 Delta Watermaster report specifically discussed the application of the California reasonable use law in the context of the need for additional instream freshwater flows into the Sacramento–San Joaquin Delta. In doing so, the Delta Watermaster report suggested that a legal analysis of the reasonableness or wastefulness of water used for agriculture may hinge in part on an assessment of the extent to which it can be shown that such diversions are resulting in unreasonably adverse instream impacts.

Racanelli Decision, Salinity and Seawater Intrusion

In its 1986 decision in *United States* v. *State Water Resources Control Board*, the California Court of Appeal addressed the question of whether the State of California could modify the existing water rights permits (issued to the Bureau of Reclamation for the federal Central Valley Project and to the California DWR for the State Water Project) to provide additional flow into the Sacramento–San Joaquin Delta to maintain water quality standards.[11] More specifically, the California Court of Appeal decision (which became known as the "Racanelli decision" after Judge Racanelli, who authored the opinion) considered whether California reasonable use/waste law provided the State Water Board with an independent basis to reduce Delta water exports so additional fresh water could remain instream to reduce salinity levels from saltwater intrusion.

In the 1986 Racanelli decision, the California Court of Appeal held:

> Here, the Board determined that changed circumstances revealed in new information about the adverse effects of the projects upon the Delta necessitated revised water quality standards. Accordingly, the Board had authority to modify the projects permits to curtail their use of water on the ground that the project use and diversion of water had become unreasonable .... Curtailment of project activities through reduced storage and export was eminently reasonable and proper to maintain the required level of water quality in the Delta. We perceive no legal obstacles to the Board's determination that particular methods of use have become unreasonable by their deleterious effects upon water quality.

The Racanelli decision clarified that, consistent with California reasonable use law, the State Water Board has independent authority to restrict freshwater diversions to maintain instream water quality and salinity levels.

EDF and Alternate Points of Diversion

In its 1980 *Environmental Defense Fund* v. *East Bay Municipal Utility District* (*EDF*) decision, the California Supreme Court considered issues related to a 1968 agreement between East Bay Municipal Utility District (EBMUD) and the United States Bureau of Reclamation to construct Auburn Dam on the American River (a tributary to the Sacramento River).[12] Pursuant to this 1968 agreement, EBMUD agreed to purchase up to 150,000 acre-feet of water, which would be delivered to EBMUD through the Folsom South Canal that diverts water from the upper American River.

EBMUD's proposed diversion of such quantities of water from the upper American River raised concerns about adverse impacts on water quality and fisheries in the lower American River, and led to proposals for EBMUD to instead divert water via a new proposed canal (the Hood Clay Connection) that would be located on the Sacramento River below the confluence of the American River with the Sacramento River. In response to these fishery concerns, the State Water Board imposed certain instream flow conditions in the appropriative permits issued to the United States Bureau of Reclamation for Auburn Dam. More specifically, in 1971 the State Water Board issued Decision No. 1400 imposing minimum flows for the protection of fish in the American River and retaining jurisdiction to determine whether the EBMUD diversion of water though the Folsom South Canal (as opposed to the alternative Hood Clay Connection) constituted an unreasonable method of diversion.[13]

In *EDF*, the California Supreme Court clarified that the State Water Board and the California courts have "concurrent" jurisdiction to prevent unreasonable water use or unreasonable methods of water diversion, and on this basis granted EDF leave to amend its complaint against EBMUD to allege that the diversion of water through the Folsom South Canal rather than the proposed Hood Clay Connection constituted an unreasonable method of diversion.

EDF therefore lends support to the independent and concurrent authority of California courts and the State Water Board to evaluate whether the selection of particular points of diversion constitutes an unreasonable method of diversion due to adverse instream impacts on fisheries.

Frost Protection Diversions and Stream Flow

The question of freshwater diversions for frost protection arose first in the 1976 California Court of Appeal's decision in *State Water Resources Control Board*

v. *Forni* (*Forni*).[14] Although this decision did not focus specifically on fisheries, it did focus on instream impacts. In *Forni*, the Court noted:

> [T]he State Water Resources Control Board initiated this action to enjoin certain vineyards in the Napa Valley from drawing water directly from the Napa River to their vineyards for frost protection. The complaint charges that the diversion of water during the frost period extending from March 15 through May 15 each year constitutes an unreasonable method of diversion within the meaning of article XIV, section 3, of the California Constitution and section 100 of the Water Code . . . it is alleged, direct diversion during the frost season may at time dry up the river.

On this set of facts, the *Forni* Court concluded:

> It is readily apparent that the claim that respondent's direct diversion of water constitutes an unreasonable use and an unreasonable method of use of water is predicated on the very premise that the direct pumping results in great temporary scarcity of water during the crucial frost period . . . the direct diversion of water for frost protection in the crucial period constitutes an unreasonable use and an unreasonable method of use within the purview of the Constitution and statutory provisions . . . . [W]e find no merit in respondent's assertion that the Board has exceeded its authority by declaring that [] the direct diversion of water in the frost period constitutes an unreasonable method of use within the meaning of the Constitution and the Water Code.

More recently, in December 2011, the State Water Board adopted a new regulation (Regulation 862) pertaining to salmon and diversions of water from the Russian River for vineyard frost protection.[15] The introductory paragraph to this regulation explains:

> During a frost . . . the high instantaneous demand for water for frost protection by numerous vineyardists and other water users may contribute to a rapid decrease in stream stage that results in the mortality of salmonoids due to stranding. Stranding mortality can be avoided by coordinating or otherwise managing diversions to reduce instantaneous demand. Because a reasonable alternative to current practices exist, the Board has determined these diversions must be conducted in accordance with this section.

The central component of the 2011 Russian River frost protection regulation is the requirement that diverters of water from the Russian River stream system must prepare and submit a Water Demand Management Program (WDMP) to the State Water Board. Among other information, the WDMP must include data regarding "acreage frost protected and acres frost protected by means other than water diverted from the Russian River Stream system" and the "rate

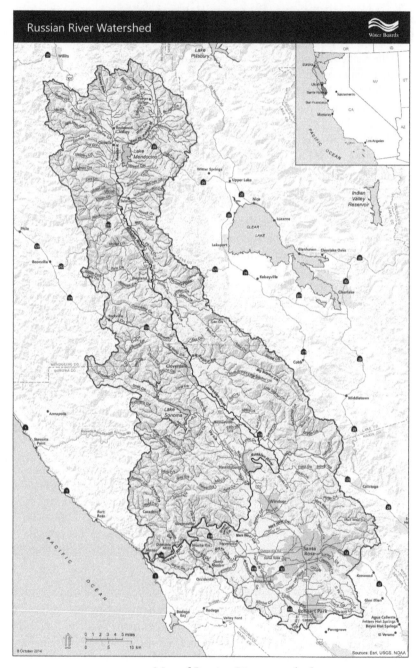

MAP 2.1 Map of Russian River watershed

of diversion, hours of operation, and volume of water diverted during each front event for the year." If it is determined that the frost diversions described in the WDMP have the potential to cause salmonoid stranding mortality, "corrective actions" (such as the construction of off-stream storage facilities) may be required to prevent such stranding mortality.

The closing paragraph of the 2011 Russian River frost protection regulation states:

> The diversion of water in violation of this section, including the failure to implement the corrective actions included in any corrective action plan developed by the governing body, is an unreasonable method of diversion and use and a violation of Water Code section 100, and shall be subject to enforcement by the Board.

State Water Board Regulation 862 was challenged in a lawsuit filed in Mendocino County Superior Court.[16] In its 2013 decision in *Light* v. *State Water Board*, Mendocino County Superior Court struck down the regulation as unlawful on two primary grounds. First, the trial court held that California reasonable use law applies only to appropriative water rights holders and not to riparian water rights holders (and petitioner Light was a riparian water rights holder). Second, the trial court held that although courts could rely on California reasonable use law on a case-by-case basis to bring enforcement actions for violating reasonable use standards, the State Water Board could not rely upon California reasonable use law to enact regulations applying to general categories of water usage or water diversion.

The 2013 Mendocino County Superior Court decision in *Light* v. *State Water Board* was appealed to the California Court of Appeal for the First District. In its briefing to the California Court of Appeal, the State Water Board relied extensively on the 1976 holding in *Forni* (upholding reliance on California reasonable use law as a basis for regulating diversions for frost protection).[17] In contrast, the petitioners opposing the Russian River frost protection regulation sought to distinguish *Forni* on a number of grounds, including the assertion that the *Forni* decision is limited to appropriative water rights holders and does not apply to riparian right diverters, and that *Forni* recognized the State Water Board's authority to bring enforcement actions but not its authority to adopt reasonable use regulations.[18]

In its briefing to the California Court of Appeal for the First District, the State Water Board met these *Forni*-related arguments head-on, focusing on the language in former section 659 (of the California Code of Regulations) that imposed conditions on frost protection diversions from the Napa River. In its reply brief, the State Water Board contended:

In this case the trial court erred in its efforts to distinguish *Forni*. First, the trial court incorrectly concluded that "section 659 on its face only applied to appropriative rights holders – an important distinction from the present case." While it is true that the second sentence of former section 659 is directed to appropriative right permit holders, the first sentence declared that the direct diversion of water from the Napa River during the frost period was unreasonable. The respondents in *Forni* who challenged the validity of section 659 were riparian diverters. There is simply no basis to conclude that section 659 did not apply to all water users, including riparians.[19]

In an opinion issued on June 16, 2014, the California Court of Appeal for the First District reversed the Mendocino County Superior Court.[20] In regard to the application of California reasonable use law to riparian water rights holders, the Court of Appeal held that the petitioner's argument that riparian rights are vested rights exempt from the application of reasonable use has been "rejected repeatedly" by the California Supreme Court, and that this precedent establishes that "riparian users' vested water rights extend only to reasonable beneficial water use, which is determined at the time of use." The June 16, 2014 opinion further clarified that the State Water Board "is charged with acting to prevent unreasonable and wasteful uses of water, regardless of the claim of right under which the water is diverted."

In regard to the authority of the State Water Board to enact regulations to prevent unreasonable use of water, the Court of Appeal found:

In finding that the Board lacked the authority to enact [Regulation 862], the trial court recognized the Board has regulatory authority over the unreasonable use of state waters. It held, however, that this authority was limited, at least as to riparian users, to pursuing enforcement actions in the courts against allegedly unreasonable users, rather than enacting regulations to preclude unreasonable use. Neither decisional law nor the government statutes support the trial court's limited vision of the Board's regulatory authority.[21]

In this vein, the Court of Appeal opinion continued:

It appears that in many, or perhaps most circumstances, diversion for frost protection purposes from the Russian River is biologically harmless. Yet on those occasions when it might be damaging, it has the potential to inflict long-lasting damage on already fragile salmon populations. Restricting the Board to post-event litigation deprives it of any effective regulatory remedy, since the damage will have been done and the critical circumstances may not arise again for months or years. It is difficult to imagine what effective relief a court could grant, other than a broad and inflexible injunction against future diversions for purposes of frost protection, a ruling that would be in the interest of neither the enjoined growers nor the public. Efficient regulation of the state's water resources in these circumstances demands that the Board have the authority to enact tailored regulations.[22]

In upholding the lawfulness of the Russian River frost protection regulation in *Light*, the California Court of Appeal established new precedent for reliance on California reasonable use law as an independent basis for the State Water Board to adopt policies and regulations of broad applicability to reduce the adverse impacts of out-of-stream diversions on instream fisheries.

Emergency Drought Instream Flow Requirements

More recently, the 2014 *Light* decision served as the basis for the California Court of Appeals' June 2020 ruling in *Stanford Vina Ranch Irrigation Company* v. *State of California* (*Stanford Vina*). In the *Stanford Vina* litigation, the plaintiff challenged the State Water Board's issuance of temporary emergency regulations in 2014 and 2015, during the height of one of the most severe droughts in California's history. The challenged regulations established minimum flow requirements on three tributaries of the Sacramento River, including Deer Creek, in order to protect two threatened species of anadromous fish, Chinook salmon and steelhead trout, during their respective migratory cycles. These emergency instream flow regulations reduced the amount of water from Deer Creek available for diversion and irrigation use by the plaintiff.

The State Water Board had adopted the emergency drought instream flow regulations based on its reasonable use authority under the California Constitution and the California Water Code, and the plaintiff claimed that this reliance on reasonable use authority was misplaced.

In *Stanford Vina*, the California Court of Appeal noted:

> Again returning to *Light*, *supra*, 226 Cal.App.4th 1463, in upholding the Board's regulatory authority to adopt the challenged regulation declaring diversions of water for purposes of frost protection to be per se unreasonable when done in contravention of the regulation, the First Appellate District concluded: "Given the Board's statutory charge to 'prevent waste, unreasonable use, unreasonable method of use, or unreasonable method of diversion of water in this state' (§ 275) and the recognized power of the Legislature to pass legislation regulating reasonable uses of water (*California Trout*, *supra*, 207 Cal.App.3d at pp. 624–625.), the Board's grant of authority to 'exercise the regulatory functions of the state' (§ 174) necessarily includes the power to enact regulations governing the reasonable use of water." (*Light*, *supra*, 226 Cal.App.4th at pp. 1484–1485.)

The California Court of Appeal then went on to hold:

> Similarly, here, the Board adopted regulations setting minimum flow requirements for three creeks during certain time periods, and when certain protected fish were present in the creeks, in order to enable those fish to survive their yearly migration through the creeks during severe drought conditions. Diversions that threatened to drop the flow of water below the minimum flow requirements were declared per se unreasonable and subject to curtailment by the Board. As in *Light, supra*, 226 Cal.App.4th 1463, we conclude the adoption of these regulations was within the Board's regulatory authority as they furthered the Board's constitutional and statutory mandate to "prevent waste, unreasonable use, unreasonable method of use, or unreasonable method of diversion of water in this state." (§ 275; art. X, § 2.) Also like *Light*, we reject Stanford Vina's assertion the Board's authority in this regard was limited by the fact the company manages riparian and pre–1914 water rights. "[T]he Board is charged with acting to prevent unreasonable and wasteful uses of water, *regardless of the claim of right under which the water is diverted*." (*Light, supra*, 226 Cal.App.4th at p. 1482, italics added.)[23]

The 2020 *Stanford Vina* decision therefore expands upon the earlier *Light* decision, reaffirming that the reasonable use authority under the California Constitution and the California Water Code provides the State of California with broad authority to adopt regulations of general applicability to ensure adequate instream flows to maintain fisheries.

MORE A QUESTION OF POLITICS THAN LAW

As documented herein, there is a well-developed body of California law suggesting that the reasonable use/waste provisions of the California Constitution and the California Water Code can provide a proper and independent basis for courts and the State Water Board to address agricultural irrigation practices with impacts both in the field (such as flood irrigation, high levels of evaporation and canal spills/tailwater) and in the stream (such as insufficient flow to maintain water quality/salinity standards, instream impacts associated with particular points of diversion, and prevention of fish mortality).

Moreover, at this point there is a substantial body of scientific evidence establishing high rates of water evapotranspiration on California farms (particularly in the Southern Central Valley),[24] and there is a substantial body of scientific evidence establishing the adverse impacts of freshwater diversions on instream salinity levels and instream temperatures needed by native fisheries.[25]

These two considerations, taken together, suggest that whether the State Water Board decides to act on and implement the agricultural irrigation efficiency recommendations set forth in the 2011 Delta Watermaster's report may therefore hinge more on politics than law. If the political will is present to act on and implement these recommendations, the State Water Board appears to be on solid legal ground to move forward. As to whether such political will exists, that remains to be seen. There are unfolding developments that may offer some insights in this regard.

For instance, pursuant to California's Agricultural Efficient Water Management Act, by 2013, agricultural water suppliers were required to submit agricultural water management plans to the California Department of Water Resources. These plans call for the inclusion of information about water efficiency and conservation efforts, and therefore might provide the basis for the State Water Board to further evaluate whether particular agricultural irrigation operations might qualify as unreasonable or wasteful.[26]

As another example, in 2013, California Senate Bill 103 (S.B. 103) was adopted, which provides $2.5 million in funding to the State Water Board "for drought related water rights and water conservation actions, including establishing and enforcing requirements to prevent the waste or unreasonable use of water."[27] S.B. 103 does not expressly call for the creation of the "reasonable water use unit" proposed in the 2011 Delta Watermaster report, but seems to provide funding and the discretion for such an undertaking by the State Water Board.

In sum, given that agricultural irrigation presently represents the lion's share of freshwater usage in California, and given the increasing instream and out-of-stream demands on California fresh water, the issue of agricultural water efficiency is likely to remain a central part of water debates in the state. The extent to and ways in which California reasonable use law will factor into these debates, however, is still an open question.

Outside of California, the question of frost protection water use and other agricultural irrigation practices will not be considered in the particular "reasonable use" framework that is unique to California constitutional and statutory law. But this does not mean that the reasonableness of methods of diversion and the nature of water use, and their impacts on instream flows and fisheries, will not be a subject of legal and policy contention in other states and in other countries.

For example, a 2005 decision by the Court of Appeals of Michigan clarified that "reasonable use" determinations are part of Michigan law principles for resolving disputes about the exercise of riparian water rights. In *Michigan Citizens for Water Conservation* v. *Nestle Waters North America Inc.*

(*Michigan Citizens for Water Conservation*), the Court considered a challenge to diversions from the Dead Stream by a water bottling company that resulted in a 24 percent loss of instream flow. In its decision, the Court noted:

> The trial court determined that this reduction in flow would raise the stream's temperature and cause the stream to become choked with plant life. The trial court further found the loss of flow would cause a narrowing of the channel by at least four feet over a period of time. The trial court determined that these effects would impair the Dead Stream's aesthetic value and its usefulness as a fishery, and would impair recreational navigation of the stream .... Therefore, taking all of the factors outlined into consideration, we determine that defendant's proposed withdrawal of 400 gpm (gallons per minute) would be unreasonable under the circumstances.[28]

As the holding in *Michigan Citizens for Water Conservation* illustrates, wherever and whenever the diversion of instream flow is diverted in regions of water scarcity, and particularly where fisheries are dependent on such instream flows, the reasonableness of such diversions and resulting uses of diverted waters will come under scrutiny by the agencies, laws, and courts tasked with managing water resources. It would be unreasonable to expect otherwise.

Notes

1. Anne Krebiehl, *Fighting Frost in Vineyards*, WINE ENTHUSIAST (January 2, 2018).
2. *San Luis v. Jewell*, Case No. 11–15871 (March 13, 2104, decision of the United States Court of Appeal for the Ninth Circuit).
3. Ellen Hanak et al., MANAGING CALIFORNIA'S WATER: FROM CONFLICT TO RECONCILIATION (Public Policy Institute of California, 2011), p. 88.
4. *The Reasonable use Doctrine & Agricultural Water Efficiency* (January 2011 report by Delta Watermaster Craig Wilson to the State Water Resources Control Board and the Delta Stewardship Council).
5. 200 Cal. 81 (1926).
6. 3 Cal. 2d 489 (1935).
7. 22 Cal.App.3d at 585.
8. 186 Cal.App.3d 1160 (1986).
9. 186 Cal.App.3d at 1163.
10. 186 Cal.App.3d at 1164.
11. 182 Cal.App.3d 82 (1986).
12. 26 Cal.3d 183 (1980).

13. 26 Cal.3d at 190.
14. 54 Cal.App.3d 743 (1976).
15. Section 862, Division 3, Title 23, California Code of Regulations.
16. Mendocino County Superior Court, Case No. A138440.
17. Case No. A138440, *Light* v. *California State Water Resources Control Board*, Court of Appeal of the State of California, First Appellate District, Division One, Appellant State Water Resources Control Board's Opening Brief, pp. 32–34. Appellant State Water Resources Control Board's Reply Brief, pp. 11–14.
18. Case No. A138440, *Light* v. *California State Water Resources Control Board*, Court of Appeal of the State of California, First Appellate District, Division One, Appellee Rudolf and Linda Light's Opposition Brief.
19. Case No. A138440, *Light* v. *California State Water Resources Control Board*, Court of Appeal of the State of California, First Appellate District, Division One, Appellant State Water Resources Control Board's Opening Brief, p. 33.
20. Opinion by Judge Margulies, Judges Dondero and Banke concurring, http:/bit/ly/iqmdIfh; see also Paul Stanton Kibel, *Frost Protection Diversions and Stranded Salmon – The California Court of Appeal Affirms State Water Board Reliance on Reasonable Use Law to Maintain Instream Flow*, California Water Law Journal (June 24, 2014).
21. Page 14, June 16, 2014 opinion of the Court of Appeal of the State of California, First Appellate District.
22. Pages 19–20, June 16, 2014 opinion of the Court of Appeal of the State of California, First Appellate District.
23. June 18, 2020 decision by the Third Appellate District Court of Appeal in *Stanford Vina Ranch Irrigation Company* v. *State of California* (Case No. C085762).
24. Blaine Hanson, *Irrigation of Agricultural Crops in California* (paper on file with author), reporting particularly high rates of evaporation for alfalfa, cotton, and rice grown in California.
25. Ellen Hanak et al., *Managing California's Water: From Conflict to Reconciliation* (Public Policy Institute of California, 2011), pp. 200–205 (for discussion of reduced instream flow on native salmon and smelt fisheries). See also STATE WATER RESOURCES CONTROL BOARD, DEVELOPMENT OF FLOW CRITERIA FOR THE SACRAMENTO-SAN JOAQUIN DELTA ECOSYSTEM, PREPARED PURSUANT TO THE SACRAMENTO-SAN JOAQUIN DELTA REFORM ACT OF 2009 (adopted August 3, 2010).
26. Sections 10900–10904, California Water Code.
27. Section 14(2), S.B. 103.
28. *Michigan Citizens for Water Conservation* v. *Nestle Waters North America Inc.*, 269 Mich.App. 25 (Court of Appeal of Michigan, 2005).

3

Instream Rights and Dams

For obtaining a free course for fish thro' such Caulds, Dams or Damheads as are already erected or hereafter may be made in the River Tweed or other rivers connected with.[1]

August 1, 1805 Mission Statement of the Western Association, main advocate for passage of the 1807 River Tweed Act

TWO CENTURIES OF SALMON NAVIGATING HYDRO

There is a tendency to think of the impacts of hydropower facilities on salmon stocks as a more recent phenomenon, as an issue that emerged in the mid-twentieth century in the period when most of the large-scale onstream dams were constructed in the United States and elsewhere. As evidenced by the quote here relating to the passage of the 1807 River Tweed Act by the British Parliament, however, the law has struggled to reconcile the interests of salmon and hydropower for more than two centuries.[2]

The River Tweed forms the eastern border between England and Scotland and is one of the most productive salmon and sea trout fisheries in the United Kingdom. As its name suggests, it is associated with the woolen textile mills that began to operate along the waterway in the late 1700s and the early 1800s, mills that were powered by waterwheels. The textile mills along the River Tweed were often built upland away from the river's edge, and water was diverted to the off-stream waterwheels adjacent to the mills through instream construction of impoundments called "caulds" to collect water, which was then diverted through channels to the water-wheels and then returned downstream back to the river.[3] To the consternation of both commercial and recreational salmon fishermen, these instream mill caulds often blocked the upstream and downstream passage of salmon and sea trout.[4]

To address this problem, in 1807 the British Parliament passed the River Tweed Act, establishing the River Tweed Commissioners and providing them with authority to undertake certain measures to safeguard salmon and sea trout stocks. More particularly, to address the problem of instream impoundments to collect and deliver water to textile mill waterwheels, Article XI of the 1807 River Tween Act provides as follows:

> All mills dams/dikes/weirs and other permanent obstructions in the river to be altered or constructed to allow the free run of fish. If proprietors/occupiers do not comply, Commissioners & Overseers to give notice in writing to do so within 14 days. If nothing happens, Commissioners & Overseers may order the work to be done at the expense of the proprietor/occupier.[5]

Pursuant to Article XI of the River Tweed Act (which remains in effect today), we see that as early as 1807 there were provisions in English law that provided not only that it was unlawful for instream hydropower facilities to obstruct the "free run of fish" but also that it was the financial responsibility of the operators of such instream hydropower facilities to modify their facilities to ensure such fish passage. If the operators of the facility refused to make these modifications with two weeks' notice, the River Tweed Commissioners were authorized under the 1807 River Tweed Act to make modifications themselves and send the operator the bill.[6]

In the United States, the approach to reconciling the relationship between salmon stocks and hydropower facilities has been quite different to the approach reflected in the River Tweed Act. Compared to 1807, we now have a much more advanced understanding of the particular habitat needs of salmon and how these habitat needs are impacted by onstream dams. For instance, we now better appreciate that cold-water fish like salmon cannot survive higher water temperatures and higher water temperatures are often associated with reduced downstream flow due to the diversion and impoundment of water upstream. As a second example, we now know that salmon require the presence of gravel instream for spawning habitat yet such gravel is often trapped behind upstream impoundments. Finally, there is now scientific literature showing that salmon are particularly suited to spawning in the higher elevation reaches of a watershed, but upstream passage to and downstream passage from such higher elevation reaches is often blocked by impoundments.

Despite our more advanced understanding of the ways that onstream hydroelectric facilities can adversely impact salmon stocks, in the United States it has proven difficult to establish regulatory mechanisms to ensure that such facilities are operated in a manner that provides for the upstream/

downstream passage of salmon and salmon's habitat needs. In this respect, twenty-first-century hydro regulation in the United States has been slow to incorporate the principles and remedies reflected in the 1807 River Tweed Act.

With this broader historical context in mind, this chapter will review efforts in the United States to better address the relationship between the condition of fisheries and the operation of onstream dams. More specifically, it will review the fishery-related aspects of the Federal Power Act (FPA). The FPA requires operators of most existing onstream hydroelectric facilities in the United States to periodically apply to the Federal Energy Regulatory Commission (FERC) to relicense such facilities.

As detailed later, the FERC hydro relicensing process in the United States has often provided an effective mechanism to modify the terms of dam operations to reduce the adverse impacts on fisheries, particularly impacts on wild Pacific Coast salmon. This experience with the FERC relicensing suggests that a transparent and scientifically rigorous regulatory framework to periodically review and modify the way dams operate can play a critical role in the restoration of wild fish stocks.

INSTREAM CONDITIONS NEEDED BY WILD PACIFIC COAST SALMON

To understand the relationship between the FERC hydro relicensing and wild salmon stocks, there are two preliminary points that need to be explained at the outset. The first point is to identify the life cycle and particular habitat needs of wild Pacific Coast salmon. The second point is to recount historic reliance on hatchery salmon as an anticipated replacement for wild salmon in the context of the initial approval and licensing of many Pacific Coast hydro facilities.

Wild Pacific Salmon Habitat Needs

All wild Pacific Coast salmon are anadromous, which means they spawn and spend the first period of their life in freshwater rivers, streams, and creeks. The juvenile salmon then migrate downstream to the ocean, where they spend several years in salt water, ultimately returning upstream to their natal freshwater river, stream, or creek to reproduce and die. The following sections discuss some of the conditions wild Pacific Coast salmon need to complete this life cycle and provide an overview of how onstream dams can impact these conditions.

Downstream and Upstream Passage

To make the journey from their upstream freshwater spawning grounds to the ocean, wild Pacific Coast salmon need downstream passage from these grounds to the sea. Such downstream passage for salmon can be adversely impacted by dams in two ways. First, if no water is being released from a dam, salmon migrating downstream will find themselves trapped and confined to the reservoir located behind the dam. Second, if water is being released into high-speed turbines to generate hydroelectric power, salmon migrating downstream can be killed as they pass through the spinning turbines. Some dams include fish ladders that enable some outgoing salmon to go around the dam or avoid being pulled into the turbines. Sometimes outgoing salmon are collected upstream of the turbines and then trucked below the dam where they are then released.

On their return journey from the ocean to their natal freshwater spawning grounds, wild Pacific Coast salmon need upstream passage. Such upstream passage can be blocked by dams, preventing salmon from reaching their natal spawning grounds to reproduce. Some dams include fish ladders which enable some returning salmon to navigate their way upstream around the impoundment. Sometimes returning salmon are collected below the dam, and then trucked above the dam where they are then released.

Maintaining Cold-Water Temperatures

Salmon are cold-water fish with limited tolerance for higher water temperatures. They prefer water temperatures below 55 °F, suffer reduced growth and survival rates as water temperatures get close to 60 °F, and are generally unable to survive in water warmer than 60 °F.

Instream water temperatures tend to be hottest in the summer, which is also when water stored in reservoirs behind dams is used most intensely for agriculture and irrigation. The result is that there is often reduced release of upstream water from dams at the time of year when increased air temperatures are pushing water temperatures up. The reduced volume of water flowing downstream causes downstream waters to warm, increasing salmon mortality rates.

Increased and timely reservoir releases of cold water can help maintain the downstream cold-water habitat conditions that salmon need, but such releases are often opposed by stakeholders, who would like to divert reservoir water out of stream or would like the reservoir releases to occur only at times when hydroelectric power generation is needed.[7] Releasing reservoir water downstream during periods when the turbines are not operating is sometimes referred to as "spilling" water.

Gravel and Woody Debris

Salmon require shallow water with clean gravel beds to spawn and reproduce. Spawning can also be adversely affected if the velocity of the water where the eggs have been laid is too high, as this tends to wash the eggs out of the gravel and downstream. One of the ways the velocity of rivers, streams, and creeks can be reduced is by the presence of large woody debris (e.g. fallen trees), which can create calmer eddies with reduced flow speeds.[8]

The presence of upstream impoundments often traps gravel and woody debris behind the dam, so that the presence of these features/conditions is reduced downstream below the dam. The release of reservoir water for hydro-power generation (which is designed to maximize the velocity of the water passing through the turbine) can result in high-velocity flows below the dam, which can wash out gravel and woody debris in these downstream reaches.

Replacing Wild Salmon with Hatchery Salmon

Many of the onstream dams on salmon-bearing rivers on the Pacific Coast of the United States were built in the period 1930–1970. In this time period, there was a basic understanding of the life cycle of wild Pacific Coast salmon, and more specifically there was a recognition that wild salmon stocks would be adversely impacted by the blockage of downstream and upstream passage resulting from the dams.

At the time these dams were constructed (in the 1930–1970 period), however, the approach was generally not to consider how the design or operation of dams could be modified to maintain wild salmon stocks. Rather, at that time, the focus was on developing "hatchery salmon" facilities below the dams that would replace the wild salmon stocks that would be lost or reduced as a result of the dams. In her 2005 article, *The Salmon Hatchery Myth: When Bad Policy Happens to Good Science*, Melanie Kleiss explains: "Salmon hatcheries create their stocks by killing returning adult females, harvesting their eggs, and fertilizing them with sperm from returning males. After incubation and hatching, the offspring are then raised in a captive environment until they are ready to migrate to the ocean."[9]

Unfortunately for salmon, and the indigenous communities and fishers reliant on salmon, the salmon hatchery programs have generally not been successful, and there is a growing body of scientific data and literature on how hatchery salmon are in fact contributing to the further decline of wild salmon stocks.[10]

There are two primary reasons hatchery salmon mitigation has fallen short. First, numerous scientific studies have confirmed that hatchery salmon have lower overall survival rates than wild Pacific Coast salmon, as well as significantly lower breeding success rates than wild Pacific Coast salmon. Second, when large numbers of juvenile hatchery salmon are released into rivers from their captive environment, they are particularly aggressive at this stage and tend to outcompete wild juvenile salmon for food. The result of these two dynamics is that hatchery salmon tend to displace and further deplete wild salmon stocks, but these hatchery salmon then later have trouble surviving and reproducing.[11]

These tendencies and interactions were not well understood when most Pacific Coast dams were initially approved and constructed in the 1930–1970 period. Going forward, however, in the context of proceedings to relicense hydro facilities, there is no longer a credible scientific basis to rely on hatchery salmon programs to effectively offset the loss of wild salmon stocks. This recognition has led to an increasing focus on how the design and operation of existing hydro facilities can be modified to restore wild salmon stocks. It is in this context, of the previous experience with misplaced reliance on hatchery salmon mitigation, that the FERC relicensing process can assume a pivotal role.

FISHERY ASPECTS OF HYDRO RELICENSING IN THE UNITED STATES

FPA Provisions Regarding Fisheries

The requirements of the FPA apply to all nonfederal hydro facilities operated on navigable waters in the United States. Although hydro facilities operated by the United States Bureau of Reclamation (a federal agency) are outside the scope of the FPA, there are many other hydro facilities operated by nonfederal entities that the FPA covers. For instance, in California there are onstream hydro facilities operated by such nonfederal entities as the California Department of Water Resources (a state agency), the San Francisco Public Utilities Commission and the East Bay Municipal Utility District (local/ regional public agencies), and the Pacific Gas and Electric Company (a private water utility).

Under the FPA, the FERC issues initial hydro facility licenses for periods of 30 to 50 years.[12] Once an initial license is set to expire, the project operator must apply for a new license through the relicensing process.[13] During relicensing, the FERC evaluates the project and determines whether continuing to operate the project is in the public interest and, if so, under what conditions.

Between 1990 and 2010, the FERC relicensed about 500 hydro projects in the United States. Of these 500 relicensed hydro facilities, it required fish passage improvements or other fish restoration improvements in more than 40 percent of the new licenses.[14] The FERC's authority and obligation to include these fish restoration conditions in the relicensing process derives from Sections 10(a), 10(j), and 18 of the FPA.[15] The last of these two sections of the FPA (discussed later) set forth how the FERC's relicensing authority interacts with the authority of the two other federal agencies, with main authority for fishery management, the National Marine Fisheries Service (NMFS) and the United States Fish and Wildlife Service (USFWS).

Section 10(a) of the FPA provides that a project must serve the public interest in the river basin, not just the licensee's interest in hydropower generation. More specifically, Section 10(a) requires that a license must ensure that the project adopted "will be best adapted to a comprehensive plan for improving or developing a waterway or waters for the use of benefit of interstate or foreign commerce, for the improvement and utilization of water-power development, and for the *adequate protection, mitigation, and enhancement of fish and wildlife (including related spawning grounds and habitat)*" (italics added).

Section 10(j) of the FPA requires that an FERC license "adequately and equitably protect, mitigate damages to, and enhance fish and wildlife (including related spawning grounds and habitat) affected by the development, operation and management of the project." NMFS, USFWS, or a state fish and wildlife department may recommend such conditions. If timely submitted, the FPA provides that FERC must generally include such conditions in the license.

Section 18 of the FPA, NMFS, or USFWS prescribes a facility for fish passage (such as a fish ladder or a trapping site to recollect fish for truck transport), operation, and maintenance of the facility, and any other conditions necessary to ensure effective passage. A Section 18 prescription may apply to upstream or downstream passage.[16] As with Section 10(j) of the FPA, FERC must generally incorporate a Section 18 fish passage prescription submitted by NMFS or USFWS.

Rights of Non-Operator Stakeholders in Hydro Relicensing Proceedings

The operator of the hydro facility applying for relicense and FERC are often not the only parties to the relicensing process. Other interested parties, such as environmental, fishery groups, and indigenous tribes, are permitted to file an administrative motion with FERC to intervene in FERC licensing and relicensing proceedings. So long as this motion is timely filed with FERC, the FPA provides that this motion to intervene will be automatically granted.[17]

An intervenor has two fundamental rights in connection with FERC licensing proceedings: (1) it will be served with all of the documents that are filed in the proceeding because the intervenor will be included in the service list; (2) it may file a motion with FERC during the administrative proceedings or, on a final decision, seeking rehearing or judicial review.[18] The active and effective participation of intervenors often plays an important role in the scope of issues considered during the proceedings as well as the terms and conditions proposed in the final license.[19] For instance, an intervenor may assert that the absence of relicense terms providing for fish passage or minimal release flows is the violation of the FPA or other environmental laws, and that it will seek judicial review of license if such terms are not included. The right of an intervenor to seek judicial review of license terms can provide incentives for both the FERC and the applicant to meaningfully address the concerns raised by an intervenor.

NEPA, ESA, and Clean Water Act Applied to Hydro Relicensing

The implementation of Sections 10(a), 10(j), and 18 of the FPA is closely related to compliance with three other federal laws: the National Environmental Policy Act (NEPA), Endangered Species Act (ESA), and Clean Water Act.

In connection with the FERC's relicensing decision, NEPA requires the preparation of an environmental impact statement that must consider alternatives and mitigation measures to reduce the adverse impacts of the project on fisheries. Under the ESA, if the continued operation of the hydro project will result in death or injury to fisheries listed as endangered, NMFS or USFWS must prepare a biological opinion that includes conditions to ensure the project does not jeopardize the survival of the species. The alternatives and mitigation measures identified in the environmental impact statement (prepared pursuant to the NEPA), and the conditions set forth in the biological opinion (prepared pursuant to the ESA), often serve as the basis for the fishery restoration terms later included in FERC's relicensing decision.[20]

Section 401 of the Clean Water Act requires that all discharges into navigable waters must comply with state water quality standards. Hydro facilities licensed under the FPA are subject to Section 401 water quality certification requirements (sometimes referred to as "401 Certification"). State water quality standards often relate to fishery habitat conditions, such as adequate instream flow or water temperatures. If a state government denies water quality certification for a hydro facility located in the state, the FERC may not issue a license for the facility. Similarly, if a state government issues water quality certification for a hydro facility subject to certain terms and conditions, FERC must include these terms and conditions in its license.[21] For instance, a state government could deny a requested 401 Certification for a hydro facility on the grounds that the facility does not provide sufficient flows below the dam to maintain fisheries in good condition, or it could issue a water quality certification that required certain enhanced downstream releases of water for fisheries. In this way, the 401 Certification process provides states with legal authority to insist that FERC-licensed hydro facilities operate in a manner that is sufficiently protective of fisheries.

Relicensing in Action: Case Studies on Hydro and Wild Salmon

Oroville Hydro Relicensing on the Feather River in California

Oroville Dam was built in the 1960s by the California Department of Water Resource (DWR) on the Feather River north of Sacramento, California. The Feather River flows south/southwest until it empties into the Sacramento River, and the Sacramento River flows south to San Francisco Bay and eventually out to the Pacific Ocean. The initial 1957 Oroville permit was for 50 years (until 2007).

At the time Oroville Dam was built, it was already known that there were extensive salmon spawning grounds upstream of where the dam would be located. Oroville Dam is 770 feet high, the tallest dam in the United States, with no fish ladders to provide for upstream or downstream passage of salmon. Lake Oroville has a water storage capacity of over 3.5 million acre-feet. For the reasons discussed earlier, at the time Oroville Dam was built, DWR proposed to develop a hatchery salmon program below the dam to compensate for the dam's anticipated adverse impacts on wild salmon. Although hatchery salmon now account for the majority of salmon on the lower Feather River, the overall numbers of salmon on the lower Feather River have declined drastically since Oroville Dam was built (and for the reasons noted earlier). There are studies indicating that the hatchery salmon may be contributing to the decline of wild salmon stocks on the lower Feather River.[22]

During the Oroville relicensing proceedings, there was considerable focus on what could and should be done to restore wild salmon runs. In 2006, after several years of negotiations between FERC, DWR, and fishery stakeholders, an agreement was reached over the terms and conditions to be included in the new license.

Given the height of Oroville Dam, the prospect of installing fish ladders to provide for upstream and downstream salmon passage was generally viewed as a cost-prohibitive and unfeasible modification. Instead of fish passage, the new relicensing terms focused on a three-pronged approach to improve habitat for wild salmon in the portions of the Feather River below Oroville Dam.

The first prong of the Oroville relicensing wild salmon restoration conditions concentrated on flow and water temperature improvements. Under the terms of the new license, sufficient water from Lake Oroville (the reservoir behind Oroville Dam) must be released to maintain water temperatures in the lower Feather River at or below 56 degrees Fahrenheit from September 1–30, and below 55 degrees Fahrenheit from October 1–May 31. These periods cover the main spawning and migration seasons for salmon on the Feather River.

The second prong of the Oroville relicensing wild salmon restoration conditions concentrated on gravel supplementation. As discussed earlier, salmon spawn in gravel in clear shallow water. Oroville Dam blocks 97 percent of the gravel from passing downstream to the lower Feather River which has reduced salmon spawning habitat. Under the terms of the new license, DWR will deliver and deposit 8,300 cubic yards of gravel in specified locations below the dam.

The third prong of the Oroville relicensing wild salmon restoration conditions concentrated on supplementation of large woody debris. Large woody debris (such as fallen trees) creates essential habitat elements for salmon like pool and eddies with reduced water velocity. Oroville Dam currently blocks the downstream movement of large woody debris in the lower Feather River. The new Oroville relicensing terms require placement of several hundred pieces of large woody debris in locations on the lower Feather River that maximizes benefits for salmon.

If fully implemented, collectively these measures hold the prospect of contributing significantly to the restoration of wild salmon stocks that spawn in the lower Feather River. The value of these fish restoration improvements, over the course of the new license, has been estimated at around $450 million (US).[23] While this figure may initially appear to be a significant amount of money, it represents a small percentage of the value of the hydroelectricity and water that will be delivered during this same license period.

Pelton Hydro Relicensing on the Deschutes River in Oregon

The Pelton Round Butte Project (Pelton Dam) is located on the Deschutes River in North Central Oregon. The Deschutes River, with a robust historic sockeye salmon fishery, flows in a northerly direction to its confluence with the Columbia River. The Columbia River then flows east where it empties into the Pacific Ocean. Pelton Dam was completed in 1965 pursuant to a fifty-year license, and is owned and operated jointly by Portland General Electric

Company (PGE) and the Warm Spring Confederated Tribes. Pelton Dam (whose official name is the Round Butte Development) stands 440 feet tall and creates a reservoir (Lake Billy Chinook) with a gross storage capacity of 535,000 acre-feet of water. It is therefore considerably smaller (in terms of both height and reservoir storage capacity) than Oroville Dam.

Like Oroville Dam, a hatchery salmon program was instituted at the same time Pelton Dam was built, to help offset some of the wild salmon stock losses anticipated to result once the dam was completed. Unlike Oroville Dam, however, Pelton Dam was designed with an adjacent fish ladder to assist wild salmon with upstream and downstream passage around the dam. Unfortunately, due to the slack water and circular currents in Lake Billy Chinook behind the dam, outbound juvenile salmon were usually unable to find the adjacent fish ladder that would provide them with downstream passage to the Pacific Ocean. When Pelton Dam came up for relicensing, a main focus of study and contention was on how to modify the design and/or operation of the facility to improve downstream migration of wild salmon.[24]

The solution that emerged became known as the "Selective Water Withdrawal" (SWW) facility. The SWW is a 273-foot tall underwater tower in Lake Billy Chinook capped by an intake module that collects fish migrating downstream and separately sends water to the turbines to generate hydroelectricity. At the intake structure, fish are collected into two screens and sorted. Non-anadromous fish (such as bull trout) are returned to Lake Billy Chinook. Juvenile salmon move into a floating fish transfer facility, and are then loaded into a truck for transport and released below the dam to continue their migration to the Pacific Ocean.[25]

The SWW was completed in 2009 and in its first five years of operation, significant increase in salmon returns occurred. The SWW cost $108 million to build. As with the costs associated with the salmon restoration efforts related to the Oroville Dam relicensing, this $108 million figure represents a small percentage of the value of the hydroelectricity and water that will be delivered during the license period.[26]

The SWW component of the Pelton Dam relicensing represents an innovative effort to improve downstream passage for wild salmon, but the experimental nature of the proposed solution will require careful monitoring. More specifically, there remain questions about how the collection and truck transport of the juvenile salmon under the SWW approach may affect their long-term survival and reproduction rates. It should be remembered that there were also initially high hopes for the effectiveness of hatchery salmon programs, and in the early years these hatcheries produced increased numbers of salmon heading downstream. The shortcomings of hatchery salmon operations were not fully understood until smaller salmon returned that often failed to reproduce.

Notwithstanding these concerns, the SWW can still be seen as an attempt to address the downstream passage failures of the original design and operation of Pelton Dam. Because the SWW includes a rigorous monitoring program, there should be opportunities to revisit and modify wild salmon restoration strategies related to Pelton Dam if the SWW proves less successful than anticipated.

La Grange Hydro Relicensing on the Tuolumne River in California

La Grange Dam is located on the Tuolumne River in California, which is tributary to the San Joaquin River that flows into San Francisco Bay and then to the Pacific Ocean. The dam was constructed in the 1890s by the Modesto Irrigation District and the Turlock Irrigation District to store and divert water for agricultural irrigation. In the 1920s, a hydroelectric power station was added to the facility. La Grange Dam is built of cyclopean rubble masonry and stands 127.5 feet high and 336 feet wide. It presently provides no downstream or upstream fish passage.

La Grange Dam was constructed many years before the FPA went into effect, and therefore was not required to receive a FERC license before being built. In 2012, FERC issued an order to the dam's operators requiring them (for the first time) to apply for a license.[27] In this sense, the FERC regulatory posture for La Grange Dam is initial licensing for an existing hydro facility rather than relicensing for a previously licensed facility.

The wild salmon and anadromous steelhead trout stocks on the Tuolumne River have been in decline for several decades. In 2009, the NMFS released a report titled *Public Draft Recovery Plan for Evaluation of Significant Unites of Sacramento River Winter Run Salmon and Central Valley Spring-Run Chinook Salmon and Distinct Population Segments of Central Valley Steelhead.*[28] This 2009 NMFS report found that a primary stressor leading to salmon and steelhead decline was the blockage of access to historical upstream habitat by La Grange Dam.

Under the FPA's relicensing procedures, one of the first steps is for FERC to determine the issues and areas that need to be evaluated by the applicant in connection with its application. In their initial study proposal to FERC, the operators of La Grange Dam did not propose to conduct studies concerning modifying facility design or operations to allow fish passage to or from above the dam. In the context of the La Grange relicensing, several conservation groups that were intervenors to the proceeding (including American Rivers, California Sportfishing Protection Alliance, California Trout, Friends of the River, Golden

West Women's Flyfishers, Northern California Federation of Flyfishers, Pacific Coast Federation of Fishermen's Associations, Trout Unlimited, and the Tuolumne River Trust) and NMFS submitted comments to FERC urging that the operators of the dam be required to conduct a fish barrier assessment and evaluate the alternative of installing fish passage facilities.[29]

As per NMFS December 14, 2014 comment letter to FERC explained as follows: "The completion of La Grange Dam in 1894 constituted a permanent and complete blockage to upstream anadromous fish migrations to their historical spawning and rearing grounds. The La Grange Diversion Dam is a 125 ft. tall dam that completely lacks any fish passage structures or improvements – these are indisputable facts, as is the conclusion that La Grange Diversion Dam and the Project have continued to the present day to act as a complete barrier to upstream anadromous fish migration ... NMFS Recovery Plan identifies the upper Tuolumne River above La Grange [] as candidate area for reintroducing California Central Valley steelhead and spring-run Chinook salmon ... it is clear that a comprehensive evaluation of fish passage should be conducted as part of the La Grange ILP [Integrated Licensing Proceeding]."[30]

On February 2, 2015, FERC issued its study plan determination in the La Grange licensing proceeding, agreeing with the NMFS and the intervenor conservation groups that the operators of the facility will be required to conduct both a *Fish Passage Facilities Alternative Assessment* and a *Fish Passage Barrier Assessment*.[31] In making this determination, the FERC noted that "The information collected in this study would help define the nature and degree to which the dam and powerhouse are barriers and impediments to the upstream migration of anadromous salmonoids."

At this point, it remains to be seen what analysis or findings will be included in the fish passage/fish barrier studies prepared in connection with the La Grange licensing proceeding, and how the results of these fish passage/fish barrier studies may ultimately affect the terms and conditions that FERC includes in the license for the La Grange facility. However, based on the La Grange FERC licensing proceeding to date, it can be expected that NMFS and the aforementioned conservation groups that are intervenors in the proceeding will press for the incorporation of fish passage modification terms in the license to help restore the declining salmon and steelhead runs on the Tuolumne River.

CITIZEN ENFORCEMENT OF WATER QUALITY CERTIFICATION STANDARDS

As discussed earlier, a little over a decade ago FERC relicensed Pelton Dam on the Deschutes River in Oregon. As part of the license issued for

Pelton Dam, the Oregon Department of Environmental Quality issued a water quality certification pursuant to Section 401 of the federal Clean Water Act.

Since that FERC relicensing was completed, a lawsuit was filed by the Deschutes River Alliance under the citizen suit provision and section 401 of the federal Clean Water Act, alleging violations of the State of Oregon's water quality certification standards by the operator Portland General Electric. Among other things, these water quality certification standards related to the maintenance of cold-water temperatures for salmon and trout.

In response to the lawsuit filed by the Deschutes River Alliance, Portland General Electric filed a motion to dismiss in which the company alleged that only FERC and the state government that issued the water quality certification had authority to bring suit for noncompliance with the standards set forth in the certification. The federal district court did not accept Portland General Electric's cramped reading of the Clean Water Act's citizen suit which is as follows:

> PGE concludes, Congress authorized citizen suits to enforce the require-
> ment under section 401 of the CWA to obtain a certification but not to
> enforce any conditions that are included within any certification. PGE
> maintains that any such enforcement authority resides only in the hands of
> the federal permitting or licensing entity. The Court rejects PGE's inter-
> pretation, which rewrites the statute. The plain reading of the citizen suit
> provision is that it authorizes a citizen to initiate suit against anyone alleged
> to be in violation – that is, currently violating – certification under section
> 401. The definition does not expressly limit its application to obtaining
> certification.[32]

The 2017 holding in the *Deschutes River Alliance* v. *Portland General Electric* case suggests that, going forward, there may be more lawsuits filed by environmental groups focused on noncompliance with the standards in state water quality certification issued in the context of FERC hydropower. Such litigation holds the promise of serving as an effective mechanism to ensure not only that hydro relicensing includes new operational standards to help restore wild salmon stocks but that there is also actual compliance with these new operational standards.

HYDRO AND THE FREE RUN OF FISH

Dams occupy an interesting place in the physical terrain as well as the political terrain. Although dams and the reservoirs behind dams are man-made structures, structures that can be modified or even removed, this is not often how we come to view them over time.

Particularly for dams and reservoirs that have been present for a few generations, and in which there are few if any living people that can remember what the river or land looked like before such dams and reservoirs were there, these structures appear today almost as if they were a part of the natural order. The longer they are there, the more the "lakes" named for the reservoirs behind dams can seem like naturally occurring lakes, and the more the dams themselves can seem like organic geologic extensions of the rock to which they are abutted.

When Bill Clinton was President of the United States, Daniel Beard served as Commissioner of the United States Bureau of Reclamation, an agency that operates many dams. In a 2017 interview, Beard observed: "Once we build a dam, we somehow think it is a permanent part of the landscape. But it's not."[33] If the original design of a dam or the original operational parameters of a dam no longer comport with current economic and ecological needs, the design and operational parameters of a dam can be appropriately modified. As Daniel Beard suggests, there is nothing fixed or permanent about these things.

In the United States, many Pacific Coast dams were initially designed and approved on the assumption that hatchery salmon programs would replace the lost wild salmon stocks caused by the dams. The hydro relicensing process set forth in the FPA provides an important opportunity to reexamine the ways dams operate now that this initial assumption has proven faulty. This hydro relicensing process allows such questions as fish passage and downstream flows to be considered anew with improved science and fresh eyes.

The broader legal and policy takeaway from the United States experience with relicensing under the FPA is that the operation and design of hydro facilities can be modified over time to greatly reduce adverse impacts on fisheries. Such modifications are unlikely to occur, however, unless there is an effective regulatory mechanism in place to force operators of existing dams to periodically and systemically identify and incorporate feasible fish restoration measures. Without such a mechanism, the faulty fishery assumptions and chronic operational flaws of existing hydro facilities may continue in perpetuity.

The FERC hydro relicensing process therefore offers a way to bring the principles and remedies reflected in Article XI of the 1807 River Tweed Act[34] into the modern era, so the "free run of fish" and the condition of our wild salmon stocks moves from the periphery to the mainstream of the law's efforts to define the obligations of those who are granted permission to operate onstream hydropower facilities on our rivers.

Notes

1. Caroline Balfour, THE EARLY DAYS OF THE RIVER TWEED COMMISSIONERS (published by the River Tweed Commissioners, 2007), p. 31.

2. *Act to amend and rent more effectual three Acts, made in the Eleventh, Fifteenth and Thirty-seventh years of His present Majesty, for the Regulation and Improvement of the River Tweed* (adopted April 25, 1807, hereinafter referred to as the 1807 River Tweed Act). See generally Caroline Balfour, THE EARLY DAYS OF THE RIVER TWEED COMMISSIONERS (published by the River Tweed Commissioners, 2007).

3. See generally Caroline Balfour, THE EARLY DAYS OF THE RIVER TWEED COMMISSIONERS (published by the River Tweed Commissioners, 2007). In this text a "cauld" is defined as a "weir, or dam-head, built across the river in order to achieve a sufficient head of water to allow the run-off of a mill-stream, or lade, to power a mill."

4. See generally Caroline Balfour, THE EARLY DAYS OF THE RIVER TWEED COMMISSIONERS (published by the River Tweed Commissioners, 2007).

5. *Act to amend and rent more effectual three Acts, made in the Eleventh, Fifteenth and Thirty-seventh years of His present Majesty, for the Regulation and Improvement of the River Tweed* (adopted April 25, 1807, hereinafter referred to as the 1807 River Tweed Act). See Caroline Balfour, THE EARLY DAYS OF THE RIVER TWEED COMMISSIONERS (published by the River Tweed Commissioners, 2007), p. 44.

6. *Act to amend and rent more effectual three Acts, made in the Eleventh, Fifteenth and Thirty-seventh years of His present Majesty, for the Regulation and Improvement of the River Tweed* (adopted April 25, 1807, hereinafter referred to as the 1807 River Tweed Act). See Caroline Balfour, THE EARLY DAYS OF THE RIVER TWEED COMMISSIONERS (published by the River Tweed Commissioners, 2007), p. 44.

7. Paul Stanton Kibel, *A Salmon Eye Lens on Climate Adaptation*, 19 OCEAN AND COASTAL LAW JOURNAL 65, 71–72 (2013) ("Additional quantities of cold water from upstream dams/reservoirs can be released to reduce the temperature of downstream waters .... The additional release of reservoir water for this purpose, however, may be resisted by agricultural and municipal users of water stored in reservoir behind such dams.")

8. California Department of Water Resources, *Oroville Facilities – Highlights of the Settlement Agreement for Licensing* (2008).

9. Melanie E. Kleiss, *The Salmon Hatchery Myth: When Bad Policy Happens to Good Science*, 6 MINNESOTA JOURNAL OF LAW, SCIENCE AND TECHNOLOGY 433 (2005).

10. See generally Jim Lichatowich, SALMON WITHOUT RIVERS: A HISTORY OF THE PACIFIC SALMON CRISIS (Island Press, 1999).

11. Edward D. Weber and Kurt D. Fausch, *Interactions between Hatchery and Wild Salmonids in Streams: Differences in Biology and Evidence for Competition*, 60 Canadian Journal of Fisheries and Aquatic Science 1018 (2003).

12. Section 6 of the Federal Power Act, 16 U.S.C. §799; Hydropower Reform Coalition, *Citizen Toolkit for Effective Participation in Hydropower Relicensing* (2005), p. 1.

13. Hydropower Reform Coalition, *Citizen Toolkit for Effective Participation in Hydropower Relicensing* (2005), p. 1.

14. Hydropower Reform Coalition, *Citizen Toolkit for Effective Participation in Hydropower Relicensing* (2005).

15. Sections 10(a), 10(j) and 18 of the Federal Power Act, 16 U.S.C. §§ 791–832 (Part I) and §§ 824–824n (Part II).

16. Section 18 of the Federal Power Act, 16 U.S.C. §§ 791–832 (Part I) and §§ 824-824n (Part II).

17. 18 C.F.R. § 385.2010; Hydropower Reform Coalition, *Citizen Toolkit for Effective Participation in Hydropower Relicensing* (2005), pp. 62–64.

18. 18 C.F.R. 385.214(a); Hydropower Reform Coalition, *Citizen Toolkit for Effective Participation in Hydropower Relicensing* (2005).

19. Hydropower Reform Coalition, *Citizen Toolkit for Effective Participation in Hydropower Relicensing* (2005).

20. Hydropower Reform Coalition, *Citizen Toolkit for Effective Participation in Hydropower Relicensing* (2005).

21. Hydropower Reform Coalition, *Citizen Toolkit for Effective Participation in Hydropower Relicensing* (2005).

22. California Department of Water Resources, *Oroville Facilities – Highlights of the Settlement Agreement for Licensing* (2008); Ted Sommer, Debbie McEwan, and Randall Brown, *Factors Affecting Chinook Salmon Spawning in the Lower Feather River* (Fish Bulletin No. 197).

23. Settlement Agreement for Licensing of the Oroville Facilities (2006); California Department of Water Resources, *Oroville Facilities – Highlights of the Settlement Agreement for Licensing* (2008).

24. Low Impact Hydropower Institute, *LIHI Certificate #25 – Pelton Round Butte Project, Oregon* (Certified on March 28, 2007).

25. Deschutes River Conservancy, *Return of the Sockeye Salmon to Pelton Round Butte Complex* (August 2012 Bulletin).

26. Deschutes River Conservancy, *Return of the Sockeye Salmon to Pelton Round Butte Complex* (August 2012 Bulletin); Pelton Round Butte Hydroelectric Project Settlement Agreement, FERC Project No. 2004 (July 13, 2004).

27. John Holland, *La Grange Dam Catches the Eye of Government*, Modesto Bee (December 31, 2012).

28. National Marine Fisheries Service, *Public Draft Recovery Plan for Evaluation of Significant Units of Sacramento River Winter Run Salmon and Central Valley Spring-Run Chinook Salmon and Distinct Population Segments of Central Valley Steelhead* (2009).

29. Water and Power Law Group, *Comments on Behalf of Conservation Groups Regarding Pre-Application Document and Scoping Document and Study Request for La Grange Project* (July 22, 2104 Filing on behalf of American Rivers, American Whitewater, California Sportfishing Protection Alliance, California Trout, Central Sierra Environmental Resource Center, Friends of the River, Golden West Women's Flyfishers, Merced Fly Fishing Club, North California Federation of Flyfishers, Pacific Coast Federal of Fishermen's Association, Trout Unlimited, and the Tuolumne River Trust); National Marine Fisheries Service, *Comments on Proposed Study Plan for the LaGrange Hydroelectric Project*, P-14581–00 (December 4, 2015).

30. National Marine Fisheries Service, *Comments on Proposed Study Plan for the LaGrange Hydroelectric Project*, P-14581–00 (December 4, 2015).

31. Federal Energy Regulatory Commission, *Study Plan Determination for the La Grange Hydroelectric Project* (February 2, 2015).

32. March 27, 2017 Opinion and Order, in *Deschutes River Alliance v. Portland General Electric* (Case No. 3:16-cv-1644-SI, United States District Court of the District of Oregon).

33. Jeremy P. Jacobs, Dams: 'Relics' or Vital to an "All of the Above" Fix, Greenwire, June 10, 2017.

34. *Act to amend and rent more effectual three Acts, made in the Eleventh, Fifteenth and Thirty-seventh years of His present Majesty, for the Regulation and Improvement of the River Tweed* (adopted April 25, 1807, hereinafter referred to as the 1807 River Tweed Act). See Caroline Balfour, THE EARLY DAYS OF THE RIVER TWEED COMMISSIONERS (published by the River Tweed Commissioners, 2007).

4

Instream Rights and Watershed Governance

In many river basins around the world, the instream flows in the mainstem rivers are often determined by the contribution of water to these mainstem rivers from tributaries. Notwithstanding the somewhat obvious hydrologic reality that the contribution of water from tributaries helps determine the instream flow of mainstem rivers, the law often treats mainstem rivers as if they were hydrologically distinct from tributaries. That is to say, legal rights of diversion of water on mainstem rivers are often determined without taking into proper account how diversion of water on upstream tributaries impacts the volume of water in mainstem rivers.

Perhaps the most glaring example of this disconnect between hydrology and the law is the case of the multistate legal regime (often referred to as the "Law of the River") to allocate the Colorado River in the United States. Pursuant to the Law of the River, California was granted the right to divert 4.4 million acre-feet (MAF) of water from the Colorado River, while Arizona was granted the right to divert 2.8 MAF of water from the Colorado River. In the 1963 case of *Arizona* v. *California*, the United States Supreme Court considered California's claim regarding how this allocation should be affected by Arizona's diversion of water from the Gila River, a tributary to the mainstem of the Colorado.[1] California alleged, in a position grounded in basic hydrology, that since Arizona's diversions from the upstream Gila River reduced the volume of flow from this tributary into the mainstem of the Colorado River, such diversions from the Gila River should count against Arizona's 2.8 MAF rights to water from the Colorado River.

In its ruling in *Arizona* v. *California*, the United States Supreme Court rejected California's position regarding the Gila River, concluding that the pertinent federal legislation made clear that California's 4.4 MAF allocation and Arizona's 2.8 MAF allocation referred only to rights of diversion from the "mainstream" and left each state free to divert intrastate tributaries to this "mainstream."[2] From a legal standpoint this holding was likely correct, although from a hydrological standpoint it was somewhat delusional.

In the years since *Arizona* v. *California* was decided in 1963, and as Arizona has continued to divert a significant amount of water from the Gila River, there have predictably been significant reductions in the instream flow of the mainstem of the Colorado River below the confluence with the Gila River. This reduction in instream flow below the Colorado River's confluence with the Gila River has in turn had adverse impacts on fisheries and water quality as well as impaired the ability of the United States to meet its downstream Colorado River water deliver obligation to Mexico. These are the types of consequences that ensue when the legal rules by which we manage watersheds are at odds with the ways watersheds actually operate.

The challenge of developing legal rules that operate at the watershed level, which are consistent with the ways that the mainstems of rivers and the tributaries to such mainstems interact, is not unique to the United States. It is a global challenge for watersheds, and our inability to regulate at the watershed level can result in excessive tributary diversions and corresponding reduced mainstem instream flow.

1878 *ARID LANDS* REPORT BY JOHN WESLEY POWELL

In 1878, John Wesley Powell, the first director of the United States Geological Survey, published his *Report on the Lands in the Arid Regions of the United States*. In his *Arid Lands Report*, Powell foresaw the essential role that water would play in the development of the American West and the challenges faced in managing watersheds that included not only mainstem rivers but also networks of tributaries that contributed water to mainstem rivers.

The San Joaquin River–Sacramento River–San Francisco Bay basin in California illustrates the hydrology and landscape that Powell described. The mainstem of the San Joaquin River drains into the Carquinez Strait and then to San Francisco Bay but the flow of the San Joaquin River is itself a product of the flows of the Stanislaus, Tuolumne, and Merced Rivers that contribute to it. Similarly, the mainstem of the Sacramento River also drains into the Carquinez Strait and then to San Francisco Bay but the flow of the Sacramento River is itself a product of the flows of Feather River and American River that contribute to it. Moreover, anadromous salmon and steelhead trout fisheries in this basin often originate in the tributaries before heading downstream to the mainstems of the San Joaquin and Sacramento Rivers and through San Francisco Bay and then retrace this route back upstream when they return to spawn.[3]

In light of the ways that the flows of mainstem rivers are dependent on the contributing flows of tributaries, and in light of how fisheries such as salmon and steelhead trout migrate downstream and upstream between mainstem rivers and tributaries, what did Powell recommend? Powell advocated for the creation of governmental entities with authority to manage water resources and water supply at the "watershed" level to enable them to take account of the interrelationship between tributaries and mainstem rivers. He even went so far as to recommend drawing the borders of states to correspond to major watersheds/drainage basins.[4]

Although Powell's proposal to designate state borders in the American West on a watershed basis came too late, as most of the state borders were already established by the time his *Arid Lands Report* was published in 1878, his concept of watershed-based governance lies at the root of more recent actions by California's State Water Resources Control Board.

On September 15, 2016, the State Water Board released its draft of a proposed update to the *Water Quality Control Plan for the San Francisco Bay/Sacramento-San Joaquin Delta Estuary*, often referred to as the *Bay Delta Water Quality Plan*. The update to the *Bay Delta Water Quality Plan* is being undertaken pursuant to requirements under the federal Clean Water Act and California's Porter-Cologne Water Quality Act. To ensure adequate water conditions for fisheries (such as salmon, steelhead trout, and smelt) that are present in and migrate through the Bay Delta, the September 15, 2016 draft of the *Bay Delta Water Quality Plan* update recommended that a range of between 30 and 50 percent (with a starting point of 40 percent) of the "unimpaired flows" of the Stanislaus, Tuolumne, and Merced Rivers be left instream until their confluence with the San Joaquin River.

According the State Water Board, "Unimpaired flow is the rate and volume of water that would be produced by the rain and snow accumulating in a watershed absent any diversion, storage or use of water. An unimpaired flow approach generally mimics the natural variability of California's river flows that support native fish like salmon and steelhead and for which they have evolved."[5]

Although current data suggest that average base flow for the Stanislaus River is already about 40 percent of unimpaired flow, the average flows for the Tuolumne River and Merced River are currently 21 percent and 26 percent, respectively, of unimpaired flow.[6] The State Water Board's proposed base flows for the Tuolumne River and Merced River, if implemented, would therefore result in a measurable increase in water left instream in these San Joaquin River tributaries and presumably a corresponding decrease in the amount of water available for diversion from these waterways.

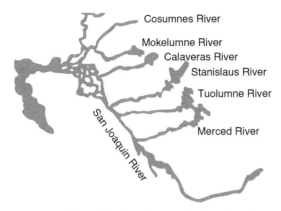

Cosumnes River

Mokelumne River
Calaveras River
Stanislaus River

Tuolumne River

San Joaquin River

Merced River

MAP 4.1 Map of the San Joaquin basin tributaries

On December 12, 2018, the State Water Board approved the draft San Joaquin tributary base instream flows that had been proposed in draft form back in 2016. In early 2019, these tributary base flows were challenged in lawsuits filed by water users that may face reductions in water supply from the tributaries, as well as by the Trump Administration in connection with potential impacts on the federal New Melones Dam located on the Stanislaus River. As this chapter discusses, the State Water Board's adoption of base flows for the San Joaquin River tributaries, and the litigation challenging these base flows, are taking place in the broader context of efforts to implement watershed governance. That is, to regulate water resources in the Sacramento River–San Joaquin River–San Francisco Bay Delta watershed on the scientific recognition that the levels of instream flow of the tributaries to the Sacramento River and the San Joaquin River ultimately affect the instream flows of the Sacramento River and the San Joaquin River and into the Bay Delta.

SAN JOAQUIN RIVER WATERSHED, MAINSTEM, AND TRIBUTARIES

2010 *Public Trust Flow Criteria for the San Joaquin River*

The State Water Board's reliance on numeric unimpaired flow benchmarks did not first emerge in the September 2016 proposed update to the *Bay Delta Water Quality Plan*. Rather, as discussed in greater detail in Chapter 1 of this book, numeric unimpaired flow benchmarks were relied upon previously by the State Water Board in 2010 with the issuance of its public trust Bay Delta flow criteria. An understanding of the legal and policy context for the prior issuance of the 2010 public trust Bay Delta flow criteria is necessary to understand the approach taken by the State Water Board in the September 2016 base flow proposals for the San Joaquin River tributaries.[7]

California's 2009 Delta Reform Act added section 85086 to the California Water Code. Section 85086 provides in pertinent part:

> *The [Water Board] shall, pursuant to its public trust obligations, develop new flow criteria for the Delta ecosystem necessary to protect public trust resources. In carrying out this section, the board shall review existing water quality objectives and use the best available scientific information. The flow criteria for the Delta ecosystem shall include the volume, quality and timing of water necessary for the Delta ecosystem under different conditions. The flow criteria shall be developed in a public process by the board within nine months of the enactment of this division. This public process shall be in the forum of an informational proceeding.[8]*

As an informational proceeding, as opposed to a water rights proceeding, the public trust flow criteria developed pursuant to section 85086 of the California Water Code would not modify any existing rights of diversion. The purpose of the public trust flow proceeding mandated in the 2009 Delta Reform Act was therefore not to directly curtail diversions but rather to compel the State Water Board to identify the inflow from the San Joaquin River and the Sacramento River needed to fully protect the salmon, steelhead trout, and smelt fisheries (the public trust resources in question) present in the Bay Delta.

At the time the 2009 Delta Reform Act was enacted, this approach was referred to as "flow first" – start with an informational science-based assessment of how much water the Bay Delta fisheries and ecosystem need and then use this assessment as a reference point for later adjustments of diversions through subsequent water rights or regulatory proceedings. As the April 14, 2010 comment letter to the State Water Board from the Bay Institute and the Natural Resources Defense Council explained as follows: "It is important to be clear as to what this proceeding is and is not. It is clearly not intended to be a regulatory proceeding to review existing permits and conditions under the authority of the SWRCB or other permitting entities. On the contrary, this proceeding was intentionally decoupled by the legislature to any specific permitting action precisely in order to allow the SWRCB to freely determine the flow necessary to fully protect public trust species in the Delta without considering the impact of such criteria on any particular interest."[9]

In August 2010, after a nine-month process of public comments and hearings, the State Water Board adopted its final public trust Bay Delta flow criteria report. In section 1.1 of the report (titled "Legislative Directive and

State Water Board Approach"), the State Water Board explained that pursuant to section 85086, its flow criteria were based only on the needs of public trust resources and did not take into account consumptive use of water for irrigation or municipal purposes, noting: "The State Water Board does not make any determination regarding the feasibility of the public trust criteria . . .. Any balancing of public trust values and water rights would be conducted through an adjudicative or regulatory proceeding. Instead, the State Water Board's focus here is solely on identifying the flow criteria as directed by section 85086."[10] The August 2010 public trust Bay Delta flow criteria report determined as follows:

> *In order to preserve the attributes of the natural variable system to which native fish species are adapted, many of the criteria developed by the State Water Board are crafted as percentages of natural or unimpaired flows. These criteria include:*
>
> * *75 percent of unimpaired Delta outflow from January through June;*
> * *75 percent of unimpaired Sacramento River inflow from November through June; and*
> * *60 percent of unimpaired San Joaquin River inflow from February through June.*[11]

The State Water Board's 2010 public trust Bay Delta flow criteria report thus found that, to fully protect and restore the fisheries and ecosystem of the Bay Delta, 60 percent of the unimpaired flow of the San Joaquin River should be kept instream until it empties into the Carquinez Strait. The August 2010 public trust flow criteria report was silent on how to balance this 60 percent unimpaired flow criteria with consumptive uses of San Joaquin River basin water, and was also silent as to the extent to which the San Joaquin River's main tributaries (the Stanislaus, Tuolumne, and Merced Rivers) may need to increase their inflow into the San Joaquin River to enhance the San Joaquin River's downstream inflow into the Bay Delta. These two open questions set the stage for the State Water Board's proposed approach to the San Joaquin River's main tributaries in its update to the *Bay Delta Water Quality Plan.*

Base Flows in 2016 Draft Update to Bay Delta Water Quality Plan

The initial *Bay Delta Water Quality Plan* was adopted in the mid-1990s and updated in 2006. The 2006 update to the *Bay Delta Water Quality Plan* included flow objectives for the lower San Joaquin River. These flow objectives were based on monitoring conducted just upstream of where the

San Joaquin River empties into the Carquinez Strait. There was no flow monitoring on or flow objectives for the main tributaries to the mainstem. The San Joaquin River flow standards in the 2006 update to the *Bay Delta Water Quality Plan* were developed in reference to unimpaired flows but were not expressed as a base percentage (or range of percentages) of unimpaired flows. Instead, the 2006 San Joaquin River flow objectives referenced unimpaired flows to provide a narrative/qualitative sense of the ways flow can contribute to the health and recovery of the Bay Delta fisheries. The continuing decline of salmon, steelhead trout, and smelt fisheries in the period between 2006 and 2016 indicated that the more narrative/qualitative approach to San Joaquin River flows in the 2006 update to the *Bay Delta Water Quality Plan* was inadequate.

In conjunction with its September 15, 2016 draft of the San Joaquin River portion of its update to the *Bay Delta Water Quality Plan*, the State Water Board also released a draft of a substitute environmental document (SED).[12] The draft SED was prepared to satisfy the requirements of the California Environmental Quality Act (CEQA). A central focus of the draft SED was the impact of the proposed San Joaquin River tributaries base flows on instream temperatures for the Stanislaus, Tuolumne, and Merced Rivers. The draft SED noted the extensive body of science confirming that mortality rates for salmon and steelhead trout, cold-water fisheries present in the Bay Delta and San Joaquin River watershed, rise steeply when water temperatures reach 60.8 degrees Fahrenheit.[13]

The draft SED included Table ES-15, titled *Summary of Mean Annual Temperature Benefits with Increased Flows February-June in All Years*. As explained in the text of the SED that accompanied Table ES-15, the proposed San Joaquin River tributary flows would have a substantial positive impact on keeping instream temperatures below 60.8 degrees Fahrenheit, the "temperature target" for salmon and steelhead:

> *Temperature targets are already achieved much of the time under baseline [existing conditions] during the cold weather and high flow months of December and January. The biggest improvements [with the proposed 40 percent of unimpaired flow for the San Joaquin River tributaries] occur for the core rearing life stage in April and May. Under baseline, temperature targets in the three tributaries are achieved 69 and 54 percent, respectively, for this critical core rearing life stage. Attainment [of the 60.8 degree Fahrenheit temperature target] increases to 83 and 73 percent of the time, respectively for April and May with 40 percent unimpaired flows. This summary statistic of temperature improvement for all year types, however, masks the benefits in critically dry years when baseline flows are lowest.*

Table ES-16 [titled Summary of Mean Annual Temperature Benefits with Increased Flows February-June in Critically Dry Years] shows the average number of mile-days that these temperature targets are achieved in all three tributaries, combined, under baseline [existing conditions] and also for unimpaired flows of 20, 30, 40, 50 and 60 percent, for only critically dry years. The improvements from baseline are much bigger than the average for all years. That is important because low flow conditions in dry years currently have a negative effect on salmon survival. Under baseline core rearing temperature targets in the three tributaries are attained 38 and 22 percent of the time in April and May, respectively in critically dry years. Attainment of the temperature criteria increases to 64 and 46 percent of the time, respectively, for April and May with 40% unimpaired flow. The temporal and spatial attainment of the temperature targets more than doubles in May.[14]

On September 15, 2016, the State Water Board also released a document titled *Summary of Proposed Updates to the Bay Delta Water Quality Control Plan*. This document explained the relationship between the recommendations in the 2010 public trust Bay Delta flow criteria report and the recommendations in the 2016 draft update to the *Bay Delta Water Quality Plan*. This document noted as follows:

> *As part of the 2009 Delta Reform Act, the [California] Legislature directed the State Water Board to develop flow criteria for the Delta ecosystem necessary to protect public trust uses. In keeping with the narrow focus of the legislation, the State Water Board's 2010 Delta Flow Criteria Report only presents a technical assessment of flow and operational requirements to provide fishery protection under existing conditions. The report does not do the analysis to inform the consideration of competing uses that is required by the California Water Code. The Delta Flow Criteria Report determined that 60 percent of the unimpaired San Joaquin River flow from February-June was necessary to preserve the attributes of a natural, variable system to which native species are adapted.*[15]
>
> . . .
>
> *As recommended in the Delta Flow Criteria Report, the new flow objectives would be based on percentages of unimpaired flows at locations on each tributary . . . The proposal does not contemplate flow requirements equal to natural, pre-development conditions or even the 60 percent threshold identified in the Delta Flow Criteria Report. Instead, the draft proposes narrative and numeric flow objectives, expressed as a range from 30 to 50 percent of unimpaired flow, for February through June, for the Stanislaus, Tuolumne and Merced Rivers through to the San Joaquin River near Vernalis.*
>
> *The proposal recommends a 30 to 50 percent adaptive flow range, with a starting point of 40 percent, because the State Water Board's analysis*

shows that range will provide a reasonable protection of fish and wildlife while moderating impacts to water supply for drinking water and agriculture.[16]

The *Summary of Proposed Updates to the Bay Delta Water Quality Control Plan* also noted the adaptive management advantages of reliance on a range of percentages tied to unimpaired flow rather than on a uniform fixed percent of unimpaired flow: "The unimpaired flow proposal does not require rigid adherence to a fixed percent of unimpaired flows but can be thought of as a water budget. The draft proposes a block of water that can be 'shaped' or shifted in time to best align instream flows with the needs of fish and wildlife throughout the year. As such, the flow proposal accommodates an adaptive implementation process that allows the magnitude and timing of flows to be adjusted, within a prescribed range, provided that such changes protect the fishery."[17]

Like the San Joaquin River public trust flow criteria adopted in 2010, the State Water Board's 2018 base flows for San Joaquin River tributaries opted to define flow standards as a numeric percentage of unimpaired flow. The 2018 base flows differ from the 2010 public trust flow criteria, however, in three noteworthy ways. First, the 2018 base flows apply to San Joaquin River tributaries while the 2010 public trust flow criteria applied to San Joaquin River inflow into the Bay Delta. Second, the 2018 base flows for San Joaquin River tributaries were based on the State Water Board balancing of the needs of fisheries with the consumptive water demands of agricultural and municipal users while the State Water Board's 2010 public trust flow criteria were based solely on an assessment of the needs of fisheries. Third, the 2018 base flows for San Joaquin River tributaries were based on a 30 to 50 percent prescribed range of unimpaired flow while the 2010 public trust flow criteria adopted a fixed percentage of 60 percent of San Joaquin River inflow to the Bay Delta.

December 2018 Adoption of Tributary Base Flows by the State Water Board

As noted earlier in this chapter, on December 12, 2018, the State Water Board adopted the San Joaquin tributary base flows proposed in the 2016 draft. The adoption was challenged in lawsuits filed by both water users and by the Trump Administration. The focus of these lawsuits was the allegation that the SED prepared in connection with the adoption of the base flows was not consistent with the requirements of CEQA. Under California law, a court's invalidation of the CEQA SED might also result in the court's voiding of the adoption of the tributary base flows.

The arguments raised in the lawsuits filed by water users and the Trump Administration, therefore, did not directly challenge the State Water Board's adoption of the tributary base flows but rather challenged the adequacy of the environmental review associated with this adoption.

For example, in the lawsuit filed by the San Joaquin Tributaries Authority (a joint power authority consisting of the Oakdale Irrigation District, South San Joaquin Irrigation District, Turlock Irrigation District, and the City and County of San Francisco), it was alleged that the CEQA SED failed to adequately consider how reduced diversions and water supply might impact recreational resources and landscaping. The petition and complaint filed by the San Joaquin Tributaries Authority claimed: "Increased rationing ... and the consequent reduction in outdoor water use and resulting loss in park vegetation, landscaping, and trees (the urban forest) would result in significant environmental impacts that the SED did not analyze, including but not limited to ... the loss of vegetation in parks and other public and private outdoor spaces ... would have an adverse effect on aesthetic resources and result in reduced use and enjoyment of these spaces."[18]

In a similar vein, the petition and complaint filed by the San Joaquin Tributaries Authority claimed: "Numerous state and local policies encourage green infrastructure, i.e. landscaping and open space areas, in order to provide social and environmental benefits ... Increased water rationing would have the effect of degrading landscaping and open spaces ... The SED fails to identify, discuss, and reconcile the inconsistencies with applicable state and local plans that promote green infrastructure."[19]

Although recreation and parks and green infrastructure may not be a primary concern of the water use agencies constituting the San Joaquin Tributaries Authority, this is a CEQA issue that it believes may succeed in litigation.

The lawsuit filed by the Trump Administration focused on the potential impacts of the San Joaquin tributary base flows on the operation of the federal New Melones Dam on the Stanislaus River. New Melones Dam is operated by the United States Bureau of Reclamation as part of the federal Central Valley Project, and stores and delivers water to agricultural users in California's Southern Central Valley. The complaint filed by the Trump Administration alleged that the CEQA SED did not include adequate discussion and analysis of the impacts on "agricultural resources", claiming: "The new flow objectives in the Amended Plan would significantly reduce the amount of water available in New Melones reservoir for meeting congressionally authorized purposes of the New Melones Project including irrigation ... The reduced water available for New Melones Project purposes would also impair Reclamation's delivery of water under contracts it presently holds with irrigation and water districts."[20]

Interestingly, the State Water Board's adoption of the San Joaquin tributary base flows was done in part to comply with requirements established by two other federal agencies (the United States Fish and Wildlife Service and the National Marine Fisheries Service) to maintain habitat for fish species protected under the federal Endangered Species Act (ESA). Significantly, the position staked out by the Trump Administration in its lawsuit makes no mention of the role of the federal ESA in protecting endangered fisheries, or of the role of the two federal agencies responsible for implementing the federal ESA, preferring instead to focus on the interests of the Bureau of Reclamation in storing, diverting, and delivering water.

SUSTAINABLE WATERSHED MANAGEMENT PLANS

In 2019, the Public Policy Institute of California (PPIC) published a report titled *A Path Forward for California's Freshwater Ecosystems.*[21] The 2019 PPIC Report included the suggestion that California's State Water Resources Control Board take the lead in promoting the preparation of "sustainable watershed management plans." According to the 2019 PPIC Report,

> This process could be modeled on SGMA [California's Sustainable Groundwater Management Act], which requires that water users in priority basin achieve sustainable groundwater management by the early 2040s. Water users self-organize into groundwater sustainability agencies (GSAs), which in turn prepare and administer groundwater sustainability plans (GSPs). If an agency either does not prepare an acceptable plan or fails to meet sustainability goals, SGMA authorizes the State Water Board to draft its own plan for the basin, which may include limits on pumping and fees to support management actions.
>
> Sustainable watershed management plans – modeled after GSPs – could take many forms, but they include . . . [State Water Board] setting criteria for the plans, encouraging comprehensive agreements, setting timelines, and adopting plans that meet water quality control plan goals and objectives.[22]
>
> . . .
>
> Following the approach of SGMA, if a [sustainable watershed management] plans is insufficient or inadequately implemented, the [State Water Board] would exercise its authority to set biological and water quality standards and use its water rights authorities to achieve the plan's objectives.[23]

The Public Policy Institute of California's proposal for the preparation and implementation of Sustainable Watershed Management Plans throughout

California would provide an opportunity to manage the interactions of the mainstems of rivers and tributaries to rivers statewide, and with an eye toward ensuring that water quality and fisheries conservation objectives are better aligned with diversion/impoundment practices throughout the state (as opposed to just in the San Joaquin River basin).

FLOWS AND FISHERIES AT THE WATERSHED LEVEL

The adoption of the 2018 base flows for San Joaquin River tributaries represents an important step in efforts to manage water resources at the watershed level. They also confirm that the "flow first" 2010 public trust Bay Delta flow criteria worked as designed, establishing a scientifically grounded methodology and baseline for the full protection of fisheries that could then be relied upon as a credible reference point in subsequent regulatory proceedings such as the *Bay Delta Water Quality Plan* update. Even so, as evidenced by the lawsuits filed, not all of the responses to the San Joaquin tributary base flows have been positive.

Some environmental and fishery conservation groups criticized the proposed 40 percent/30 to 50 percent range of unimpaired flow standard as being too low to restore and sustain salmon, steelhead trout, and smelt fisheries, and have suggested that the 60 percent of unimpaired flow standard set forth in the 2010 public trust flow criteria report is more in line with the supporting science.[24] Some environmental and fishery conservation groups have also raised questions as to whether in times of drought the State Water Board will simply grant temporary emergency waivers to allow levels of diversion that result in base flows below 30 percent of unimpaired flow range.[25] This latter concern is based on the experience during the 2012–2015 drought, when the State Water Board granted a series of temporary emergency waivers for compliance with water quality standards.[26]

Some agricultural water users have criticized the proposed 40 percent/30 to 50 percent range of unimpaired flow standard as economically unfeasible given current reliance on diversions from the Tuolumne River and Merced River for irrigation.[27] Such users have also suggested that meeting the 60.8 degrees temperature target may not by itself be sufficient to restore and maintain cold-water fisheries because of other non-temperature related stressors such as pollution and invasive aquatic species.[28] With the State Board's final approval of the tributary base flows in December 2018, and the lawsuits filed challenging this approval, these critiques by water users continue.

Amidst these criticisms and concerns and litigation, however, important areas of consensus have emerged. Scientifically, there is now consensus that, independent of such other non-temperature fishery stressors such as pollution and invasive aquatic species, the survival rates of salmon and steelhead trout decline sharply once instream temperatures rise above 60.8 degrees Fahrenheit. Hydrologically, there is now consensus that adequate flows from the San Joaquin River and Sacramento River into the Bay Delta (at whatever levels they are set) cannot be ensured without also ensuring there is adequate flow contributed from these rivers' main tributaries. There is nothing in the 2019 lawsuits filed by the San Joaquin Tributaries Authority or the Trump Administration that counters these points.

These points of consensus, reflected in the State Water Board's final December 2018 base flows for the San Joaquin River tributaries, represent tangible movement in the direction of watershed-based governance. This is a water policy trajectory of which John Wesley Powell would have approved.

Notes

1. 373 U.S. 546 (1963).
2. 373 U.S. 546 (1963) at 567–575.
3. Patrick Wright, *Fixing the Delta: The CALFED Bay-Delta Program and Water Policy Under the Davis Administration*, 31 GOLDEN GATE UNIVERSITY LAW REVIEW 331 (2001).
4. John Wesley Powell, *Report on the Lands of the Arid Regions of the United States* (1878).
5. California State Water Resources Control Board, *Summary of Proposed Updates to the Bay-Delta Water Quality Control Plan* (September 15, 2016) p. 3.
6. California State Water Resources Control Board, *Summary of Proposed Updates to the Bay-Delta Water Quality Control Plan* (September 15, 2016) p. 4.
7. Paul Stanton Kibel, *The Public Trust Navigates California's Bay Delta*, 51 NATURAL RESOURCES JOURNAL 35 (2011).
8. Section 85086 of California Water Code.
9. Closing Comments of the Bay Institute and Natural Resources Defense Council for the Informational Proceeding to Develop Flow Criteria for the Delta Ecosystem to Public Trust Resources (submitted to the State Water Resources Control board, April 14, 2010).
10. California State Water Resources Control Board, DEVELOPMENT OF FLOW CRITERIA FOR THE SACRAMENTO-SAN JOAQUIN DELTA ECOSYSTEM, PREPARED PURSUANT TO THE SACRAMENTO-SAN JOAQUIN DELTA REFORM ACT OF 2009 (adopted August 3, 2010).
11. California State Water Resources Control Board, DEVELOPMENT OF FLOW CRITERIA FOR THE SACRAMENTO-SAN JOAQUIN DELTA

Ecosystem, Prepared Pursuant To The Sacramento-San Joaquin Delta Reform Act Of 2009 (adopted August 3, 2010).

12. Substitute Environmental Document (SED) on *Evaluation of San Joaquin River Flow and Southern Delta Water Quality Objectives and Implementation* (September 2016).

13. Substitute Environmental Document (SED) on *Evaluation of San Joaquin River Flow and Southern Delta Water Quality Objectives and Implementation* (September 2016), Chapter 7 on Aquatic Biological Resources, pp. 15–16, 105–131.

14. Substitute Environmental Document (SED) on *Evaluation of San Joaquin River Flow and Southern Delta Water Quality Objectives and Implementation* (September 2016) pp. ES-42 to ES-43.

15. California State Water Resources Control Board, *Summary of Proposed Updates to the Bay-Delta Water Quality Control Plan* (September 15, 2016) pp. 2–3.

16. California State Water Resources Control Board, *Summary of Proposed Updates to the Bay-Delta Water Quality Control Plan* (September 15, 2016) pp. 3–4.

17. California State Water Resources Control Board, *Summary of Proposed Updates to the Bay-Delta Water Quality Control Plan* (September 15, 2016) p. 4.

18. Petition for Writ of Mandamus and Verified Complaint for Declaratory and Injunctive Relief (*San Joaquin Tributaries Authority* v. *California State Water Resources Control Board*, Case No. CV62094, Tuolumne County Superior Court, filed January 12, 2019) at pp. 41–42.

19. Petition for Writ of Mandamus and Verified Complaint for Declaratory and Injunctive Relief (*San Joaquin Tributaries Authority* v. *California State Water Resources Control Board*, Case No. CV62094, Tuolumne County Superior Court, filed January 12, 2019) at p. 43.

20. Complaint for Declaratory and Injunctive Relief (*United States of America* v. *State Water Resources Control Board*, Case No. 2:19-at-00236, United States District Court for the Eastern District of California-Sacramento Division, filed March 3, 2019) at pp. 4, 10 and 15.

21. *A Path Forward for California's Freshwater Ecosystems* (December 2019 Report by the Public Policy Institute of California).

22. *A Path Forward for California's Freshwater Ecosystems* (December 2019 Report by the Public Policy Institute of California) pp. 23–24.

23. *A Path Forward for California's Freshwater Ecosystems* (December 2019 Report by the Public Policy Institute of California) p. 24.

24. Doug Obegi, *State Water Board's Flow Proposal Falls Short* (September 15, 2016 Press Release from the Natural Resources Defense Council).

25. Doug Obegi, *State Water Board's Flow Proposal Falls Short* (September 15, 2016 Press Release from the Natural Resources Defense Council).

26. Order Approving in Part and Denying in Part a Petition for Temporary Urgency Changes to the License and Permit Terms and Condition Requiring Compliance with the Delta Water Quality Objectives in Response to Drought Conditions (February 3, 2105, California State Water Resources Control Board).
27. California Farmwater Coalition, *Reactions to State Board Unimpaired Flows Action* (September 16, 2016).
28. California Farmwater Coalition, *Reactions to State Board Unimpaired Flows Action* (September 16, 2016).

5

Instream Rights as Federal Law Recedes

Many of California's anadromous and freshwater fisheries are now in sharp decline. Salmon and steelhead trout runs throughout the state, as well as the delta smelt, are currently designated as endangered under federal law.

In addition to the biodiversity loss associated with the decline of these fisheries, the collapse of California's salmon stocks has had severe economic impacts on the state's commercial fishery sector – from the fishermen who catch the salmon, to those who service salmon fishing boats, to those who ultimately sell salmon to customers in markets and restaurants. All of these people whose jobs and livelihoods are involved in California's fishing sector have taken a financial hit as the state's salmon stocks have plummeted. As explained by the Golden State Salmon Association, an organization that works on behalf of commercial salmon fishermen in Northern California, "For many of us, salmon provides the income we use to keep a roof over our family's head."[1]

In recent decades, commercial fishermen, Native American tribes, and other fishery conservation stakeholders have relied extensively on a set of federal laws and federal agencies to keep water instream for California fisheries. However, following the results of the 2016 federal elections, with a Republican-controlled Congress and a new president that has pledged to reduce the scope of federal environmental protections, these federal laws and federal agencies are playing a more limited role in this regard in the near-term. Under these circumstances, commercial fishermen and other stakeholders focused on conserving California's fisheries may increasingly turn their attention to state law and state agencies.

This shift in focus for fishery stakeholders in California, from the federal law to state law protections, may have been prompted by the 2016 election results but is part of a broader and more long-standing debate about federalism and nature resource regulation. There is a well-developed body of legal scholarship that addresses such federalism questions as the distinction between federal law floors and federal law ceilings in the natural resource regulatory arena, the ways that federal law floors can prevent a race-to-the-bottom in terms of state natural resource standards, and how federal law floors can preserve a place for state law innovation in terms of natural resource management. More recently, with the election of Donald Trump, there has been legal scholarship and policy debate about what has been called the "new progressive federalism" and the opportunities to use sources of state law and authority to advance policies often associated with the political left. Although preventing the decline of fisheries (particularly commercial fisheries such as salmon) is an economic policy objective that cuts across traditional right/left political categories, the fisheries conservation and federalism questions considered in this article can be understood as part of the larger field of legal scholarship on the respective roles of state law and federal law when natural resources are involved.

This chapter examines the ways that federal law and federal agencies have in recent decades provided a legal basis to keep water instream for California fisheries, and the ways that California water law may be in a position to fill the regulatory gap that may be left if federal water law and federal agencies recede.

Although the focus of this chapter is on California fisheries, California water law and California water agencies, much of the analysis set forth may also be pertinent to other states. By studying California's response, other states may be able to develop their own strategies for effectively deploying state law and state agencies to maintain instream flow for fisheries regardless of what happens at the federal level in the coming years.

FIVE SOURCES OF FEDERAL AUTHORITY

There are at least five sources of federal law that have provided a legal foundation to maintain instream flow for fisheries in California: the federal Clean Water Act; federal Endangered Species Act; federally recognized tribal fishing rights; the National Environmental Policy Act and the Federal Power Act.

Federal Clean Water Act Section 303

Under §303 of the federal Clean Water Act, states have authority to propose "beneficial uses" for waterways and propose "water quality standards" subject to review and approval by the United States Environmental Protection Agency.[2]

Pursuant to §303, California's State Water Resources Control Board has designated the "beneficial uses" for the Sacramento River, the San Joaquin

River, and the Bay Delta to include fish spawning, rearing, and migration.[3] In recent years, the United States Environmental Protection Agency has pressed for enhanced compliance with California's water quality standards, particularly as they relate to fisheries present in or that migrate through the Sacramento River, the San Joaquin River, and the Bay Delta.

More specifically, in 2014 the United States Environmental Protection Agency sent a letter to its sister federal agency, the United States Bureau of Reclamation, commenting on a Reclamation proposal for changed operations for the Central Valley Project in California. The United States Environmental Protection Agency's 2014 letter on the proposal for future Central Valley Project operations stated as follows:

> We are concerned that the actions proposed ... may result in violations of the Clean Water Act water quality standards and further degrade the ecosystem ... The primary premise of the [proposed action by United States Bureau of Reclamation] appears to be hypothesis that endangered and threatened fish population in the San Francisco estuary can be protected from further degradation by 'habitat restoration' without increasing freshwater flow to the Estuary. This habitat restoration-only premise is inconsistent with broad scientific agreement ... that existing freshwater flow conditions in the San Francisco Estuary are insufficient to protect the aquatic ecosystem and multiple fish species, and that both increased freshwater flows and aquatic habitat restoration are needed to restore ecosystem processes in the Bay Delta and protect native and migratory fish populations.[4]

In response to issues raised in the 2014 United States Environmental Protection Agency letter regarding compliance with Clean Water Act §303, California's State Water Resources Control Board began preparing an update to the Bay Delta Water Quality Plan. As part of its update to the Bay Delta Water Quality Plan, in September 2016, California's State Water Resources Control Board proposed base instream flows for the three main tributaries to the San Joaquin River – the Stanislaus, the Tuolumne, and the Merced Rivers. The proposed base flows for the San Joaquin River tributaries are designed to protect salmon by reducing the days when and locations where instream temperatures exceed 60 degrees Fahrenheit.[5]

Endangered Species Act Section 7

The United States Bureau of Reclamation operates the Central Valley Project and the California Department of Water Resources operates the State Water Project. Both of these projects involve the operation of water diversion facilities and onstream storage dams in the Sacramento River and San Joaquin River watersheds.

Pursuant to §7 of the federal Endangered Species Act, in 2008, the United States Fish and Wildlife Service (USFWS) issued its delta smelt Biological Opinion for joint operations plan for the Central Valley Project and State Water Project.[6] Later, in 2009, the National Marine Fisheries Service (NMFS) issued its salmon Biological Opinion for joint operations plan for the Central Valley Project and State Water Project.[7] The 2008 and 2009 Biological Opinions for delta smelt and salmon, respectively, contained "jeopardy determinations" and included instream flow conditions to maintain salinity (for delta smelt) and water temperature (for salmon).[8]

Agricultural water users filed suit to challenge the instream flow/salinity provisions in the delta smelt Biological Opinion. In 2014, this litigation concluded when the Ninth Circuit Court of Appeals upheld instream flow/salinity conditions in the 2008 delta smelt Biological Opinion. In *San Luis & Delta-Mendota Water Authority* v. *Jewell*, the Ninth Circuit held:

> [A]s the combined pumping operations of the SWP [State Water Project]/ CVP [Central Valley Project] remove hundreds of gallons of fresh water from the Bay Delta, X2 [the upper salinity level at which smelt can survive] ... shifts eastward toward the Delta. The Bi-Op determined that the 'long-term upstream shift in X2 ... has caused a long-term decrease in habitat area availability for the delta smelt.'[9]

In January 2015, the United States Supreme Court denied certificate to review the Ninth Circuit Court of Appeal's decision in *San Luis & Delta-Mendota Water Authority* v. *Jewell*.[10]

Federal Tribal Fishing Rights

The Trinity River in Northern California is tributary to the Klamath River and Lewiston and Trinity Dams on the Trinity River are part of the Trinity River Division of the federal Central Valley Project. The water stored in the reservoirs behinds Lewiston and Trinity Dams is diverted by pipeline out of the Klamath–Trinity watershed, where it is deposited into the Sacramento River for use by cities and farmers outside of the Klamath–Trinity basin. Slack water conditions on the lower Klamath River previously led to outbreak of Ich parasite that decimated salmon runs. These slack water conditions were caused, in part, by minimal releases from Lewiston and Trinity Dams.[11]

The reservations of the Hoopa and Yurok tribes are located along the Trinity River and the Klamath River. In its 1995 decision in *Parravano* v. *Babbitt*, the

Ninth Circuit Court of Appeals recognized the Hoopa and Yurok tribes' fishery rights under federal law to salmon on the Trinity and Klamath Rivers.[12] In this case, the federal government, acting as trustee for the tribes, imposed restrictions on the ocean catch of salmon to ensure enough fish returned to the areas along the reservation.[13] The court in *Parravano* upheld these ocean fishing restrictions, finding as follows:

> For generations, the Hoopa Valley and Yurok Indian tribes have depended on the Klamath chinook salmon for their nourishment and economic livelihood.[14]
>
> . . .
>
> We have noted, with great frequency, that the federal government is the trustee of the Indian tribes' rights, including fishing rights. See e.g. *Joint Board of Control v. United States*, 862 F.2d 195, 198 (9th Cir. 1988). This trust responsibility extends not just to the Interior Department, but attaches to the federal government as a whole. *Eberhardt*, 789 F. 2d at 1363 (Beezer, J. concurring); see *also Pyramid Lake Paiute Tribe v. United States Department of Navy*, 98 F.2d 1410 (9th Circ. 1990); *Covelo Indian Community v. FERC*, 895 F. 2d 581, 586 (9th Circ. 1990). In particular, this court and the Interior Department have recognized a trust obligation to protect the Yurok and Hoopa Valley Tribes' rights to harvest Klamath chinook. See *Eberhardt*, 789 F. 2d at 1359–63; Interior Solicitor's Opinion, at 29.[15]
>
> . . .
>
> The Klamath chinook is an anadromous species. As a result, successful preservation of the Tribes' on-reservation fishing rights must include regulation of ocean fishing of the same resource. Indeed, allowing ocean fishing to take all the chinook available for harvest before the salmon can migrate upstream to the Tribes' waters would offer no protection to the Indians' fishing rights.[16]

In part to address the Yurok and Hoopa Valley tribes' fishing rights recognized in the *Parravano* case, in 2015, the United States Bureau of Reclamation released its draft of *Long-Term Plan for Protecting Late Summer Adult Salmon in the Lower Klamath River* (and proposed enhanced releases from Lewiston and Trinity Dams to help prevent a reoccurrence of the Ich parasite outbreak that earlier damaged salmon stocks in the Klamath River basin).[17] The draft plan notes that the current criteria require flow augmentation [additional releases from dams operated by the United States Bureau of Reclamation] in the lower Klamath River "to a minimum of 2,500–2,800 cfs [cubic feet per second] when the cumulative harvest of Chinook salmon in the Yurok tribal fishery in the estuary areas meets or exceeds a total of 7,000 fish,[18] and then recommended increasing flow augmentation to a "minimum of 2,800 cfs" under the same circumstances.[19]

Much like the ocean fishing restrictions that were the subject of the *Parravano* decision, the *Long-Term Plan for Protecting Late Summer Adult Salmon in the Lower Klamath River* is based on the position that to meet its trustee obligations to the Yurok and Hoopa Valley tribes, the federal government must take appropriate actions to ensure a healthy salmon fishery in tribal waters. More specifically, section 5 of the 2015 draft *Long-Term Plan for Protecting Late Summer Adult Salmon in the Lower Klamath River* on "Statutory Authority" states that Reclamation's actions pursuant to the plan are "consistent with Reclamation's obligations to preserve tribal trust resources."[20]

National Environmental Policy Act

The National Environmental Policy Act (NEPA) requires environmental impact statements (EISs) prepared by federal agencies to evaluate a range of alternatives to avoid significant adverse impacts. More specifically, §4332(2)(E) of NEPA provides that the range of alternatives evaluated in an EIS needs to address "unresolved conflicts" regarding significant environmental impacts (e.g. conflicts regarding the effects of reduced instream flows on fisheries).[21]

The Fourth Circuit Court of Appeals 2005 decision in *National Audubon Society* v. *Department of the Navy* is instructive on this question. In this case, the Fourth Circuit reviewed a challenge to an NEPA EIS prepared in connection with a decision to construct an aircraft training facility adjacent to a National Wildlife Refuge. The Court found that the EIS failed to comply with NEPA for, among other reasons, failing to substantively evaluate alternative locations other than one so close to protected wildlife resources:

> We note at the outset that the proximity of the proposed [aircraft facility] to the Pocosin Lakes National Wildlife Refuse bears heavily on our inquiry in this case. We cannot divorce this fact from the sufficiency of the agency's environmental analysis . . . The Navy's "hard look" in this case must therefore take particular care to how its actions will affect the unique biological features of this congressionally protected area . . . The Navy did not meet this burden. The deficiencies in each of the Navy's analysis would not, on their own, be sufficient to invalidate the EIS. But a review of the various components of the EIS taken together indicates that the Navy did not conduct the "hard look" that NEPA requires.[22]

The California WaterFix was a proposed project to move the main point of diversion for Central Valley Project and State Water Project to the north of delta and to construct two underground tunnels to transport water from new diversion point to farms/cities south of delta. Once new north delta point of diversion and tunnels are operational, California WaterFix does not include provisions to commit to reduced Central Valley Project/State Water Project diversions that would increase instream flow through the Bay Delta. Because the California WaterFix would be undertaken in part by the United States Bureau of Reclamation that operates the Central Valley Project, an NEPA EIS is being prepared in connection with the proposed project.[23]

Fishery conservation groups have criticized the proposed California WaterFix, alleging a failure to evaluate an alternative that commits to increase flow/reduce diversions to avoid adverse impacts on salmon and delta smelt. For instance, in a joint September 29, 2015 comment letter to the State Water Resources Control Board on the California WaterFix, Natural Resources Defense Council, Defenders of Wildlife, Pacific Coast Federation of Fishermen's Association, The Bay Institute, Golden Gate Salmon Association and Friends of the Estuary stated:

> [T]he existing flow and water quality standards have proven inadequate to achieve the salmon doubling objective in the existing water quality control plan, and the [State Water Resources Control Board] must ensure that the "appropriate flows" required pursuant to section 85086(b)(2) [of the California Water Code] will be sufficient to achieve this objective of the water quality plan. Alternative 4A in the California WaterFix fundamentally fails to meet . . . the salmon doubling objective of the existing Bay-Delta Water Quality Plan.[24]

In his August 23, 2016 article, titled *Why California WaterFix is a Path to Extinction for Native Fisheries*, Doug Obegi, attorney for the Natural Resources Defense Council, explained:

> [O]nce the tunnels are operational, water temperatures below Shasta dam will be so high that they will likely be lethal for endangered winter-run Chinook salmon during the critical spawning and eff incubation season more than 40 percent of the time in August, 50 percent of September and more than 90 percent of October, with the most adverse effects happening in drier years.
>
> . . .
>
> [I]nstead of helping salmon migrate through the delta, the [ESA] biological assessment estimates that the tunnels are likely to reduce survival of juvenile winter-run salmon as they migrate downstream through the Delta and out to sea. Salmon are already threatened by low survival rates as they migrate through the Delta, yet the assessment shows that survival would worsen with the tunnels.

. . .

[N]ew scientific data and analysis from state and federal agencies shows that more Delta outflow in the spring and summer is needed to protect the delta smelt. Yet the biological assessment completely ignores this data and the effects of reduced flows on delta smelt.[25]

At this point, with a new secretary of the interior in the administration of Donald Trump, it remains to be seen whether or not the United States Bureau of Reclamation will revise the NEPA EIS for the California WaterFix to include an alternative that would reduce diversions and increase instream flow to maintain fisheries.

Federal Power Act Section 10

Under the Federal Power Act, nonfederal dams on navigable rivers are relicensed by the Federal Energy Regulatory Commission.[26] Federal Energy Regulatory Commission relicensing proceedings are now underway for La Grange Dam in California, which is operated jointly by the Modesto Irrigation District and the Turlock Irrigation District on the Tuolumne River – a tributary to the San Joaquin River.[27]

Section 10(j)(1) of the Federal Power Act requires that a federal hydropower license "adequately and equitably protect, mitigate damages to, and enhance fish and wildlife (including related spawning grounds and habitat) affected by the development, operation and management of the project."[28] The National Marine Fisheries Service, United States Fish and Wildlife Service, or a state fish and wildlife department may recommend such conditions, and if timely submitted, the Federal Power Act requires that the Federal Energy Regulatory Commission must generally include such conditions in the hydropower license.[29]

In terms of La Grange Dam on the Tuolumne River, it means that if the USFWS or the NMFS recommend additional downstream releases from the dam to protect salmon and smelt below the dam, §10 of the Federal Power Act provides that the Federal Energy Regulatory Commission must generally include these release conditions in the new license issued to the operators of La Grange Dam.

FIVE SOURCES OF STATE AUTHORITY

Following the 2016 federal elections, there are indications that the administration of Donald Trump is reducing the role of federal law and federal agencies in managing water resources in general, and more specifically the role that federal law and federal agencies play in ensuring instream flow to maintain fisheries. As federal law and federal agencies play a diminished role in this regard in the near future, California is turning its attention to state laws and state agencies to ensure there are adequate instream flows in its rivers, streams, and creeks. That is, with the current political ebb and flow between the respective roles of the federal government and state government in water resource governance, California authority is advancing as federal authority recedes.

There are at least five sources of California law and legal authority that provide a basis to maintain instream flow for fisheries: California's Porter Cologne Water Quality Act; California public trust law[30]; California reasonable use law; section 5937 of the California Fish and Game Code; and California water quality certification authority. These sources of California law and authority are well-positioned to serve as the legal foundation for efforts to keep water instream for California fisheries regardless of what the administration of Donald Trump and the new Congress may do.

California's Porter-Cologne Water Quality Act

What if the United States Environmental Protection Agency stops pressing California to update and enforce its water quality standards for fisheries pursuant to Clean Water Act §303, or what if federal legislation is passed limiting application of Clean Water Act §303 to the Bay Delta watershed or Central Valley Project operations?

California's 1969 Porter-Cologne Water Quality Act predates the federal Clean Water Act and provides California's State Water Board with independent authority to establish and enforce water quality standards to protect use of watercourses for fish spawning, rearing, and migration.[31]

This means that the State Water Resources Control Board has authority under state law to proceed with its update to the Bay Delta Water Quality Plan and to adopt base instream flows for the tributaries of the San Joaquin River – regardless of whether the United States Environmental Protection Agency exercises its reviewing authority under §303 of the Clean Water Act, and regardless of whether the new Congress and the administration of Donald Trump may try to limit the application of §303 of the Clean Water Act.

California Public Trust Law

What if revised ESA §7 salmon and delta smelt Biological Opinions are issued by Donald Trump's administration that reach "no jeopardy" determinations, or what if federal legislation is enacted by Congress that limits application of ESA §7 to Central Valley Project and State Water Project operations?

This hypothetical scenario became reality in October 2019, when the Trump administration (acting through NMFS and the USFWS) issued new ESA Biological Opinions for salmon and delta smelt related to Central Valley Project and State Water Project operations. As discussed in more detail in Chapter 14 of this book, the new October 2019 ESA Biological Opinions reached "no jeopardy" determinations, thereby voiding the mitigation measures included in the earlier Biological Opinions. Lawsuits challenging the "no jeopardy" determinations in the October 2019 ESA Biological Opinions have been filed by both the State of California and conservation/fishery groups, but the outcome of this litigation is yet to be determined.

In the landmark 1983 *National Audubon* case, the California Supreme Court held that under California law, the public trust requires the State of California to fully protect instream public trust resources (such as fisheries) whenever feasible. In *National Audubon*, the California Supreme Court clarified:

> Once the state has approved an appropriation, the public trust imposes a duty of continuing supervision over the taking and use of the appropriated water. In exercising its sovereign power to allocate water resources in the public interest, the state is not confined by past allocation decisions which may be incorrect in light of current knowledge or inconsistent with current needs.[32]

In the 2014 case of *Environmental Law Foundation* v. *State Water Resources Control Board*, the Sacramento County Superior Court affirmed that public trust law applies to diversions that harm fisheries in navigable waters. This case involved pumping that reduced instream flow on the Scott River along California's North Coast. In *Environmental Law Foundation* v. *State Water Resources Control Board*, the court stated:

> The Scott River located in Siskiyou County is a navigable waterway used for boating and fishing. In the past two decades the Scott River experienced decreased flows caused in part by groundwater pumping ... As a result of these decreased flows, the Scott River is often "dewatered" in the summer and early fall. The river is then reduced to a series of pool. This, in turn, has injured the river's fish populations.
> ...
> The public trust doctrine would prevent pumping directly out of the Scott River harming public trust uses. So too under *National Audubon*, the public trust doctrine would prevent pumping a non-navigable tributary of the Scott River harming public trust uses of the river. The court finds no reason why the

analysis of *National Audubon* would not apply to the facts alleged here. The court thus finds that public trust doctrine protects navigable waters from harm caused by the extraction of groundwater, where the groundwater is so connected to the navigable water that its extraction adversely affects public trust uses.

The Superior Court's holding in *Environmental Law Foundation v. State Water Resources Control Board* was affirmed in 2018 by the California Court of Appeal, which held:

> [T]he trial court's finding is unremarkable and well supported by the facts and logic of National Audubon and the precedent upon which it relies. The most notable similarity between this case and National Audubon is the fact that nonnavigable water was diverted or extracted. In National Audubon, the diversion of nonnavigable tributaries had a deleterious effect on Mono Lake, a navigable waterway. (National Audubon, supra, 33 Cal.3d at pp 424–425.) Similarly, ELF alleges in this case that the extraction of groundwater potentially will adversely impact the Scott River, also a navigable waterway. The fact the tributaries themselves were not navigable did not dissuade the Supreme Court from concluding the public trust doctrine protects the navigable water (Mono Lake) from harm by diversion of nonnavigable tributaries. (Id. at p. 437.) Nor does the fact that nonnavigable groundwater rather than nonnavigable tributaries is at issue here dissuade us where, in both cases, it is alleged the removal of water will have an adverse impact on navigable water clearly within the public trust.[33]

The recent rulings in the *Environmental Law Foundation* litigation evidence that public trust law remains alive and well in California, and is being robustly applied to diversions impacting instream flow. Therefore, pursuant to state public trust law, regardless of what happens at the federal level regarding the application of §7 of the Endangered Species Act, California state agencies and California courts have independent public trust authority to modify existing water rights to protect salmon and smelt by requiring adequate instream flow for these fisheries.

California Reasonable Use Law

What if the administration of Donald Trump orders the United States Bureau of Reclamation to discontinue or delay work with the Hoopa and Yurok Valley tribes on the salmon plan for the lower Klamath River, or what if the new president's administration otherwise decides not to increase releases from Trinity and Lewiston Dams to give effect to the Hoopa and Yurok Valley tribes' fishing rights?

California Constitution Article XI and California Water Code §100 both provide the following: "The right to water or to use the flow of water in or from any natural stream or watercourse . . . shall be limited to such water as shall be reasonably required . . . and such right does not and shall not extend to the waste or unreasonable use or unreasonable method or use or unreasonable method of diversion of water."

In 2014, in its decision in *Light* v. *State Water Resources Control Board* (*Light*) the California Court of Appeal affirmed that the State Water Resources Control Board may rely on its reasonable use authority to implement regulatory program to ensure diversions in Russian River watershed do not reduce instream flow so as to imperil salmon. In its 2014 decision in *Light*, the Court rejected plaintiff's argument that reasonable use law only allowed for "post-event" judicial enforcement and did not support "pre-event" preventative administrative regulation, holding as follows:

> "Restricting the [State Water Resources Control Board] to post-event litigation deprives it of any effective regulatory remedy, since the damage will have been done and the critical circumstances may not arise again for many months or years. It is difficult to imagine what effective relief a court could grant, other than a broad and inflexible injunction against future diversions . . . a ruling that would in the interest of neither the enjoined growers or the public. Effective regulation of the state's water resources in these circumstances demands that the [State Water Resources Control Board] has authority to enact tailored regulations."[34]

In 1986, in what became known as the "Racanelli Decision" (after Judge Racanelli who authored the opinion), the California Court of Appeal affirmed that California's Water Board could rely on its reasonable use authority to modify the Central Valley Project and State Water Project water rights to ensure sufficient freshwater flow to prevent seawater intrusion.[35] The Racanelli Decision held:

> " . . . the [Water] Board had the authority to modify the projects' permit to curtail their use of water on the ground that the projects' use and diversions of water had become unreasonable . . . We perceive no legal obstacles to the [Water] Board's determination that particular methods of use have become unreasonable by their deleterious effects upon water quality."[36]

So, in the event the administration of Donald Trump does not seek to increase releases from Lewiston and Trinity Dams to give effect to the Hoopa and Yurok Valley tribes' fishing rights, the State Water Resources Control Board can rely on its state reasonable use law authority to compel such releases from Lewiston and Trinity Dams.

California Fish and Game Code Section 5973

What if the administration of Donald Trump does not require the United States Bureau of Reclamation to revise the NEPA EIS for the California WaterFix to evaluate an increased flow alternative, or what if federal legislation is enacted by Congress that exempts the California WaterFix from NEPA's requirements?

The administration of Donald Trump has already taken steps that signal a narrow rather than a broad interpretation of federal agency environmental impact assessment obligations under NEPA. On August 15, 2017, Donald Trump signed Executive Order 13807, titled *Establishing Discipline and Accountability in the Environmental Review Process for Infrastructure Projects*. Among other things, Executive Order 13807 calls upon the Council on Environmental Quality (CEC) to identify actions that will "ensure that agencies apply NEPA in a manner that reduces unnecessary burdens and delays as much as possible, including by using CEC's authority to interpret NEPA to simplify and accelerate the NEPA review process."[37] Narrowing the scope of alternatives considered in the NEPA environmental documents might be a way to achieve Executive Order 13807's objective of simplifying and accelerating the NEPA review process.

As explained here, the California WaterFix would alter the federal Central Valley Project, the largest water diversion project in California.[38] The federal Central Valley Project operates in a coordinated fashion with the State Water Project which is operated by the California Department of Water Resources. For instance, these federal and state water projects share diversion facilities near the city of Tracy, California that divert water from the Sacramento–San Joaquin Delta into the two projects' water delivery system.

Section 5937 of the California Fish and Game Code requires that "[T]he owner of any dam shall allow sufficient water at all time to pass through a fishway, or in the absence of a fishway, allow sufficient water to pass over, around or through the dam, to keep in good condition any fish that may be planted or exist below the dam."[39] In the 2004 case of *NRDC v. Patterson*, the federal district court in Sacramento considered whether §5937 requirements applied to the United States Bureau of Reclamation's operation of Friant Dam on the San Joaquin River, which is a key piece of water storage infrastructure for the federal Central Valley Project. Writing for the court, Judge Lawrence Karlton explained as follows:

> The Bureau built Friant Dam across the upper San Joaquin River, northwest of Fresno, in the early 1940s as part of the Central Valley Project. Construction began in 1939 and was largely completed by the mid-1940s[40] ... Friant Dam blocked upstream access to a portion of the San Joaquin River's spawning habitat for salmon and steelhead; however, it was not the construction of the

Dam that terminated the salmon runs. For several years after Friant Dam was in place, the Bureau released sufficient water to sustain the salmon fishery.[41]

. . .

By the late 1940s, however, the Bureau's operation of Friant Dam had caused long stretches of the River to dry up [citation omitted]. In the spring of 1948, the California Division of Fish and Game responded with a dramatic fish rescue in an attempt to save the River's spring-run Chinook salmon. About 2,000 up-migrating Chinook were trapped in the lower portion of the River, hauled by truck around the dewatered stretch of the River, and released at a point from which they would migrate upstream to deep pools just below Friant Dam. The salmon were able to hold over the summer in these pools, and to spawn successful below Friant Dam in the fall, but their offspring perished in early 1949 when they attempted to out-migrate through the dried-up River bed.

With the completion of the Friant-Kern Canal, the Bureau in 1949 further increased diversions, leaving even less water for the San Joaquin River [citation omitted]. The last of the upper San Joaquin River's fall-run Chinook salmon were reported in a pool below Mendota Dam in 1949 [citations omitted]. Spring-run Chinook salmon disappeared from the San Joaquin River after unsuccessful salmon rescue attempts in 1949 and 1950 [citations omitted]. For most of the last 50 years, the Bureau has diverted virtually all of the River's flows [citations omitted]. While salmon continue to return and spawn until 1949, after that, "the San Joaquin chinook was extirpated in its southernmost range." [citation omitted]

Some sixty miles of the River upstream of its confluence with the Merced [River] now lie continuously dry, except during rate flood event [citation omitted]. The spring-run Chinook – once the most abundant race of salmon in the Central Valley – appear to have been extirpated from the length of the River. [citation omitted].[42]

In his decision, Judge Karlton also noted how the lack of releases from Friant Dam was also adversely affecting salmon in the lower portions of the San Joaquin River (below the confluence with the Merced River) by reducing the instream flows needed to maintain water temperatures at which cold-water fish such as salmon can survive, observing that "Reduced flows in the San Joaquin River below Friant Dam have ... increased the temperature of the water that is available."[43] Judge Karlton continued:

In *California v. United States*, 438 U.S. 645 (1978), the Supreme Court explained that the "cooperative federalism" mandated by §8 [of the federal Reclamation Act] required the United States to comply with state water laws unless that law was directly inconsistent with clear congressional directives regarding the project. *Id.* at 650 ("The history of the relationship between the Federal Government and the States in the reclamation of arid lands of the Western

States is both long and involved, but through it run the consistent thread of purposeful and continued deference to state water law by Congress.").[44]

In *NRDC* v. *Patterson*, Judge Karlton then went on to conclude that the United States Bureau of Reclamation's operation of Friant Dam violated §5937 of the California Fish and Game Code:

There is no genuine dispute, however, as to whether the Bureau has released sufficient water to maintain historic fisheries, and the record, in any event, is clear that the Bureau has not.[45]

. . .

The Bureau, by its own admission, releases no water for this purpose and long-stretches of the River downstream are dry most of the time.

. . .

Historically, the upper San Joaquin River supported a large spring-run of chinook salmon. The annual spawning run of these fish numbered in the tens of thousands as late as the mid-1940s.

. . .

The extinction of these San Joaquin stocks can be directly attributed to inadequate instream flows, specifically those which enable adult salmon to migrate upstream. The [Friant Dam] project diverted nearly the entire river and a long reach of the waterway has been dried up.[46]

Therefore, in the event that the United States Bureau of Reclamation does not consider an increased flow alternative as part of its evaluation of the California WaterFix – either because the administration of Donald Trump does not require the agency to consider the increase flow alternative or because the new Congress exempts the California WaterFix from NEPA – §5937 may provide the State Water Resources Control Board with authority to require, for example, additional releases from Shasta Dam to help maintain water temperatures below the dam at 60 degrees Fahrenheit or lower to protect salmon and steelhead trout cold-water fisheries. Reliance on §5937 in this instance would presumably be premised on evidence establishing that releases from Shasta Dam to prevent water temperatures from rising above 60 degrees Fahrenheit are consistent with the United States Bureau of Reclamation's obligation to release sufficient water to maintain salmon and steelhead trout fisheries below Shasta Dam in "good condition."

California Water Certification Authority

What if under the administration of Donald Trump, the USFWS and NMFS do not propose licensing terms for La Grande Dam to the FERC to ensure additional downstream releases for California fisheries?

Clean Water Act §401 provides that "states" are responsible for certifying that projects approved by federal agencies (such as the Federal Energy Regulatory Commission) do not violate state water quality standards.[47] For example, pursuant to Clean Water Act §401, water quality certification by the California State Water Board is required for federal relicensing of La Grange Dam on the Tuolumne River (tributary to the San Joaquin River).[48]

In its 1994 decision in the case of *City of Tacoma* v. *Washington Department of Ecology*, the United States Supreme Court held – in a decision authored by Justice Sandra Day O'Connor and joined by Chief Justice William Rehnquist – that state water quality certification may include relicensing terms to maintain instream flow for fisheries. In this case, pursuant to its water quality certification authority, the State of Washington imposed instream flow conditions to protect salmon on a municipal dam from being relicensed by the Federal Energy Regulatory Commission. In her opinion in *Washington Department of Ecology*, Justice O'Connor wrote:

> Petitioners assert that [state water quality certification] is only concerned with water 'quality' and does not allow the regulation of water 'quantity.' This is an artificial distinction. In many cases, water quantity is closely related to water quality; a sufficient lowering of the water quantity in a body of water could destroy all of its designated uses, be it for drinking water, recreation, navigation or, as here, as a fishery.[49]

Under the administration of Donald Trump, it is foreseeable that the USFWS and the NMFS may not use their authority under Section 10 of the Federal Power Act to require the inclusion of downstream releases for fish in federal hydropower licenses, such as the license now being considered for La Grange Dam on the Tuolumne River in California.

Under this scenario, however, California's State Water Board can still rely on its state water quality certification authority to require the Federal Energy Regulatory Commission to include fishery conservation measures related to instream flow when relicensing nonfederal dams in California such as La Grange Dam.

FLOORS, CEILINGS, AND THE NEW PROGRESSIVE FEDERALISM

The prospect of increased reliance on California law and authority to keep water instream for fisheries raises federalism concerns that arise in a broader context, both in terms of legal scholarship and public policy. Although a comprehensive discussion of this broader context is beyond the scope of this chapter, there are two points that may help to better situate the chapter's preceding analysis and discussion.

First, going back several decades, there is a body of federalism and environmental law scholarship that focuses on the distinction between federal laws that create "floors" but allow state law standards with more stringent standards for environmental and natural resource protection, and federal laws that create "ceilings," which prohibit state law from adopting standards for environmental and natural resource protection that are more stringent than federal standards.[50] There is an aspect of federal preemption with both federal floors and federal ceilings, but this preemption works quite differently depending on whether a floor or a ceiling is involved. As Georgetown Law School Professor, William Buzbee, explained the following in his 2007 paper titled *Asymmetrical Regulation: Risk, Preemption and the Floor/Ceiling Distinction*:

> Typically the debate focused on the federal standards setting where federal law allows states to increase the stringency of regulation, but prohibits state from more lenient regulation.[51]
>
> . . .
>
> Elimination of state and local authority to regulate risks may have been a rarity, but several recent legislative and regulatory actions purport or propose to impose a federal "ceiling," where the federal action would displace any additional potential by other actors, be they states or even common law regimes.[52]

Professor Buzbee continues:

> [I]s there a principled rationale for distinguishing federal standard setting that set a federal floor or a ceiling? At first blush, the two appear to be mere flip sides of the same federal power, only distinguished by their different regulatory preferences for a world a minimized risk (with floors) or higher levels of risk (with ceilings) . . . However, these two central regulatory choices are fundamentally different. Floors embrace additional and more stringent state and common law actions, while ceilings actually are better labeled a "unitary federal choice."

Unitary federal choice ceiling preemption is an institutional arrangement that threatens to produce poorly tailored regulation and public choice distortions of the political process, whether it is before the legislature or a federal agency. Floor preemption, in contrast, constitutes a partial displacement of state choice in setting a minimum level of protection, but leaves room for other actors and additional regulatory action. Floors anticipate and benefit from the institutional diversity they permit.[53] In the event that President Trump and Congress were to enact legislation that federally preempted the application of California law to maintain levels of instream flow beyond that required by federal law, such legislation would be an example of what Professor Buzbee and other legal scholars of federalism and environmental regulation would refer to as federal "ceiling" preemption. Consider a federal law that forbids California from applying its public trust law and unreasonable use law, or applying Section 5973 of the California Fish and Game Code, to surface water instream flows and fisheries in the state. The preemption provisions in such federal legislation would constitute, in the words of Professor Buzbee, a "unitary federal choice" in regard to instream flow and fisheries protection in California.

This "unitary federal choice" approach to California water resources and fisheries would represent a significant departure from the cooperative federalism approach reflected in §8 of the Reclamation Act, §10 of the Federal Power Act, and §401 of the Clean Water Act, in which states have traditionally been given latitude to adopt standards for instream flow and fisheries protection that are more stringent than federal standards.

Second, since the 2016 elections, there has been increasing policy discussion of the prospect of a new progressive federalism. In a February 2017 article in THE NEW REPUBLIC, titled *From California, A Progressive Cry for State's Rights*, Daniela Blei reported:

> It might seem predictable that California, land of liberals, is leading the charge against the new administration. But the Golden State is also the birthplace of the modern conservative movement and was once an enduring source of anti-government populism. Decades before California launched the political careers of Richard Nixon and Ronald Reagan, its business conservatives – agriculture barons and utility executives – organized in opposition to the New Deal, purporting to defend citizens from the tyranny of the federal government ... In a twist of history, California's leftist leaders are now embracing state's rights, decrying Washington as a threat to a local way of life.[54]

A leading legal scholar on the concept of new progressive federalism is Professor Heather Gerken, who was recently appointed Dean of Yale Law School.[55] In a January 2017 article, Gerken observed:

> Progressives have long thought of federalism as a tool for entrenching the worst in our politics. But it is also a tool for changing our politics. Social movements have long used state and local policymaking as an organizing tool, a rallying cry, a testing ground for their ideas.[56]

Similarly, an August 2017 article in New York Magazine, titled *A New Romance: Trump Has Made Progressives Fall in Love with Federalism*, noted:

In the aftermath of the [November 2016] election, [Gerken] co-authored a user's guide in the journal *Democracy* on how localities can best harness the power of federalism to serve progressive ends. That's not to say that Democratic enclaves will necessarily carry this flag for the long haul. In an interview, she told me that people on both sides of the political spectrum tend to opportunistically wield federalism for their partisan ends – and not because of some high-minded constitutional commitment. "Both sides are fair-weather federalists. Both sides use it instrumentally to achieve their goals," she said.[57]

Proposals to use California law to keep water instream for fisheries in the face of receding federal law protection are taking place within the larger policy discussion around new progressive federalism, where there is a recognition that federalism positions have previously been used by the political right to under-mine efforts to better protect natural resources, and a recognition that if and when political circumstances change (e.g. when Democrats may control Congress and the White House), they may well be used in this manner again. This recognition, understandably, creates some apprehension and caution among progressives about the precedent they may be establishing in relying on federalism arguments to resist the policy agenda of the administration of Donald Trump.

STATE WATER LAW ADVANCING

With the prospect of federal law and federal agencies potentially receding from their role in keeping water instream for fisheries, California law and California agencies are well positioned to step in to fill the void. There is ample state law and ample state government authority to maintain instream flow for California's fisheries regardless of what the administration of Donald Trump and Congress may do. This explains why fishery conservation stakeholders, including com-mercial fishermen and others whose jobs and income are tied to the health of California's salmon fishery, may increasingly focus on how to effectively bolster and deploy California water law to maintain California's fisheries.

Increased reliance on California law to keep water instream for this purpose can perhaps be understood as an example of the new progressive federalism discussed by Yale Law School Dean Heather Gerken, although many of the commercial fishermen whose interests are involved might in fact view such state regulation as more conservative than progressive. Again, regulation to preserve jobs in the commercial fishery sector through instream flow standards does not fit neatly into the right/left political and public policy categories that often seem to underlie writings on new pro-gressive federalism.

The experience in California suggests that, in the era of the administration of Donald Trump, stakeholders interested in keeping water instream for fisheries need to pay as much attention to opportunities at the state level as obstacles at the federal level. That is, in addition to resisting efforts to reduce the role of federal law and federal agencies in maintaining instream flow, such stakeholders must also work to strengthen state water law and state water agencies to maintain instream flow.

The strong assertion and deployment of state water law to maintain instream flows for fisheries may in itself be an effective political strategy to counter efforts to reduce the role of federal law and federal agencies in ensuring such flows. This assertion and deployment highlight that, when state water law and state water agencies are available and ready to plug the holes left when federal water law and federal water agencies retreat, a reduced role for federal law and federal agencies may not in fact translate into additional water actually becoming available for out-of-stream diversion and usage. And if that is the case, this begs the question of what is the point of reducing the role of federal law and federal agencies in the first place?

Notes

1. Golden Gate Salmon Association, *Why We Work for Salmon*, https://goldenstatesalmon.org/why-we-work-for-salmon-2/.
2. Clean Water Act Section 303.
3. Dan Bacher, *Tunnel Opponents Applaud EPA's Scathing Comment Letter*, DAILY KOS (August 30, 2014). www.dailykos.com/stories/2014/08/30/1325955/-Tunnel-opponents-applaud-EPA-s-scathing-comment-letter.
4. Dan Bacher, *Tunnel Opponents Applaud EPA's Scathing Comment Letter*, DAILY KOS (August 30, 2014). www.dailykos.com/stories/2014/08/30/1325955/-Tunnel-opponents-applaud-EPA-s-scathing-comment-letter.
5. Paul Stanton Kibel, *Truly a Watershed Event: California's Water Board Proposes Base Flows for the San Joaquin River Tributaries*, CALIFORNIA WATER LAW JOURNAL (October 2016).
6. United States Fish and Wildlife Service, FORMAT ENDANGERED SPECIES ACT CONSULTATION ON THE COORDINATED OPERATIONS OF THE CENTRAL VALLEY PROJECT AND STATE WATER PROJECT (December 15, 2008). www.fws.gov/sfbaydelta/documents/SWP-CVP_OPs_BO_12–15_final_signed.pdf.
7. National Marine Fisheries Service, ESA BIOLOGICAL OPINION ON LONG-TERM OPERATIONS OF THE CENTRAL VALLEY PROJECT AND THE STATE WATER PROJECT (June 4, 2009). www.westcoast.fisheries.noaa.gov/publications/Central_Valley/Water%20Operations/Operations,%20Cr

iteria%20and%20Plan/nmfs_biological_and_conference_opinion_on_the_long-term_operations_of_the_cvp_and_swp.pdf.

8. United States Fish and Wildlife Service, FORMAT ENDANGERED SPECIES ACT CONSULTATION ON THE COORDINATED OPERATIONS OF THE CENTRAL VALLEY PROJECT AND STATE WATER PROJECT (December 15, 2008). www.fws.gov/sfbaydelta/documents/SWP-CVP_OPs_BO_12–15_final_signed.pdf.

9. *San Luis & Delta-Mendota Water Authority v. Jewell*, 747 F.3d 581, 622 (9th Cir. 2014).

10. *San Luis & Delta-Mendota Water Authority v. Jewell*, 747 F.3d 581 (9th Cir. 2014), cert denied sub nom, 135 S.Ct 948 (January 12, 2015).

11. United States Bureau of Reclamation, *Long-Term Plan for Protecting Late Summer Adult Salmon in the Lower Klamath River* (April 2015).

12. 70 F.3d 59 (9th Cir. 1995).

13. 70 F.3d 59 (9th Cir. 1995).

14. 70 F.3d 59 (9th Cir. 1995).

15. 70 F.3d 59 (9th Cir. 1995).

16. 70 F.3d 59 (9th Cir. 1995).

17. United States Bureau of Reclamation, *Long-Term Plan for Protecting Late Summer Adult Salmon in the Lower Klamath River* (April 2015).

18. United States Bureau of Reclamation, *Long-Term Plan for Protecting Late Summer Adult Salmon in the Lower Klamath River* (April 2015), p. 17.

19. United States Bureau of Reclamation, *Long-Term Plan for Protecting Late Summer Adult Salmon in the Lower Klamath River* (April 2015), p. 9.

20. United States Bureau of Reclamation, *Long-Term Plan for Protecting Late Summer Adult Salmon in the Lower Klamath River* (April 2015), p. 23.

21. 42 U.S.C. §4332(2)(E).

22. 422.F.3d 174, 186–187 (4th Cir. 2005).

23. State Water Resources Control Board, *Fact Sheet for California WaterFix – Water Right Change Petition and Water Quality Certification Process* (updated July 21, 2016).

24. *Preliminary Comments Regarding the Notice, Fat Sheet and Petition for Change in Point of Diversion for the California WaterFix* (September 29, 2015 Letter to State Water Resources Control Board from Natural Resources Defense Council, Defenders of Wildlife, Pacific Coast Federation of Fishermen's Association, The Bay Institute, Golden Gate Salmon Association, Friends of the Estuary).

25. Doug Obegi, *Why California WaterFix Is a Path to Extinction for Native Fisheries*, WATER DEEPLY (August 23, 2016). www.newsdeeply.com/water/community/2016/08/23/why-california-water-fix-is-a-path-to-extinction-for-native-fisheries.

26. 16 U.S.C. §§803(a), (j).

27. Paul Stanton Kibel, *Passage and Flow Considered Anew: Wild Salmon Restoration Via Hydro Relicensing*, 37 PUBLIC LAND AND RESOURCES LAW REVIEW 65, 81–84 (2016). See also National Marine Fisheries Service, *Comments on Proposed Study Plan for the La Grange Hydroelectric Project*, P-14581–000 (December 4, 2015).

28. 16 U.S.C. §§803(a), (j).

29. 16 U.S.C. §§803(a), (j). See also Paul Stanton Kibel, *Passage and Flow Considered Anew: Wild Salmon Restoration Via Hydro Relicensing*, 37 PUBLIC LAND AND RESOURCES LAW REVIEW 65, 81–84 (2016).

30. 33 Cal.3d 419 (1983). See also Paul Stanton Kibel, *The Public Trust Navigates California's Bay Delta*, 51 NATURAL RESOURCES JOURNAL 35 (2011).

31. 1969 Porter-Cologne Water Quality Act, California Water Code, Section 7.

32. 33 Cal.3d 419 (1983).

33. *Environmental Law Foundation v. State Water Resources Control Board*, California Court of Appeal-Third Appellate District (Case No. C083239).

34. 226. Cal.App.4d 1463, at 1486–87.

35. 182 Cal.App.3d 82 (1986).

36. 182 Cal.App.3d 82, 130 (1986).

37. Executive Order 13807, Establishing Discipline and Accountability in the Environmental Review and Permitting Process for Infrastructure Projects (signed on August 15, 2017, published in Federal Register on August 24, 2017).

38. See generally *Coordinated Long-Term Operations of the Central Valley Project and State Water Project* (August 2011), Project Description, pp. 1–108.

39. Section 5937, California Fish and Game Code.

40. 333 F.Supp.2d 909.

41. 333 F.Supp.2d 909–910.

42. 333 F.Supp.2d 910.

43. 333 F.Supp.2d 911.

44. 333 F.Supp.2d 914.

45. 333 F.Supp.2d 924.

46. 333 F.Supp.2d 925.

47. 33 U.S.C. §1341.

48. Paul Stanton Kibel, *Passage and Flow Considered Anew: Wild Salmon Restoration Via Hydro Relicensing*, 37 PUBLIC LAND AND RESOURCES LAW REVIEW 65, 81–84 (2016). See also National Marine Fisheries Service, *Comments on Proposed Study Plan for the La Grange Hydroelectric Project*, P-14581–000 (December 4, 2015).

49. 511 U.S. 700, 732 (1994).

50. William W. Buzbee, *Asymmetrical Regulation: Risk, Preemption and the Floor/Ceiling Distinction*, Emory University School of Law Public Law &

Legal Theory Research Paper Series (Research Paper No. 07–9, 2007); Jerome Organ, *Limitation on State Agency Authority to Adopt Environmental Standards More Stringent than Federal Standards: Policy Considerations and Interpretive Problems*, 54 MARYLAND L. REVIEW 1373 (1995); Kristen H. Engel, *Harnessing the Benefits of Dynamics Federalism in Environmental Law*, 56 EMORY L. J. 159 (2006).

51. William W. Buzbee, *Asymmetrical Regulation: Risk, Preemption and the Floor/Ceiling Distinction*, Emory University School of Law Public Law & Legal Theory Research Paper Series (Research Paper No. 07–9, 2007) at p. 5.

52. William W. Buzbee, *Asymmetrical Regulation: Risk, Preemption and the Floor/Ceiling Distinction*, Emory University School of Law Public Law & Legal Theory Research Paper Series (Research Paper No. 07–9, 2007) at p. 6.

53. William W. Buzbee, *Asymmetrical Regulation: Risk, Preemption and the Floor/Ceiling Distinction*, Emory University School of Law Public Law & Legal Theory Research Paper Series (Research Paper No. 07–9, 2007) at p. 1.

54. Daniela Blei, *From California, A Progressive Cry for State's Rights*, THE NEW REPUBLIC (February 14, 2017).

55. Heather Gerken, *A New Progressive Federalism*, 24 DEMOCRACY JOURNAL 37 (2012); Heather Gerken, *Slipping the Bonds of Federalism*, 128 HARVARD LAW REVIEW 85 (2014); Heather Gerken and Ari Holtzblatt, *The Political Safeguards of Horizonal Federalism*, 113 MICHIGAN LAW REVIEW 57 (2014).

56. Heather Gerken, *We're About to See State's Rights Used Defensively against Trump*, VOX (January 20, 2017).

57. Christian Farias, *A New Romance: Trump Has Made Progressives Fall in Love with Federalism*, NEW YORK MAGAZINE (August 24, 2017).

6

Instream Rights as Water Temperatures Rise

In terms of climate change law and policy, at present there are efforts under-way at the state, federal, and international levels to curb greenhouse gas (GHG) emissions. These efforts to reduce GHG emissions (and thereby mitigate global warming and other climate changes resulting from such GHG emissions) are generally referred to as "climate mitigation" laws and policies.

In addition to climate mitigation, however, there is increasing recognition that the global warming and climate changes resulting from past and present GHG emissions are happening now and will continue to happen for many decades to come, regardless of whether we are successful in curbing GHG emissions going forward. This recognition has led to the development of legal and policy responses to anticipate and plan for the global warming and climate changes that are taking place. Efforts to anticipate and plan for the effects of past and present GHG emissions are generally referred to as "climate adapta-tion" laws and policies.

In the water resources sector, to date much of the climate adaptation focus has been on water supplies for out-of-stream uses (such as agriculture and municipal/urban uses) and on instream use of water for hydro-electric facilities – that is, on how climate change is affecting the supply of water we use for irrigation, drinking water, and electric power generation.

Less attention, however, has so far been given to how climate change is impacting and will continue to impact fisheries due to rising water temperat-ures. These impacts are particularly acute for cold-water fisheries such as salmon and steelhead trout, which have limited biological capacity to adapt when instream temperatures rise. There are ways to help counter these climate-induced impacts on water temperatures, such as the curtailing diver-sions of instream flow, the releases of colder water from upstream reservoirs, and fish passage to allow salmon to spawn in the cooler upper reaches of watersheds. But the regulatory mechanisms to ensure the adoption and implementation of such climate adaptation strategies remain poorly developed at present, at least in California and the United States.

This chapter discusses this current gap in climate adaptation law and policy, with emphasis on the potential role that the National Environmental Policy Act (NEPA) and Endangered Species Act (ESA) may play in filling this gap. It focuses on the provisions in these laws that establish that agency planning, and decision making should be based on the best available science, and the notes confirm that GHG emission-induced climate change is happening now and will continue during this century. The article posits that the most appropriate and effective way to factor expected climate change into NEPA and ESA analysis and determinations may be through the use of "future baseline conditions" against which project impacts are evaluated. The use of such future baseline conditions can provide a legal mechanism to ensure that climate adaptation strategies to protect cold-water fisheries are properly incorporated into agency plans and projects.

Although the starting point for the chapter's assessment is cold-water fisheries in California, this assessment identifies regulatory questions and offers recommendations that may apply to cold-water fisheries in other states and nations as well. For instance, salmon spawn in and are present in the freshwater rivers and streams of many northern countries, such as Canada, Iceland, Ireland, Japan, Norway, Russia, and Scotland. Like California, if these nations wish to maintain their salmon stocks in the face of global warming, they will need to develop their own climate adaptation strategies, of which maintenance of instream flows may be a central component.

DIRE FORECASTS FOR SALMON AND STEELHEAD

In recent years, leading studies on water and climate change impacts in California have taken note of the nexus between rising instream temperatures and the fate of our state's cold-water fisheries. These studies present a dire picture of how climate change will impact these fisheries in the years ahead.

The Public Policy Institute of California reported in its 2011 book *Managing California's Water: From Conflict to Reconciliation* that "[w]arming is likely to significantly complicate the management of water to maintain adequate habitat for such fish as salmon and steelhead, now confined to the lower-elevation portions of rivers and streams because of dams. ... The frequency of releases of warm water from reservoirs is likely to increase as conditions warm, increasing the temperatures of rivers and worsening conditions for many species of fish."[1]

The California Natural Resources Agency found in its 2009 *California Climate Adaptation Strategy* that "[i]n many low-elevation and middle-elevation streams today, summer temperatures often approach the upper tolerance for salmon and trout. Higher air and water temperatures will exacerbate this problem. Thus, climate change might require dedication of more water, especially cold water stored behind reservoirs, to simply maintain existing fish habitat."[2]

And in *Beyond Season's End: A Path Forward for Fish and Wildlife in the Era of Climate Change*, also published in 2009, a collaborative research initiative of conservation groups and the Association of Fish and Wildlife Agencies noted that "[w]ater temperature that is within the preferred range of coldwater fish, generally 50° to 65°F, may be the most critical characteristic of high-quality habitat. Physiological effects of warm water on trout and salmon include increased metabolic demands, increased stress due to reduced levels of dissolved oxygen [and] greater susceptibility to toxins, parasites and disease."[3]

Other studies have gone beyond acknowledging the general interrelationship between rising instream temperatures and declining cold-water fisheries, and have run more detailed simulations to quantify these effects. The results of these simulations reveal a grim scenario for our salmon and steelhead. For instance, Trout Unlimited found in its 2007 report *Healing Troubled Water: Preparing Trout and Salmon Habitat for a Changing Climate* that "[m]odels of Pacific Northwest salmon populations predict losses of 20–40% by the year 2050 because of the effects of climate change. In California, where high temperatures and water availability already pose a significant source of stress, greater declines are likely."[4] These findings echo those of a 2002 joint study by Defenders of Wildlife and the Natural Resources Defense Council (NRDC), titled *Effects of Global Warming on Trout and Salmon in U.S. Streams*, which estimated that "individual species of trout and salmon could lose 5–17% of their existing habitat by the year 2030, 14–34% by 2060, and 21–42% by 2090. . . . For salmon, significant losses are projected throughout the current geographic range, with greatest losses expected for California."[5]

METHODOLOGIES TO DOWNSCALE GLOBAL WARMING

Our ability to anticipate (and therefore potentially plan for) the effects of GHG emission-induced global warming on cold-water fisheries has been greatly enhanced in recent years through the development of improved "downscaling" methodologies. "Downscaling" in context is the process of deriving finer-resolution data about warming impacts from a coarser-resolution data set. Such downscaling methodologies now enable climatologists to better predict the particular impacts of global warming on air and instream temperatures on a watershed basis, and even on a creek-by-creek or stream-by-stream basis. Such information, when considered alongside information regarding salmon and steelhead migration patterns and spawning locations and the specific temperature related tolerance/vulnerability of particular cold-water species, can provide the scientific basis for more localized and geographically specific climate adaptation strategies.

Downscaling tools are becoming more widely available for use in climate change planning. For example, the US Department of Interior's Bureau of Reclamation, the Lawrence Livermore National Laboratory, the Santa Clara University Civil Engineering Department, Climate Central, and the Institute for Research on Climate Change and its Societal Impacts have teamed up to develop a data set of Global Climate Model simulation downscaled over the entire United States. The data set is available as a public archive, and it is increasingly being used in planning studies to characterize and analyze climate change impacts.[6]

These downscaling methodologies are now being incorporated into climate change/global warming assessments prepared by the California Climate Action Team (created by the California Governor's Executive Order S-3–05 in 2005) and the Cal-Adapt program of the California Energy Commission. For instance, in 2012, the California Natural Resources Agency (in conjunction with the Cal-Adapt program) co-authored the publication *California Adaptation Planning Guide: Understanding Regional Characteristics*. This publication included separate downscaled assessments of projected climate change impacts (including warming temperatures) for each of the different regions in the state.

COLD-WATER FISHERY CLIMATE ADAPTATION STRATEGIES

In terms of on-the-ground (or perhaps 'on-the-river') strategies to maintain healthy salmon and steelhead fisheries in the face of rising instream temperatures, the literature suggests three primary alternatives. These climate adaptation strategy alternatives are not mutually exclusive and can be used in combination. If implemented, such adaptation strategies could help alleviate some of the adverse impacts that climate change will have on these species.

Reservoir Releases

Additional quantities of cold water from upstream dams/reservoirs can be released to reduce the temperature of downstream waters. These releases can be timed to ensure that quantities of cold water are flowing below the dam at the times cold-water fisheries need it most. Additionally, if the water released from the reservoir can come from the lower/deeper columns of the reservoir the water released will be colder than water taken from the upper/shallower columns. Because many dams' spillage facilities are designed for hydropower generation (in which water is dropped to create head to spin turbines), they tend to release warmer water from the upper/shallower columns of reservoirs. The additional release of reservoir waters for this purpose may be resisted by existing agricultural and municipal water users of such waters, however.

Upstream Passage

The air and water temperatures in any given watershed tend to rise as the waters move further away from high elevation headwaters into lower reaches. To the extent that higher-elevation reaches of a watershed have lower instream water temperatures, one strategy to counter higher downstream water temperatures is to provide salmon and steelhead with improved access upstream. Presently, access to such higher-elevation upstream reaches is often blocked by dams that provide little or no fish passage. Implementing these climate adaptation strategies for cold-water fisheries may therefore require modifying (or in some cases removing) existing dams. The modification and/or removal of dams for this purpose may be resisted by the owners of such dams and by water users and hydro-electric consumers that may be impacted by such changes.

Riparian Shading

Particularly in the narrower and bankside reaches of streams and creeks that support salmon and steelhead runs, trees and vegetation can provide enhanced shading that keeps instream temperatures cooler. The cold-water fishery benefits of enhanced riparian shading can be particularly pronounced for those waters that serve as spawning grounds, given the particular vulnerability of salmon and steelhead eggs to higher instream temperatures. Whether such riparian/bankside areas are located on private or public lands, the question arises as to how to fund (and who should fund) such riparian shading projects.

CLIMATE ADAPTATION UNDER NEPA AND THE ESA

Despite the consistent warnings that scientists have been providing for more than a decade about the threat climate change poses for cold-water fisheries, our environmental laws – and the government agencies tasked with implementing them – have been somewhat slow to react. Laws such as NEPA and the ESA are flexible enough in their design to allow agencies to effectively analyze and address emerging conditions like climate change, but to date climate adaptation has not been addressed in such a manner. Nevertheless, the potential for these laws to be used to identify and implement effective climate adaptation strategies exists. Several recent developments suggest that, going forward, agencies may be more prepared to acknowledge and take into account the emerging scientific evidence on climate change impacts on cold-water fisheries.

One potential legal mechanism to do so is to include projected instream warming and related impacts in the baseline conditions under which NEPA environmental analyses are performed. If such impacts are included in the environmental baseline against which the impacts of water resource projects are evaluated, then the projects can incorporate needed adaptation measures to help impacted fisheries survive in a warmer climate.

NEPA

National Environmental Policy Act requires federal agencies to evaluate the environmental impacts of actions that they approve or carry out. There are several types of federal agency actions subject to NEPA environmental review that may involve impacts on cold-water fisheries, including water storage and diversion facilities projects operated by the US Bureau of Reclamation (such as dams/pumps that are part of the Central Valley Project in California) and onstream hydro-electric projects licensed by the Federal Energy Regulatory Commission (FERC).

There are presently no provisions in the NEPA statute, in the Council on Environmental Quality (CEQ) NEPA implementing regulations, or in formal NEPA policy guidance that explicitly address the issue of climate adaptation – i.e., the extent to which NEPA environmental impact assessment documents can or must consider the ways in which anticipated changes resulting from GHG emissions are expected to alter the environmental effects of a particular project.

The current absence of any explicit guidance does not mean that the issue of climate change adaptation has not arisen in the NEPA context, however. The CEQ has issued draft guidance suggesting that federal agencies consider how climate change will affect a project's environmental impacts, and that considering climate change in the articulation of baseline conditions may be an appropriate way to accomplish this result. Subsequent

NEPA analyses for specific projects affecting cold-water fisheries have been something of a mixed bag, however, with some failing altogether to address climate change impacts on fish habitat and others doing so in a stand-alone fashion that is often detached from core elements of environmental impact assessment.

The 2010 Draft NEPA Guidance on Climate Adaptation

In February 2010, the CEQ released its *Draft NEPA Guidance on Consideration of the Effects of Climate Change and Greenhouse Gas Emissions (2010 Draft NEPA Guidance)*.[7] Although to date no action has been taken to formally adopt this draft guidance, the document offers some insight into how the CEQ believes that climate adaptation considerations should be incorporated into NEPA documents.

The *2010 Draft NEPA Guidance* recognizes that the NEPA process can be used "to reduce vulnerability to climate change impacts, adapt to changes in our environment, and mitigate the impacts of Federal agency actions that are exacerbated by climate change."[8] The document goes on to recommend that the articulation of "baseline conditions" may be the appropriate place in NEPA analysis to factor in the anticipated effects of global warming. More specifically, the *2010 Draft NEPA Guidance* states "it may also be useful to consider the effects of any proposed action or its alternatives against a baseline of reasonably foreseeable future conditions that is drawn as distinctly as the science of climate change effects will support."[9] That is, instead of evaluating the environmental effects of a proposed action solely against the conditions that exist at the time the NEPA document is prepared, it may be advisable to evaluate such environmental effects against the conditions that are expected to exist in the future as a result of climate change.

The *2010 Draft NEPA Guidance* also notes that in projecting the impact of climate change on environmental conditions, "the outputs of coarse-resolution global climate models, commonly used to project climate change scenarios at a continental or regional scale, require downscaling ... before they can be used in regional or local impact studies."[10] The document acknowledges, however, that the NEPA incorporates a "rule of reason" regarding the extent of research and analysis that an agency must undertake in its environmental analyses, and recognizes that "agencies need not undertake exorbitant research or analysis of projected climate change impacts in the project area or on the project itself ..." The development and availability of downscaling data and methodologies, such as the one developed by the US Department of the Interior/Lawrence Livermore National Laboratory (discussed earlier), may make it increasingly difficult for federal action agencies to credibly claim that "exorbitant" research and analysis is required to downscale projected climate change impacts to the regional or local level.

With the election of Donald Trump as President in 2016, no action has been taken by the CEQ to finalize this draft guidance. The preparation of the draft, however, evidences CEQ staff's growing recognition that for NEPA to remain scientifically credible climate adaptation considerations must be better factored into the NEPA environmental assessment process. The draft guidance also reflects CEQ's initial thinking that the use of future environmental baseline may be the most appropriate way to achieve this incorporation.

The 2012 EIS for Middle Fork American River Hydro-electric Project
In July 2012, FERC released its draft environmental impact statement (DEIS) in connection with a hydropower license for the Middle Fork American Hydroelectric Project in California. The project will impact cold-water salmon and steelhead fisheries on the American River, and it is projected to have a lifetime of 30 to 50 years based on the terms of the license. Although the DEIS recognizes that climate change is an important environmental challenge facing these fisheries,[11] the FERC did not follow the future baseline approach to climate adaptation recommended by the CEQ in the 2010 *Draft NEPA Guidance*.

The FERC did undertake an analysis of the effects of the proposed project on instream water temperatures, and it acknowledges the relationship between instream water temperature and cold-water fisheries. To address the potential water temperature impacts of the project, the draft environmental impact report (DEIR) calls for implementation of a proposed "Water Temperature Monitoring Plan" to "confirm whether flows are protective of the basin plan designated beneficial uses of cold freshwater habitat . . ." which would be used as a "key input" to monitor project impacts on cold-water fisheries whose "distribution and population vitality . . . are strongly related to water temperature."[12] But the document analysis relied on "existing conditions" as the benchmark for evaluating the impacts of the project on instream temperature change and the resulting impacts on cold-water fisheries. That is, in contrast to the climate adaptation approach suggested in the 2010 *Draft NEPA Guidance*, the FERC DEIS does not adopt a baseline (for instream water temperatures) that reflects the anticipated rise in instream water temperatures due to GHG emissions that is expected to occur during the 30–50-year term of the licensed project.

Additionally, the 2012 *Draft FERC DEIS* analysis makes no attempt to downscale the effects of climate change on increased instream water temperatures in the project area, nor is there analysis of the effects of such increased instream water temperatures on cold-water fisheries in the project area. As a result, no alternatives or mitigation were proposed in the 2012 *Draft FERC DEIS* to explicitly address these climate adaptation considerations.

The 2012 Bay Delta Conservation Plan Draft EIS

In February 2012, the US Bureau of Reclamation released its administrative draft of an EIS for the Bay Delta Conservation Plan (BDCP) prepared pursuant to NEPA. The BDCP proposes (among other things) a new "isolated conveyance facility" – a canal and/or tunnel – that would divert substantial portions of water from the higher elevation/upstream reaches of the Sacramento River. This proposed isolated conveyance facility would replace current water diversions that occur in the lower elevation/downstream reaches of the Sacramento River near the Bay Delta or where the Sacramento and San Joaquin Rivers converge.

One of the rationales presented for the BDCP isolated conveyance facility was that fewer juvenile salmon and steelhead were anticipated to become entrained in the diversion pumps if the pumps were relocated further upstream. However, as noted earlier, the higher elevation/upstream reaches of a watershed tend to have colder instream temperatures than the lower elevation/downstream reaches. Therefore, while the relocation of diversion structures to points further upstream may reduce entrainment of salmon and steelhead, the increased diversion of the colder water upstream (in areas that are prime cold-water fishery habitat) could have other potential adverse impacts on salmon and steelhead.

The 2012 *BDCP EIS* devotes a chapter to climate change adaptation considerations. The chapter "analyzes changes in future climate that could affect the water conveyance facilities and natural resources in the Plan Area," and evaluates how the various action alternatives evaluated in the EIR/EIS would affect the project area's resiliency to climate change impacts. In doing so, the document explains that "[t]he current environmental setting for climate change is the baseline conditions detailed in the other resource chapters."[13]

The 2012 *BDCP EIS* finds that "future changes in water temperatures of rivers below Central Valley Project (CVP) and State Water Project (SWP) reservoirs are likely to occur as a result of the combination of changes in reservoir operations caused by the BDCP Delta operations and by climate change effects." It notes further that such increased water temperatures "may have adverse effects on fish spawning (reduced egg survival) and may reduce the habitat zone (reduced abundance) of fish that are sensitive to high temperatures. . . ."[14] It also projects that less water may be available from the reservoir each year as a result of such impacts, because "[i]ncreased water temperatures can alter reservoir stratification and reduce the cold water volume (i.e. volume with temperatures of less than 55°), which may increase the minimum carryover storage required to protect downstream fish spawning and rearing." But the document concedes that none of the project alternatives considered would "provide additional resiliency to this climate change effect."

In this instance, while the NEPA document did not adopt the future baseline suggested in the 2010 *Draft NEPA Guidance*, it nonetheless did contain some substantive analysis of how global warming is expected to increase instream water temperatures in the project area, and these projected increases in instream water temperatures were then considerations built into the models to assess the impacts of the BDCP alternatives on cold-water fisheries. Moreover, the document contains an express acknowledgement that the BDCP as currently conceived does not include measures/components to increase the ability of cold-water fisheries to adapt to such rising instream temperatures.[15]

On the one hand, therefore, the draft 2012 *BDCP EIS'* inclusion of more substantive analysis of climate change impacts on instream water temperatures and cold-water fisheries can be seen as an improvement over the NEPA analysis in the 2012 *Draft FERC DEIS* discussed earlier. However, there still remains a disconnect between this climate adaptation analysis and the alternatives and mitigation set forth in the draft 2012 *BDCP EIS*. That is, the analysis did not lead to the inclusion of appropriate climate adaptation strategies, alternatives, or mitigation in the proposed project (e.g. additional reservoir releases, improved upstream passage, expanded riparian shading on creeks/stream).

This disconnect appears to have been by design rather than by oversight, as the introductory section to the climate change adaptation chapter in the 2012 *Draft BDCP EIS* acknowledges: "This chapter is organized differently from the other resource chapters because analyzing the effect of climate change on the study area is a fundamentally different analysis than those presented in the other resource chapters. Whereas the other chapters are organized to identify effects of the action alternatives and how to mitigate them, this chapter's function is to analyze and disclose how the action alternatives affect the project area's resiliency to expected changes in climate."[16] This acknowledgement evidences the ways that, even within NEPA documents, climate adaptation unfortunately continues to be treated as a stand-alone question somehow unrelated to traditional NEPA environmental impact assessment rather than a critical component of such assessment.

ESA

The ESA requires, among other things, that federal agencies ensure that any actions they approve or carry out will not jeopardize the continued existence of any endangered or threatened species, or result in adverse impacts such as species' critical habitat.[17] These federal agency responsibilities are administered jointly by the United States Fish and Wildlife Service (USFWS) and the National Marine Fisheries Services (NMFS). There are several types of USFWS/NMFS actions under the ESA that may involve assessment of impacts on cold-water fisheries, including issuance of Biological Opinions (BiOp) regarding whether federal agency actions will cause "jeopardy" to a listed species or adversely modify the species' critical habitat; decisions on whether to list or delist species as "endangered" or "threatened"; and approval of incidental take permits and habitat conservation plans. Several recent court cases have determined that USFWS and NMFS need to take into account the growing body of scientific evidence regarding the effects of climate change when taking such actions. These decisions bode well for the prospects of incorporating climate change adaptation into water resource management decisions affecting cold-water fisheries.

Litigation on Bay Delta NMFS/USFWS Biological Opinions

In the past decade, there has been extensive ESA litigation over the effects of the federal CVP and California's SWP on the condition of salmon, steelhead, and smelt fisheries in the Sacramento River/San Joaquin River/San Francisco Bay Delta watershed. The litigation has challenged the BiOp issued by USFWS and NMFS evaluating the projects' impacts on these species and their habitat. In two prominent decisions – NRDC v. *Kempthorne*, 506 F. Supp.2d. 322 (2007) and *Pacific Coast Federation of Fishermen's Association (PCFFA)* v. *Gutierrez*, 606 F. Supp.2d. 1122 (2008) – the former Judge, Oliver Wanger, of the federal District Court for the Central District of California invalidated the BiOp because they failed to adequately address the anticipated effects of climate change on the habitat of the endangered cold-water fisheries.

In NRDC v. *Kempthorne*, the court observed that there were a number of studies in the record predicting that anticipated climate change will adversely impact future water availability, which suggested that climate change will be an important aspect of the problems facing fish species (such as the endangered delta smelt) in the project area that should be analyzed in the BiOp. But the BiOp did not provide any meaningful discussion of the issue, and failed to evaluate the potential effect of climate change on Delta hydrology. The court therefore held that USFWS acted arbitrarily and capriciously, explaining that "[t]he absence of any discussion in the Biological Opinion of how to deal with climate change is a failure to analyze a potential 'important aspect of the problem.'"[18]

In PCFFA v. Gutierrez, the court noted readily available scientific data showing that climate change is projected to greatly reduce the Sierra snowpack and summer stream flow. But the BiOp did not discuss the data or indicate that NMFS had considered it. Instead, the BiOp relied on past hydrology and temperature models assuming that historical temperature, hydrologic and climate conditions experienced from 1922 through 1994 will continue for the 25-year duration of project operations.[19] The court set aside the BiOp and remanded it back to NMFS to address these deficiencies.

These cases do not explicitly hold that BiOp must always consider the effects of GHG emission-induced rising instream temperatures on coldwater fisheries protected under the ESA. Nevertheless, the cases do establish generally that ESA BiOp may not lawfully rely on historical data regarding instream flow and temperatures if there is substantial evidence that such flow and temperatures will be significantly altered by global warming during the term of the project.

Litigation on Proposed Grizzly Bear Delisting

In its 2011 decision in *Greater Yellowstone Coalition v. Servheen*, 665 F.3d 1015, the Ninth Circuit Court of Appeals affirmed a Montana district court ruling that blocked the USFWS from removing Yellowstone grizzly bears from the ESA's threatened species list because the agency had failed to consider the potential impacts of climate change on the bears' continued survival.

The USFWS has delisted the grizzly bears in the Greater Yellowstone Area based on an increase in their population from a range between 136–250 at the time of the listing in 1975 to around 580 in 2007. The district court invalidated the delisting because it found that the USFWS had failed to adequately consider the anticipated impacts of global warming on the whitebark pine, an important food source for grizzly bears. In affirming this ruling, the Ninth Circuit noted that the USFWS itself had found that whitebark pine seeds were the important food source of grizzly bears' survival; that a well-documented association exists between reduced whitebark pine seed abundance and increased grizzly mortality; and that global warming was expected to lessen whitebark pine abundance. The Ninth Circuit went on to find that "the best science indicates that whitebark pines are expected to decline" due to global warming, and that the USFWS failed to articulate "a rational connection" between the best available science and the conclusion that grizzly bears would be able to adapt to the decline of whitebark pines. The Ninth Circuit explained that the USFWS "must rationally explain why the uncertainty regarding the impact of whitebark pine loss on the grizzly counsels in favor of delisting now, rather than, for example, more study. . . . Otherwise, we might as well be deferring to a coin flip."[20]

The decision in *Greater Yellowstone Coalition* did not directly address fisheries, fisheries habitat, or rising instream temperatures. However, the case does stand for the more general proposition that to the extent the best available science indicates that anticipated global warming may affect the survival of a particular species protected under the ESA, a decision by USFWS or NMFS to delist a particular species must directly and meaningfully address such impacts and provide a rational explanation for why delisting is nonetheless warranted.

Litigation Regarding Leavenworth National Fish Hatchery

The Leavenworth National Fish Hatchery (Leavenworth Hatchery) is operated by the US Bureau of Reclamation (Reclamation) on Icicle Creek in the state of Washington. Icicle Creek is tributary to the Wenatchee River which is part of the Columbia River watershed. There are Chinook salmon and steelhead trout runs below the Leavenworth Hatchery, and the instream habitat of these fisheries is impacted by diversions to and releases from the hatchery.

Pursuant to the ESA, Reclamation engaged in consultation with NMFS is the proposed operation of Leavenworth Hatchery during dry years. The NMFS' BiOp relied solely on historical data concerning stream flow water temperatures and containing no analysis of the anticipated impacts of climate change on these fish habitat parameters. The group Wild Fish Conservancy sued NMFS in federal district court regarding the BiOp for Leavenworth Hatchery, alleging that the agency's failure to address anticipated climate change impacts was a violation of the ESA.

In a November 22, 2016 order, the federal district court agreed with plaintiff Wild Fish Conservancy, holding as follows:

> Defendants' argument that NMFS did not need to consider climate change in its analysis miss the mark here. The best available science indicates that climate change will affect stream flow and water conditions throughout the Northwest. The fact there is not a model or study specifically addressing the effects of climate change on Icicle Creek does not permit the agency to ignore this factor.
>
> The problem with NMFS' analysis is not that it used recent historical streamflow data to model the effects of hatchery operations and water use at different flow levels. The problem here is that NMFS included no discussion

whatsoever of the potential effects of climate change in the [Biological Opinion's] analysis of the Hatchery's future operations and water use. NMFS discusses the effects of climate change generally and then proceeds on the apparent assumptions that there will be no change to the hydrology of Icicle Creek. NMFS does not necessarily need to conduct a study or build a model addressing the impacts of climate change on the Icicle Creek watershed. But its analysis must consider the best available science, which it discusses elsewhere in the [Biological Opinion], suggests that baseline historical flow averages may not be effective predictors of future flow.[21]

. . .

Because NMFS failed to consider the potential effects of climate change on stream flows in Icicle Creek in connection with its analysis of the effects of the Hatchery's operations and water use on listed salmonids and critical habitat, NMFS failed to consider an important aspect of the problem, and the [Biological Opinion] is arbitrary and capricious.[22]

The federal district court's holding in *Wild Fish Conservancy* v. *Irving* suggests that an ESA BiOp may not simply ignore and disregard best available science indicating that stream flows and other instream conditions such as temperature will be impacted by climate change.

MOVING CLIMATE ADAPTATION INTO THE MAINSTREAM

The impact of climate change-induced rising instream temperatures is likely to be devastating on cold-water fisheries such as salmon and steelhead unless effective climate adaptation strategies are implemented. These climate adaptation strategies include increased releases of cold water from upstream reservoirs to downstream waterways, improved fishery passage around existing dams to reach colder upstream waters, and increased shading along streams and creeks whose waters serve as cold-water fishery spawning grounds. The first two of these climate adaptation strategies – reservoir releases and fish passage – relate closely to instream flow, and can be understood as securing the instream flow conditions salmon need to maintain the cooler water temperatures they need to survive.

Although there are now improved data and methodologies to downscale the effects of climate change to anticipate temperature rises in particular watersheds and rivers/streams, and although there is now an improved scientific understanding of how rising instream temperatures adversely affect cold-water fisheries, we are still at a relatively early stage in terms of integrating such information and analysis into environmental laws such as NEPA and the ESA.

Going forward, if NEPA and the ESA are interpreted to require more quantified analysis of the impacts of rising instream temperatures on cold-water fisheries, and also to require formulation of specific project design and mitigation to address such impacts (such as measures to maintain instream flows and provide for fish passage), these laws may play an increasingly important role in the development and implementation of effective climate adaptation strategies to help already imperiled salmon and steelhead fisheries weather the hotter days that lie ahead.

Notes

1. Hanak et al., MANAGING CALIFORNIA'S WATER: FROM CONFLICT TO RECONCILIATION (Public Policy Institute of California, 2011), pp. 146–147.
2. 2009 *California Climate Adaptation Strategy: A Report to the Governor of the State of California in Response to Executive Order S-13–2008* (California Natural Resources Agency), p. 81.
3. *Beyond Seasons' End: A Path Forward for Fish and Wildlife in the Era of Climate Change* (2009 Report prepared by Bipartisan Policy Center for Ducks Unlimited, Trout Unlimited, BASS/ESPN Outdoors, Izaak Walton League of America, Association of Fish and Wildlife Agencies, Coastal Conservation Association, American Sportfishing Association, Pheasants Forever, and Boone & Crockett Club), p. 34.
4. *Healing Troubled Waters: Preparing Trout and Salmon Habitat for a Changing Climate* (Trout Unlimited, October 2007 Report), p. 3.
5. *Effects of Global Warming on Trout and Salmon in U.S. Streams* (May 2002 Report by Defenders of Wildlife and Natural Resources Defense Council), pp. 3–4.
6. California Department of Water Resources (DWR) 2010 report *Climate Change Characterization and Analysis in California Water Resources Planning Studies*, p. xv.
7. *Draft NEPA Guidance on Consideration of the Effects of Climate Change and Greenhouse Gas Emissions* (Council on Environmental Quality, February 2010).
8. *Draft NEPA Guidance on Consideration of the Effects of Climate Change and Greenhouse Gas Emissions* (Council on Environmental Quality, February 2010), p. 2.
9. *Draft NEPA Guidance on Consideration of the Effects of Climate Change and Greenhouse Gas Emissions* (Council on Environmental Quality, February 2010), p. 7.
10. *Draft NEPA Guidance on Consideration of the Effects of Climate Change and Greenhouse Gas Emissions* (Council on Environmental Quality, February 2010), p. 8.

11. *Draft Environmental Impact Statement for Hydropower License* (Middle Fork American River Hydroelectric Project, FERC Project No. 20179–069, July 2012), p. 96 ("The American River population is classified at a high risk of extinction; increasing demands for water and the potential effects of climate change are likely to increase this risk").
12. *Draft Environmental Impact Statement for Hydropower License* (Middle Fork American River Hydroelectric Project, FERC Project No. 20179–069, July 2012), pp. 125–130.
13. *Administrative Draft of EIR/EIS for Bay Delta Conservation Plan* (February 2012, California lead agency, California Department of Water Resources; federal co-lead agencies, Bureau of reclamation, U.S. Fish and Wildlife Service and National Marine Fisheries Service), at p. 29–2.
14. *Administrative Draft of EIR/EIS for Bay Delta Conservation Plan* (February 2012, California lead agency, California Department of Water Resources; federal co-lead agencies, Bureau of reclamation, U.S. Fish and Wildlife Service and National Marine Fisheries Service), at p. 29–20.
15. *Administrative Draft of EIR/EIS for Bay Delta Conservation Plan* (February 2012, California lead agency, California Department of Water Resources; federal co-lead agencies, Bureau of reclamation, U.S. Fish and Wildlife Service and National Marine Fisheries Service), at pp. 29–23, 29–25.
16. *Administrative Draft of EIR/EIS for Bay Delta Conservation Plan* (February 2012, California lead agency, California Department of Water Resources; federal co-lead agencies, Bureau of reclamation, U.S. Fish and Wildlife Service and National Marine Fisheries Service), at pp. 29–1.
17. 16 U.S.C. § 1536(a)(2).
18. 506 F.Supp.2d 322, 367–370.
19. 606 F.Supp.2d 1122, 1183.
20. *Great Yellowstone Coalition* v. *Servheen*, __ F. 3d __, 2011 WL 5840646, p. 9 (9th Cir. 2011).
21. Order Granting in Part and Denying in Part Plaintiff's and Defendants' Motions for Summary Judgments (Case No. 2:14-CV-0306-SMJ, United States District Court for the Eastern District of Washington, issued November 22, 2016), at pp. 16–17.
22. Order Granting in Part and Denying in Part Plaintiff's and Defendants' Motions for Summary Judgments (Case No. 2:14-CV-0306-SMJ, United States District Court for the Eastern District of Washington, issued November 22, 2016), at pp. 17–18.

7

Instream Rights as Sea Levels Rise

The basic environmental impact assessment paradigm, under the federal National Environmental Policy Act (NEPA) and state laws such as the California Environmental Quality Act (CEQA), is as follows: set forth an accurate project description, describe baseline environmental conditions at the time the project is being considered for approval, assess the impacts of the proposed project on baseline environmental conditions, and then present a reasonable range of alternatives and feasible mitigation to reduce the significant adverse impacts of the project on baseline environmental conditions. The critical temporal assumption to this basic environmental impact assessment paradigm is that appropriate alternatives and mitigation will be determined in reference to a set of baseline environmental conditions at a fixed point in time when the environmental impact assessment is being prepared.

This critical temporal assumption is found not only in environmental impact assessment laws in California and the United States but also in environmental impact assessment regimes around the world. In general, the impacts of a proposed project or policy are evaluated against the baseline conditions that exist at the time the environmental impact assessment is undertaken.

At the time NEPA and CEQA were adopted, around 1970, this temporal assumption made sense. In 1970, it was perhaps difficult to envision a situation where a lead agency could credibly predict future changes in background conditions that would occur independent of the project being considered or similar nearby proposed projects. Grounding environmental impact assessment on a comparison of project impacts against existing conditions was a logical approach.

The effects of climate change, however, present a challenge to the viability of this basic environmental impact assessment paradigm, particularly for projects that will operate many decades into the future. With climate change, the background environmental conditions against which long-term projects operate will change: air and water temperatures will be higher, the snowpack will be smaller, and sea levels will rise. As these background environmental conditions shift during the project's operation, the project's impacts on the environment will also change and may become more severe. Yet, if the environmental impact assessment remains tethered to the baseline conditions when the environmental impact assessment was prepared, and disregards the ways such baseline conditions will shift as a result of climate change, the assessment will fail to identify the true impacts of the project during its anticipated lifetime. Thus, effective alternatives and mitigation to address these true impacts will not be considered or incorporated into the project.

In 2013, the California Supreme Court issued a landmark CEQA holding that authorized state and local agencies in California to depart from the basic environmental impact assessment paradigm to more effectively address changes in baseline conditions that are expected to occur during the lifetime of a proposed project. In its decision in *Neighbors for Smart Rail* v. *Exposition Metro Line Construction Authority* (*Smart Rail*), the Court reviewed an environmental impact report (EIR) for a Los Angeles urban light rail project, which considered air quality and traffic impacts against a future environmental baseline that included anticipated population increases in the vicinity of the project.[1] The use of this future baseline had been affirmed by the California Court of Appeal, which held: "[t]he important point, in our view, is the reliability of the projections and the inevitability of the changes on which those projections are based . . . Population growth, with its concomitant effects on traffic and air quality, is not hypothetical in Los Angeles County; it is inevitable."[2]

On review, the issue was presented to the California Supreme Court in *Smart Rail* as an "either/or" question: when is it appropriate to use a future baseline for CEQA analysis in lieu of an existing conditions baseline? A key aspect of the Court's 2013 *Smart Rail* decision was its rejection of this proposed "either/or" framework for evaluating the relationship between existing and future baselines. Instead, the Court focused on the appropriate use of "multiple" baselines in CEQA documents.

That is, in *Smart Rail*, the Court held that it is permissible for a lead agency to use a future baseline when there are inevitable changes in the environmental setting that will occur during the duration of the project. Although this is very important holding, the Court made clear that while there may be situations where it is permissible or even advisable for a lead CEQA agency to use a future baseline in its environmental impact analysis, this does not mean that the lead agency is generally allowed to forgo analysis of the project's impact as compared to existing conditions.

As the Court explained in *Smart Rail*, "nothing in CEQA law precludes an agency ... from considering both types of baselines – existing and future conditions – in its primary analysis of the project's significant adverse impact."[3] The California Supreme Court then further elaborated:

> Even when a project is intended and expected to improve conditions in the long term – 20 or 30 years after an EIR is prepared – decision makers and members of the public are entitled under CEQA to know the short- and medium-term environmental costs of achieving that desirable improvement ... Though we might rationally choose to endure short- or medium-term hardship for a long-term, permanent benefit, deciding to make that tradeoff requires some knowledge about the severity and duration of the near-term hardship. An EIR stating that in 20 or 30 years the project will improve the environment, but neglecting, without justification, to provide any evaluation of the project's impacts in the meantime, does not give due consideration of both the short-term and long-term effects of the project.[4]

The Court cautioned that allowing CEQA lead agencies to ignore near-term effects on existing conditions "would sanction the unwarranted omission of information on years or decades of a project's environmental impacts and open the door to gamesmanship in the choice of baselines."[5]

From this holding, we understand that the Court's multiple baselines approach is grounded in CEQA's requirement that both short-term and long-term project impacts must be evaluated. Otherwise, if a CEQA lead agency were allowed only to focus on a distant point in time in the future with changed baseline conditions, it would be allowed to bypass analysis of the more immediate effects of the project on existing conditions. With *Smart Rail*, it is now generally permissible for a lead CEQA agency to employ a future baseline in addition to an existing baseline. The anticipated and inevitable shifts in environmental conditions (e.g. rising temperatures, snowpack reduction, sea level rise) resulting from climate change, due to their inevitable nature, appear to fall within *Smart Rail*'s bounds of when the use of such multiple baselines would be permissible.

The question left open by *Smart Rail* is whether there are situations where CEQA not only *permits* the use of a future baseline but *requires* it. Although in one sense this is a CEQA-specific question, the answer to this question may also have implications for how climate change is addressed under NEPA and other non-California state environmental impact assessment laws. As such, these other jurisdictions may look to California's answer and approach as guidance and persuasive precedent.

This chapter suggests that this open question may be addressed in litigation challenging the CEQA climate change analysis for the Bay Delta Conservation Plan (BDCP), a fishery restoration-water supply project proposed in California. To understand the relevant CEQA climate change issues related to the BDCP, our starting point is the 2008 Biological Opinion issued by the US Fish & Wildlife Service (USFWS) for the delta smelt, a fish species protected under the federal Endangered Species Act (ESA).

NEXUS BETWEEN X2 AND DELTA FISHERIES

In 2008, pursuant to the ESA, the United States USFWS issued its biological opinion (BiOp) for the delta smelt in connection with the proposed "coordinated operations" of the federal Central Valley Project (CVP) and California's State Water Project (SWP). The CVP and SWP, which deliver water to agricultural and urban water users throughout the state, both divert significant amounts of water from and upstream of the Bay Delta where the fresh water of the Sacramento and San Joaquin Rivers flow into San Francisco Bay. In this 2008 BiOp, the USFWS determined that it could not issue an incidental take permit for the proposed CVP–SWP coordinated operations unless these operations ensured adequate fresh water flows into the Delta.

According to the USFWS, adequate fresh water flows would be met if "X2," which represents the distance salt water has traveled into the Delta by measuring "the intrusion of water with a salinity level of two parts per thousand," was located at a distance of 74–81 kilometers eastward of the Golden Gate Bridge.[6]

This BiOp determined that maintaining X2 at this particular locational range was needed to ensure the survival and recovery of the endangered delta smelt. This decision was based on data showing a strong correlation between increases in salinity levels beyond X2 levels and decreases in suitable abiotic habitat for delta smelt. The BiOp explained that the location of "X2 is largely determined by Delta outflow, which in turn is largely determined by the difference between total Delta inflow and the total amount of water exported,"[7] and that the effects of the proposed CVP–SWP coordinated operation on X2 will have "significant adverse direct and indirect effects on delta smelt."[8]

The BiOp contained a graph indicating that the proposed CVP–SWP coordinated operations would cause X2 to shift upstream to approximately 90 kilometers east of the Golden Gate Bridge.[9] The USFWS found that a shift of X2 upstream to this location, which was nearly 15 percent farther upstream than the current average location of X2, could cause the delta smelt to go extinct.[10]

The 2008 USFWS BiOp for the delta smelt was challenged in federal court, and in April 2014, this BiOp was upheld by the Ninth Circuit Court of Appeals. In its ruling in *San Luis v. Jewell*, the Ninth Circuit found that "[a]s the combined pumping operations of the SWP/CVP remove hundreds of gallons of fresh water from the Bay Delta, X2 . . . shifts eastward towards the Delta . . . . The Bi-Op determined that the 'long-term upstream shift in X2 . . . has caused a long-term decrease in habitat area availability for the delta smelt' and it set forth an adaptive management program to minimize the effect of project pumping on X2."[11] In November 2014, the US Supreme Court denied cert to review the Ninth Circuit Court of Appeals' decision in *San Luis v. Jewell*.

NEXUS BETWEEN X2 AND SEA LEVEL RISE

In September 2014, the Bureau of Reclamation released a report titled *Sacramento and San Joaquin Basins Climate Impact Assessment* (*Climate Impact Assessment*).[12] Reclamation prepared the Climate Impact Assessment in connection with the operations of its CVP, which diverts, stores, and delivers waters from the Sacramento River and the San Joaquin River watersheds and includes such structures as Shasta Dam on the Sacramento River and Friant Dam on the San Joaquin River. The report focused on how projected salinity increases induced by sea level rise would impact CVP agricultural and urban water supplies, rather than impacts on smelt or fisheries.

The "Delta Salinity" section of the 2014 Reclamation *Climate Impact Assessment* contains a table showing salinity measurements and projections. This table focuses on two salinity monitoring locations in the Delta, one at a location called Emmaton and the other at a location upstream called Jersey Point. The table shows the anticipated twenty-first century increases in salinity levels at these locations resulting from climate change-induced sea level rise and saltwater intrusion.

For the period from 2041–2070, the delta salinity table projects a 28–56 percent increase in salinity levels at Emmaton and an 18–38 percent increase in salinity levels at Jersey Point.[13] For the period from 2071–2099, the table projects an 83–88 percent increase in salinity at Emmaton, and a 53–65 percent increase in salinity at Jersey Point. Taken together, these data indicate that, as a result of climate change-induced sea level rise, salinity levels in these two Delta locations are expected to rise by 53–88 percent over the coming century.

Keep in mind, these are not the projections of environmental groups or the US Environmental Protection Agency or the USFWS. These are the projections of the Bureau of Reclamation, which operates the CVP.

While there was no mention in the delta salinity table of the 2014 Reclamation *Climate Impact Assessment* of the current location of X_2 or of the upstream location where X_2 is projected to shift as a result of climate change-induced sea level rise, the implications of the table for X_2 are plain to see. If sea level rise will cause salinity levels in the Delta to increase by 53–88 percent in the coming century, then it follows that sea level rise will also cause X_2 to shift much farther upstream.

The information presented in the delta salinity table of the 2014 Reclamation *Climate Impact Assessment* is therefore quite bad news for the delta smelt.

THE 2013 DRAFT EIS

Overview of BDCP

There are two underlying purposes of the BDCP, which are often referred to as the coequal goals of the BDCP. These coequal goals are: (i) to restore the Delta's ecosystem and fisheries; and (ii) to improve water supply reliability.

The BDCP was drafted as a multispecies habitat conservation plan (HCP) to satisfy the requirements of Section 10 of the federal ESA. As an HCP, the focus of the BDCP was on the restoration of several ESA-listed fisheries in the Delta, namely the endangered delta smelt and several endangered salmon and steelhead trout runs.

Additionally, the BDCP proposed a series of components that would guide the activities of the Bureau of Reclamation's CVP and the California Department of Water Resources' SWP for many decades, perhaps as long as 50 years out. The components of the BDCP (as presented in the draft environmental impact assessment document issued in late 2013) include the following main three items. First, the BDCP proposes moving the main point of Delta diversion for the CVP and SWP from the south Delta to the north Delta and construction of two new tunnels to transport water from the new north point of diversion to agricultural and urban water users south of the Delta.[14] Second, the BDCP outlines a series of riparian enhancement projects designed to improve spawning habitat for fisheries. Third, the BDCP anticipates a potential 18 percent increase in the amount of fresh water diverted out of or upstream of the Delta – diversions sometimes called Delta exports.[15] An 18 percent increase in freshwater diversions out of the Delta would result in a significant decrease in the amount of fresh water flowing both into and through the Delta.

There are four lead agencies for the BDCP – the federal Bureau of Reclamation, USFWS, National Marine Fisheries Service, and California's Department of Water Resources (DWR). Because the BDCP is a joint undertaking of these agencies, a joint EIR–(environmental impact statement) EIS is being prepared pursuant to the NEPA and CEQA. The analysis below focuses on the CEQA-specific analysis in the December 2013 Draft EIR–EIS for the BDCP ("Draft EIR–EIS") rather than the NEPA-specific analysis in this document.

Appendix 2C of the BDCP

Appendix 2C of the BDCP was titled "Climate Change Implications and Assumptions" and reports: "Scenarios modeled by the California Climate Action Team project sea level rise increases along the California coast of 1.0 to 1.5 feet by 2050, and 1.8. to 4.6 feet by 2100. However, if California's sea level continues to mirror global trends, increases in sea level during this century could be considerably greater." So in Appendix 2C of the BDCP DWR acknowledges that the best available evidence indicates that by the end of the century sea level rise could be 4.6 feet (54 inches) and possibly higher.[16]

Appendix 29A of the Environmental Impact Assessment for the BDCP

Appendix 29A of the Draft EIR–EIS for the BDCP is titled "Effects of Sea Level Rise on Delta Tidal Flows and Salinity." Figure 29A-13 presents a chart showing how projected increases in sea level rise are expected to shift the location of X_2.

According to this chart, a 30-centimeter sea level rise would cause X_2 to shift approximately 1–2 kilometers upstream, a 45-centimeter sea level rise would cause X_2 to shift 2–4 kilometers upstream, and a 140-centimeter sea level rise would cause X_2 to shift 6–11 kilometers upstream.[17] As noted previously, Appendix 2C of the Draft BDCP environmental impact assessment acknowledged that sea level may rise more than 4.5 feet (or 140 centimeters). Reading Appendix 2C and Appendix 29A together, the Drafts BDCP and EIR–EIS therefore concede that climate change-induced sea level rise may cause the location of X_2 to shift as much as 11 kilometers upstream from its current location.

Yet, pursuant to the analysis and methodology in the 2008 USFWS BiOp, if X_2 were to shift 11 kilometers upstream (to a location approximately 90 kilometers east from the Golden Gate Bridge), the delta smelt faces the likelihood of extinction. The projected upstream shift in X2 due to sea level rise places X2 close to the location where the USFWS has determined that delta smelt cannot survive, and the only way to counteract this anticipated upstream shift in X2 would be to ensure that additional fresh water flows into the Delta.

Appendix 2C and Appendix 29A of the Drafts BDCP and EIR–EIS, respectively, therefore disclose the effect that climate change-induced sea level rise will have on salinity levels and the location of X2. These appendices, however, do not then contain subsequent analysis of how these expected changes in salinity levels and the location of X2 will impact the recovery and survival of the endangered delta smelt.

The CEQA Baseline in the BDCP Documents

As noted earlier, DWR (which operates California's SWP) was the lead CEQA agency in connection with the Draft EIR–EIS prepared for the BDCP. In Appendix 3D's of the BDCP EIR–EIS, DWR explains the baseline conditions it would be using in connection with its CEQA environmental impact analysis.

In Appendix 3D's, DWR states: "The CEQA baseline for assessing the significance of impacts of any proposed project is normally the environmental setting, or existing conditions, at the time the NOP [Notice of Preparation] is issued (State CEQA Guidelines Section 15125) . . . This directive was recently interpreted and applied by the California Supreme Court (*Neighbors for Smart Rail*). . . . According to the Court [in *Smart Rail*], the CEQA Guidelines establish the default of an existing baseline conditions even for projects expected to be in operation for many years or decades . . . [A]ny sole reliance on such a future baseline is only permissible where a CEQA lead agency can show, based on substantial evidence, that an existing conditions analysis would be misleading or without informational value . . . The CEQA baseline [for the BDCP] is existing conditions at the time of the NOP [February 2009]."[18]

This characterization of the *Smart Rail* holding is not wholly inaccurate but is certainly an incomplete and arguably misleading description of the decision. More specifically, the characterization of *Smart Rail* in Appendix 3D's of the EIR–EIS fails to mention the California Supreme Court's express endorsement of the use of multiple baselines (that include future as well as existing baseline conditions) as a preferred approach to sole reliance on a future baseline. Appendix 3D's characterization of *Smart Rail* suggests that CEQA would somehow prohibit or preclude DWR from using a future baseline to consider the effects of climate change-induced sea level rise on Delta fisheries, and this is erroneous. The California Supreme Court's decision in *Smart Rail* lends no support to this characterization and in fact contradicts it. In *Smart Rail*, the California Supreme Court expressed reservations about the use of a future baseline conditions in lieu of an existing baseline conditions, and not the use of a future baseline conditions *in addition to* an existing baseline conditions.

The definition of the CEQA baseline presented in Appendix 3D of the BDCP EIR–EIS was also set forth in a December 2013 document coprepared by DWR titled *Highlights of Bay Delta Conservation Plan Environmental Impact Report/Environmental Impact Statement* (*BDCP Highlights*). The section of *BDCP Highlights* on "Water Supply" explained that "[s]ea level rise will push salt water further east into the Delta, requiring upstream water releases to push seawater out of the Delta and achieve in-Delta water quality standards. These operational changes, would in turn, decrease available water supply for south of Delta users." The section of the *BDCP Highlights* on "Water Quality" then finds that "seawater intrusion caused by sea level rise or decreased Delta outflow ... can increase the concentration of salts. Conversely, Delta outflow can decrease the effects of seawater intrusion."[19] *BDCP Highlights* thus explicitly and repeatedly notes how sea level rise will impact Delta salinity levels and how increasing fresh water flows in the Delta would help counter this seawater intrusion.

However, after noting that sea level rise will require additional instream flow to push saltwater intrusion back, the section of *BDCP Highlights* labeled "Environmental Baseline" provides as follows: "In order to measure the magnitude of any impact, agencies must first identify a baseline condition to serve as a point of impact comparison ... The CEQA baseline standard normally requires a project to review its impacts relative to 'change from existing conditions.'" The section of *BDCP Highlights* on "Water Quality" also goes on to clarify: "Existing conditions ... are the conditions at the time the NOP [CEQA Notice of Preparation] was issued – that is, 2009. These conditions do not include projections of future sea level rise and climate change ... "[20] Again, this characterization of CEQA baseline conditions does not take into account the California Supreme Court's endorsement of multiple baselines in *Smart Rail*, which permits CEQA lead agencies to use a future baseline conditions, in addition to an existing baseline conditions.

Similar to Appendix 2C of the BDCP and Appendix 29A of the Draft EIR–EIS, the *BDCP Highlights* document acknowledges the ways sea level rise will impact Delta salinity and how this will require increased instream fresh water flow into the Delta, while simultaneously taking the position that this information regarding sea level rise will not be considered in the CEQA environmental impact assessment analysis of the BDCP.

As a result of DWR's exclusive reliance on an existing baseline conditions for its CEQA analysis in the Draft EIR–EIS, notwithstanding the disclosure in Appendix 2C of the BDCP and Appendix 29A of the Draft EIR–EIS that confirm the impacts of sea level rise on salinity levels and X2, the CEQA analysis in the Draft EIR–EIS does not factor the information on sea level rise and salinity levels into its significance determinations, alternatives analysis, or mitigation analysis. That is, the information in Appendix 2C and Appendix 29A is not then integrated into the rest of the CEQA analysis. This information is, so to speak, left out in the cold of the appendices. More to the point, the CEQA analysis does not consider (in the context of severity of project impacts, alternatives or mitigation) how additional fresh water flows into the Delta (and a corresponding reduction in the amount of freshwater diversion) would be needed to prevent the upstream shift of X2 resulting from sea level rise.

One possible explanation for this disregard of the sea level rise impacts on delta smelt is hinted at in Appendix 3D of the Draft EIR–EIS. More specifically, Appendix 3D disclosed:

> DWR did not assume full implementation of a particular requirement of the [2008] delta smelt BiOp, known as the 'Fall X2' salinity standard, which in certain water year types can require large upstream reservoir releases in fall months for wet and above normal wet years to maintain the location of 'X2' as approximately 74–81 river kilometers inland from the Golden Gate Bridge . . . DWR determined that full implementation of the Fall X2 salinity standard was not certain to occur within a reasonable near-term time frame because of a recent court decision . . . . As of [spring 2011], in litigation challenging the delta smelt BiOp filed by various water users, which DWR intervened, the United States District Court found that the USFWS failed to full explain the pecific rationale used to determine the location for Fall X2 included in the RPA and remanded to the USFWS . . . . This uncertainty, together with CEQA's focus on existing conditions, led to the decision to use a CEQA baseline without the implementation of the Fall X2 action in the draft EIR/ EIS.[21]

Putting aside the question of the credibility of this explanation, with the 2014 reversal of the referenced federal district court decision by the Ninth Circuit Court of Appeals in *San Luis* v. *Jewell* and the US Supreme Court's denial of review, there is now no longer any uncertainty as to the status of the X2 requirements in the 2008 USFWS delta smelt BiOp. The X2 requirements in the BiOp have now been upheld by the courts, so it would then follow that

DWR should now assume (in its CEQA analysis) that these X2 requirements will be fully implemented.

It is also perhaps understandable why DWR and the contractors that receive water from the SWP are reluctant to engage in environmental analysis which would demonstrate that more fresh water needs to be left instream to flow into the Delta, since this would result in reduced SWP water exports above and out of the Delta. However, the omission of this analysis renders the CEQA analysis in the Draft EIR–EIS legally vulnerable. Given that Appendix 2C of the BDCP and Appendix 29A of the Draft EIR–EIS expressly concede and document the extent to which climate change-induced sea level rise will move X2 upstream, and given the well-established link between the position of X2 and the survival of the endangered delta smelt, DWR may have a difficult time convincing a court that there is substantial evidence to support the remainder of its CEQA fisheries impact analysis which assumes that X2 will remain in the same location. Such reliance on an assumption explicitly acknowledged by a lead CEQA agency to be incorrect may constitute an unlawful abuse of discretion.

A POTENTIAL TEST CASE ON SHIFTING BASELINES

As noted earlier, the effects of climate change present unique challenges to the basic environmental impact assessment paradigm, particularly for projects that will operate well into the future. This is because under the basic environmental impact assessment paradigm, the determination of significant adverse impacts and the identification of appropriate alternatives and mitigation to address such impacts are developed in reference to a single set of baseline conditions. Yet, with climate change, the baseline conditions against which long-term projects operate will shift. This means that the severity of the project's impacts and the measures needed to effectively counter these more severe project impacts will shift too.

In this context, the BDCP may serve as an important test case to assess whether, under circumstances where climate change impacts are inevitable and quantifiable, the lack of consideration of future baseline conditions (alongside existing baseline conditions) may constitute a violation of CEQA. The BDCP may be the right test case on this question because the failure to consider the impacts of sea level rise on the survival of the endangered fisheries that are a primary focus of the BDCP arguably taints the remaining fisheries impact analysis of the project.

Without the use of such a future baseline, the CEQA analysis of how much freshwater instream flow is needed to restore the delta smelt becomes delusional. The fisheries impact analysis remains tethered to long-term assumptions of saltwater intrusion and X2 that everyone (including the agencies that operate the CVP and SWP) knows to be incorrect. More specifically, in this instance, the failure to use a future baseline results in fundamental flaws in the CEQA analysis of how the BDCP's proposed export of an additional 18 percent of fresh water from the Delta is likely to impact the endangered delta smelt. Under these circumstances, a reviewing court may be persuaded that the use of a future baseline to address expected sea level rise is not merely permissible under CEQA but required.

The recognition of such a requirement under CEQA could in turn help influence the way sea level rise specifically and climate change more generally is factored into other non-California environmental impact assessment laws. This would help shift the standard environmental impact assessment paradigm to take full account of how the impacts of long-term projects will change as climate change alters the background conditions against which such projects operate.

As noted at the beginning of this chapter, environmental impact assessment regimes are not unique to California or even the United States. Many nations and international institutions around the world use environmental impact assessment to inform decision making, and are working to modify environmental impact assessment methodologies to take better account of climate change projections for the years to come.

For example, Khe San Dam is located in Vietnam and the reservoir behind the dam is filled with waters from Dong Ngan Stream and its tributary creeks. The World Bank is now considering funding for Khe San Dam and Reservoir Rehabilitation Project, which among other things would reinforce the earthen dam and include improvements in the spillway that discharges waters from the reservoir. These proposed upgrades provide an opportunity to modify the way the facility operates, in terms of both the collection of waters in and the discharge of waters from the reservoir.

As required by both the World Bank's Environmental Assessment Policy and Vietnam's Law on Environmental Protection, in May 2019, an Environmental and Social Impact Assessment (ESIA) was prepared for the rehabilitation project.[22] The current draft of the ESIA for the Khe San Dam and Reservoir Rehabilitation Project, however, does not take account of how climate-induced global warming will change the baseline conditions under which the facility will operate in the coming years. The use of a future baseline in the ESIA would provide a mechanism to factor in how climate change will alter the impacts of the facility, and would help identify appropriate mitigation measures to lessen the facility's adverse effects on Dong Ngan Stream and its tributary creeks.

The California experiences recounted in this chapter suggest that the use of future baselines based on climate change projections may be an effective technique to embed climate change considerations into traditional environmental impact assessment. This, in turn, may better enable us to forecast and provide the instream flows that fisheries will need in light of climate impacts such as sea level rise and increased seawater intrusion.

Notes

1. 57 Cal.4th 439 (2013).
2. 141 Cal.Rptr.3d 1, 17–18 (Cal Ct. App. 2012).
3. 57 Cal.4th 4393, 454 (2013).
4. 57 Cal.4th 4393, 455 (2013).
5. 57 Cal.4th 4393, 456 (2013).
6. U.S. FISH AND WILDLIFE, FORMAL ENDANGERED SPECIES ACT CONSULTATION ON THE COORDINATED OPERATIONS OF THE CENTRAL VALLEY PROJECT AND STATE WATER PROJECT (December 15, 2008), http://fws.gov?sfbaydelta/documents/SWP-CVP_Ops_BO_12–15_final_signed.pdf, at 282.
7. U.S. FISH AND WILDLIFE, FORMAL ENDANGERED SPECIES ACT CONSULTATION ON THE COORDINATED OPERATIONS OF THE CENTRAL VALLEY PROJECT AND STATE WATER PROJECT (December 15, 2008), http://fws.gov?sfbaydelta/documents/SWP-CVP_Ops_BO_12–15_final_signed.pdf, p. 236.
8. U.S. FISH AND WILDLIFE, FORMAL ENDANGERED SPECIES ACT CONSULTATION ON THE COORDINATED OPERATIONS OF THE CENTRAL VALLEY PROJECT AND STATE WATER PROJECT (December 15, 2008), http://fws.gov?sfbaydelta/documents/SWP-CVP_Ops_BO_12–15_final_ signed.pdf, p. 237
9. U.S. FISH AND WILDLIFE, FORMAL ENDANGERED SPECIES ACT CONSULTATION ON THE COORDINATED OPERATIONS OF THE CENTRAL VALLEY PROJECT AND STATE WATER PROJECT (December 15, 2008), http://fws.gov?sfbaydelta/documents/SWP-CVP_Ops_BO_12–15_final_signed.pdf, p. 265, figure E-19.
10. U.S. FISH AND WILDLIFE, FORMAL ENDANGERED SPECIES ACT CONSULTATION ON THE COORDINATED OPERATIONS OF THE CENTRAL VALLEY PROJECT AND STATE WATER PROJECT (December 15, 2008), http://fws.gov?sfbaydelta/documents/SWP-CVP_Ops_BO_12–15_final_signed. pdf pp. 235, 237.
11. 747 F.3d 581 (9th Cir. 2014).
12. UNITED STATES BUREAU OF RECLAMATION, U.S. DEPARTMENT OF THE INTERIOR, SACRAMENTO AND SAN JOAQUIN BASINS CLIMATE

IMPACT ASSESSMENT (September 2014), http://www.usbr.gov/Water SMART/wcra/docs/ssjbia.pdf.

13. UNITED STATES BUREAU OF RECLAMATION, U.S. DEPARTMENT OF THE INTERIOR, SACRAMENTO AND SAN JOAQUIN BASINS CLIMATE IMPACT ASSESSMENT (September 2014), www.usbr.gov/WaterSMART/ wcra/docs/ssjbia.pdf, p. 40, table 7.

14. CALIFORNIA DEPARTMENT OF WATER RESOURCES, BAY DELTA CONSERVATION PLAN ENVIRONMENTAL IMPACT REPORT/ ENVIRONMENTAL IMPACT STATEMENTS HIGHLIGHTS (December 2013).

15. CALIFORNIA DEPARTMENT OF WATER RESOURCES, BAY DELTA CONSERVATION PLAN ENVIRONMENTAL IMPACT REPORT/ ENVIRONMENTAL IMPACT STATEMENTS HIGHLIGHTS (December 2013).

16. UNITED STATES BUREAU OF RECLAMATION, UNITED STATES FISH & WILDLIFE SERVICE, NATIONAL MARINE FISHERIES SERVICE CALIFORNIA DEPARTMENT OF WATER RESOURCES, 2013 PUBLIC DRAFT BAY DELTA CONSERVATION PLAN, 2.C-12.

17. UNITED STATES BUREAU OF RECLAMATION, UNITED STATES FISH & WILDLIFE SERVICE, NATIONAL MARINE FISHERIES SERVICE CALIFORNIA DEPARTMENT OF WATER RESOURCES, 2013 PUBLIC DRAFT BAY DELTA CONSERVATION PLAN, Appendix 29.

18. UNITED STATES BUREAU OF RECLAMATION, UNITED STATES FISH & WILDLIFE SERVICE, NATIONAL MARINE FISHERIES SERVICE CALIFORNIA DEPARTMENT OF WATER RESOURCES, 2013 PUBLIC DRAFT BAY DELTA CONSERVATION PLAN, 3D-1.

19. CALIFORNIA DEPARTMENT OF WATER RESOURCES, BAY DELTA CONSERVATION PLAN ENVIRONMENTAL IMPACT REPORT/ ENVIRONMENTAL IMPACT STATEMENTS HIGHLIGHTS (December 2013).

20. CALIFORNIA DEPARTMENT OF WATER RESOURCES, BAY DELTA CONSERVATION PLAN ENVIRONMENTAL IMPACT REPORT/ ENVIRONMENTAL IMPACT STATEMENTS HIGHLIGHTS (December 2013).

21. UNITED STATES BUREAU OF RECLAMATION, UNITED STATES FISH & WILDLIFE SERVICE, NATIONAL MARINE FISHERIES SERVICE CALIFORNIA DEPARTMENT OF WATER RESOURCES, 2013 PUBLIC DRAFT BAY DELTA CONSERVATION PLAN, 3D-1.

22. Environmental and Social Impact Assessment for the Khe San Dam and Reservoir Project in Vietnam (May 2019).

8

Instream Rights and Groundwater Extraction

A HIDDEN CONNECTION

In California and many other countries and jurisdictions, surface waters have historically been regulated as if they were unconnected to groundwater. Yet in reality, surface waters and groundwater are often hydrologically connected. Many of the rivers that support fisheries are hydrologically dependent on tributary groundwater to maintain instream flow. This means that when there is an intensive pumping of tributary groundwater, the result can be reductions in instream flow and damage to fisheries.

Consider the Scott River in Northern California, part of the larger Klamath River basin, where nearby groundwater contributes to the Scott River. When high volumes of groundwater are extracted from nearby wells, it depletes the Scott River's instream flow with adverse impacts on salmon and steelhead trout.[1] This has led to litigation over the application of California public trust law to groundwater extraction affecting Scott River instream flows, and efforts to use California's Sustainable Groundwater Management Act (SGMA) to ensure that groundwater pumping near the Scott River is compatible with the instream flow needs of fisheries. Situations similar to the Scott River surface and groundwater basin are unfolding throughout California.

The problem of groundwater extraction impacts on interconnected surface flows is not only limited to California but is also faced by other states and other regions around the world. For example, in 2007, the Australian Government published a report titled *The Impact of Groundwater Use on Australia's Rivers*, which noted:

> In much of Australia, groundwater and surface water are interconnected and interchangeable resources. This common reality, however, is not reflected in our water management systems whereby groundwater and surface water are generally managed as separate resources. The implications of this separate management are that the one resource is often allocated to both surface water

users and to groundwater users. This 'double allocation' is not well understood and the extent of the problem throughout Australia is poorly quantified. More significantly the environment is the principal loser, as often the resulting effect is reduced flow in rivers and in some cases even complete drying out of some rivers.[2]

As another example from outside California, there is the situation in the Puget Sound region in the State of Washington, where salmon runs are central to the culture and economy of tribes such as the Lummi Nation.[3] In its 2016 report titled *State of our Watersheds*, the Northwest Indian Fisheries Commission noted:

> Washington state instream flow rules allocate river flow for ecological requirements, but state law allows new wells to withdraw 5,000 gallons of groundwater per day without a permit if water is legally available. Groundwater withdrawals can cumulatively affect streamflows, especially in late summer when flows are naturally low.
>
> . . .
>
> Unchecked growth and its associated increased demand for groundwater must be addressed, if implementation of the Puget Soundsalmon recovery strategy is to successfully move forward.[4]

On a statewide basis in California, how pervasive is the effect of groundwater pumping on surface water flows? Research by Maurice Hall of the Environmental Defense Fund, utilizing the California Department of Water Resources' Central Valley Groundwater Surface Flow Model (MODFLOW), provides us with some sense of the magnitude of the problem. In a May 2018 presentation, Hall reported:

> What the model showed us is that early in the 1900s, 1940s and 1950s, the Sacramento River received a net inflow from the groundwater of something like 1 million-acre feet a year . . . Since that time, the groundwater levels have gone down, and the amount of water that has flowed into the Sacramento River from the surrounding groundwater has gone down accordingly to the point that when we were doing this modeling around 2010, it appeared that on average, the Sacramento River lost just about as much as it gained from the surrounding groundwater in the valley floor. This is the Sacramento River and all of its tributaries upstream of the Sacramento . . . So the net effect over that period is there was roughly on average 900,000 acre-feet per year less water showing up in the Sacramento River at Sacramento.[5]

In 2017, SGMA was enacted in California.[6] Pursuant to SGMA, by June 2017, a groundwater sustainability agency was required to be designated for each groundwater basin in California. Each groundwater sustainability agency in high and medium priority basins must prepare and adopt a Groundwater Sustainability Plan (SGMA Groundwater Plan) by 2020 if the basin is deemed to be in a critical state of overdraft or 2022 for all remaining high and medium priority basins. Each SGMA Groundwater Plan must detail how the groundwater basin will be managed to avoid overdraft conditions and, importantly for fisheries, to avoid significant adverse impacts on hydrologically connected surface waters.

Although groundwater sustainability agencies and fishery stakeholders recognize that the groundwater–surface water connection needs to be addressed in SGMA Groundwater Plans, at present, there is limited guidance on how to do this. That is, what are the specific types of information, modeling, monitoring, and pumping provisions that should be included in SGMA Groundwater Plans to ensure that groundwater extraction does not cause significant adverse impacts to fisheries?

THE CONNECTION HAS BEEN THERE ALL ALONG

The Sustainable Groundwater Management Act is part of the larger body of California water law, which has developed its own set of terms and distinctions. One of the key distinctions in California water law is between surface water and groundwater.

In California, surface water use is regulated pursuant to the twin doctrines of riparian water rights and prior appropriation water rights. Since 1914, all prior appropriation water rights are issued by the State Water Resources Control Board (State Water Board). Use of groundwater in California, however, is subject to a different set of legal doctrines – overlying and non-overlying groundwater rights – and generally is not subject to the appropriative permitting authority of the State Water Board. The exception to this rule is found in the State Water Board's assertion of permitting authority over certain "subterranean" waters located in close proximity to surface waters, although the precise scope and limits of this permitting authority over such "subterranean" waters has been subject to longstanding debate.

In 2002, the late Professor Joseph Sax (at the University of California– Berkeley's Boalt Hall Law School), a leading authority on California water law, completed a report assessing the permitting authority of State Water Board over groundwater and subterranean waters. Professor Sax's 2002 report, titled *Review of Laws Establishing the SWRCB's Permitting Authority over Appropriations of Groundwater Classified as Subterranean Streams and the SWRCB's Implementation of Those Laws*, included the following analysis that provides a useful framework for evaluating the ways SGMA Groundwater Plans should consider impacts on surface waters:

> My analysis reveals that the legislative purpose [of granting the State Water Board permitting authority over subterranean water in close proximity to surface waters] was to protect the permitting authority of the permitting agency's jurisdiction over surface stream adjudications by preventing unpermitted taking of groundwater that appreciably and directly affects surface stream flows. The concern was essentially to close a loophole that would have been left if any taking of water from a subsurface location would leave the permitting agency powerless in the face of wells or tunnels that were effectively underground facilities for withdrawing stream water.
>
> . . .
>
> My conclusion is that the legislation was designed to create an impact test (impact of pumping on surface stream flows) rather than seeking to identify a physical entity with a specific shape despite the conventional "subterranean stream" language the law picked up from the old treaties. I conclude that a test designed to identify appreciable and direct impact of groundwater diversion on surface streams represents a more faithful implementation of the legislative purposes than any catalog of physical characteristics.[7]

The "impact test" described by Professor Sax in 2002 was intended to define the reach of the State Water Board's permitting authority over groundwater pumping and was based on the premise that to effectively regulate surface water the State Water Board needed permitting authority over pumping that directly reduced surface water flows.[8] Professor Sax's reasoning and proposed "impact test" apply with equal force in the context of SGMA Groundwater Plans, only in a different way. For an SGMA Groundwater Plan to effectively regulate groundwater resources, it must include information that explains the surface–groundwater interaction at pumping locations, addresses how this interaction affects fish that are present, and set forth measures to mitigate adverse impacts.

The "impact test" described by Professor Sax is consistent with the approach taken by the California Supreme Court in its 1909 decision in the case of *Hudson* v. *Dailey*.[9] As noted water rights attorney Kevin O'Brien explained in a May 2018 presentation, in *Hudson* v. *Dailey*, the California Supreme Court held that when groundwater is tributary to surface waters, the two sources need to be viewed as a "common supply." O'Brien explains:

> Mrs. Hudson sued the groundwater pumpers and basically said, I'm riparian, I have a paramount right, you groundwater pumpers, you have to curtail. And the California Supreme Court ultimately said no, in this situation these are

overlying landowners and they have overlying rights, you are a riparian and you have a riparian right, so you essentially stand on equal footing from a water rights standpoint, and we're going to take all that groundwater and surface water and put it together and we're going to determine water rights as a common supply. So while California does have separate water rights systems for groundwater and surface water, I think this concept of the common supply rule is going to be more and more prominent as we move forward and will remain relevant to issues that will arise under SGMA.[10]

In his 2002 law review article, titled *We Don't Do Groundwater; A Morsel of California Legal History*, Professor Sax also noted the fairness considerations involved by requiring surface water diverters to comply with bypass flow requirements for fisheries but allowing groundwater extraction to occur with no regard for bypass flow impacts:

> While California has a system in place that averts crisis and system collapse, it continues to suffer a variety of dysfunctional results growing out of a system that is at odds with hydrologic reality. One example that has drawn a good deal of attention recently arises from assertions that groundwater pumpers are depriving streams of water needed to meet downstream environmental flow requirements, even though regular surface water users are meeting the bypass flow requirements that have been imposed on them.[11]

In this sense, SGMA's mandate to address the impacts of groundwater pumping on surface waters is not really new from a conceptual or policy standpoint. Professor Sax's 2002 report for the State Water Board made clear that it has long been understood and recognized that groundwater pumping can reduce surface flows, and as early as 1909, the California Supreme Court acknowledged that there were times when groundwater and surface water formed a "common supply." Moreover, Professor Sax's 2002 law review article recognized that it was fair that groundwater pumpers impacting surface water flows be subject to bypass flow requirements just like direct surface water diverters. Under SGMA, this interconnection and these common supply and fairness concerns must now be addressed explicitly and meaningfully in SGMA Groundwater Plans.

PICTURING THE CONNECTION

To understand the potential impact of groundwater pumping on surface waters and fisheries, it is helpful to first picture the ways that groundwater and surface water can interact, and to become familiar with some of the common terminology used to discuss these interactions.

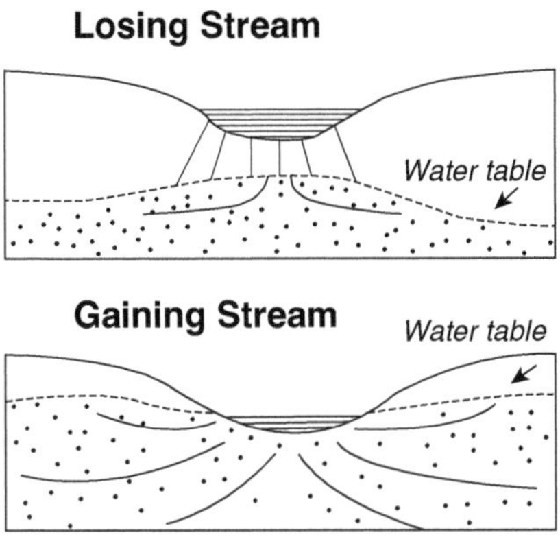

Losing Stream

Gaining Stream

MAP 8.1 Map of gaining stream and losing stream

One of the key conceptual distinctions involved in groundwater–surface water interaction is the distinction between "gaining streams/reaches" and "losing streams/reaches." A gaining stream/reach is one that receives water from subterranean aquifers. Or put another way, in a gaining stream/reach groundwater discharge contributes to surface flows. In contrast, a losing stream/reach is one where surface flows are lost or drained into an aquifer. Or put another way, in a losing stream/reach surface waters flow into the aquifer.

Whether a surface stream/reach is "gaining" or "losing" depends on the respective elevations of the groundwater and surface water involved. This means that the status of surface water as "gaining" or "losing" is not static or fixed but is subject to intra- and inter-annual variation. That is, during a period when the groundwater table in an aquifer is higher and surface flows are lower, the surface water may be gaining; but during a period when the groundwater table in an aquifer is lower and surface flows are higher, the surface water may be losing. During periods when there is simultaneously intensive groundwater pumping (e.g. in late summer when irrigation needs are highest) and reduced surface flows, a gaining stream/reach can become a losing one.

It is also important to understand that, along a particular surface watercourse, there may be some reaches where it is a gaining stream and other reaches where it is a losing stream. Whether the reach is gaining or losing depends on the proximity of and connection between the groundwater and surface water, and the respective elevations of the groundwater table and the surface water.

The concept of gaining and losing streams/reaches presents particular challenges for developing hydrologic models, water budgets, monitoring programs, and pumping provisions in the context of SGMA Groundwater Plans.

In addition to the question of gaining and losing streams/reaches, when it comes to fisheries, there is also the question of how the relative contributions of surface water and groundwater affect fish habitat parameters. For instance, a critical component of salmon and steelhead habitat is water temperature. These are cold-water fish – for instance, Chinook salmon eggs incubate most successfully at temperatures below 55 degrees Fahrenheit and experience increased mortality and negative sublethal effects as water temperatures rise. Importantly, instream temperatures tend to rise when ambient air temperatures rise (e.g. late summer) and whenever ambient conditions allow increased sunlight penetration (e.g. unshaded areas). Even when higher ambient air temperatures tend to raise the temperature of surface waters, the temperature of groundwater tends to remain stable and cooler. Therefore, if groundwater is tributary to surface waters, the influx of cooler groundwater tends to keep instream surface waters cooler, a dynamic that is particularly important for cold-water fish in late summer/early fall when ambient air temperatures tend to be warmer.

As another example, anadromous fish such as salmon and steelhead migrate downstream at particular times of the year and their need for surface flows is more acute during these seasonal migration periods. To protect and restore spring and fall runs of salmon and steelhead, the State Water Board has conditioned water rights on bypass flow requirements and restrictions on diversions for certain water year types.

As a final illustration, to escape warm summer and early fall temperatures on the mainstem of larger surface waters such as the Klamath River, migrating salmon and steelhead often retreat from the exposed mainstem into smaller, shaded tributary creeks until mainstem temperatures have declined. In this way, fish use tributary creeks as "coldwater refuges" (sometimes also referred to as "thermal refugia") to escape warmer mainstem waters.

However, these tributaries only provide suitable refuges for fish migrating during summer/early fall if flows are sufficient to maintain connectivity with the mainstem so fish do not become isolated from or trapped within the creeks. Connectivity between the mainstem and coldwater refuges can be lost due to increased groundwater pumping near tributary creeks in the late summer/ early fall (a period of high irrigation demand) when groundwater pumping can transform a gaining reach into a losing reach and turn tributary creeks into isolated ponds.

In terms of assessing the impacts of groundwater pumping on fisheries, groundwater sustainability agencies need to consider specific habitat needs and timing in developing SGMA Groundwater Plans that will effectively regulate groundwater pumping to prevent impacts to fish. This requires robust hydrologic models, water budgets, monitoring, and groundwater pumping provisions that consider the biological and physical needs of fish. The good news is that there are now tested and readily available methods to address these factors related to the groundwater–surface water connection and fisheries impacts, and to incorporate these factors into SGMA Groundwater Plans. To do this effectively, groundwater sustainability agencies will need to understand both the spatial and temporal impacts that groundwater pumping has on instream flows, as well as the instream conditions protective of fish species in their basin.

One of the best resources for how to analyze and model groundwater pumping-surface water flows interactions in SGMA Groundwater Plans is the 2012 United States Geological Survey (USGS) Circular 1376, titled *Streamflow Depletion by Wells – Understanding and Managing the Effects of Groundwater Pumping on Streamflow* (USGS *Circular 1376*). It provides a catalog of scientifically accepted programs and methodologies that can be used to determine the impact of groundwater pumping on surface stream flows, which in turn can be relied upon to manage groundwater pumping to avoid significant adverse impacts on surface stream flows and the fisheries that depend on such flows. As USGS *Circular 1376* explains the following at the outset:

> One of the primary concerns related to the development of groundwater resources is the effect of groundwater pumping on streamflow. Groundwater and surface-water systems are connected, and groundwater discharge is often a substantial component of the total flow of a stream. Groundwater pumping reduces the amount of groundwater that flows to streams and, in some cases, can draw streamflow into the underlying groundwater system. Streamflow reductions (or depletions) caused by pumping have become an important water-resource management issue because of the negative impacts that reduced flows can have on aquatic ecosystems.
>
> . . .
>
> [B]ecause precipitation rates, pumping rates, and other hydrologic stresses vary with time, it is possible for a particular stream reach to switch from a gaining to a losing condition or from a losing to a gaining condition from one period of time to the next.

United States Geological Survey Circular 1376 provides guidance on ways to model and quantify groundwater pumping-surface water flow interactions:

> The most common way to describe streamflow depletion has been to report the changes in the instantaneous flow rate of the stream, which is expressed in units of volume of streamflow per unit of time, such as cubic feet per second . . . . A related approach is to report the rate of stream-flow

depletion as a fraction of the pumping rate of the well, which is a dimensionless quantity ... The streamflow depletion that results from pumping the well is shown in units of cubic feet per second, which is the unit most often used in reporting streamflow.

...

More commonly ... pumping schedules vary with time, either in response to changing water supply demands or for the maintenance and overall operation of the water supply system. Pumping schedules can vary on an hourly and daily basis response to short-term fluctuations in demand and over longer-term cycles in response to factors as seasonal and annual climate variability and irrigation demands.

USGS Circular 1376 goes on to explain why traditional groundwater management concepts, such as "safe yield" and "overdraft avoidance," may not be appropriate benchmarks for determining groundwater pumping's impacts on surface flows and fisheries. This is because the concepts of "safe yield" and "overdraft avoidance" focus on a particular variable – maintaining the groundwater table over the long term. The groundwater management objectives of "safe yield" and "overdraft avoidance" do not capture the seasonal or year-to-year (e.g. drought) impacts of groundwater pumping on surface stream flows, in which the periodic/short-term combination of low surface flows and increased groundwater pumping can have devastating adverse impacts on fisheries. As *UGGS Circular* 1376 notes: "[t]here has been a tendency in parts of the United States to view groundwater development in an aquifer to be 'sustainable' or 'safe' when the overall rate of groundwater extraction does not exceed the long-term average rate of recharge to the aquifer."[12]

Given SGMA's mandate that groundwater plans evaluate and address impacts on fisheries, not just long-term maintenance of the aquifer, we need to rethink what "sustainable" and "safe" groundwater pumping means.

Fortunately, there are programs, methodologies, and software available that allow groundwater sustainability agencies to address the correlation between reduced surface water flows and impacts on fisheries in SGMA Groundwater Plans. For instance, in the case of surface stream flow and temperature impacts on salmon, many agencies and fishery scientists in California now rely on SALMOD software, which was initially developed by the USGS in 1994 to address stream flow impacts on salmon in the Klamath River–Trinity River watershed in Northern California. As explained in a 2004 article by USGS Fishery Biologist John M. Bartholow, titled *Modeling Chinook Salmon with SALMOD on the Sacramento River, California*:

SALMOD is a computer model that simulates the dynamics of freshwater salmonid populations. The conceptual model was developed using fish experts concerned with Trinity River Chinook restoration ... The model's premise is that egg and fish mortality are directly related to spatially and temporally variable micro- and macro-habitat limitations, which themselves are related to the timing and amount of streamflow and other meteorological variables. Habitat quality and capacity are characterized by the hydraulic and thermal properties of individual mesohabitats, which are used as spatial "computation units" in the model. The model tracks a population of spatially distinct cohorts that originate as eggs and grow from one life stage to another as a function of local water temperature.[13]

In addition to SALMOD, California water managers and fishery biologists sometimes rely on the Interactive Object-Oriented Simulation Model ("IOS Model") to evaluate the impact of surface water flows and surface water temperatures on fisheries such as salmon and steelhead. In a 2012 article by Steven C. Zueg et al., titled *Application of a Life Cycle Simulation Model to Evaluate Impacts of Water Management and Conservation Actions on an Endangered Population of Chinook Salmon*, the authors explain how life cycle models like the IOS Model work:

> Life cycle models utilize available time-series data as well as values taken from laboratory studies or other sources to parameterize model relationships, thereby utilizing the greatest amount of data available to dynamically simulate responses of populations across multiple life stages to changes in environmental variables or combinations of environmental variables at specific times and locations.[14]

Moreover, in cases where groundwater pumping is causing surface waters to go dry altogether, reliance on SALMOD and the IOS Model is not needed to determine that there are significant adverse impacts on fisheries otherwise present in these areas. The complete disappearance of surface waters to groundwater pumping, by itself, renders these dried-out surface water reaches unsuitable for fish (because fish need water) and results in a loss of connectivity for fish in the portions of the watershed downstream and upstream of the dried-out reaches.

The availability of SALMOD and the IOS Model, which enable groundwater sustainability agencies to model the effects of reduced surface stream flow and changes in surface stream temperatures on fish, makes it difficult for groundwater sustainability agencies to credibly claim that it is not feasible or it is too speculative to meaningfully address the impacts of groundwater pumping on fisheries in SGMA Groundwater Plans.

FRAMING THE CONNECTION

Under SGMA, groundwater sustainability agencies are required to prepare groundwater sustainability plans that establish the water basin setting and describe how the agency will manage and use groundwater "in a manner that can be maintained during the planning and implementation horizon without causing undesirable results."[15] In addition to depletion of groundwater supply or storage and degradation of water quality, the definition of "undesirable result" includes "depletion of interconnected surface water that have significant and unreasonable adverse impacts on beneficial uses of the surface water."[16] Fisheries propagation, rearing, and/or migration are designated beneficial uses in most basins.

Under SGMA, groundwater plans must contain certain elements, including but not limited to "a description of the water basin setting and geographic area covered by the plan." The basin setting is one of the key elements of an SGMA Groundwater Plan. The setting serves "as the basis for defining and assessing reasonable sustainable management criteria and projects and management actions."[17] For this reason, an accurate description of the setting – including data gaps and areas of uncertainty – is critical to the success of any plan.

As part of defining the basin setting, each groundwater sustainability agency is required to develop a hydrogeologic conceptual model based on technical studies and qualified maps that characterizes the physical components and interaction of the surface water and groundwater systems in the basin. In addition, the conceptual model must describe the current and historical groundwater conditions in the basin, including "identification of interconnected surface water systems within the basin and an estimate of the quantity and timing of depletions of those systems."[18]

The identification of interconnected surface water systems and estimates of the quantity and timing of depletions are important to understanding the effects of groundwater pumping on fisheries. There are certain types of information and data that can serve as the foundation for developing hydrologic models and water budgets to understand groundwater–surface water interaction in a given basin, and these hydrologic models and water budgets can then serve as the foundation for the adoption of groundwater pumping provisions to prevent depletion of surface water flows and prevent associated adverse impacts on fisheries.

Given that SGMA represents the first time groundwater will be comprehensively regulated in California, the statute anticipates there will be gaps in existing monitoring data and understanding of the ground and surface water interconnection. The statute adopts a "best available science" standard for information relied upon in developing SGMA Groundwater Plans. "Best available science" is defined as "the use of sufficient and credible information and data, specific to the decision being made and the time frame available for making that decision, that is consistent with scientific and engineering professional standards of practice."[19]

There may be stakeholders that will resist the inclusion of specific and quantitative limitations on groundwater pumping to avoid surface stream depletion based on the claim that there is incomplete data to support such limitations. This line of reasoning does not square with SGMA's grounding in "best available science," or with the obligation of groundwater sustainability agencies to adopt thresholds for groundwater pumping to prevent continuing depletion of surface streams and continuing harm to fisheries based on the information and data that are available. Under SGMA, the quest for improved and more complete underlying data on groundwater pumping impacts on surface water flows and fisheries (which can be obtained through additional monitoring) is not a valid justification for delaying or avoiding the adoption of quantitative thresholds and groundwater pumping conditions in an SGMA Groundwater Plan to avoid the "undesirable result" of "depletions of interconnected surface water."

Groundwater models such as MODFLOW and SALMOD can help bridge some of the gaps in existing data. Indeed, reliance on such models has become standard in the management of groundwater systems, and will be key to implementing SGMA. Groundwater models serve as simplified versions of real-world systems. Such models can provide an improved conceptual understanding of the system, including the essential processes and properties influencing the system. They support decision making by facilitating the exploration of alternative management actions and, when calibrated appropriately, can forecast short- and long-term changes to the groundwater system resulting from management actions or changing environmental conditions.

As noted in a 2016 article by Tara Moran of the Stanford University Water in the West program, titled *Projecting Forward – A Framework for Groundwater Model Development Under the Sustainable Groundwater Management Act*:

> Groundwater models in California are developed using predominantly two model codes. Of the respondents that reported model codes, the [United States Geologic Survey's] MODFLOW and [California Department of Water Resources'] IWFM model codes account for more than 95 percent of the reported groundwater models used across the state. The consistency in model codes used across the state may aid in groundwater model coordination efforts under SGMA.[20]

In December 2016, Department of Water Resources (DWR) published a series of Best Management Practices (BMPs) to assist in the preparation of SGMA Groundwater Plans. Some of these BMPs addressed techniques and considerations related to how plans can prevent groundwater pumping causing significant and unreasonable depletion of interconnected surface waters.

An important component of the basin setting is the water budget, which is defined in the *DWR Modeling BMP* as "an accounting and assessment of the total annual volume of groundwater and surface water entering and leaving the basin, including historical, current and projected water budget conditions, and the change in the volume of water stored." The *DWR Modeling BMP* further provides:

> The water budget shall quantify the following, either through direct measurements or estimates based on following data:
>
> 1. Total surface water entering and leaving a basin by water source type.
> 2. Inflow to the groundwater systems by water sources type, including subsurface groundwater inflow and infiltration of precipitation, applied water, and surface water systems, such as lakes, streams, rivers, canals, springs, and conveyance systems.
> 3. Outflows from the groundwater system by water use sector, including evapotranspiration, groundwater extraction, groundwater discharge to surface water sources, and subsurface groundwater outflow.[21]

The *DWR Water Budget BMP* addresses the potential interplay of groundwater pumping and stream depletion that must be included in the water budget:

> Another important water budget consideration is stream depletion due to groundwater pumping. In basins with *interconnected surface water* systems, if inflows (recharge) to the basin remain fixed while the amount of groundwater extraction increases, the increased volume of groundwater extraction, while initially resulting in a decline in the volume of *aquifer* storage, will eventually be balanced by decreases in the groundwater flow to springs, gaining streams, groundwater-dependent ecosystems or an increase in discharge from losing streams. Shallow production wells in close proximity to surface water systems commonly capture flow directly from the surface water system through induced recharge. Stream depletion associated with pumping wells further removed from surface water systems is more commonly the result of the indirect capture of groundwater flow that would otherwise have discharged to the surface water system sometime in the future. In both situations, streamflow depletion will continue until a new equilibrium between the outflow

associated with groundwater extraction and the inflow from surface water depletion is established.

The *DWR Water Budget BMP* describes how the water budget may change over time:

> The transition from storage depletion to stream depletion will affect water budget accounting over time ... In many basins, stream depletion due to groundwater extraction will continue for decades prior to reaching a new equilibrium. Because of this transitional process, a water budget based on "average conditions" will not reflect this slow and progressive change. It is also important to recognize that water budget accounting during the early stages of groundwater basin development will have different storage and basin outflow values than water budget for a later time period, when the basin is approaching equilibrium ... To accurately identify and evaluate the various inflow and outflow components of the water budget, it is important to adequately characterize the interaction between surface water and groundwater systems through sufficient monitoring of groundwater levels and streamflow conditions.[22]

In the context of drafting and implementing an SGMA Groundwater Plan, the preparation of a water budget can accurately reveal tensions between objectives, or "undesirable results" as defined under SGMA, such as the potential tension between avoidance of adverse impacts on agriculture of reducing groundwater pumping in late summer/drought years and the reduction of surface flows for fish that can result from intensive groundwater pumping in late summer/drought years. Disclosing such potential tensions will enable groundwater sustainability agencies and other stakeholders to make informed decisions. For instance, it may be that for certain times of year (e.g. late summer) or under certain conditions (e.g. drought) the need for groundwater as an irrigation supply may need to yield to the need to maintain adequate surface flows for fisheries. A rigorous and robust water budget in an SGMA Groundwater Plan can frame these potential tensions and trade-offs in a way that allows for more informed and transparent decision making.

Echoing the guidance provided by the DWR BMPs, the Union of Concerned Scientists (UCS) has stated that "water budgets" are an "essential component" of an SGMA Groundwater Plan:

> The water budget is a critical element of a GSP [Groundwater Sustainability Plan]. Water budgets track a variety of important pieces of information and can be used to help estimate a groundwater basin's sustainable yield, the amount of water that can be drawn out without causing an undesirable

result ... A water budget is like a household budget. It accounts for all of the water that enters and leaves your groundwater basin, by category. Your sources of income are inflows, and your expenses are outflows.[23]

In regard to the groundwater–surface water interconnection, as discussed earlier, the concepts of "gaining streams/reaches" and "losing streams/ reaches" relate to the accounting of "outflows" and "inflows" in water budgets. That is, when a surface watercourse "gains" water from an aquifer, this is reflected as an "outflow" in the groundwater basin budget, and when a surface watercourse "loses" water to an aquifer (perhaps as a result of the water table falling due to groundwater pumping), this is reflected as an "inflow" in the groundwater basin budget. The UCS Guide makes clear why the water budgets included in SGMA Groundwater Plans need to include an accurate accounting of the inflow and outflows between aquifers and surface waters.

In addition to the *DWR Modeling BMP* and the *DWR Water Budget BMP*, there is also a *DWR BMP on Monitoring Networks and Identification of Data Gaps* (*DWR Monitoring/Data Gaps BMP*).[24] Sustainable Groundwater Management Act requires that each Groundwater Plan include monitoring protocols to assess progress in meeting the sustainability goals established in the Plan. Each groundwater sustainability agency must develop a monitoring network capable of collecting sufficient data to demonstrate short-term, seasonal, and long-term trends in groundwater and related surface conditions and yield representative information about groundwater conditions as necessary to evaluate Plan implementation "along with specific monitoring network objectives."[25] Agencies are to report their monitoring data to DWR annually.

According to the guidance provided in the *DWR Monitoring/Data Gaps BMP*: "Depletions of Interconnected Surface Water: The minimum thresholds for depletions of interconnected surface water shall be the rate or volume of surface water depletions caused by groundwater use that has adverse impacts on beneficial uses of the surface water and may lead to undesirable results." The *DWR Monitoring/Data BMP* goes on to state:

> Monitoring of the interconnected surface water depletions requires the use of tools, commonly modeled approaches, to estimate the depletions associated with groundwater extraction. Models require assumptions be made to constrain the numerical model solutions. These assumptions should be based on empirical observations determining the extent of the connection of surface water and groundwater systems, the timing of those connections, the flow dynamics of both surface water and groundwater systems, and hydrogeologic properties of the geologic framework connecting these two systems.[26]

This guidance in the *DWR Monitoring/Data BMP* is particularly relevant in terms of the monitoring networks required in SGMA Groundwater Plans. More specifically, this guidance suggests that when there are known or potential groundwater–surface water interactions, the plan should include monitoring (both for volume and temperature to assess fishery-related impacts) of surface waters that may be impacted by groundwater pumping. This stream gauge/temperature monitoring should be done on a seasonal rather than annual basis, to account for the ways that seasonal groundwater pumping and surface flow fluctuations affect surface water flows and temperatures.

THE PUBLIC TRUST CONNECTION

Groundwater sustainability agencies' obligations to prepare SGMA groundwater plans that address the impact of groundwater pumping on surface flows and fisheries are based on a source of law outside of SGMA and its implementing regulations – California public trust law. The application of California public trust law has become apparent as a result of recent litigation involving groundwater pumping in California's Scott River Basin.

As noted at the beginning of this chapter, there is evidence that groundwater extraction from wells near the Scott River depletes surface flows with adverse impacts on the salmon and steelhead fisheries present. To address this situation, the Environmental Law Foundation (ELF) sued Siskiyou County and the State Water Board in Sacramento County Superior Court under California public trust law.[27] California public trust law applies to public trust resources (which include fisheries such as salmon and steelhead) and public trust uses (which include noncommercial fishing for salmon and steelhead).

The Superior Court held California public trust law applies to groundwater that is tributary to navigable surface waters such as the Scott River that contain public trust resources and support public trust uses. Relying on the California Supreme Court's 1983 *National Audubon* decision[28] concerning the public trust, the court explained:

> The public trust doctrine would prevent pumping directly out of the Scott River harming public trust uses. So too under National Audubon the public trust doctrine would prevent pumping a non-navigable tributary of the Scott River harming public trust uses of the river. The court finds no reason why the analysis of National Audubon would not apply to the facts alleged here. The court thus finds the public trust doctrine protects navigable waters from harm caused by extraction of groundwater, where the groundwater is so connected to the navigable water that its extraction adversely affects public trust uses.[29]

The court also held that public trust obligations apply not only to the State Water Board and other state agencies but also to local governments like Siskiyou County:

> There is no conflict between authorizing the County to adopt a groundwater management plan, and requiring it to comply with the public trust doctrine. The public trust doctrine applies when the extraction of groundwater harms navigable waters and the public's use for trust purposes. If the County's issuance of well permits will result in extraction of groundwater adversely affecting the public's right to use the Scott River for trust purposes, the County must take the public trust into consideration and protect public trust uses when feasible. Such a requirement does not conflict with the County's discretion to decide whether or not to implement an overall groundwater management plan.[30]

Siskiyou County appealed the decision, arguing that the State Water Board "has neither the authority nor the duty to consider how the use of groundwater affects the public trust in the Scott River; nor does the County have a public trust duty to consider whether groundwater uses by new wells affect public trust uses in the Scott River."[31] The Court of Appeal rejected these challenges, upholding the trial court's holding.

The Court of Appeal concluded that the public trust doctrine applies to groundwater extractions that adversely affect navigable waterways. In rejecting the County's arguments that the doctrine applied to surface water diversions but not groundwater extractions, the court stated: "the dispositive issue is not the source of the activity, or whether the water that is diverted or extracted is itself subject to the public trust, but whether the challenged activity allegedly harms a navigable waterway."[32] It added, "*National Audubon* and its progeny recognize that government has a duty to consider the public trust interest when making decisions impacting water that is imbued with the public trust."[33]

The Court of Appeal also concluded that enactment of SGMA did not displace the public trust doctrine. It stated that, by its own terms, SGMA did not comprehensively regulate groundwater, and certainly was not as comprehensive as the appropriative water rights system. The court stated that even if SGMA was deemed comprehensive, it still would not displace the public trust doctrine, explaining as follows:

> *National Audubon* teaches the two systems can live in harmony. If the expansive and historically rooted appropriative rights system in California did not subsume or eliminate the public trust doctrine in the state, then certainly SGMA, a more narrowly tailored piece of legislation, can also accommodate the perpetuation of the public trust doctrine.[34]

In addition to the SGMA requirements for how groundwater plans must address the impacts of groundwater extraction on surface waters and fisheries, groundwater sustainability agencies may also be required to take into account California public trust law. Following the 2018 *ELF* v. *State Water Board* decision, it is clear that groundwater sustainability agencies have a separate, fiduciary duty under the public trust doctrine, independent of SGMA, to consider the impacts of groundwater pumping that reduces the instream flow of navigable rivers needed to maintain fisheries or other public trust uses.

For example, the groundwater sustainability agency designated for the Scott River Valley Groundwater Basin is the Siskiyou County Flood Control and Water Conservation District.[35] Over the next few years the district will be preparing an SGMA Groundwater Plan that covers groundwater wells that are impacting the Scott River's instream flow and salmon fisheries. The district's preparation of the SGMA Groundwater Plan provides an opportunity to see how California public trust law overlies SGMA. Under SGMA, in every basin where groundwater extraction is adversely impacting surface flows and fisheries, the SGMA Groundwater Plan drafting and approval process provides a key opportunity for fishing and conservation organizations to press for provisions that effectively recognize the public trust law obligations in the *ELF* v. *Siskiyou County* case.

Overlaying the public trust doctrine to the implementation of SGMA could enhance the legal obligations of groundwater sustainability agencies in several ways. For example, California public trust law calls for full protection of public trust resources whenever feasible.[36] If it can be demonstrated that it is feasible for groundwater sustainability agencies to develop hydrologic models and water budgets that account for the impacts of groundwater pumping on surface flows, and fisheries dependent on such surface flows, the failure of a groundwater sustainability agency to factor these considerations into the hydrologic models and water budgets in an SGMA Groundwater Plan may constitute a violation of California public trust law independent of SGMA's requirements.

As another example, if it can be demonstrated that it is feasible to conduct seasonal surface stream monitoring of flows and temperatures to track the impacts of groundwater pumping on fisheries, the failure of a groundwater sustainability agency to require such seasonal surface stream monitoring in an SGMA Groundwater Plan may constitute a violation of California public trust law independent of SGMA's requirements.

Furthermore, if it can be demonstrated that it is feasible to adopt thresholds for groundwater pumping that provide for full protection of fisheries from the adverse impacts of groundwater pumping-induced surface stream depletion, the failure of a groundwater sustainability agency to adopt such thresholds may constitute a violation of California public trust law independent of SGMA's requirements.

This suggested approach to the relationship between public trust law and SGMA was also endorsed in Kate Fritz's 2019 article (in Environmental Law News) titled *Shoring Up SGMA: How Advocates Might Use the Holding in Environmental Law Foundation v. SWRCB to Support Groundwater Management in California.* Fritz begins by noting: "It seems possible, based on the *ELF* holding, that an adequate public trust analysis might require more than what would be required under SGMA alone ... Public trust analysis requires that agencies protect public trust resources whenever economically feasible, while there is no such requirement under SGMA."[37]

Fritz continues: "Advocates might use the *ELF* holding to argue that adequately considering the public trust requires GSAs to make more rigorous, evidence-based showings about the groundwater-surface water interaction than might have been required under SGMA alone ... For example, groundwater sustainability advocates might urge that GSAs must use some of the most technically-sophisticated data collection tools available for monitoring groundwater-surface water interaction in order to adequately carry out their public trust obligations."[38]

GIVING SUBSTANCE TO THE CONNECTION

In his 2002 report to the State Water Board, Professor Sax offered the following observation about California water law:

> Water underground may, at one place or during one season, seep into a river through its banks (a gaining river), and at another place or time seep out from the banks and into the underground (a losing river). It all depends on whether the saturated area of the ground is above or below the river bank at that point.
>
> The categories that statutes and judicial opinions use, such as "underflow," "subflow," "subterranean streams," and "percolating groundwater," bear little if any relationship to these geological realities. Indeed, these water law terms are geographic conceptions fundamentally at odds with science's understanding of water's movements.[39]

The Sustainable Groundwater Management Act provides an opportunity to bring California's regulation of water into closer alignment with the "geological realities" noted by Professor Sax, by ensuring that SGMA Groundwater

Plans are implemented that effectively prevent groundwater extraction from resulting in surface water depletions and the adverse impacts on fisheries associated with reduced surface water flows. In essence, SGMA Groundwater Plans are a regulatory means to give effect to the guidance provided by the California Supreme Court more than a century ago in its 1909 decision in *Hudson* v. *Dailey*, to treat groundwater and surface water as a "common supply" when groundwater is tributary to surface flows.

California is not the only jurisdiction struggling with how to improve management of groundwater and surface water that are interconnected. As noted at the beginning of this chapter, Australia is now also turning its attention to the problem of "double accounting" of such interconnected waters, to the reality that although the law may often treat groundwater and surface waters as separate sources, hydrologically they often constitute a "common supply." Similarly, as also noted at the beginning of this chapter, the State of Washington is now confronting the problem of how unpermitted groundwater extraction wells are depleting streamflows and frustrating salmon recovery efforts. The Sustainable Groundwater Management Act's approach to such interconnected waters, and its relation to public trust law, therefore merits study by other states and other nations.

Notes

1. *Envtl. Law Found.* v. *State Water Res. Control Bd.*, 26 Cal. App. 5th 844, 870 n. 7 (Ct. App. 2018), review denied (November 28, 2018).
2. Dr. Richard Evans, *The Impact of Groundwater Use on Australia's Rivers* (2007 Report for Land & Water Australia) at page 4.
3. Northwest Indian Fisheries Commission, *State of our Watersheds* (2016 Report), p. 81.
4. Northwest Indian Fisheries Commission, *State of our Watersheds* (2016 Report), p. 18.
5. Hall, Maurice and O'Brien, Kevin, *Sustainable Groundwater Management: Can California Successfully Integrate Groundwater and Surface Water under SGMA?* (May 16, 2018 article posted on Maven's Notebook website reporting on the presentations by Maurice Hall and Kevin O'Brien at the 2018 Anne J. Schneider Memorial Lecture Series). https://mavensnotebook.com/2018/05/16/sustainable-groundwater-management-can-california-successfully-integrate-groundwater-and-surface-water-under-sgma/.
6. Sustainable Groundwater Management Act is a three-bill legislative package signed into law by Governor Brown on September 16, 2014.

Assemb. B. 1739, 2014–2015, Reg. Sess. (Cal. 2014); S.B. 1168, 2014–2015, Reg. Sess. (Cal. 2014); S.B. 1319, 2014–2015, Reg. Sess. (Cal. 2014). California Water Code, Section 10720 et seq. California Code of Regulations, Title 23, Sections 350 et seq.

7. Sax, Joseph, *Review of Laws Establishing the SWRCB's Permitting Authority over Appropriations of Groundwater Classified as Subterranean Streams and SWRCB's Implementation of Those Laws* (2002 Report to the California State Water Resources Control Board).

8. Sax, Joseph, *Review of Laws Establishing the SWRCB's Permitting Authority over Appropriations of Groundwater Classified as Subterranean Streams and SWRCB's Implementation of Those Laws* (2002 Report to the California State Water Resources Control Board).

9. *Hudson v. Dailey*, 156 Cal. 617, 627 (1909).

10. Hall, Maurice and O'Brien, Kevin, *Sustainable Groundwater Management: Can California Successfully Integrate Groundwater and Surface Water under SGMA?* (May 6, 2018 article posted on Maven's Notebook website reporting on the presentations by Maurice Hall and Kevin O'Brien at the 2018 Anne J. Schneider Memorial Lecture Series). https://mavensnotebook.com/2018/05/16/sustainable-groundwater-management-can-california-successfully-integrate-groundwater-and-surface-water-under-sgma/.

11. Sax, Joseph, *We Don't Do Groundwater: A Morsel of California Legal History*, 6 University of Denver Water Law Review 269 (2002).

12. United States Geological Survey, *Circular 1376 – Streamflow Depletion by Wells: Understanding and Managing the Effects of Groundwater Pumping on Streamflow* (2012).

13. Bartholow, John, Modeling Chinook Salmon with SALMOD on the Sacramento River, California, Hydroecol (2004).

14. Zeug, Steven C. et al., Application of a Life System Simulation Model to Evaluate Impacts of Water Management and Conservation Actions on an Endangered Population of Chinook Salmon, Springer Science and Business Media (February 2012).

15. SGMA section 10721, SGMA regulation 350.4.

16. (SGMA section 10721).

17. (SGMA Regulation 354.12).

18. (SGMA Regulation 354.16).

19. (SGMA Regulation 351).

20. Moran, Tara, *Projecting Forward – A Framework for Groundwater Model Development Under the Sustainable Groundwater Management Act* (Stanford University Water in the West Program, 2016).

21. California Department of Water Resources, Best Management Practices for the Sustainable Management of Groundwater: Modeling BMP (December 2016).

22. California Department of Water Resources, Best Management Practices for the Sustainable Management of Groundwater: Water Budget BMP (December 2016).
23. Union of Concerned Scientists, Getting Involved in Groundwater: A Guide to California's Groundwater Sustainability Plans (2017).
24. California Department of Water Resources, Best Management Practices for the Sustainable Management of Groundwater: BMP on Monitoring Networks and Identification of Data Gaps (December 2016).
25. (SGMA Regulation 354.34).
26. California Department of Water Resources, Best Management Practices for the Sustainable Management of Groundwater: BMP on Monitoring Networks and Identification of Data Gaps (December 2016).
27. Superior Court for Siskiyou County, *Environmental Law Foundation v. Siskiyou County et al.* (2014 decision in Case No. 34–2010–80000583).
28. *National Audubon Society* v. *Superior Court of Alpine County*, 658 P.2d 709 (1983).
29. Superior Court for Siskiyou County, *Environmental Law Foundation v. Siskiyou County et al.* (2014 decision in Case No. 34–2010–80000583).
30. Superior Court for Siskiyou County, *Environmental Law Foundation v. Siskiyou County et al.* (2014 decision in Case No. 34–2010–80000583).
31. *Envtl. Law Found. v. State Water Res. Control Bd.*, 26 Cal. App. 5th 844, 870 n. 7 (Ct. App. 2018), review denied (November 28, 2018) at 8.
32. *Envtl. Law Found. v. State Water Res. Control Bd.*, 26 Cal. App. 5th 844, 870 n. 7 (Ct. App. 2018), review denied (November 28, 2018) at 14.
33. *Envtl. Law Found. v. State Water Res. Control Bd.*, 26 Cal. App. 5th 844, 870 n. 7 (Ct. App. 2018), review denied (November 28, 2018) at 15.
34. *Envtl. Law Found. v. State Water Res. Control Bd.*, 26 Cal. App. 5th 844, 870 n. 7 (Ct. App. 2018), review denied (November 28, 2018) at 22.
35. Initial Notification of Groundwater Sustainability Plan Development for the Scott Valley Basin (issued on May 7, 2018 by the County of Siskiyou Flood Control and Water Conservation District).
36. See *National Audubon Society* v. *Superior Court of Alpine County*, 658 P.2d 709 (1983).
37. Kate Fritz, *Shoring Up SGMA: How Advocates Might Use the Holding in Environmental Law Foundation v. SWRCB to Support Sustainable Groundwater Management in California*, 28 ENVIRONMENTAL LAW NEW 3 (2019) at 7.
38. Kate Fritz, *Shoring Up SGMA: How Advocates Might Use the Holding in Environmental Law Foundation v. SWRCB to Support Sustainable*

Groundwater Management in California, 28 ENVIRONMENTAL LAW NEW 3 (2019) at 8.

39. Sax, Joseph, *Review of Laws Establishing the SWRCB's Permitting Authority over Appropriations of Groundwater Classified as Subterranean Streams and SWRCB's Implementation of Those Laws* (2002 Report to the California State Water Resources Control Board).

9

Instream Rights and Old Canals

One of the instream uses of waterways is for navigation, and waterways are sometimes characterized in statutes and state constitutions as "common highways" open to all. In the case of man-made waterways such as canals, however, the notion of these channels as "common highways" has often been muddled or lost, as control of such canals has often been turned over to private companies.[1] As some of these older canals have become less economically viable as corridors for commercial shipping, however, perceptions of these waterways have begun to change. These waterways are viewed less as privatized artificial conduits and more as public natural space.

When thinking about the concept of protected natural areas, there is often a tendency to consider such protected natural areas in contrast to or in opposition to artificial man-made structures. Similarly, when thinking about the concept of protected natural areas, there can be a tendency to assume that the appropriate location for such areas is geographically remote from the more built-up urban environment.

As author Anne Whiston Spirn noted in her book *The Granite Garden: Urban Nature and Human Design*, "The belief that the city is an entity apart from nature and even antithetical to it has dominated the way in which the city is perceived and continues to affect how it is built. The city must be recognized as part of nature and designed accordingly"[2] In a similar vein, the International Union for the Conservation Nature (IUCN) advised: "As our cities continue to grow, we must not abandon the protection of natural areas to the pressures of urbanization, but should instead defend such places, and indeed try to create new space for nature within the urban fabric – even within the centers of cities."[3]

The story of the Manchester Ship Canal in England challenges the traditional assumptions and thinking described by Anne Whiston Spirn, and forces us to reassess nature's place in the urban context as Spirn and the

IUCN advocate. With the Manchester Ship Canal, we find an artificial man-made watercourse constructed at the end of the nineteenth century that, over time, has in both appearance and function become more like a natural river, and that has become the setting for a series of canal-side nature parks that are reshaping the identity and economy of Greater Manchester. It is an adaptation of industrial infrastructure to new urban uses: a blue-green space parallel to the creation of greenspaces on brownfield land.

The experience with the Manchester Ship Canal, of an urban man-made watercourse that comes to be viewed as part of the natural landscape, is also happening in other cities, such as Los Angeles, California and Portland, Oregon in the United States. In Los Angeles, the natural Rio de Porciuncula (also known as the Los Angeles River) was straightened and encased in a uniform concrete trapezoidal cover in the 1940s, and renamed by government authorities as the Los Angeles County Flood Control Channel. Yet, in recent decades, concrete has been removed from portions of the channel, more regular instream flows have been restored, parks and bike paths have been built along its banks, and the greening of the Los Angeles River has become a source of civic pride.[4]

In Portland, annual floods south of the Columbia River created a network of marshes and wetlands adjacent to the river. From 1919–1921, in an effort to drain the area south of the Columbia River for farming and built structures, settlers built levees to prevent annual floods that profoundly affected the character of the floodplain. The natural marsh ecosystem was transformed into a highly managed system of agricultural lands and an earthen channel (which collected rainwater and irrigation runoff). The levees' elimination of spring freshets dried out lakes and ponds and prevented salmon from migrating into and out of the former marsh. Yet more recently, to increase flows into the earthen channel and restore connectivity, water from the Columbia River is now being diverted into the earthen channel to support spawning salmon and a dense riparian habitat, and these flows are then returned to the river. The earthen channel has been rechristened with the more poetic name "Columbia Slough" and is now used by the community for canoeing and kayaking.[5]

On an even grander scale, there is also the Erie Canal in New York State. Constructed in the early 1800s, the Erie Canal quickly became obsolete as a commercial shipping route when the railroads replaced canal transport. However, the Erie Canal is now part of an extensive corridor of parks and trails that extend from Albany to Buffalo, forming urban blue and greenways through cities such as Syracuse and Rochester. Sometimes called the "Artificial River," the Erie Canal has been absorbed into the urban and natural landscape of upstate New York.[6]

In this sense, the Manchester Ship Canal, the Los Angeles River, the Columbia Slough, and the Erie Canal stories represent a new variation of the established architectural concept of "adaptive re-use." Adaptive re-use has generally referred to the ways that older vacant historic industrial buildings have been reclaimed and modified for new uses, such as residences, restaurants, and art galleries. The adaptive re-use concept seems equally applicable to the transformation of use of older underemployed canals only this re-use takes place in an expansive outdoor landscape rather than within the walls of a building.[7]

This chapter begins with the history of the Manchester Ship Canal, both in terms of its decline as a shipping corridor and as a setting for canal-side open spaces such as Moore Nature Reserve, Wigg Island, and Woolston Eyes Nature Reserve. The chapter then compares the shipping and parks experience of the Manchester Ship Canal with that of the Erie Canal in the United States.

With both the Manchester Ship Canal in England and the Erie Canal in the United States, what we see is a changing landscape and new emerging open space roles for shipping canals that have outlived or expanded beyond their originally intended economic purpose. Part of this transition involves the public asserting new claims to public open space, both on the water and on canal-side lands. The stories of the Manchester Ship Canal and Erie Canal hold potential lessons for other cities that may also be looking to re-envision and repurpose deteriorating older underemployed man-made watercourses as new urban environmental amenities.

A CANAL REPURPOSED

There was a time when the prosperity of Manchester, England seemed to hinge on its ability to economically export the city's manufactured goods and to import raw cotton for the region's textile mills. In this era, the 36-mile Manchester Ship Canal, which provided a pathway for vessels to move between the city and the Irish Sea at the mouth of the River Mersey, was viewed as a critical piece of transport infrastructure.[8] Completed in 1894, the canal enabled Manchester's factories to avoid paying the additional costs for goods to be carried by road or rail to the docks at the Port of Liverpool, where the Port of Liverpool then imposed further charges on its more industrially productive Merseyside neighbor. With the Manchester Ship Canal, it was Manchester straight to the world.

This history explains why the badge of Manchester City Football Club includes a ship, a somewhat strange symbol for a city not on the coast unless one knows about the Manchester Ship Canal. The placement of a ship on the Manchester City badge may also have been a defiant gesture to the Liverpool and Everton football clubs based in Liverpool (in reference to the hefty shipping charges the Port of Liverpool would impose on Manchester factories).

When the United Kingdom's Queen Victoria opened the Manchester Ship Canal in 1894, into which flow the rivers Mersey and Irwell, it was the largest river navigation canal in the world. With the canal's completion, the newly created Port of Manchester became Britain's third busiest port despite being inland, handling a wide range of commercial vessels from bulk cargo sailing ships to towed barges and later mid-sized ocean-going container ships.

The annual amount of freight moving through the Manchester Ship Canal peaked in 1958 at 18 million long tons, but changes in the shipping sector resulted in declines in the 1970s and 1980s. With the shift in commercial shipping from bulk cargo to larger containers, the vessels became increasing larger. The Manchester Ship Canal was not wide enough or deep enough to accommodate the modern container ships. Moreover, there were numerous bridges that spanned the Manchester Ship Canal, although most were swing bridges that open to allow ships to pass, some high-level bridges that were fixed. Such high-bridges, the existing locks, and channels began to be too small to accommodate the increased height of the modern container ships. This meant that goods that were destined for ocean transport (to destinations around the world) on vessels that plied the canal from Manchester would need to be off-loaded and reloaded onto larger vessels at the Port of Liverpool. With this change, the market advantage to Manchester provided by canal transport was greatly diminished and use of the canal began to wane. By 1984, ship activity through the canal had fallen such that Salford Docks, the former heart of the Port of Manchester, were closed.

The declining use of the Manchester Ship Canal coincided with a more general decline in the manufacturing sector in Manchester. For instance, in 1945 it was estimated that there were 75,000 workers employed in Manchester's Trafford Park industrial estate. By 1967, manufacturing employment in Trafford Park had fallen to 50,000, and by 1976 it had fallen to 15,000.[9] However, a revival in employment was triggered by the Trafford Park Development Corporation after 1987, with some 30,000 people working there by 2016.[10]

As commercial vessel traffic on the Manchester Ship Canal declined, however, the trees and vegetation along the canal prospered due to seepage from the bed and banks. Although not a natural watercourse, for much of its length, the lush and forested landscape along the canal began to take on a natural quality, serving as habitat for birds and wildlife and as scenic recreational waterfront resource for people in the Liverpool–Manchester corridor. Such conservation groups as the Royal Society for the Protection of Birds (RSPB), Manchester Groundwork and Mersey Forest began to take a growing interest in canal-side lands.

Over time, as it became part of the regional landscape and ecosystem, the appearance of the Manchester Ship Canal became increasingly like that of an actual river.[11] And what could be more appropriate along what appeared to be a river than the creation of riverside (or canal-side) parks.

Moore Nature Reserve

Established in 1991, the 200-acre Moore Nature Reserve is located between the Manchester Ship Canal and the River Mersey near the town of Warrington. The site of the reserve is a former gravel and sand quarry. When the quarry was exhausted, an initial planting occurred and then it was left for nature to take over. Moore Nature Reserve contains woodlands, lakes, and wildflower meadows, and serves as habitat for an array of birds and dragonflies. Walking paths wind through the terrain and the reserve is used by local school and universities as an educational resource.

Although open to the public, the reserve is owned and managed by a private company, FCC Environment. This company also operates the nearby Arpley Landfill that borders the reserve. The vessels on the Manchester Ship Canal and the proximity to the landfill place these lands in a strange yet for some striking context.[12] The current policy is to retain and manage the existing mosaic of woodland, grassland, and open water on Moore Nature Reserve, and to ensure any new planting complements important open grassland habitat for ground-nesting birds in the area and maintains the views of the Mersey estuary.[13]

Wigg Island

Like the Moore Nature Reserve, 59-acre Wigg Island (also known as Wigg Island Community Park) near the town of Runcorn, lies between the

Manchester Ship Canal and the River Mersey. The park, which opened in 2002, is located on land with a rich industrial and wartime history.

The park is named after Charles Wigg, who established alkali works on the site in the 1860s to extract copper from its ore. As a potential deterrent to Nazi chemical warfare, mustard gas was produced from 1938 at Wigg Island works. Due to these previous uses, the site was heavily contaminated and had to undergo extensive environmental remediation before it could be re-used as public open space.

Wigg Island is reached via a swing bridge over the Manchester Ship Canal. The park has a network of paths along both the Mersey River and the canal, is known for the bee orchid and other wildflowers found there and is frequented by birdwatchers. At the 2002 opening of the park, the then Mayor of Halton commented "It's great to have a green space slap bang in the middle of a very urban area."[14] Wigg Island, like Moore Nature Reserve, is changing the way people think about nature. Contrary to most expectations, here the former industrial use of the site and its close proximity to current industrial uses creates its value to the local community, rather than its remoteness from such industry.

Woolston Eyes

A third nature reserve lies east of Warrington, again between the Ship Canal and the River Mersey. Regarded as one of the top twenty UK resources for seeing wildlife, the 667-acre Woolston Eyes Nature Reserve is a Site of Special Scientific Interest (SSSI) and has been described as "A post-industrial Gem, an oasis in the tangled wreckage" of the urban landscape.[15] The reserve extends for almost 4 km along the northern bank of the Canal and is accessible by footpaths from both the Woolston and Grappenhall areas of Warrington. It is the premier UK site for breeding Black-necked Grebes (*Podiceps nigricollis*), which first colonized the area in 1987.[16] A wide range of other bird species is found there.

Woolston Eyes is in a sequence of old meanders of the River Mersey which were altered in the eighteenth and nineteenth centuries to improve the Mersey River navigation and then changed further by the construction of the Ship Canal. Originally farmland, a chemical works and a gunpowder mill were established in the eighteenth century, but they ceased activity before the Canal was built. Since the 1920s, material dredged from the canal has been dumped on the marshy floodplain lands.[17] Today much of the area is wooded and several large waterbodies exist within the old meanders.

IF THE SHIPS RETURN

Although the narrow width and shallow depth of the Manchester Ship Canal and the height of fixed bridges across it precludes passage of larger taller container ships, there are now efforts to expand commercial container traffic on the canal. The most recent effort in this regard is the Port Salford project, a component of the larger Ocean Gateway project in North England.[18] The Ocean Gateway project calls for the investment of US $65 billion over 50 years in the economic development of the Greater Manchester–Liverpool corridor. Since 1984, the Salford Docks have been re-invented as a commercial, entertainment, media, and residential area. The Port Salford project, launched in 2011 by the Peel Group and Peel Ports, who respectively own the land where the Port Salford project will be located and operate the canal, plans to construct a modern canal freight terminal near the Trafford Park industrial estate to expedite loading and off-loading of vessels and to provide more efficient linkage with trucks and rail.

In addition to the Port Salford project, the Ocean Gateway has also promoted business activities in Greater Manchester that use the Manchester Ship Canal, providing synergy with the plans for the new freight terminal. For instance, in 2007, the British supermarket chain Tesco began transporting its wine imports from South America, Australia, and the United States through the Manchester Ship Canal, and the grain company Rank Hovis MacDonald (RHM) now ships more 100,000 tons of wheat annually from the Royal Seaforth Grain Terminal at the Port of Liverpool to its mill in Trafford Park.[19] With Tesco wines and RHM grain, the canal is being used to bring goods into Manchester rather than as a route for Manchester exports.

In 2010, a total of 8,000 shipping containers were transported along the Manchester Ship Canal. With the Port Salford project, and more deals like the Tesco wine shipments and RHM wheat shipments in place, the Peel Group and Peel Ports hope to increase that figure to 100,000 shipping containers by 2030.[20]

An increase in commercial vessel traffic on the Manchester Ship Canal would have a number of implications for nature parks and reserves in the area, some of which may be at cross-purposes and some of which may be supportive. On the one hand, there is interest not only in creating parkland and wildlife habitat along the lands adjacent to the Manchester Ship Canal but also in potentially opening up the canal to noncommercial boating, such as canoes, kayaks, and small sailboats. Given its narrowness, a revival and expansion of commercial traffic on the canal may not be consistent with such recreational boating from a safety standpoint. Peel Ports currently imposes extensive restrictions and requirements on the use of the Manchester Ship Canal by "pleasure craft" and it is foreseeable that such requirements may become more stringent if commercial vessel traffic increases as a result of the Port Salford project.[21]

On some summer weekends tourist passenger ferry boat cruises are operated by Mersey Ferries along the Manchester Ship Canal between Liverpool and Manchester. However individual paddleboats (such as canoes and kayaks) and smaller motorboats must seek prior approval and a "Certificate of Seaworthiness." The primary safety concern is "about narrowboats 'lacking stability' – [Peel Ports] are clearly worried about narrowboats tipping over if/ when a large vessel passes."[22] There are also Peel Ports requirements that smaller "narrowboats" be able to communicate via radio with the larger vessel, in order to avoid possible collisions and the small boats capsizing in the waves created by larger vessels.[23] These considerations create legitimate safety concerns and have made it difficult to obtain permission to launch smaller boats on the Manchester Ship Canal. The Bridgewater Canal, an eighteenth century precursor of the Ship Canal, now is actively used by canal narrow boat enthusiasts and others to travel from Manchester to Runcorn as part of the Cheshire Canal "Ring" route.

On the other hand, a resurgent economy in the Manchester–Liverpool corridor may be better able to attract and retain people in the region if there are high quality regional scenic environmental amenities nearby, such as Moore Nature Preserve and Wigg Island Community Park. In this sense, the creation and maintenance of open space and parkland along the Manchester Ship Canal can be viewed as part of the Ocean Gateway project's broader vision, of making the Manchester–Liverpool corridor a place people want to live and work.

OLD ERIE CANAL IN NEW YORK

A 1995 review of the positive potential impacts of riverside parks on local economies found that: "Rivers, trails and greenway corridors are traditionally recognized for their environmental protection, recreational values and aesthetic appearance. These corridors also have the potential to create jobs, enhance property values, expand local business, attract new or relocating businesses, increase local tax revenue, decrease government expenditures and promote a local community."[24] In short, nature parks along the Manchester Ship Canal may help support the success of such urban economic revitalization initiatives in the Liverpool–Manchester corridor as the Ocean Gateway Project. In the context of the Ocean Gateway project, Moore Nature

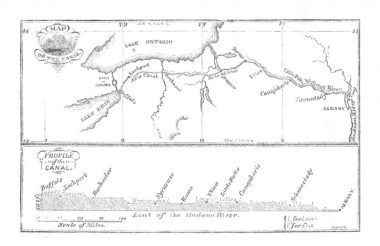

MAP 9.1 Map of the Erie Canal

Reserve and Wigg Island may become open space landmarks and sources of regional pride and identity for a new revitalized Manchester.

The Manchester Ship Canal is not the first man-made shipping canal to have faced the question of economic obsolescence and is not the first canal where parks have risen along adjacent lands. Completed in 1821 in the United States, the Erie Canal (formerly known as the New York State Barge Canal) runs 362 miles from the city of Albany on the Hudson River to the city of Buffalo on Lake Erie. Importantly, the Erie Canal provided a navigable water route between the Great Lakes and New York City and the Atlantic Ocean. Constructed in an era when there were no railways and transport of bulk goods was limited to pack animals, the canal provided a cost-effective and greatly expedited way to move goods in the United States between the eastern seaboard and farms, factories, and cities in the interior of the new nation.

In addition to playing a role in the economic development of New York City (whose port now had a major advantage over other Northeast coast ports such as Boston, Philadelphia and Baltimore), the transport of goods and people via the Erie Canal also contributed to growth of such Great Lakes cities as Buffalo, Cleveland, Detroit, and Chicago.

The original Erie Canal, built 70 years before the Manchester Ship Canal, had a channel that was only 42 feet wide and 4 feet deep and was designed to handle flat bulk goods barges and passenger packet boats that were towed by teams of horses and mules. The horses and mules walked along towpaths on each side of the canal and pulled the barges and packet boats behind them. With the development of the railroad and railways, however, the Erie Canal soon had competition. Moreover, the canal was too narrow and too shallow to handle the larger steamboats and paddleboats that might be in a position to better compete with the "iron horse" locomotive.

The limitations of the Erie Canal were recognized in the decades after its completion, and two enlargement project were undertaken to make it more competitive with the railroads. The first enlargement projected was completed in 1862, when the canal channel was widened to 68 feet and deepened to 6 feet. Later on, the canal channel was widened to 120 feet and deepened to 12 feet. These enlargement projects, however, did not prevent the railroads from overtaking the Erie Canal as the less expensive and more efficient means of transport in the period from 1850–1900. The opening of the Baltimore and Ohio Railroad in 1853, establishing a rail link between the east coast and the Great Lakes (via the Ohio River) can with hindsight be seen as the beginning of the end for the Erie Canal as a financially viable shipping route.

During much of the 1900s, as use of and investment in the Erie Canal declined, the infrastructure of the canal began to deteriorate. The sides of the canal were lined with stones set in clay and over time these sides began to crack, shift, and leak. The leakage of water from the sides of the canal led to the establishment of a corridor of dense trees and vegetation (and corresponding wildlife habitat) along the canal. Just as with the Manchester Ship Canal, from a scenic and ecosystem standpoint, the man-made Erie Canal increasingly came to resemble a natural river at the same time the commercial and passenger traffic on the waterway declined. Professor Carol Sheriff provides a sense of how perceptions of the Erie Canal began to change over time: "In the intervening decades, the artificial river had in many respects become of a part of the natural topography" and adds that "In many towns the artificial river replaced the main street as the principal thoroughfare, the facades of the new buildings overlooked the Erie Canal rather than the streets that ran beside it". The waters and banks of the Erie Canal came to be viewed as what Sheriff describes as "a sort of *middle landscape* between the extremes of civilization and wilderness."[25]

Today, the Erie Canalway National Heritage Corridor includes the entire length of the Erie Canal. Within the Erie Canalway National Corridor is the Erie Canalway Trail as well as a collection of several local and state parks, including the 362-mile Old Erie Canal State Historic Park between the cities of Syracuse and Rome. The Erie Canalway Trail is part of the larger New York State Canalway Trail, which includes former tow roads not only along the Erie Canal but also along the Oswego, Cayuga-Seneca, and Champlain canals (that all link to the Erie Canal). This broader canal-side trail system is being constructed and maintained by a partnership of government and private entities, including Parks and Trails New York and the New York State Canal Corporation. In 1995, the New York State Canal Corporation issued a comprehensive recreation plan which offered a vision not only for the former towpaths but also for the expanded recreational boating and fishing on the canals.

As part of the Old Erie Canal State Historic Park, the towpaths along the canal have been resurfaced with asphalt and stone and are now suitable for biking. One can now cycle along the roads where teams of horses and mules once pulled the bulk good barges and passenger packetboats on the canal.[26]

With the Erie Canal, we see the transformation of a man-made waterway from a vital transport corridor for goods and people, to a decaying and largely abandoned piece of infrastructure whose initial raison d'être was superseded by the railway (and later by the automobile and trucks), to its more modern reclamation as a historic, recreational, and ecological resource. The Manchester Ship Canal was built in a different era to serve different purposes, and its economic decline was caused by different forces and different technologies. But the rise and demise and rebirth of the Erie Canal echoes aspects of the unfolding story of the Manchester Ship Canal – dual tales of engineering marvels that were economically displaced, and of the ways these marvels were absorbed into the ecology and landscape where they were built.

NEW PUBLIC BLUE-GREEN SPACE

With the Ocean Gateway Project, there are indications that there may be an uptick in vessel traffic on the Manchester Ship Canal in the coming years. As such, unlike with the Erie Canal in New York, the Manchester Ship Canal is not simply an abandoned historical relic. It is a waterway that is still struggling to find its place as a commercially viable route of transport in today's economy.

Even if the Ocean Gateway Project vision for the Manchester Ship Canal comes to pass, however, it is unlikely the canal will ever return to the shipping prominence it had a century ago. There are too many things working against it – its narrowness, its shallowness, the low bridges that span it, the demise of Manchester-based manufacturing, and the low-costs and flexibility of transporting goods by truck. These are not types of limitations that can be easily overcome.

It is therefore foreseeable that, notwithstanding a potential increase in vessel traffic in the decades ahead, perceptions of the value and appropriate uses of the Manchester Ship Canal and its adjacent lands will continue to shift. As the canal is viewed more as a permanent element of the natural landscape and not just a transport route for goods, investments will continue to be made in the parks and nature reserves that line it. Interest will continue to grow in the habitats that these parks and preserves provide and the wildlife they support. As recreational use of these parks and preserves grows and becomes part of people's routines and sense of place, they will come to see an environmental dimension of local and regional significance and importance to the Manchester Ship Canal. The canal and its adjacent lands will transform from a simple privately managed water transport corridor for private vessels to a more complex new form of public blue-green space.

That is, we can expect the process of "adaptive re-use" of the canal to continue. When viewed as environmental amenities, the series of parks rising along the Manchester Ship Canal have the potential to not only re-incorporate nature into the urban landscape but also to serve as a catalyst and engine for urban economic investment and recovery.[27]

In this sense, the continued presence of a ship on the Manchester City Football Club badge seems proper because the Manchester Ship Canal remains part of the essential fabric of the City of Manchester. The nature of the relationship between the city and the canal is changing, but the canal's centrality to the city's identity remains fixed.

Like the experience with the Erie Canal before it, the "middle landscape" that the Manchester Ship Canal presently occupies, located somewhere between notions of wilderness and notions of civilization, is now just an accepted and familiar part of the greater landscape of the City of Manchester, in the same way that the River Irwell and the River Mersey are part of this greater landscape. The distinctions between the natural and the man-made have blurred over time.[28]

An appreciation of this "middle landscape," perhaps even an embrace of it, is something other cities with deteriorating under-used man-made watercourses (such as the Los Angeles River and the Columbia Slough) should consider. Rather than viewing such older canals simply as poorly maintained outdated private infrastructure, the experience with the Manchester Ship Canal and the Erie Canal suggests that such watercourses can also be viewed as the scenic and ecological foundations for new public urban open space. That is, vibrant new water-connected habitats and landscapes emerging from the decay of the built environment.

Notes

1. Timothy M. Mulvaney, *Instream Flows and the Public Trust*, 22 TULANE ENVIRONMENTAL LAW JOURNAL 315, 346–347 (2009).

2. A. W. Spirn, THE GRANITE GARDEN: URBAN NATURE AND HUMAN DESIGN (New York: Basic Books, 1984).

3. T. Trzyna, *Urban Protected Areas – Profiles and best practice guidelines*, IUCN Best Practice Protected Area Guidelines Series No. 22, Gland CH: **The International Union for Conservation of Nature** (IUCN), 2014.

4. B. Gumprecht, THE LOS ANGELES RIVER: ITS LIFE, DEATH AND POSSIBLE REBIRTH (Baltimore: Johns Hopkins University Press, 2001).

5. Portland Bureau of Environmental Services, *Columbia Slough: About the Watershed* (2008); Susan Barthel, *A Brief History of the Columbia Slough* (on file with author, provided by Mike Houck, Director of the Urban Greenspaces Institute in Portland, Oregon); Columbia Slough Watershed Council, A PADDLER'S ACCESS GUIDE TO COLUMBIA SLOUGH (Portland OR: Environmental Services, City of Portland, 2009), www.portlandoregon.gov/bes/articles/42677 [Accessed April 18, 2019].

6. C. Sheriff, THE ARTIFICIAL RIVER: THE ERIE CANAL AND THE PARADOX OF PROGRESS (New York: Hill & Wang, 1996).

7. L. Wong, ADAPTIVE RE-USE (Basel: Birkhäuser, 2017); C. Zaitzevsky, and G. Burnell, BUILT TO LAST: A HANDBOOK ON RECYCLING OLD BUILDINGS (Washington: Preservation Press, 1977).

8. D. A. Farnie, THE MANCHESTER SHIP CANAL AND THE RISE OF THE PORT OF MANCHESTER (1894–1975) (Manchester: Manchester University Press, 1980); D. E. Owen, *The Manchester Ship Canal* (Manchester: Manchester University Press, 1983); E. Gray, A HUNDRED YEARS OF THE MANCHESTER SHIP CANAL, Chicago: Aurora Publishing, 1993).

9. D. A. Farnie, THE MANCHESTER SHIP CANAL AND THE RISE OF THE PORT OF MANCHESTER (1894–1975) (Manchester: Manchester University Press, 1980); D. E. Owen, *The Manchester Ship Canal* (Manchester: Manchester University Press, 1983); E. Gray, A HUNDRED YEARS OF THE MANCHESTER SHIP CANAL (Chicago: Aurora Publishing, 1993); C. J. Wood, MANCHESTER'S SHIP CANAL: THE BIG DITCH (Stroud: Tempus Publishing, 2005).

10. B. Robson, "The resurgent entrepreneurial city," in A. Kidd and T. Wyke (eds.) MANCHESTER: MAKING THE MODERN CITY' (Liverpool: Liverpool University Press, 2016), 347–396.

11. C. J. Wood, MANCHESTER'S SHIP CANAL: THE BIG DITCH (Stroud: Tempus Publishing, 2005).

12. FCC Environment (2019) *Moore Nature Reserve*, www.fccenvironment.co
.uk/waste-processing/landfill/arpley-landfill/moore-nature-reserve/ [Accessed April 18, 2019].

13. Mersey Forest, MORE FROM TREES: THE MERSEY FOREST PLAN (Warrington: The Mersey Forest, 2019) [Accessed May 12, 2019].

14. Natural England, *Wigg Island – Local Nature Reserves* (2016). https://de
signatedsites.naturalengland.org.uk/SiteLNRDetail.aspx?SiteCode=
L1083066&SiteName=Wigg%20Island&countyCode=&responsiblePers
on=&SeaArea=&IFCAArea= [Accessed April 24, 2019].

15. Woolston Eyes Conservation Group (2019) *Woolstone Eyes Nature Reserve* (www.woolstoneyes.com/) [Accessed May 12, 2019].

16. Martin and J. Smith, *A Survey of Breeding Black-Necked Grebes in the UK: 1973–2004*, 100 BRITISH BIRDS (2007), 368–378.

17. S. K. Price, H. F. Burke, R. L. Terrington, H. Reeves, D. Boon, and A. J. Schieb, *The 3D Characterization of the Zone of Human Interaction and the Sustainable Use of Underground Space in Urban and Peri-Urban Environments: Case Studies from the UK*, 161 ZEITSCHRIFT DER DEUTSCHEN GESELLSCHAFT FUR GEOWISSENSCHAFTEN 2 (2012), 219–235, DOI: 10.1127/1860-1804/2010/0161-0219.

18. www.oceangateway.co.uk/ [Accessed May 12, 2019].

19. D. Ward, *Wine on the Water as Tesco Turns to Barges to Cut Emissions*, THE GUARDIAN (October 19, 2007), www.theguardian.com/environment/
2007/oct/19/carbonemissions.uknews [Accessed April 17, 2019].

20. Peel Group, *Port Salford*, https-//web.archive.org/web/20120427195451/htt
p-//www.peel.co.uk/media/Land%20and%20Property/key%20projects/Po
rt_Salford_Interactive_Brochure.pdg (2015) [Accessed April 24, 2019].

21. Peel Ports, *Manchester Ship Canal Instructions to Vessels, Pleasure Craft Induction Pack* (2017).

22. *Manchester Ship Canal General Boating*, post on www.canalworld.net website (September 13, 2013).

23. *Manchester Ship Canal General Boating*, post on www.canalworld.net website (September 13, 2013).

24. National Park Service (1995) *Economic Impacts of Protecting Rivers, Trails and Greenway Corridors. Rivers Trails and Conservation Assistance*, National Park Service, Fourth Edition (Revised). https://conservation
tools-production.s3.amazonaws.com/library_item_files/126/147/Econo
mic_Impacts_of_Protecting_Rivers__Trails__and_Greenway_Corrido
rs-_A_Resource_Book.pdf?AWSAccessKeyId=AKIAIQFJLILYGVDR4
AMQ&Expires=1556130564&Signature=NIPCri9ST8fXuK6KTs933aQ
po2Y%3D [Accessed April 24, 2019].

25. C. Sheriff, THE ARTIFICIAL RIVER: THE ERIE CANAL AND THE PARADOX OF PROGRESS (New York: Hill & Wang, 1996), pp. 198, 115 and 191.

26. Parks & Trails New York (2015) *Closing the Gaps: A Progress Report on the Erie Canalway Trail*, https://ptny.org/application/files/8714/5935/3322/2015-Closing-the-Gaps-Report.pdf [Accessed April 18, 2019].

27. A. W. Spirn, THE GRANITE GARDEN: URBAN NATURE AND HUMAN DESIGN (New York: Basic Books, 1984); T. Trzyna, *Urban Protected Areas – Profiles and best practice guidelines*, IUCN Best Practice Protected Area Guidelines Series No. 22 (Gland CH: **The International Union for Conservation of Nature** (IUCN), 2014); National Park Service (1995) *Economic Impacts of Protecting Rivers, Trails and Greenway Corridors. Rivers Trails and Conservation Assistance*, National Park Service, Fourth Edition (Revised). https://conservationtools-production.s3.amazonaws.com/library_item_files/126/147/Economic_Impacts_of_Protecting_Rivers__Trails__and_Greenway_Corridors-_A_Resource_Book.pdf?AWSAccessKeyId=AKIAIQFJLILYGVDR4AMQ&Expires=1556130564&Signature=NIPCr i9ST8fXuK6KTs933aQpo2Y%3D [Accessed April 24, 2019].

28. C. Sheriff, THE ARTIFICIAL RIVER: THE ERIE CANAL AND THE PARADOX OF PROGRESS (New York: Hill & Wang, 1996).

10

Instream Rights and Water as an Investment

In considering the status of water as an investment under international trade agreements, the concept of grasping seems particularly on point for several reasons. First, many international trade lawyers have conceptual difficulty grasping the nature and scope of private legal interests in the use of water. Second, many water lawyers have conceptual difficulty grasping the nature and scope of investor protections under international investment and trade agreements. Then there are recent efforts of private water users to secure recognition of entitlements to water under international trade agreements. These efforts represent a type of grasping as well.

This question is also now an important focal point for academic work in the field of international law, as evidenced by Oxford University Press' 2005 book *Freshwater and International Economic Law*, a collection of essays by leading international law scholars from around the world.[1] The debate over the scope of private interests in water under international law is therefore global in nature.

STREAMS OF PUBLIC INTERNATIONAL LAW

Within the broader field of public international law, there are many subfields, including those of international environmental law and international economic law. Because public international law often emerges through regional legal developments and because public international law is not subject to the discipline of a single global legal entity, its evolution often lacks coherence. Different regions develop different legal principles and institutions to govern other subfields.

In terms of international environmental law and international economic law, we are now confronted with a somewhat turbulent confluence between public international law on cross-border freshwater resources (cross-border water law) and public international law on foreign investment (foreign invest-ment law). Globally, these two streams of public international law are inter-secting with increasing frequency, giving rise to uncertainty. The essence of this uncertainty hinges on the extent to which water allocation provisions in cross-border water treaties may establish rights enforceable against nation States pursuant to foreign investment treaties, and the extent to which standing requirements and dispute resolution mechanisms under cross-border water treaties may differ from those established under foreign investment treaties.

In North Africa, for instance, claims regarding the Nile River were allocated pursuant to the 1959 Agreement for the Full Utilization of the Nile Waters (1959 Nile Agreement).[2] Pursuant to the 1959 Nile Agreement, Egypt was allocated 55 billion cubic meters (annually) of the main Nile, Sudan was allocated 18.5 billion cubic meters (annually), and upstream nations such as Ethiopia were implicitly prohibited from diversions that threatened Egypt's or Sudan's numerical allocations. According to water researchers, Ethiopia's headwaters and snowpack contribute the majority of the water that feeds the main Nile, but Ethiopia presently utilizes less than 1 percent of the Nile Basin's waters.[3]

To meet crop irrigation and drinking water needs, Ethiopia has recently proposed plans to divert additional waters from highland Nile tributaries – plans that could potentially affect water supplies downstream in Sudan and Egypt and thus give rise to potential claims of noncompliance with the 1959 Nile Agreement.

In 2000, however, the agreement between the Government of the Federal Republic of Ethiopia and the Government of the Republic of the Sudan on the Reciprocal Promotion and Protection of Investment (2000 Ethiopia–Sudan Investment Treaty) was signed.[4] The 2000 Ethiopia–Sudan Investment Treaty defines "investment" to include "concessions to search for, cultivate, extract or exploit *natural resources*" (italics added) and pro-vides that "prompt, adequate and effective compensation" may be due if one nation takes "any measures of expropriation, nationalization or any other measures having the same nature or same effect against investment of Investors of the other Contracting Party." Under the 2000 Ethiopia–Sudan Investment Treaty, disputes are to be resolved through either submission to a three-person Arbitral Tribunal or to the International Centre for Settlement of Investment Disputes ("ICSID"), both of which are empowered to issue "final and binding" awards.

The central question here is whether parties may bring claims against Ethiopia pursuant to the 2000 Ethiopia–Sudan Investment Treaty to the extent that Ethiopian upstream diversions diminish the downstream waters available such that Sudan's freshwater allocation under the 1959 Nile Agreement is impaired.

In South America, as another example, Ecuador and Peru entered into a treaty in 1998 to allocate the waters of the cross-border Zarumilla River and Canal.[5] The 1998 Agreement on the Basis for the Administration of the Zarumilla/Rules for the Administration of the Zarumilla Feed and Utilization of Water (1998 Zarumilla River Agreement) built on a previous water-sharing agreement negotiated between Ecuador and Peru in 1944 that obligated Peru to "guarantee the supply of water necessary for the life of the Ecuadorian villages" on the right bank of the river. There were longstanding allegations by Ecuador of Peruvian noncompliance with its water supply obligations under the 1944 water-sharing agreement. Pursuant to the 1998 Zarumilla River Agreement, Ecuador was allocated rights to 55 percent of the water in the flow channel and Peru was allocated 45 percent. Disputes over compliance with this freshwater allocation regime are to be referred to a Permanent Binational Commission composed of Ecuadorian and Peruvian sections.

One year later, however, in 1999, Ecuador and Peru entered into a bilateral investment treaty.[6] The treaty between the Government of the Republic of Peru and the Government of the Republic of Ecuador for the Promotion and Reciprocal Protection of Investments (1999 Ecuador–Peru Investment Treaty) defines "investment" to include "concessions for the prospecting, exploration and exploitation of *natural resources*" (italics added) and provides that "rapid adequate and effective compensation" may be due if one nation takes an action that "has equivalent effect of expropriation or nationalization" of the investments of the citizens of the other nation. Under the 1999 Ecuador–Peru Investment Treaty, a complaining party can seek "final and binding arbitration" against the alleged offending nation before the ICSID.

Could the water allocations under the 1998 Zarumilla River Agreement provide the basis for a claim under the 1999 Ecuador–Peru Investment Treaty in connection with alleged improper river diversions?

In North America, this confluence of subfields of public international law is no longer theoretical but instead was directly at issue in an acute conflict that played out between the United Mexican States (Mexico) and private water users from the State of Texas in the United States of America (United States). This dispute centered on claims to the cross-border waters of the Rio Grande under the terms of the 1944 Rivers Treaty between Mexico and the United States and the investor protection provisions of the 1994 North American Free Trade Agreement (NAFTA) among Mexico, and the United States and Canada.

In July 2007, an international arbitral tribunal – the ICSID, the same dispute resolution body designated in the 2000 Ethiopia–Sudan Investment

Treaty and the 1999 Ecuador–Peru Investment Treaty – issued its decision in the Rio Grande case.[7] This decision represents perhaps the most significant consideration of the legal relationship between cross-border water law and foreign investment law to date. This chapter deconstructs the arguments ultimately accepted (and rejected) by the July 2007 ICSID tribunal for the Rio Grande dispute, with an eye toward what the Rio Grande case may signal for similar public international law conflicts emerging in other regions over competing claims to cross-border freshwater resources.

This chapter begins by outlining the hydrologic and legal restraints to private ownership of water resources. It then details the provisions of NAFTA that pertain to private rights in water, and reports on two high profile water entitlement cases that have arisen under NAFTA's foreign investor protection regime. The piece concludes by observing that the experience of United States federal courts with state water law may provide a jurisprudential template to bring NAFTA into better alignment with existing domestic water law and international water treaties.

PRIVATE RIGHTS TO WATER: ELUSIVE BY NATURE AND LAW

North American Free Trade Agreement was approved by Canada, the United States, and Mexico in 1993 and went into effect on January 1, 1994. The bulk of NAFTA's provisions focus on the transnational trade in goods and products. Early on, however, the NAFTA parties recognized that water did not fit neatly within accepted notions of what constituted a good or product under traditional trade law terminology. This recognition led the parties to issue a joint statement in 1993 concerning NAFTA's application to water resources (1993 NAFTA Statement).[8] The 1993 NAFTA Statement provides:

> The governments of Canada, the United States and Mexico, in order to correct false interpretations, have agreed to state the following jointly and publicly as Parties to NAFTA … The NAFTA creates no rights to the natural water resources of any Party to the Agreement. Unless water, in any form, has entered into commerce and become a good or product, it is not covered by the provisions of any trade agreement including the NAFTA. And nothing in the NAFTA would oblige any NAFTA party to either exploit its water for commercial use, or to begin exporting water in any form. Water in its natural state in lakes, rivers, reservoirs, aquifers, water basins and the like is not a good or product, is not traded, and therefore is not and never has been subject to the terms of any trade agreement. International rights and obligations respecting water in its natural state are contained in separate treaties and agreements negotiated for that purpose. Examples are the United States-Canada

Boundary Waters Treaty of 1909 and the 1944 Boundary Waters Treaty between Mexico and the United States.

Within the NAFTA regime, we can therefore see that Canada, Mexico, and the United States have long agreed that there is something fundamentally different about water compared to other items that may cross national boundaries – something that eludes and often precludes traditional notions of private ownership. Although the 1993 NAFTA Statement does not spell out exactly what it is about water that warrants this special treatment, it may have to do with certain characteristics that are somewhat unique to water.

First, there are peculiar hydrologic uncertainties and fluctuations inherent with water resources. Precipitation and temperature levels during any given period will affect how much water is stored as snowpack, the amount of precipitation that remains as snowpack versus the amount of precipitation that melts to become runoff that makes its way into creeks, streams, rivers, and underground aquifers, when such runoff occurs, and how much surface water is lost due to evaporation.

Second, the availability of a water resource for a particular party is often contingent on how other parties divert the resource. If two parties are withdrawing groundwater from the same underground aquifer, the withdrawals of one party may affect the groundwater available to the other party. The same is true for surface water diversions by multiple parties – reduction in instream flow caused by one diverter reduces the remaining flow for other diverters and for instream uses and users (i.e. fisheries and fishermen).

Finally, water has long been considered by most domestic legal systems to be a resource that is public, or at least quasi-public. As Professor Michael Hanemann of the University of California, Berkeley, recently observed: "The public good nature of water ... has had a decisive influence on the legal status of water. In Roman Law, and, subsequently, in English and American common law, and to an extent in Civil Law systems, flowing waters are treated as common to everyone (res communis omnium), and are not capable of being owned."[9] A few local examples from California and the American West illustrate the public or quasi-public domestic legal status of water resources.

The California Supreme Court's 1983 decision in *National Audubon Society* v. *Superior Court* confirmed that all surface waters in the state are subject to the public trust doctrine. The public trust doctrine restricts the ability of the state of California – acting through its state water board – to grant private entitlements to divert waters that significantly impair the public's interest in maintaining adequate instream flows. In setting aside a series of state agency permits allowing the city of Los Angeles to divert waters away from

Mono Lake, the court clarified that "before state courts or state agencies approve water diversions they should consider the effect of such diversions upon interests protected by the public trust, and attempt, so far as feasible, to avoid or minimize any harm to those interests."[10]

In June 2006, in the case of *Allegretti* v. *Imperial County*, the California Court of Appeal rejected the argument that a county's application of groundwater anti-overdraft pumping restrictions constituted a physical taking of a landowner's water under the Fifth Amendment of the US Constitution. A "physical taking" covered by the Fifth Amendment entitles a property owner to "just compensation" for the property taken. The court in *Allegretti* held:

> [The] County's action with respect to *Allegretti* – in the present case imposition of a permit condition limiting the total quantity of groundwater available for *Allegretti*'s use-cannot be characterized as or analogized to the kinds of permanent physical occupancies or invasions sufficient to constitute a categorical physical taking. [The] County did not physically encroach on *Allegretti*'s property or aquifer and did not require or authorize any encroachment; it did not appropriate, impound or divert any water.[11]

In 2005, in the case of *Klamath Irrigation District* v. *United States*, the United States Court of Claims rejected a Fifth Amendment takings claim, finding that the plaintiff's entitlement to divert water from the Klamath River (located in California and Oregon) under contracts with the US Bureau of Reclamation was subject to compliance with the habitat protection provisions of the Federal Endangered Species Act 8. The Court of Claims held: "[T]he court is mindful that … this ruling may disappoint a number of individuals who have long invested effort and expense in developing their lands based upon the expectation that the waters of the Klamath Basin would continue to flow, uninterrupted, for irrigation. But, those expectations, no matter how understandable, do not give those landowners any more property rights as against the United States."[12]

In three recent California court decisions – *Planning and Conservation League* v. *California Department of Water Resources* in 2000[13], *Santa Clarita Organization for Planning and the Environment* v. *County of Los Angeles* in 2003[14], and *Vineyard Area Citizens for Responsible Growth, Inc.* v. *City of Rancho Cordova* in 2005[15] – the courts recognized a distinction between "wet water" and "paper water." These three cases clarified that "wet water" is water supply that is actually and physically available for diversion and use, while "paper water" are water supply entitlements that are referenced in documents (such as delivery contracts with California's State Water Project) but that do not in fact exist due to hydrological realities, environmental restraints, or uncompleted infrastructure. As the court in the *Planning and Conservation League* case explained, State Water Project entitlements represent nothing more than hopes, expectations, water futures or, as the parties refer to them as "paper water," which always was an illusion. "Entitlements" is a misnomer, for contractors surely cannot be entitled to water nature refuses to provide or the body politic refuses to harvest, store, and deliver.

These domestic law conceptions of water provide the backdrop for understanding the 1993 NAFTA Statement. They explain the difficulty in applying standard notions of property, ownership, and entitlement to alleged private claims to a specific quantity of water.

WATER AND INVESTMENT UNDER NAFTA CHAPTER 11

Chapter 11 of NAFTA is designed to protect foreign investors from appropriation of their property by host nations. More specifically, Chapter 11 prohibits a host nation from taking measures that are "tantamount to nationalization or expropriation" of an "investment" except on "payment of compensation" based on "fair market value."[6] Foreign investors who believe that a host nation has taken such measures may initiate binding arbitration proceedings that can result in an enforceable damages award. There is no requirement that a foreign investor first exhaust domestic legal remedies available in the host nation before initiating a Chapter 11 claim.

Chapter 11's use of the term "investment," instead of the term "goods" or "products," makes a confusing application to water resources. Although the 1993 NAFTA Statement provides that water generally should not be considered a good or product for NAFTA purposes, it does not directly address the question of how this characterization might affect claims regarding an investment in water brought pursuant to Chapter 11. More specifically, the 1993 NAFTA Statement on water leaves open the possibility of claims regarding investments in water that might exist independent of claims that water itself is a good or product subject to private ownership.

Article 1139 of NAFTA attempts to offer some guidance on what might be considered an investment for Chapter 11 purposes. Article 1139(g) provides that the term "investment" may include "real estate or other property acquired in the expectation or used for the purpose of economic benefit."[7] Yet given the body of domestic law establishing that any private right "acquired" to use water is subject to significant limitations, the definition provided in Article 1139(g) is not particularly helpful when applied to water resources. It merely begs the underlying question of whether, and if so to what extent, a private party can acquire water as property.

Article 1139(h) of NAFTA similarly attempts to offer guidance by providing that an investment may include "interests arising from the commitment of capital or other resources in the territory of a Party to economic activity in such territory."[18] As with the use of the term "acquired" in Article 1139(g), the use of the term "interests" in this context raises more questions than it answers when applied to water resources. Once again, given the body of domestic law establishing that any private interest to use water is subject to significant limitations, what type of interest in water can a private party be said to possess?

Chapter 11's definition of "investor" in Article 1139 also provides little help. This definition provides that an "investor of a Party" means a "Party or state enterprise thereof, or a national or an enterprise of such Party, that seeks to make, is making or has made an investment."[19] As to what constitutes an investment for purposes of determining who constitutes an investor in the context of Chapter 11 claims involving water resources, we are left again with the ambiguities of Article 1139's definition of investment. In light of the uncertain relationship between the 1993 NAFTA Statement and Chapter 11, and the less-than-helpful water-related definitions of "investment" provided in Article 1139 of NAFTA, it is not surprising that disputes have arisen over Chapter 11's application to foreign investment appropriation claims involving water resources.

To date, there have been two NAFTA Chapter 11 cases where claims regarding water resources have been front and center.

Claim by California's Sun Belt against Canada

Sun Belt Water Inc. (Sun Belt) is a California corporation created to provide additional water supply to real estate developments in California. In 1990, Sun Belt entered into a joint venture with Snowcap Waters Limited (Snowcap), a company based in British Columbia, Canada. The joint venture called for the diversion of water from the Fraser River in British Columbia. The bulk water exports would be transported by retrofitted oil supertankers down the Pacific Coast to California where Sun Belt would market the water.

In 1991, the government of British Columbia – concerned about the impacts of these diversions and exports on instream flow, fishery resources, and water quality – passed a temporary ban on bulk water exports and refused to award Snowcap its requested permit. This ban rendered the Snowcap–Sun Belt endeavor unviable. Because Snowcap was a Canadian company and not a foreign investor, it could not use Chapter 11 against Canada. Over many years, Sun Belt attempted unsuccessfully to reach a settlement with the government of British Columbia, and then had its claim for damages rejected by the Canadian courts.

In 1998, Sun Belt filed a Chapter 11 claim against Canada alleging $10.5 billion in damages resulting from lost profits, lost market access, and lost access to water resources.[20] The Sun Belt NAFTA claim did not proceed to arbitration, and as of this writing no final settlement has been reached.

Sun Belt's Chapter 11 claim, although unresolved, raises a fundamental question. If the Canadian courts have already reviewed its claim and determined that Sun Belt has no property interest entitling it to compensation under Canadian law, should a NAFTA Chapter 11 tribunal defer to this domestic judicial determination? Chapter 11 does not require that a foreign investor first exhaust domestic judicial remedies before bringing a Chapter 11 claim. Nevertheless, the lack of a domestic exhaustion requirement does not establish that a Chapter 11 tribunal can or should disregard a previous domestic judicial ruling in the host county that directly addressed the question of whether regulation of a specified natural resource in a particular manner gave rise to a governmental duty to compensate a particular party.

The issue here is not so much whether a previous domestic court ruling acts to deprive a NAFTA panel of jurisdiction to consider a Chapter 11 claim. Rather, the issue is what degree of deference a NAFTA panel owes a domestic court in the event that a Chapter 11 claimant's alleged property interest has already been examined and ruled upon.

Claim by Texas Farmers against Mexico

To understand the Texans' Chapter 11 Rio Grande claim against Mexico, a brief review of the 1944 Waters Treaty is required. The 1944 Waters Treaty between Mexico and the United States established separate allocation regimes for the Colorado River and the Rio Grande.

In the case of the Rio Grande, the largest tributary to the river, the Rio Conchos, has its headwaters in Northern Mexico. Therefore, the Rio Grande allocation regime set forth in the 1944 Waters Treaty obligates Mexico to allow certain flows to reach the United States. A converse regime was established under the 1944 Waters Treaty for the Colorado, which flows from the United States to Mexico, which calls upon the United States to release certain flows.

The 1944 Waters Treaty allocated one-third of the flow of the tributaries in Mexico that reach the Rio Grande to the United States. Except in times of "extraordinary drought," this one-third allocation is not to be less than 350,000 acre feet (AF) annually, averaged over a five-year period.[21] If the five-year period averages less than 350,000 AF due to drought conditions, then Mexico is left with a "water debt." Under the terms of the treaty, Mexico must pay back an accumulated "water debt" in the next five-year period through increased releases.[22] The 1944 Waters Treaty is silent as to the specific timeframe or schedule for making these increased releases, and the agreement is also silent about what happens if extraordinary drought conditions occur in back-to-back five-year periods.

Under the 1944 Waters Treaty, the bilateral institution entrusted with overseeing the allocation regime for both the Colorado River and the Rio Grande is the International Boundary and Waters Commission (IBWC). In the 1992–1997 five-year period, and then again in the 1997–2002 period, Mexico did not provide an annual average of 350,000 AF. Mexico maintained that drought conditions prevented it from making these deliveries. At the end of the 1997–2002 five-year cycle, Mexico had accumulated a 1.3 million AF water debt. With assistance from the IBWC, in March 2005, the United States and Mexico agreed on a schedule for Mexico to discharge its Rio Grande water debt through additional releases.

Although the US government was satisfied with this resolution, a group of farming irrigation districts in Texas (Texas farmers) was not satisfied. These Texas farmers initiated a NAFTA Chapter 11 claim against Mexico in late 2004, seeking close to $700 million in damages.[23] The thrust of the Texas farmers' Chapter 11 claim is that they had and continue to have a legal entitlement to the minimum 350,000 AF, and that Mexico appropriated this entitlement by failing to provide this quantity. The Texas farmers argued that Mexico improperly relied on the treaty's drought conditions exception.

The Rio Grande NAFTA Chapter 11 dispute involves more than conflicting views of the scope and nature of the Texas farmers' property interest in water. The dispute also raises the preliminary question of whether the IBWC dispute resolution process provided for in the 1944 Waters Treaty deprives a NAFTA Chapter 11 panel of jurisdiction over the Texas farmers' claim.

Article 30 of the Vienna Convention on the Law of Treaties, entitled "Application of successive treaties to the same subject matter," suggests that NAFTA's dispute resolution procedures should govern. Article 30(3) provides in pertinent part, "When all the parties to the earlier treaty are parties also to the later treaty but the earlier treaty is not suspended or terminated … the earlier treaty applies only to the extent that its provisions are compatible with those of the later treaty."[24] Application of this provision suggests that since Mexico and the United States are both parties to the earlier 1944 Waters Treaty and to the later NAFTA, the provisions of NAFTA should govern in the event of a conflict between the two treaties.

However, other considerations of international law point to an alternative conclusion.

First, the primary focus of the 1944 Waters Treaty is on the allocation of river resources, whereas the primary focus of NAFTA Chapter 11 is on private investment. Therefore, it could be argued that the two treaties do not in fact relate to the "same subject matter" and that Article 30(3) of the Vienna Convention is therefore inapplicable. Second, Article 31(a) of the Vienna Convention provides that "[t]he context for the purpose of the interpretation of a treaty shall comprise, in addition to the text ... any agreement relating to the treaty which was made between all the parties in connection with the conclusion of the treaty."[25]

The 1993 NAFTA Statement, approved by both Mexico and the United States, declared, "International rights and obligations respecting water in its natural state are contained in separate treaties and agreements negotiated for that purpose. Examples are the United States-Canada Boundary Waters Treaty of 1909 and the 1944 Waters Treaty between Mexico and the United States." To the extent the 1993 NAFTA Statement falls within the scope of Article 31(a) of the Vienna Convention, it suggests that NAFTA was not intended to displace or replace the terms – including the dispute resolution terms – of the 1944 Waters Treaty.

Finally, another rule of treaty interpretation under customary international law, *lex specialis*, holds that a more specific treaty or treaty provision should prevail over a more general treaty or treaty provision.[26] Given that the 1944 Waters Treaty relates specifically to the question of Rio Grande allocations between Mexico and the United States, and given that NAFTA Chapter 11 relates to the more general question of appropriation of foreign investments, *lex specialis* would dictate that the dispute resolution provisions of the 1944 Waters Treaty should prevail over the dispute resolution provisions of NAFTA when allocation of the Rio Grande is at issue.

To provide a sense of the opposing positions in this case on both the jurisdictional and property interest questions, below are excerpts from the opening briefs submitted to the NAFTA Rio Grande tribunal in the summer of 2006.

Briefing Submitted by Government of Mexico
On the question of the NAFTA tribunal's jurisdiction over the dispute, the government of Mexico stated: "The claim is outside the scope of NAFTA by reason of the nature of the treaty: The breaches of NAFTA alleged by the

claimants are based exclusively on the argument that Mexico breached obligations established in the Treaty Between the United States of America and Mexico Respecting Utilization of Waters of the Colorado and Tijuana Rivers and of the Rio Grande entered into by Mexico and the United States in 1944. The Bilateral Water Treaty has its own dispute settlement mechanism, which can only be invoked by Mexico and the United States. [The Water Treaty of 1944 ... grants the [IBWC] exclusive jurisdiction."[27]

On the question of the issue of "ownership" of the alleged investment, the Government of Mexico maintained: "[N]one of the claimants even argue that they have a property right in Mexico, whether in land, water or any other assets. [Mexico's] Secretariat of Economy requested that they present a copy of the property title or other documents that proves that each one has a direct or indirect ownership or control of the investment allegedly affect. None of the claimants did so ... None of the systems, facilities, and infrastructure that they allege to own is located in Mexican territory; all are located in the United States. [Alt a more basic level, if the claimants are located in the United States and are subject to U.S. jurisdiction, specifically, to that of the State of Texas, it is perplexing at best to wonder how they can simultaneously be subject to Mexican jurisdiction ... or how it is that Mexico could have expropriated a property right created by foreign legal system and existing only in another country."[28]

Briefing Submitted by Texas Farmers

On the question of whether the IBWC has exclusive jurisdiction over the matter, to the exclusion of the NAFTA Chapter 11 tribunal, the Texas farmers argued: "The fact that Mexico may have breached a treaty obligation [under the 1944 Waters Treaty] owed to the United States does not immunize it from the separate consequences of a violation of Chapter 11 of NAFTA. Simply put, this arbitration is about national treatment, the minimum standard of treatment, and expropriation and compensation, resulting from Mexico's seizure of water owned by Claimants. As investors, Claimants have the right to pursue this claim for Respondent's adoption of measures relating to their investment, and this Tribunal has jurisdiction over this claim."[29]

On the question of ownership of water interests, the Texas farmers contended:

> Claimants are the legal owners of 1,219,521 acre-feet of the irrigation water
> wrongfully withheld and diverted from the Rio Grande by Mexico's manipu-
> lation of its dams and reservoirs as of October 2002. These water rights, as well
> as delivery facilities, irrigation works, farms, equipment, and irrigated

farming businesses of which they are an essential element, form an integrated investment, the expropriation and diversion of which has severely damaged the ability of Claimants to produce crops ... Claimants' expectations to the right to the receipt of use of the water at issue in these claims were fixed by the [1944] Treaty Between the United States of America and Mexico.[30]

On the question of the applicability of the 1993 NAFTA Statement to water, the Texas farmers maintained: "Since Claimants' water, which flows within courses of the six abovenamed Mexican tributaries before reaching the Rio Grande, where it is stored in Falcon and Amistad reservoirs, sold on the water market, and delivered through a complex of irrigation works, is clearly a good or product in commerce, it necessarily falls within the scope of NAFTA."[31] The reference by the Texas farmers to "reservoirs" in support of their argument that the Rio Grande water should be considered a "good" or "product" under the 1993 NAFTA Statement on water is particularly interesting given that the 1993 NAFTA Statement specifically provides: "Water in its natural state in lakes, rivers, reservoirs, aquifers, water basins and the like is not a good or product, is not traded, and therefore is not and never has been subject to the terms of any trade agreement." The Merriam-Webster Dictionary defines a "reservoir" as "an artificial lake where water is collected and kept in quantity for use." To the extent the Texas farmers contend that water stored in a "reservoir" is not "water in a natural state," this interpretation would appear to render the inclusion of the word "reservoir" in the 1993 NAFTA Statement nonsensical since a reservoir is by definition an artificial man-made impoundment (as opposed to a naturally occurring aquifer or lake).

In its briefing to the Tribunal, Mexico took a fairly hard line. There were risks, however, with this approach. As Kyla Tienhaara from the Institute for Environmental Studies at Vrije University in Amsterdam observed in an article dated November 2006 in *Global Environmental Politics*: "The uncertainty created by the current framework for investor-state dispute settlement, coupled with the high cost associated with arbitration proceedings, can leave governments in developing countries in a precarious position. When faced with a decision on whether to risk millions of dollars for an unknown outcome, many countries may opt instead to retract, amend or fail to enforce an environmental regulation."[32]

The 2007 Tribunal Decision

On June 19, 2017, the ICSID NAFTA Chapter 11 Tribunal issued its decision on the Texans' water claim against Mexico. The majority of the Tribunal's decision was devoted to assessing the Texans' "integrated investment" theory, which could serve as the proper basis for jurisdiction over the claim. As the excerpt below indicates, the Tribunal had conceptual difficulty with the premise of this theory:

> The Tribunal considers that in order to be an "investor" within the meaning of NAFTA Article 1101(a), an enterprise must make an investment in another NAFTA state, not its own ... The simple fact that an enterprise in one NAFTA State is *affected* by measures taken in another NAFTA State is not sufficient to establish the right of that enterprise to protection under NAFTA Chapter Eleven: it is the relationship, the legally-significant connection, with the State taking measures that establishes the right to protection, not the bare fact that the enterprise is *affected* by the measures.
>
> In the opinion of the Tribunal, it is quite plain that NAFTA Chapter Eleven was not intended to provide substantive protection or rights of action to investors whose investment are wholly confined to their own national States, in circumstances where those investments *may be affected* by another NAFTA State Party. The NAFTA should not be interpreted as to bring about this unintended result. (italics added.)
>
> It is clear that the words "territory of the Party" [in Article 1101(b) of NAFTA] do not refer to the territory of the Party of whom the investors are nationals. It requires investment in the territory of another NAFTA Party – the Part that adopted or maintained the measures challenged. In short in order to be an "investor" under Article 1139 one must make an investment in the territory of another NAFTA state, not in one's own.[33]

In considering whether the Texans had or have an investment "in the territory" of Mexico, and how this related to jurisdiction under NAFTA Chapter 11, the Tribunal determined:

> In our view it is clear they do not. They have substantial investments in Texas, in the form of businesses, and in the context of these proceedings, more particularly in the form of the infrastructure for the distribution of water that they extract from the [Rio Grande]. They have substantial investments in the form of the water rights guaranteed by the State of Texas. They are certainly "investors"; but their investments are in Texas, and they are not investors in Mexico or vis-à-vis Mexico.
>
> In the view of this Tribunal it has not been demonstrated than any of the Claimants seeks to make, is making or has made an investment *in Mexico*. That being the case, the Tribunal does not have jurisdiction to hear any of these claims against Mexico because the Claimants have not demonstrated that their claims fall within the scope and coverage of NAFTA Chapter Eleven, as defined by NAFTA Article 1101. (italics in original.)[34]

The Tribunal's disposition of the Texans' Rio Grande claim therefore rested on the grounds that it lacked proper jurisdiction over the claim due to its determination that an investment in Mexico was not involved. Because it based its decision on these grounds, the Tribunal did not need to resolve the scope or limitations of the 1993 NAFTA Statement on Water, thereby avoiding having to reconcile potentially conflicting provisions of the 1944 Waters Treaty and NAFTA Chapter 11. On this latter question, however, the Tribunal did offer the following analysis that suggests that the 1944 Rivers Treaty might have provided an additional jurisdictional basis to deny the Texans' claim:

> The Claimants sought, with arguments of considerable subtlety and ingenuity, to identify a supervening right that overcame all such problems, by saying that in the 1944 Rivers Treaty Mexico alienated or relinquished title to one-third of the waters in [the Rio Grande's tributaries in Mexico], just as States sometimes relinquish land territory in treaties. According to this view, approximately one-third of the water [in the Rio Grande's tributaries in Mexico] belongs to the United States – although who owns what cannot be accurately determined at any given moment because of the sharing formula under Article 4 of the 1944 Treaty applies a combination of fixed amounts and percentage shares over periods of several year.
>
> The Tribunal can find no evidence in the 1944 Treaty to suggest that this imaginative interpretation of the Treaty, whose legal coherence and practical operability are open to considerable doubt, was intended by the Parties. The ordinary meaning of the Treaty is that it is an agreement to apportion such water arrive as the international watercourse.
>
> If such a diversion [by Mexico of tributaries to the Rio Grande] were to occur, it may or may not amount to a breach of the 1944 Treaty. That would be a matter for the two States, who are the *only* parties to that Treaty. If the interest of the US nation were thought to be prejudiced by any action alleged to amount to a violation of the Treaty, that is an issue which could be taken up *by the US government under the dispute resolution procedures in the 1944 Treaty. But the 1944 Treaty does not create property rights amounting to investment within the meaning of NAFTA which US nationals themselves may protect by action under NAFTA Chapter Eleven.* The Tribunal expresses no views on the interpretation or application of the 1944 Treaty in the circumstances of this case. (italics added.)[35]

The aforementioned quote suggests that the Tribunal was of the general opinion that private non-state parties (such as the Texans) did not have standing to enforce rights granted to Mexico and the United States under the 1944 Treaty, and that even such State-to-State claims would likely be governed by the dispute resolution mechanisms set forth in the 1944 Treaty. However, this passage concludes with the comments that the Tribunal "expresses no view on the interpretation or application of the 1944 Treaty in the circumstances of this case," leaving readers to sort out the legal significance of the Tribunal's observations regarding the scope and exclusivity of the 1944 Rivers Treaty.

REACHING BEYOND COMPETENCE

Stepping back from the particulars of the Rio Grande and Sun Belt NAFTA Chapter 11 claims, what is so intriguing about these disputes is the way claimants are advancing private property notions of water that are contrary to domestic water law.

In domestic water law, the past several decades have seen an increase in the legal recognition of the public interest in water resources. Fishery habitat protection for endangered species, the public trust doctrine, instream flow requirements, and the wet water/paper water distinction are all elements of this domestic water law trajectory. Yet within the framework of multilateral investment treaties such as NAFTA's Chapter 11, we are now confronted with efforts to characterize water resources again as quantitatively fixed private property. If these efforts were to prove successful, we will be left with a fundamental disconnect and divergence between domestic water law and international trade law.

If progress is to be made in bringing NAFTA Chapter 11 – and, potentially, other foreign investor protection regimes – into closer alignment with domestic law notions of the private interest in water, an analytic framework for such reconciliation might be found in the domestic litigation leading up to the California Supreme Court's 1983 decision in *National Audubon*. In this case, the California Supreme Court held that California's public trust doctrine applies to instream waters, and that this doctrine imposes an obligation on California agencies to limit the private interest in diversion of such waters to avoid and minimize adverse impacts on public trust resources. The path by which the underlying litigation in *National Audubon* made its way into the California courts may provide instructive lessons for NAFTA Chapter 11 tribunals.

The environmental plaintiffs in *National Audubon* filed their initial lawsuit in May 1979 in Mono County Superior Court against the Department of Water and Power (DWP) of the City of Los Angeles. The case was then transferred to Alpine County Superior Court. In January 1980, DWP cross-complained against several other parties, including the US federal government. Upon being named, the United States removed the case from state court to the federal district court for the Eastern District of California. However, because certain California water law questions were central to the plaintiffs' claims and DWP's defenses, Federal District Court Judge Lawrence Karlton sent these questions back to the California courts for resolution.

The California Supreme Court decision in *National Audubon* explained as follows:

> [T]he district court stayed its proceedings under the federal abstention doctrine to allow resolution by the California courts of [an] important issue of California law .... What is the interrelationship of the public trust doctrine and the California water rights system, in the context of the right of the Los Angeles Department of Water and Power ("Department") to divert water from Mono Lake pursuant to permits and licenses issues under the California water rights system? In other words, is the public trust doctrine in this context subsumed in the California water rights system, or does it function independently of that system? Stated differently, can the plaintiffs challenge the Department's permits and licenses by arguing that those permits and licenses are limited by the public trust doctrine, or must the plaintiffs challenge the permits and licenses by arguing that the water diversions and uses authorized thereunder are not "reasonable or beneficial" as required under the California water rights system?[36]

In essence, Federal District Court Judge Karlton determined that since the public trust doctrine was a matter of California law, the California courts should first be provided with an opportunity to offer further clarification on the scope of the doctrine before the federal courts took up the issue.

The US Court of Claims adopted a similar approach in its 2005 decision in *Klamath Irrigation District* v. *United States (Klamath Irrigation)*. In *Klamath Irrigation*, Judge Allegra concluded that federal courts need to take account of background principles of state water law in reviewing claims alleging a property interest in water, because otherwise the federal court result might be an award of compensation "for the taking of interests that may well not exist under state law."[37]

In NAFTA Chapter 11 tribunals' review of alleged private investments in domestic water resources, a level of restraint similar to that exercised by Judge Karlton in the *National Audubon* litigation and Judge Allegra in the *Klamath Irrigation* decision may be warranted. To the extent the existence and scope of an alleged property interest in water is contingent on domestic water law, a NAFTA Chapter 11 tribunal considering this alleged interest should properly identify and reflect such domestic water law. To the extent the existence and scope of an alleged property interest in water is contingent on an international water treaty, such as the 1944 Waters Treaty or the 1909 Boundary Waters Treaty, a NAFTA Chapter 11 tribunal considering this alleged interest needs to properly identify and reflect the provisions of the relevant international water treaty.

In short, there are sound reasons for NAFTA Chapter 11 tribunals to exercise restraint in taking upon themselves the task of interpreting water law questions more appropriately answered by domestic courts or by dispute resolution bodies (such as the IBWC) established under international water treaties. To do otherwise will only evidence the potential of NAFTA's foreign investor regime to reach into areas of domestic and international natural resource law that are outside its areas of legal expertise and competency.

Notes

1. FRESH WATER AND INTERNATIONAL ECONOMIC LAW (Edith Brown Weiss, Laurence de Boisson de Charournes & Nathalie Bernasconi-Osterwlader eds., 2005).
2. Agreement for the Full Utilization of the Nile Waters, Sudan and Egypt, November 8, 1959 [1959 Nile Agreement].
3. Cam McGrath & Sonny Inbaraj, 'Unquiet Flows the Nile' (January 15, 2009), online: Ethiopia Tecola Hagaon.
4. Agreement between the Government of the Federal Democratic Republic of Ethiopia and the Government of the Republic of Sudan on the Reciprocal Promotion and Protection of Investment, Ethiopia and Sudan, March 7, 2000.
5. Agreement on the Basis for the Administration of Canal Zarumilla and Rules for the Administration of Zarumilla Feed and Utilization of Water, Peru and Ecuador, January 19, 1998.
6. Treaty between the Government of the Republic of Peru and the Government of the Republic of Ecuador for the Promotion and Reciprocal Protection of Investments, April 7, 1999 [1999 Ecuador–Peru Investment Treaty) (entered into April 1999).
7. Award of ICSID Arbitral Panel, *Bayview Irrigation District et al.* v. *United Mexican States*, ICSID Case No. ARB (AF)/05/1 (2007) (International Centre for Settlement of Investment Disputes), at 24.
8. 1993 Joint Statements of the Governments of Canada, Mexico, and the United States.
9. W. M. Hanemann, THE ECONOMIC CONCEPTION OF WATER, in Water Crisis: Myth or Reality (Peter P. Rogers et al. eds. 2006).
10. 658 P.2d 709, 712 (Cal. 1983).
11. 42 Cal.Rptr.3d 122, 130–131 (Ct. App. 2006).
12. 67 Fed. Ct. 504, 540 (2005).
13. 100 Cal.Rptr.2d 173 (2000).

14. 131 Cal.Rptr.2d 186 (2003).

15. 25 Cal.Rptr.3d 596 (2005).

16. North American Free Trade Agreement, U.S.-Can.-Mex., December 17, 1992, 107 Stat. 2057, 32 I.L.M. 289 (1993), Article 1110.

17. North American Free Trade Agreement, U.S.-Can.-Mex., December 17, 1992, 107 Stat. 2057, 32 I.L.M. 289 (1993), Article 1139(g).

18. North American Free Trade Agreement, U.S.-Can.-Mex., December 17, 1992, 107 Stat. 2057, 32 I.L.M. 289 (1993), Article 1139(h).

19. North American Free Trade Agreement, U.S.-Can.-Mex., December 17, 1992, 107 Stat. 2057, 32 I.L.M. 289 (1993), Article 1139.

20. Sun Belt Water Inc., Notice of Intent to Submit a Claim to Arbitration Under Chapter 11 of the North American Free Trade Agreement, *Sun Belt Water Inc.* v. *Her Majesty the Queen*, U.N. Commission on International Trade (October 12, 1999).

21. Treaty Relating to the Utilization of Waters of Colorado and Tijuana Rivers and of the Rio Grande, U.S.-Mex., February 3, 1944, 59 Stat. 1219, 1226–27.

22. Treaty Relating to the Utilization of Waters of Colorado and Tijuana Rivers and of the Rio Grande, U.S.-Mex., February 3, 1944, 59 Stat. 1219, 1224–28.

23. Bayview Irrigation District, Notice of Intent to Submit a Claim to Arbitration Under Section B, Chapter 11 of the North American Free Trade Agreement, *Bayview Irrigation District et al.* v. *United Mexican States* (August 24, 2004).

24. Vienna Convention on the Law of Treaties, May 23, 1969, U.N. Doc A/ CONF. 39.27, 1155 U.N.T.S. 331 (entered into force January 27, 1980), Article 30(3).

25. Vienna Convention on the Law of Treaties, May 23, 1969, U.N. Doc A/ CONF. 39.27, 1155 U.N.T.S. 331 (entered into force January 27, 1980), Article 31(a).

26. C. Wold, S. E. Gaines, G. Block, Trade and the Environment: Law and Policy (Durham: Carolina Academic Press, 2005), p. 676.

27. Memorial on Jurisdiction Submitted by United Mexican States at 2. Before the Honorable Tribunal Established Pursuant to Chapter XI of the North American Free Trade Agreement, *Bayview Irrigation District et al.* v. *United Mexican States* (April 19, 2006).

28. Memorial on Jurisdiction Submitted by United Mexican States at 34. Before the Honorable Tribunal Established Pursuant to Chapter XI of the North American Free Trade Agreement, *Bayview Irrigation District et al.* v. *United Mexican States* (April 19, 2006).

29. Counter-Memorial of Bayview Irrigation District et al. in Support of Jurisdiction at 44, In the Arbitration between *Bayview Irrigation District et al.* v. *United Mexican States* (June 23, 2006).

30. Counter-Memorial of Bayview Irrigation District et al. in Support of Jurisdiction at 7–8, In the Arbitration between *Bayview Irrigation District et al.* v. *United Mexican States* (June 23, 2006).

31. Counter-Memorial of Bayview Irrigation District et al. in Support of Jurisdiction at 25, In the Arbitration between *Bayview Irrigation District et al.* v. *United Mexican States* (June 23, 2006).

32. Kyla Tienhaara, *What You Don't Know Can Hurt You: Investor-State Disputes and the Protection of the Environment in Developing Countries*, GLOBAL ENVIRONMENTAL POLITICS (November 2006) at 75, 96.

33. Award of ICSID Arbitral Panel, *Bayview Irrigation District et al.* v. *United Mexican States*, ICSID Case No. ARB (AF)/05/1 (2007) (International Centre for Settlement of Investment Disputes), at 24.

34. Award of ICSID Arbitral Panel, *Bayview Irrigation District et al.* v. *United Mexican States*, ICSID Case No. ARB (AF)/05/1 (2007) (International Centre for Settlement of Investment Disputes), at 25, 27.

35. Award of ICSID Arbitral Panel, *Bayview Irrigation District et al.* v. *United Mexican States*, ICSID Case No. ARB (AF)/05/1 (2007) (International Centre for Settlement of Investment Disputes), at 26.

36. 658 P.2d 709, 717 (Cal. 1983).

37. 67 Fed. Ct. 504 (2005).

11

Instream Rights and International Law

INTRODUCTION

There can be various reasons why onstream dams are constructed and operated on rivers. Some dams are built to create new water supplies for irrigation or domestic use that can be stored in the reservoirs behind the impoundments. Other dams are built to generate hydro-electric energy that can be produced by running the water stored in reservoirs through turbines. There are also dams built to regulate flows to avoid downstream flooding during storms. More often than not, there are "multipurpose" onstream dams that are designed to serve a mix of water supply, energy, and flood control purposes.

Globally, the presence of onstream dams is pervasive and extensive. A report by the World Commission on Dams in 2000 found that there were more than 45,000 dams in more than 150 countries.[1]

Some dams are geographically located in watersheds within a single nation, while other dams are located in watersheds that span multiple nations. For example, in North America, the Columbia River/Snake River watershed spans Canada and the United States, and the Colorado River watershed spans Mexico and the United States. There are numerous onstream dams in both the Columbia River/Snake River and Colorado River watersheds. Similarly, there are onstream dams located on the Mekong River (which flows through multiple nations in Southeast Asia), the Danube River (which flows through multiple nations in Europe), the Indus River watershed (which spans India and Pakistan), the Tigris/Euphrates watershed (which flows through Turkey, Syria, and Iraq in the Middle East) and the Nile River (which flows through Ethiopia, Sudan, and Egypt in northern Africa).

Regardless of the reasons why onstream dams are constructed and operated, and regardless of whether onstream dams are located in watersheds that span multiple nations, there is a set of environmental impacts commonly associated with such construction and operation. The presence and operation of dams can have significant impacts on the instream flow below the structures. More specifically, the retention of water in reservoirs behind dams can alter and often reduce downstream flows. These alterations of instream flow below dams in turn impact aquatic ecosystems, fisheries, and fishers dependent on fisheries.

This chapter will examine the impacts of onstream dams on instream flow, ecosystems, and fisheries through the dual lens of international water law and international fisheries laws, as well as international law on the obligation to assess transboundary environmental impacts.

EFFECT OF ONSTREAM DAMS ON FISHERIES AND FISHERS

Before discussing the legal frameworks for evaluating the environmental impacts of onstream dams, at the outset, it is useful to first identify the different ways that fisheries and aquatic ecosystems can be affected by such facilities. This identification will provide an ecological foundation for the legal analysis that follows.

Dams as Barriers to Passage

The presence of an onstream dam can serve as a barrier for fish that tradition-ally migrate upstream and downstream of where the dam is located. For example, on the west coast of North America, wild Pacific salmon begin their life in inland freshwaters, migrate to the ocean for several years and then return to their natal inland freshwaters to spawn. Onstream dams in the Fraser River watershed in Canada, the Columbia River/Snake River water-shed in Canada, and the United States and the Sacramento River/San Joaquin River watershed in the United States serve as downstream and upstream barriers to migratory salmon. Since the construction of these dams on the west coast of North America, the salmon fishery in the region has suffered significant declines.[2]

Slack Water Conditions above and below Dams

Onstream dams and associated reservoirs change the natural flow (velocity) of a river. This change can create "slack water" conditions both above and below the dam, in which the velocity of the natural flow of a river is greatly reduced. Slack water conditions can result in algae growth and reduced oxygen levels that impact fisheries.

The environmental impacts associated with slack water conditions on the Danube River in Europe was a central issue in the 1997 decision by the

International Court of Justice (ICJ) in the *Gabcikovo-Nagymaros* case.[3] In this case, the ICJ considered allegations that slack water conditions resulting from an onstream dam located in Slovakia had led to an algae bloom and degraded aquatic habitat for fisheries in waters located in Hungary.

The adverse effects related to slack water have also become a concern on the Volta River in Africa. There is evidence that low flow conditions below the Akosombo Dam in Ghana (on the Volta River) have resulted in the spread of weeds that harbor snails that serve as intermediate hosts for lethal intestinal diseases.[4] Research undertaken by the Volta Basin Research Project at the University of Ghana has documented the rise of these intestinal diseases and associated child mortality since Akosombo Dam was constructed in the 1960s.[5]

Water Temperature, Salinity, and Sediment Transport

When an onstream dam changes the timing or reduces the amount of water released downstream, this can result in an increase in water temperatures below the dam. The increase in water temperatures below a dam can have particularly acute adverse impacts on cold-water fisheries such as salmon. Salmon have a limited tolerance for higher water temperatures. They prefer water temperatures below fifty-five degrees (Fahrenheit), suffer reduced growth and survival rates as water temperatures get closer to sixty degrees (Fahrenheit) and are generally unable to survive in water warmer than sixty degrees (Fahrenheit).[6] Instream water temperatures tend to be hottest in the summer, which is also when water stored behind dams is in highest demand for agriculture and irrigation. The result is that there are often reduced releases of upstream water from dams at the time of year when increased air temperatures are pushing water temperatures up. The reduced volume of water flowing downstream caused downstream waters to warm and salmon mortality rates to rise.[7]

The presence of onstream dams can also affect the salinity levels of waters below the dams due to seawater intrusion. When the amount of freshwater flowing downstream is reduced by onstream dams the seawater pushes farther upstream. Rising salinity levels can affect freshwater fisheries with low tolerance for higher salt concentrations. In the United States, for instance, saltwater intrusion resulting from the operation of dams in the Sacramento River/San Joaquin River watershed in California has adversely impacted delta smelt, a freshwater fish now listed as endangered.[8]

The presence of onstream dams can also trap sand and gravel that would otherwise be carried downstream. To the extent the presence of sand and gravel serve as important elements of aquatic habitat for fisheries downstream, the interference of dams with natural sediment transport can adversely impact fisheries.

Effects on Fishers Dependent on Impacted Fisheries

In considering the harm that onstream dams can cause to fisheries, it is critical to remember that this harm goes beyond biodiversity and ecological considerations. In many watersheds, freshwater fisheries serve as an important food source for local populations and/or support local commercial fishers. The loss of fisheries caused by onstream dams can therefore affect poverty conditions in watershed communities and the economic viability of the fishing sector.

For example, in connection with Ghana's Akosombo Dam on the Volta River (discussed earlier), slack water conditions have had an adverse impact on the shrimp fishery below the dam.[9] Because many riverside communities below the Akosombo Dam rely on such shrimp as a basic food supply, the decline of the shrimp fishery on the lower Volta River has health and nutritional impacts for the local population.[10]

As another example, on the west coast of North America there are many local fishers whose livelihood is dependent on the health and abundance of fisheries such as salmon. Local fishers in this region have banded together to form the Pacific Coast Federation of Fishermen's Associations (PCFFA), which is now a leading advocate for efforts to change the way onstream dams operate (in terms of fish passage and downstream releases) to restore Pacific coast fisheries.

Recognition of how onstream dams can impact local communities and fishers dependent on fisheries is important to understanding how certain principles of international water law and international environmental law – such as equitable utilization, meeting vital human needs, avoidance of significant environmental harm, and transboundary environmental impact assessment (discussed further below) – apply to the construction and operation of onstream dams.

GENERAL PRINCIPLES OF INTERNATIONAL FISHERIES LAW

There is a well-developed body of international fisheries law, but this body of law has focused primarily on ocean fisheries or anadromous fisheries (which spend at least part of their life cycle in the ocean). Although there is little international law dealing directly with rights and obligations relating to freshwater fisheries, there are general legal principles established in the context of ocean and anadromous fisheries that may be pertinent and relevant to the evaluation of disputes over rights and obligations respecting freshwater fisheries.

UNCLOS and United Nations Straddling Stocks Treaty

In regard to ocean and anadromous fisheries, two of the primary sources of international law are the 1982 United Nations Convention on the Law of the Sea (UNCLOS) and the 1996 United Nations Treaty on Straddling and Migratory Fish Stocks (UN Straddling Stocks Treaty). Both of these treaties address the rights and obligations of nations in regard to fish stocks that are located in the international high seas, which move between the international high seas and a nation's 200 mile offshore exclusive economic zone (EEZ), or which move between different nations' EEZs. The provisions of these two agreements dealing with ocean/anadromous fish stocks that "straddle" and "migrate" between the waters of different nations may provide guidance in regard to freshwater fisheries that straddle and migrate between the waters of different nations.

Article 63(1) UNCLOS provides: "Where the same stock or stocks of associated species occur within the exclusive economic zone of two or more coastal states, these States shall seek, either directly or through appropriate subregional or regional organizations, to agree upon the measures necessary to coordinate and ensure the conservation and development of such stocks." Article 64(1) of UNCLOS is titled, "Highly migratory species" and provides: "The coastal states and other States whose nationals fish in the region for the highly migratory species listed in Annex I shall co-operate directly or through appropriate international organizations with a view to ensuring conservation and promoting the objective of optimum utilization of such species throughout the region, both with and beyond the exclusive economic zone. In regions for which no appropriate international organization exists, the coastal State and other States whose nationals harvest these species in the region shall co-operate to establish such an organization and participate in its work." Taken together Articles 63(1) and 64(1) of UNCLOS provide that coastal nations have an affirmative obligation to cooperate to ensure the conservation of fish species that straddle or migrate between multiple coastal states' offshore waters.

The UN Straddling Stocks Treaty sought to provide further guidance on the participatory rights of different nations in terms of the regional fishery management organizations described in Articles 63(1) and 64(1) of UNCLOS. These participatory rights would, in turn, help determine the respective rights and obligations of nations whose nationals actively fished in the area or for the species regulated by a particular regional fishery management organization. Article 11 of the UN Straddling Stocks Treaty provides as follows:

> In determining the nature and extent of participatory rights for new members of a subregional or regional fisheries management organization, or for new participants in a subregional or regional fisheries management organization, States shall take into account, inter alia: (a) the status of the straddling fish stocks and highly migratory fish stocks and the existing levels of fishing effort in the fishery; (b) the respective interests, fishing patterns and fishing practices of new and existing members or participants; (c) the respective contributions of new and existing members or participants to conservation and management of the stocks, and to the collection and provisions of accurate data and to the conduct of scientific research on the stocks; (d) the needs of coastal fishing communities which are dependent mainly on fishing for the stocks; (e) the needs of coastal States who economies are overwhelmingly dependent on the exploitation of living marine resources; and (f) the interests of developing States from the subregion or region in whose area of national jurisdiction the stocks also occur.

From Article 11 of the UN Straddling Stocks Treaty the following two general principles emerge that may also be relevant to freshwater fisheries. First, the extent to which a nation is contributing to the conservation of straddling/migratory fish stocks should be taken into account in the allocation of rights to catch such fish stocks. Second, when determining the respective rights of nations to catch straddling/migratory fish stocks, consideration should be given to local communities dependent on such stocks and to nations whose economies are greatly reliant on such fish stocks.

ICJ Fisheries Decision on Iceland–United Kingdom Case

In the 1970s, prior to the international codification of the 200-mile EEZ in the 1982 UNCLOS, a fisheries dispute developed between Iceland and the United Kingdom over the cod fishery offshore of Iceland. Due to concerns about overfishing of its offshore cod fishery, Iceland unilaterally extended its 12-mile offshore exclusive fishing zone to 200 miles. British fishing vessels, which had traditionally fished well within the 200-mile zone, refused to recognize Iceland's claims.

The two nations agreed to submit the dispute to the ICJ, which rendered its decision in 1974 in the *Icelandic Fisheries Case*.[11] The ICJ held as follows:

> Both states have an obligation to take full account of each other's rights and of any fishery conservation measures the necessity of which is shown to exist in

those waters. It is one of the advances of maritime international law, resulting from the intensification of fishing, that the former laissez-faire treatment of the living resources of the high seas has been replaced by a recognition of a duty to have due regard to the rights of other states and the needs of conservation for the benefits of all. Consequently, both Parties have the obligation to keep under review the fishery resources in the disputed waters and to examine together, in light of scientific and other available information, the measures required for conservation, development and equitable exploitation of those resources.

In this 1974 ruling, the ICJ articulated general international law principles that would later be incorporated into the 1982 UNCLOS. More specifically, the ruling found that nations have an affirmative obligation to work together for the conservation of fisheries, and that in fulfilling this obligation nations have a related duty to take each other's respective interest in the fishery into appropriate consideration. Taken together, these findings suggest that unilateral actions by one nation (or vessels flying that nation's flag) that undermined the conservation of fisheries or that disregarded the interest of other nations in such fisheries were inconsistent with modern international fisheries law.

Although the ICJ *Icelandic Fisheries Case* involved ocean fisheries, there is no apparent reason why the general principles noted earlier might not also apply to disputes between nations involving the conservation of and respective rights and obligations relating to freshwater fisheries or fisheries that migrate through inland waters.

Fishing Rights Grounded in Originations in Pacific Salmon Treaty

Salmon on the west coast of North America begin their life cycle in inland freshwater streams. From there, they head downstream to the Pacific Ocean where they spend several years and then return to their natal inland freshwater streams to spawn. Different salmon runs travel in different directions and routes during their life period in the ocean.

Vessels flying the Canadian and United States flags fish for salmon in offshore ocean waters. Offshore Canadian fishers often catch salmon that originate and spawn in freshwater streams in Alaska, Washington, Oregon, and California in the United States (such as the Yukon River watershed, Columbia River/Snake River watershed and Sacramento River/San Joaquin River watershed). Similarly, offshore United States fishers often catch salmon that originate and spawn in freshwater streams in British Columbia in Canada (such as the Fraser River watershed). From a practical standpoint, it is difficult if not impossible for the vessels fishing offshore to know whether they are catching salmon whose natal streams are in Canada or the United States.

In the 1995 Pacific Salmon Treaty, Canada and the United States addressed this situation by basing respective fishing rights on the concept of "originations." Pursuant to Article III(a) of the treaty, fishing rights are allocated so as to "provide for each Party to receive benefits equivalent to the production of salmon originating in its waters." This approach is consistent with Article 11(c) of the UN Straddling Stocks Treaty, which suggests in allocating the respective fishing rights of nations' consideration should be given to the extent each nation contributes to the conservation of the fish stocks in question.

According to international fisheries law scholar J.A. Yanagida:

> The purpose of the equity principle [in the Pacific Salmon Treaty] is sensible enough. It recognizes that downstream fishermen depend substantially on the country that has jurisdiction over the spawning grounds. To ensure that salmon have unimpeded access to upriver spawning grounds, the country of origin may have to remove natural obstructions, build fish passes, forgo hydro-electric development and control pollution. If stocks are to be enhanced, the party upstream is best situated to do so. To accord that party adequate incentive to undertake these responsibilities, the equity principles provides that the country of origin should receive benefits equivalent to the production of salmon in its waters.[12]

The corresponding implication of the originations approach relied upon in the Pacific Salmon Treaty is that countries whose facilities and activities reduce the amount of salmon originating in their inland freshwater stream should have their right to fish offshore for salmon reduced accordingly. The implications of the originations approach to fishing rights allocation have significant implications for onstream dams. That is, if onstream dams in Canada or the United States block the upstream/downstream passage of migrating salmon or are operated in a manner that results in downstream aquatic habitat conditions that reduce the productivity of salmon stocks, the presence and operation of such dams should provide the basis for a downward adjustment of respective salmon fishing rights.

Although the originations approach in the Pacific Salmon Treaty relates to an anadromous fishery and offshore fishing, there is no apparent reason why the originations approach might not also provide an appropriate basis for the allocation of rights to catch freshwater fisheries. To the extent there are fisheries that migrate through freshwater rivers and streams of multiple nations, when a nation constructs and operates onstream dams that reduce the productivity of the freshwater fisheries in the region, the originations approach would warrant a corresponding reduction in the fishing rights of the nation causing such injury to the fisheries.

UPSTREAM/DOWNSTREAM NATION RIGHTS AND OBLIGATIONS

With an understanding of the ways that onstream dams can adversely affect fisheries and fishers, and with an understanding of general principles of international fisheries law, we can now consider the application of general principles of international water law to the question of the impacts of onstream dams on fisheries.

Equitable Utilization and Vital Human Needs

Up until around 1900, there was some limited support for a principle of international water law known as "absolute territorial sovereignty." Pursuant to this theory, when a watercourse flowed from upstream nations through downstream nations, the upstream nations were lawfully entitled to capture or otherwise use all of the water resources that passed through its boundaries without any obligations to downstream nations. Upstream nations might voluntarily opt to enter into treaties with downstream nations regarding water resources, but such treaty arrangements were not mandated by generally accepted principles of international law. A well-known example of this approach is the 1895 opinion of US Attorney General, Judson Harmon, concerning whether the United States had any legal obligations to Mexico that curtailed the United States use of Rio Grange water. In an opinion that became known as the "Harmon Doctrine," Harmon found that the question of whether the United States' should "take any action from considerations of comity is a question which should be decided as one of policy only, because, in my opinion, the rules, principles, and precedents of international law impose no liability or obligation upon the United States."

In the twentieth century, the principle of absolute territorial sovereignty in international water law gave way to the principle of "limited territorial sover-eignty," a principle that itself was based on the concept of "equitable utiliza-tion." Equitable utilization posits that in a transboundary watershed all nations in the watershed have rights to equitably utilize the water resources, and all nations in the watershed have obligations to respect other nations' rights to such equitable usage. Further sources of international water law provided additional guidance on the scope and limits of what constituted equitable utilization.

Article 6(1) of the 1997 United Nations Convention on the Law of the Non-Navigational Uses of International Watercourses (1997 UN Watercourses Convention) presents a nonexhaustive indicative list of factors, the following of which should be considered in determining what constitutes equitable utilization of international watercourses between multiple nations:

a. Geographic, hydrographic, hydrological, climatic, ecological, and other factors of a natural character;
b. The social and economic needs of the watercourse States concerned;
c. The population dependent on the watercourse in each watercourse State;
d. The effects of the use or uses of the watercourse in one watercourse State on other watercourse States;
e. Existing and potential uses of the watercourse;
f. Conservation, protection, development, and economy of use of the water resources of the watercourse and the costs of measures taken to that effect;
g. The availability of alternatives, of corresponding value, to a particular planned or existing use.

The following Article 6(3) of the 1997 UN Watercourses Convention then explains: "The weight to be given each factor is to be determined by its importance in comparison with that of all other relevant factors. In determining what is a reasonable and equitable use, all relevant factors are to be considered together and a conclusion reached on the basis of the whole."

In connection with the impacts of onstream dams on fisheries and fishers, there are at least two potential ways that the international water law principle of equitable utilization may be implicated.

First, the international water law principle of equitable utilization can be readily paired and integrated with the international fisheries law principle of originations set forth in the Pacific Salmon Treaty and Article 11(c) of the UN Straddling Stocks Treaty. Article 6(1) of the 1997 UN Watercourses Convention provides that equitable utilization involves consideration of "ecological factors," "economic needs of the watercourse States concerned," "uses of the watercourse," and the "effects of the use or uses of the watercourse in one watercourse State on other watercourse States." All of these factors are consistent with an originations approach to the allocation of fishing rights on international watercourses, in that a nation whose onstream dams adversely impact fisheries and the fishers dependent on such fisheries would have their rights to catch such fisheries appropriately reduced vis-à-vis other nations that fish on the same international watercourse.

Second, there is a growing body of international water law which suggests that although there may be various factors to be considered in determining the equitable utilization of international watercourses, paramount consideration should be given to ensuring that "vital human needs" are met. For instance, Article 10(2) of the 1997 UN Watercourses Convention provides that a dispute between uses of an international watercourse shall be resolved "with special regard being given to the requirements of vital human needs." Consistent with Article 10(2) of the 1997 UN Watercourses Convention, international water law scholars have suggested that vital human needs should enjoy a higher priority among the various factors considered in equitable utilization determinations.[13] The recognition of a privileged place in international water law for water to meet vital human needs, however, begs the question of what water usage qualifies as a vital human need?

To date, the focus of vital human needs has been on ensuring sufficient water to meet basic drinking water and sanitation needs with an eye toward avoidance of life-threatening dehydration and of diseases associated with poor human waste sanitation. However, for nations or vulnerable populations within nations whose basic food supply is tied to the presence of freshwater fisheries, the concept of vital human needs can be expanded to include the obligation to operate onstream dams in a manner consistent with the conservation of such fisheries. To meet this obligation, nations that operate such onstream dams may need to provide for fish passage through/around dams and for sufficient downstream releases to avoid slack water conditions, salinity, and rising water temperatures below dams.

Avoidance of Significant Environmental Harm and Ecosystem Protection

In addition to the international water law principle of equitable utilization, there is also the obligation under international water law of each nation to avoid causing significant harm to other nations.

Article 7(1) of the 1997 UN Watercourses Convention provides "Watercourse States shall, in utilizing an international watercourse in their territories, take all appropriate measures to prevent the causing of significant harm to other watercourse States." Article 7(2) of the 1997 UN Watercourses Convention further adds that where significant harm nevertheless is caused to other watercourse States, the State whose use causes such harm shall take "all appropriate measures" to "eliminate or mitigate such harm and, where appropriate, to discuss the question of compensation."

Similarly, Article 12 of the International Law Association's 2004 Berlin Rules on Water Resources Law (Berlin Water Resources Law Rules) provides as follows: "Basin States shall in their respective territories manage the waters of an international drainage basin in an equitable and reasonable manner having due regard to their obligation not to cause significant harm to other basin States."

Additionally, Articles 20 and 22 of the 1997 UN Watercourses Convention address the questions of ecosystem protection and invasive species in the transboundary river basin context. Article 20 provides "Watercourse States shall, individually and where appropriate jointly, protect and preserve the ecosystems of international watercourses." Article 22 provides "Watercourse states shall take all measures necessary to prevent the introduction of species, alien or new, into an international watercourse which may have effects detrimental to the ecosystem of the watercourse resulting in significant harm to other watercourse States."

According to international water law expert Stephen McCaffrey, the "no significant harm" provision in Article 7 of the 1997 UN Watercourses Convention is likely to be construed broadly rather than narrowly to address adverse transboundary river impacts.[14] McCaffrey further notes that such significant harm is not limited to diversions or pollution of waters but could encompass other activities that result in "obstruction of fish migration" or "interference with the flow regime" or that otherwise have "negative impacts on the riverine ecosystems."[15]

Owen McIntyre, another recognized international water expert, explains that the "ecosystems approach employed enthusiastically in Articles 20–23 of the [1997 UN Watercourses Convention] might be expected to increase the likelihood of Article 7 being construed broadly, at least in relation to any ecological or environmental damage."[16]

There are several ways in which the presence and operation of onstream dams could be implicated by the aforementioned provisions and principles of international water law relating to avoidance of significant harm, ecosystem protection, and prevention of invasive species.

First, as McIntyre observes, the concept of significant environmental harm can include obstruction of fish migration and changes to instream flow regimes that negatively impact riverine ecosystems. Onstream dams frequently block the upstream and downstream migration of fish and often alter natural flow regimes creating slack water conditions, increased water temperatures, higher salinity levels, and reduced sediment/gravel transport. Depending on the severity of consequences to other watercourse nations, such impacts from onstream dams may qualify as significant harm. Pursuant to Articles 7(1) and 7(2) of the 1997 UN Watercourses Convention and Article 12 of the 2004 Berlin Rules on Water Resources Law, nations that operate onstream dams have an obligation to avoid such significant impacts on other watercourse nations and pursuant to Article 7(2) of the 1997 UN Watercourses Convention may be required to provide compensation for such harm.

Second, consistent with Articles 63(1) and 64(1) of UNCLOS, Article 11 of the UN Straddling Stocks Treaty and the ICJ's 1974 ruling in the *Icelandic Fisheries Case*, nations with fisheries that migrate and move between their respective jurisdictional waters have an obligation to cooperate in efforts to conserve and sustainably manage such fisheries. The operation by one nation of an onstream dam that undermined the conservation of a migratory fish species also present in the waters of another nation would implicate this obligation reflected in international fisheries law. More specifically, it would suggest an obligation on the part of the nation operating an onstream dam to reach agreement with other nations whose fisheries are impacted by the dam on what measures are needed to conserve the fisheries in question. Such agreement may pertain to such issues as the installation of fish passage, the timing and quantity of downstream releases of water, and the replacement downstream of sediment/gravel trapped behind the dam.

Third, there are situations where the presence and operation of onstream dams can contribute to the spread of invasive aquatic species. One example, discussed earlier, would be the invasive snails that have flourished in the Volta River in Ghana due to slack water conditions created by the Akosombo Dan.[17] Another example would be the spread of saline-tolerant fish species in rivers where reduced freshwater flow from upstream streams has led to saltwater intrusion. A final example would be where naturally muddy rivers (such as the Colorado River in North America) become increasingly clear due to sediments trapped behind dams, leading to the spread of fish adapted to clear water rather than muddy water conditions. These impacts from onstream dams would implicate Article 22 of the 1997 UN Watercourses Convention, which requires nations to take necessary measures to prevent the introduction of invasive species that "may have effects detrimental to the ecosystem of the watercourse resulting in significant harm to other watercourse States."

INTERNATIONAL ENVIRONMENTAL IMPACT ASSESSMENT LAW

Apart from the sources of international fisheries law and international water law already discussed, there are also provisions of international environmental law generally and international water law more specifically that pertain to the obligation of nations to conduct environmental impact assessments (EIA) when transnational impacts are involved. As discussed below, the sources of international law on transboundary EIA have particular application in regard to the construction and operation of onstream dams and the effects of such dams on fisheries and fishers.

In terms of general international environmental law, the 1991 Espoo United Nations Convention on Environmental Impact Assessment in a Transboundary Context (Espoo EIA Convention) sets forth several relevant provisions. At the outset, it should be noted that the provisions of the Espoo EIA Convention only apply to the list of activities provided in Appendix I to the agreement. In terms of this chapter, it is important to note that Appendix I to the Espoo EIA Convention expressly lists "Large dams and reservoirs" among the activities covered by its provisions.

Article 2(1) of the Espoo EIA Convention states, "The parties shall, either individually or jointly, take all appropriate and effective measures to prevent, reduce and control significant adverse transboundary environmental impacts from proposed activities." Article 2(3) provides, "The party of origin shall ensure that in accordance with the provisions of this Convention an EIA is undertaken prior to a decision to authorize or undertake a proposed activity listed in Appendix I that is likely to cause a significant adverse transboundary impact."

Article 4(1) of the Espoo EIA Convention states, "The environmental impact assessment documentation to be submitted to the competent authority of the Party of origin shall contain, at a minimum, the information described in Appendix II." Among other things, Appendix II requires an environmental impact assessment to include information on reasonable alternatives to the proposed activities, the potential environmental impact of the proposed activities and alternatives and an estimate of their significance, mitigation measures to keep adverse environmental impacts to a minimum, and monitoring programs for post-project analysis.

Article 7 of the Espoo EIA Convention provides additional guidance on the "post-project analysis" listed in Appendix II. Article 7(1) provides for the preparation of post-project analysis to be undertaken "with a view to achieving the objectives listed in Appendix V." Appendix V provides that the objectives of post-project analysis include "(a) Monitoring compliance with the conditions as set out in the authorization or approval of the activity and the effectiveness of mitigation measures; (b) Review of an impact for proper management and in order to cope with uncertainties; (c) Verification of past predictions in order to transfer experience to future activities of the same type."

The approach reflected in the Espoo EIA Convention is reinforced in other water-specific international agreements, such as Article 12 of the 1997 UN Watercourses Convention, Article 3(1)(h) of the 1991 Helsinki Convention on the Protection and Use of Transboundary Watercourses and International Lakes, and Article 29(1) of the Berlin Water Resources Law Rules. For example, Article 29(1) of the Berlin Water Resources Law Rules provides that nations "shall undertake prior and continuing assessment of the impact of programs, projects and activities that may have a significant effect on the aquatic environmental or the sustainable development of waters."

In regard to EIA obligations related to onstream dams, the provisions of Article 7 and Appendix V of the Espoo EIA Convention and Article 29(1) of the Berlin Water Resources Law Rules merit particular attention. These provisions highlight that the scope of EIA for onstream dams should not be limited to the initial construction of such facilities but should also encompass the continuing operations of such facilities. The "post-project analysis" provided for in the Espoo EIA Convention and the "continuing assessment" provided for in the Berlin Water Resources Law Rules speak to the ways that the continuing operations of dams can be modified and adjusted to reduce adverse environmental impacts on fisheries and fishers, and the role that ongoing environmental assessment of dam operations can ensure that such modification and adjustment takes place. For example, if post-construction monitoring demonstrates that an onstream dam is resulting in significant adverse impacts on fisheries, it may be possible to modify the dam to add appropriate fish passage or to modify water release schedules to improve downstream aquatic habitat.

The Federal Power Act in the United States offers one model of a legal regime to assess the post-construction operations of onstream dams. Under this law, operators of most dams can obtain licenses to operate from the Federal Energy Regulatory Commission (FERC) for 40 years. Five years prior to the expiration of a license, the operator must apply to FERC to relicense the dam. As part of this relicensing process, the operator of the dam must conduct studies related to fisheries, and FERC must prepare a comprehensive environmental impact assessment, consult with fishery agencies regarding changes in operation to reduce adverse impacts on fisheries, and incorporate such changes in any new license to the dam operator.[18] The relicensing process under the Federal Power Act provides a regulatory mechanism to fulfil the "post-project analysis" and "continuing assessment" objectives set forth in the Espoo EIA Convention and the Berlin Water Resources Law Rules.

ONGOING REVIEW AND MITIGATION OF DAM OPERATIONS

When drafting laws or negotiating treaties that focus on the construction and operation of onstream dams in transboundary basins, the following three considerations should be kept front and center.

First, the impact of onstream dams on fisheries is not simply a matter of ecology and biodiversity. It may also be a matter of poverty and human health. There are situations where the fisheries impacted by onstream dams serve as a basic food source for local populations, and in such situations the failure of dam operators to provide for fish passage or adequate releases of water to maintain fish habitat may improperly impinge on vital human needs under international water law principles. There may also be situations where local communities are heavily dependent economically on the fisheries impacted by onstream dams, and in such situations international water law and international fisheries law suggest the interests of such communities should be given careful consideration and that dam operators may have an obligation to compensate such communities for resulting injuries.

Second, the international fisheries law principle of originations may provide guidance on decisions regarding the construction and operation of onstream dams in transboundary watersheds. The originations principle provides that a nation's right to catch fish stocks that migrate through the waters of multiple nations should correspond to the extent to which the nation's facilities and activities contribute to or undermine the conservation of the fish stocks in question. To the extent the onstream dams in one nation reduce the abundance and health of fish stocks that migrate through the waters of another nation, the nation that operates its dams in this manner should find its right to catch such fish stocks reduced.

Finally, under international water law and general international environmental law, prior to constructing an onstream dam that may have significant environmental effects on other nations, the nation where the dam will be located has an obligation to prepare an EIA that addresses and appropriately mitigates these transboundary impacts.

Moreover, and of critical importance, consistent with the "post-project analysis" provisions of the Espoo EIA Convention and the "continuous assessment" provisions of the Berlin Water Resources Law Rules, nations that operate onstream dams have an obligation to environmentally assess the post-construction operations of such facilities. Many of the harmful effects of onstream dams can be ameliorated by modifications to how such dams operate: fish passage elements can be added; the amount and timing of water released downstream can be changed to protect fisheries habitat below the dam; sediment and gravel can be supplemented to offset sediment and gravel trapped behind the dam. Such modifications are only likely to occur if laws and treaties contain provisions obligating dam operators to conduct post-construction monitoring of impacts on fisheries and obligating the adoption of appropriate mitigation measures to address the fisheries' impacts revealed through such monitoring.

Ongoing environmental assessment of dam operations gives effect to Article 20 of the 1997 UN Watercourses Convention which calls for nations to protect the ecosystems of international watercourses. Because the aquatic ecosystems and fisheries entitled to such protection are present throughout the lifetime an onstream dam operates, the environmental assessment of the effects on such ecosystems and fisheries must continue during the lifetime of the facility as well.

Given the significant impact of dams and dam operations on downstream flow conditions in rivers, a strengthening of international law requirements for dams related to vital human needs, fisheries protection and EIA is likely to result in strengthening the legal basis for enhanced instream flows below such dams.

Notes

1. World Commission on Dams, *Dams and Development: A New Framework for Decision-Making* (2000 Report) p. 8.
2. Melanie E. Kleiss, *The Salmon Hatchery Myth: When Bad Policy Happens to Good Science*, 6 MINNESOTA JOURNAL OF LAW, SCIENCE AND TECHNOLOGY 420 (2004).
3. *Case Concerning the Gabcikovo-Nagymaros Project (Hungary/Slovakia)* (International Court of Justice, The Hague, 25 September 1997).
4. *Remediation of the Environmental Impacts of the Akosombo and Kpong Dam in Ghana* (2008 report by the Volta Basin Research Project, University of Ghana).
5. *Remediation of the Environmental Impacts of the Akosombo and Kpong Dam in Ghana* (2008 report by the Volta Basin Research Project, University of Ghana).
6. Trout Unlimited, *Healing Troubled Waters: Preparing Trout and Salmon Habitat for a Changing Climate* (2007 Report).
7. Paul Stanton Kibel, *Passage and Flow Considered Anew: Wild Salmon Restoration Via Hydro Relicensing*, 37 PUBLIC LAND & RESOURCES LAW REVIEW 1 (2016).
8. Paul Stanton Kibel, *Sea level Rise, Saltwater Intrusion and Endangered Fisheries – Shifting Baselines for the Bay Delta Conservation Plan*, 38 ENVIRONS 259 (2015).

9. *Remediation of the Environmental Impacts of the Akosombo and Kpong Dam in Ghana* (2008 report by the Volta Basin Research Project, University of Ghana).

10. *Remediation of the Environmental Impacts of the Akosombo and Kpong Dam in Ghana* (2008 report by the Volta Basin Research Project, University of Ghana).

11. 1974 I.C.J. 3 (1974).

12. J. A. Yanagida, *The Pacific Salmon Treaty*, 81(3) AMERICAN JOURNAL OF INTERNATIONAL LAW 577–592 (1987).

13. Own McIntyre, *Environmental Protection of International Watercourses under International Law* (Ashgate 2007) at 109; E. Hey, "Sustainable Use of Shared Water Resources: The Need for a Paradigmatic Shift in International Water Law", in THE PEACEFUL MANAGEMENT OF TRANSBOUNDARY RESOURCES (Graham Trotman/Martinus Nijhoff, Dordrecht/Boston/London, 1995) 127–152, at 127.

14. Stephen McCaffrey, THE LAW OF INTERNATIONAL WATERCOURSES: NON-NAVIGATIONAL USES (Oxford University Press) at 348.

15. Stephen McCaffrey, THE LAW OF INTERNATIONAL WATERCOURSES: NON-NAVIGATIONAL USES (Oxford University Press) at 348.

16. Owen McIntyre, ENVIRONMENTAL PROTECTION OF INTERNATIONAL WATERCOURSES UNDER INTERNATIONAL LAW (Ashgate 2007) at 92.

17. *Remediation of the Environmental Impacts of the Akosombo and Kpong Dam in Ghana* (2008 report by the Volta Basin Research Project, University of Ghana).

18. Paul Stanton Kibel, *Passage and Flow Considered Anew: Wild Salmon Restoration Via Hydro Relicensing*, 37 PUBLIC LAND & RESOURCES LAW REVIEW 1 (2016).

12

Instream Rights and Irrigation Subsidies

There are competing demands for fresh water. Farms look to it as an irrigation source, cities rely on it for drinking water, and fisheries and fishermen depend on it for instream flow. When governments subsidize the costs of providing fresh water for irrigation in agricultural production, such subsidization can result in tiered water pricing. With tiered pricing, agricultural producers pay the government less than other water users. This tiered pricing can distort the water marketplace in a manner that can encourage wasteful irrigation practices and that can leave insufficient water instream for fisheries.

As the authors of the book *Legal Control of Water Resources* explained, in reference to irrigation subsidies in the United States, "[S]ubsidies have lessened water users' fiscal incentive to conserve. There is far less reason to invest in expensive irrigation control or to line canals when you are receiving water for only a fraction of the costs."[1] This same dynamic is true outside of the United States, such as subsidized irrigation for rice-growing in India and Japan and subsidized irrigation for cotton-growing in Brazil. Where irrigation subsidies undercut the incentive for the agricultural sector to use water resources more efficiently, it becomes more difficult to implement policies to allow additional water to remain flowing instream.

The federal Bureau of Reclamation (Reclamation) operates water infrastructure systems throughout the western United States that provide irrigation for agriculture, and the largest Reclamation system is the Central Valley Project (CVP) in California. Construction of the CVP began in the 1940s, and today the CVP includes twenty water storage reservoirs with a combined storage capacity of approximately 11 million-acre feet and approximately 500 miles of canals and aqueducts.[2]

Central Valley Project irrigation subsidization has been the subject of domestic criticism in the United States for several decades. This criticism has come not only from environmental groups generally associated with the political left (focused on how CVP freshwater diversions have impacted California's fisheries and led to the planting of water intensive crops such as alfalfa, rice, and cotton) but also from free market advocacy groups generally associated with the political right. For instance, in 2012, the conservative Cato Institute released a paper titled *Cutting the Bureau of Reclamation and Reforming Water Markets*, which concluded that CVP irrigation pricing is "corporate welfare which comes at the expense of average taxpayers, citizens and the environment." The 2012 Cato Institute report explained:

> One early decision by the Bureau of Reclamation led to large investment inefficiencies for much of the 20th century. The 1902 legislation states 'charges shall be determined with a view of return to the reclamation fund the estimated cost of construction of the project.' In interpreting this, the Bureau decided to exclude interest costs, so that project beneficiaries would be required to pay back only the original project costs over time. The effect was to greatly reduce the real value of repayments, thus creating large subsidies on Reclamation projects.[3]
>
> ...
>
> Agriculture has received by far the largest subsidies from Reclamation projects. In calculating repayment requirements, Reclamation allocates substantial costs related to irrigation to other project beneficiaries, such as power customers and urban water customers. Also, a change in the law in 1939 allowed the bureau to reduce costs to irrigators on the basis of 'ability to pay' which has saved farmers billions of dollars over the decades.[4]

The observations in the 2012 Cato Institute report paralleled the findings in the 2005 Oxford University Press book *Fresh Water and International Economic Law*:

> In the United States ... the federal government is subsidizing irrigation systems in various ways. It incorporated a two-stage subsidy in the way it sets prices for irrigation water. First, the contractual water prices were based on an irrigator's ability to pay, rather than on the actual costs of supplying the water. Second, no interest was charged on the loans to fund construction costs. Researchers calculated a water subsidy of nearly $100 million for seventeen projects alone. The annual irrigation subsidies for the United States for such underpricing have been estimated as between $2 billion and $2.5 billion.[5]

The dispute over Reclamation irrigation subsidies, in general, and CVP subsidies in particular, may now be moving from the domestic to the international arena. The 1994 World Trade Organization Agreement on Subsidies and Countervailing Measures (WTO Subsidies Agreement) provides that one WTO member country may impose countervailing tariffs against another WTO member country that makes a financial contribution to domestic enterprises, and that "government revenue otherwise due that is foregone" can constitute a financial contribution.[6] The WTO Subsidies Agreement further provides that "government revenue ... otherwise due that is foregone" can qualify as a "financial contribution" and that governments must be paid "adequate remuneration" for goods provided.[7]

In terms of Reclamation and CVP water pricing, if subsidized irrigation is found to qualify as "foregone revenue" or "inadequate remuneration" under WTO rules, this may provide the basis for other nations to impose tariffs against US goods. Moreover, this basis for other nations to impose tariffs against the United States may apply not only to the CVP but also to other Reclamation projects in the American West.

RECLAMATION AND CVP IRRIGATION PRICING

The Reclamation Project Act of 1939 (RPA) set forth the initial authority for Reclamation to recover its investment in constructing, operating, and maintaining water projects.[8] The RPA provided for Reclamation to enter into long-term water service contracts (often for 40 years) for projects such as the CVP. The prices charged to Central Valley farmers by Reclamation pursuant to the RPA for CVP water delivery contracts fell far short of actual cost recovery.

The reasons for this shortfall were explained in a 2006 paper prepared by the Congressional Budget Office (CBO), titled *How Federal Policies Affect the Allocation of Water*. The 2006 CBO paper noted the following in regard to the CVP:

> Irrigators are responsible for paying $1.3 million of the project's federal construction cost of $3.6 billion (in nominal dollars). Originally, irrigators had renewable 40-year water service contracts that provided for water deliveries but not necessarily for repaying the $1.3 billion by the end of the contract term. The Bureau of Reclamation intended for the contract prices to cover only operation and maintenance (O&M) expenses and a portion of construction costs. However, the prices were not even sufficient to cover O&M expenses, which increased over time. Deficits accrued and no payments were made for construction costs. According to the most recent figures available, as of September 30, 2004, irrigators had met 14.2 percent of their total repayment obligation.[9]

In response to criticisms regarding the lax repayment and cost recovery terms in the CVP water delivery contracts, the federal Central Valley Improvement Act (CVPIA) was enacted in 1992.[10] Although CVPIA resulted in certain changes to the terms of renewed CVP water delivery contracts, such as reduced duration, research indicates that post-CVPIA contracts for CVP irrigation water are still well undermarket. For instance, in 2004, the Environmental Working Group published its *California Water Subsidies* report, which determined that CVP irrigation users were getting a discount of between 55–90 percent below market for the water they received:

> Depending on how the market value of the water is defined, CVP farmers are receiving between $60 million and $416 million in water subsidies each year. The first figure [$60 million] represents the subsidy if the water is priced at the Bureau of Reclamation's so-called 'full cost rate,' which in practice is much less than the actual full cost of delivering water to recipients. The higher figure [$416 million] comes from comparing the average price for CVP water to the estimated costs of replacement water supplies for proposed dams and reservoirs on the San Joaquin River. An intermediate figure is $305 million a year, reflecting the difference between the average CVP rate and the price paid for CVP water by the Environmental Water Account, a state-federal joint agency to restore fish and wildlife habitat in the Bay Delta.[11]

According to the 2004 Environmental Working Group report, whether one relies on the costs-recovery methodology or a comparative evaluation of pricing with other markets for water, CVP irrigation subsidies are substantial in monetary terms.

THE WTO RULES ON SUBSIDIES AND FOREGONE REVENUE

The WTO Subsidies Agreement is based on what is referred to as a "traffic light" system with three basic categories of subsidies. The first category is "green light" subsidies that are permitted. The second category is "red light" subsidies that are prohibited outright. The third category is "amber light" subsidies that are "actionable." "Amber light" or "actionable" subsidies can be maintained by a WTO member country but other WTO member countries may be entitled to impose "countervailing" measures against the country that maintains an "actionable" subsidy. Such countervailing measures might include equivalent tariffs imposed on the import of goods from the country maintaining the actionable subsidy.

The WTO Subsidies Agreement provides that an "amber light" subsidy may exist when a financial contribution is made to a domestic enterprise, and that "financial contributions" may include "government revenue otherwise due that is foregone." This means such a subsidy is not prohibited but that other countries injured by the subsidy may be entitled under WTO rules to impose countervailing tariffs against the country that maintains the subsidy.

The WTO Subsidies Agreement does not set forth a definition of what constitutes "government revenue otherwise due that is foregone." However, some guidance on this question can be gleaned from Article 14(d) of the WTO Subsidies Agreement, which suggests that a determination of whether the domestic government is being paid adequate remuneration for a good can often be determined in relation to "prevailing market conditions" in the country for the good. Some additional guidance can also be found in previous WTO decisions regarding domestic subsidies.

The 2002 WTO Appellate Body FSC Report

In 2002, the WTO Appellate Body issued its Report in *United States – Tax Treatment for Foreign Sales Corporation (WTO Appellate Body FSC Report)*.[12] This case involved a challenge by the European Communities against the US policy of non-taxation of income earned by entities recognized under US law as Foreign Sales Corporations. In the *WTO Appellate Body FSC Report*, a narrow construction of "revenue otherwise due" proposed by the United States was rejected. Instead, the WTO Appellate Body held as follows:

> Our examination as to whether there is revenue foregone that is 'otherwise due' must be based on actual substantive realities and not be restricted to pure formalism ... A government could opt to bestow financial contributions in the form of fiscal incentives simply by modulating the 'outer boundary' of its 'tax jurisdiction' or by manipulating the definition of the tax base to accommodate any 'exclusion' or 'exemption' or 'exception' it desired, so that there could never be a foregoing of revenue 'otherwise due.' This would have the effect of reducing [Article 1.1 of the WTO Subsidies Agreement] to 'redundancy and inutility' and cannot be the appropriate implication to draw.[13]

The report then went on to clarify: "The normative benchmark for determining whether revenue foregone is otherwise due must allow a comparison of the fiscal treatment of comparable income, in the hands of taxpayers in similar situations."[14]

To the extent the United State attempted to counter a WTO challenge to CVP irrigation pricing on the grounds that additional revenue from irrigators is not 'otherwise due' because Reclamation has not adopted policies (or entered into water deliver contracts) that require the payment of such additional revenues, this more narrow formalistic line of reasoning would run counter to the approach taken by the WTO *Appellate Body FSC Report*.

If the approach employed by the WTO *Appellate Body FSC Report* is followed in the context of a WTO challenge to CVP irrigation pricing, the focus would be on the "substantive realities" of the CVP undermarket pricing, which presumably would look more to the types of considerations and evidence highlighted in the 2004 Environmental Working Group report.

The 2003 WTO Appellate Body Softwood Lumber Report

The interpretation of Article 14(d) of the WTO Subsidies Agreement, mentioned earlier, was front and center in the 2003 WTO Appellate Body Report on *United States – Final Countering Duty Determination with Respect to Certain Softwood Lumber from Canada (WTO Appellate Body Softwood Lumber Report)*.[15] This case involved claims that Canada was providing access to public forests to Canadian logging companies at undermarket rates, and that such rates constituted actionable subsidies under the WTO Subsidies Agreement.

The *WTO Appellate Body Softwood Lumber Report* found: "Although Article 14(d) does not dictate that private prices are to be used as the exclusive benchmark in all situations, it does emphasize by its terms that prices of similar goods sold by private suppliers in the country of provision are the primary benchmark that investigating authorities must use when determining whether goods have been provided by a government for less than adequate remuneration ... This approach reflects the fact that private prices in the market of provision will generally represent an appropriate measure of the 'adequate remuneration' for the provision of goods."[16]

Although confirming that prevailing market prices for the good in question will serve as the "primary benchmark" for determining whether a government has received adequate remuneration for a good provided, the *WTO Appellate Body Softwood Lumber Report* recognized that such an approach may not be appropriate in every instance. More specifically, it noted that in a situation where there is in effect no "prevailing market conditions" for the good due to the overwhelmingly predominant role of government in providing the particular good, reference to some other comparative reference may be warranted. It therefore included some discussions of potential "alternative benchmarks." In this regard, the *WTO Appellate Body Softwood Lumber Report* found that "alternative methods for determining the adequacy of remuneration could include proxies constructed on the basis of production costs."[17]

In the context of a potential WTO challenge to CVP irrigation prices, the *WTO Appellate Body Softwood Lumber Report* may be pertinent in at least two aspects. First, the report confirmed that in most situations, prevailing market prices should serve as the benchmark for determining whether the amount paid to the government by the recipients of the benefit of this good constituted adequate remuneration. Second, the report suggested that to the extent the government's predominant role in providing the particular good makes a comparison to prevailing market prices inappropriate, an appropriate proxy "alternative benchmark" to use may be "production" costs (which in the case of the CVP might constitute construction and operation and maintenance (O&M) costs).

The 2007 WTO Cotton Subsidies Report

Another potentially informative case may be the 2007 WTO Compliance Panel report in *United States – Subsidies on Upland Cotton* (*WTO Cotton Subsidies Report*).[18] In this dispute, Brazil had alleged that the US cotton export credit program amounted to an actionable subsidy under the WTO Subsidies Agreement. In support of this position, Brazil asked the WTO Compliance Panel to recognize the export credit rates established by the Organization for Economic Cooperation and Development (OECD) as evidentiary support that the pricing under the US cotton export credit program qualified as an actionable subsidy.

The WTO Compliance Panel found that the *OECD Export Credit Arrangement* rates provided an "indication" of whether the US cotton export credit rates were "sufficient to cover the long-term operating costs and losses" of the US program. According to the Compliance Panel, the "magnitude of the difference" between the OECD export credit rates and the US export credit rates (OECD fees were on average 106 percent more than US fees) suggested that US pricing "is insufficient to cover the long-term operating costs and losses of the programme."[19]

The *WTO Cotton Subsidies Report* did not focus specifically on the "foregone revenue" provision of the WTO Subsidies Agreement. Nonetheless, the *WTO Cotton Subsidies Report*'s willingness to look to accepted outside costing standards (such as OECD export credit rates) as a basis for determining the existence of a subsidy may be pertinent to an evaluation of whether CVP irrigation pricing is WTO compliant. The ruling in the *WTO Cotton Subsidies Report* suggests that valuating CVP irrigation water pricing against accepted outside standards as costs-recovery methodology or comparative market rates may be appropriate.

NOT JUST THE CVP

Much of the preceding analysis has centered on the CVP and the extent to which Reclamation's CVP Irrigation prices may constitute an actionable amber light subsidy under the WTO Subsidies Agreement. This analysis, however, may be applicable beyond the CVP.

In addition to the CVP, there are many other Reclamation water projects in the arid west of the United States, such as the Rio Grande Project in New Mexico, the Salt River Project in Arizona, the Boulder Canyon Project on the Nevada–Arizona Border, the Newlands Project in Nevada, and the Parker–Davis Project in California. The basic methodology used in this chapter to examine whether Reclamation's prices for CVP irrigation water qualify as an actionable WTO subsidy can be employed to examine WTO compliance for other Reclamation projects.

For example, consider the case of Reclamation's Newlands Project. The Newlands Project, formerly known as the Truckee–Carson Project, predates the CVP and its initial components were constructed from 1903–1904. The project delivers irrigation water to approximately 55,000 acres of Nevada cropland in the Lahontan Valley and bench lands located in Churchill, Lyon, Storey, and Washoe counties.[20] In addition to alfalfa, a significant portion of the crops grown with Newlands Project irrigation water are cereal crops, such as barley, wheat, and oats. Just as with the irrigation pricing for the CVP, the price for Newlands Project irrigation deliveries is established pursuant to long-term water service contracts with Reclamation, which in turn are established pursuant to the regulatory pricing approach laid out in the 1902 Reclamation Act and the 1939 Reclamation Project Act (with no interest on initial construction costs and periodic reduction in prices due to farms' "ability to pay").

To evaluate whether Reclamation's Newlands Project irrigation pricing constitutes an actionable amber light subsidy under the WTO Subsidies Agreement, the following information and determinations would be involved: determination of the construction costs (in initial and current dollars) for the Newlands Project infrastructure; the Newlands Project irrigation pricing in water service contracts with Reclamation; a comparison of Reclamation's Newlands Project irrigation pricing with the construction costs and ongoing O&M costs for the Newlands Project; a comparison of Reclamation's Newlands Project irrigation pricing with prevailing water marketplace prices in the area that receives water from the project; and identification of whether there are other WTO member nations, such as those that grow and export cereal crops like barley, wheat, and oats, which are being adversely impacted by the reduced prices charged by Nevada farms growing and selling these same cereal crops.

The WTO compliance analysis presented in this chapter can therefore be replicated for other non-CVP Reclamation irrigation projects around the country.

GETTING PRICES RIGHT

Domestically in the United States, the debate over Reclamation and CVP irrigation pricing has so far played out more in the arena of politics and public policy than the law. Regardless of whether the critiques of Reclamation and CVP irrigation prices have come from groups on the political right such as the Cato Institute or groups on the political left such as the Environmental Working Group, the characterization of such undermarket prices as a "subsidy" has been used to convey the view that the pricing is unwise from a policy standpoint rather than that such pricing is unlawful.

Pursuant to WTO rules and remedies, however, it appears the designation of Reclamation and CVP water prices as a subsidy may have independent legal consequences under international law.

The United States might respond to such a WTO challenge by noting that Reclamation is contractually obligated to provide CVP irrigation at such undermarket prices. The United States' contention here might well be correct, but the fact that Reclamation may have opted to enter into long-term contracts with California farms to provide subsidized water should not immunize such undermarket pricing from being characterized as an actionable amber light subsidy under the WTO Subsidies Agreement. Per WTO rules, an otherwise actionable subsidy is not rendered non-actionable merely because it is implemented pursuant to lawful contracts.

In his 1948 book *The Thirsty Land: The Story of the Central Valley Project*, author Robert de Roos argued that California needed the CVP to "find ways to use every drop of available water, to allow none to go to waste."[21] Due to Reclamation's tiered and undermarket pricing scheme for CVP irrigation water, however, the CVP's effects have been quite different from what de Roos forecasts.

By providing farms with inexpensive access to extensive quantities of fresh water, Reclamation's CVP has itself led to wasteful irrigation practices, the planting of crops inappropriate to the Central Valley's climate, loss of instream flow to sustain native fisheries and maintain water quality, and the farming of land with unsuitable drainage. As a result, there is a growing consensus that much of CVP irrigation water is in fact wasted, and this waste comes at the expense of urban residents' water access and prices, and the sacrifice of instream flows needed to support native fisheries and fishermen. The same could be said for many other Reclamation water projects throughout the United States.

Moreover, the existing Reclamation pricing scheme for irrigation water fails to take account of the economic value associated with keeping sufficient water instream. That is, in maintaining a vibrant commercial fishery sector that depends on instream flows, and in maintaining a secure and healthy water supply for communities. These economic aspects to instream flow fall outside the assumptions that currently underlie Reclamation irrigation pricing.

Permitting recourse to WTO rules and tribunals to address the problem of Reclamation's subsidized irrigation not only holds the prospect of addressing fairness considerations between WTO trading nations but also holds the prospect of reducing wasteful irrigation practices and shifting to production of less water intensive crops in the American West. This, in turn, could make additional water available for instream use to sustain fisheries and to supplemental already strained urban water supplies – a result that many within the United States might welcome. If the United States finds itself on the receiving end of a WTO claim regarding Reclamation irrigation prices, it can therefore be anticipated that there may well be domestic environmental, fishery, and urban water interests in the United States that could align themselves with the foreign claimants.

From a domestic perspective, recourse to WTO subsidy disciplines can therefore be understood as a potential means of enlisting international trade law to return the CVP specifically, and Reclamation more generally, to their original intended purposes of preventing the wasteful use of scare freshwater resources in the American West.

As other countries outside of the United States pursue their own efforts to improve water conservation and efficiency, they may also want to assess the extent to which undermarket pricing of irrigation water undercuts such efforts. If water is truly a valuable resource, and if there needs to be a better balance struck between the value of instream flow and the value of out of stream diversions, then water used for irrigation needs to be priced accordingly.

Notes

1. Thompson, Leshy, Abrams & Zellmer, LEGAL CONTROL OF WATER RESOURCES (6th Edition, 2018) pp. 842–843.
2. Delta Vision Task Force, *Overview of the Central Valley Project Financing, Cost Allocation and Repayment Issues* (2008) at p. 4.

3. Chris Edwards & Peter J. Hill, *Cutting the Bureau of Reclamation and Reforming Water Markets* (2012 Cato Institute Report) at p̃. 3.
4. Chris Edwards & Peter J. Hill, *Cutting the Bureau of Reclamation and Reforming Water Markets* (2012 Cato Institute Report) at p. 4.
5. Nathalie Bernasconi-Osterwalder, *Water Agriculture and Subsidies* in the *International Trading System*, in Fresh Water and International Economic Law (Oxford University Press, 2005) at p. 44.
6. WTO Agreement on Subsidies, parts I-V, in Kevin Kennedy, International Trade Regulation: Readings, Cases, Notes and Problems (Wolters Kluwer, 2009).
7. WTO Agreement on Subsidies, parts I-V, in Kevin Kennedy, International Trade Regulation: Readings, Cases, Notes and Problems (Wolters Kluwer, 2009), Articles 1.1(a), 11.2, and 11.9.
8. Delta Vision Task Force, *Overview of the Central Valley Project Financing, Cost Allocation and Repayment Issues* (2008) at p. 7.
9. Congressional Budget Office, *How Federal Policies Affect the Allocation of Water* (2006) pp. 5–7.
10. Central Valley Project Improvement Act, Public Law No. 102–575, title XXXIV, 106 Stat. 4600, 4706 (1992).
11. *California Water Subsidies: Findings* (2004 Environmental Working Group Report) at pp. 15–19.
12. WTO Appellate Body Report, *United States – Tax Treatment for Foreign Sales Corporations*, WT/DS108/AB/RW (January 14, 2002).
13. WTO Panel Report, *United States – Tax Treatment for Foreign Sales Corporations*, paragraphs 8.37 and 8.39, WT/DS108/RW (August 20, 2001).
14. WTO Appellate Body Report, *United States – Tax Treatment for Foreign Sales Corporations*, WT/DS108/AB/RW (January 14, 2002), paragraphs 88 and 90.
15. WTO Appellate Body Report, *United States – Final Countervailing Duty Determination with Respect to Certain Softwood Lumber from Canada*, WT/DS257/SB/R (January 19, 2004).
16. WTO Appellate Body Report, *United States – Final Countervailing Duty Determination with Respect to Certain Softwood Lumber from Canada*, WT/DS257/SB/R (January 19, 2004), paragraph 90.
17. WTO Appellate Body Report, *United States – Final Countervailing Duty Determination with Respect to Certain Softwood Lumber from Canada*, WT/DS257/SB/R (January 19, 2004), paragraphs 104–106.
18. WTO Panel Report, *United States – Subsidies on Upland Cotton*, WT/DS267/RW (December 18, 2007).

19. WTO Panel Report, *United States – Subsidies on Upland Cotton*, WT/DS267/RW (December 18, 2007) at pp. 167–169.
20. Joe Simmons, THE NEWLANDS PROJECT (Bureau of Reclamation, 1996).
21. Robert de Roos, THE THIRSTY LAND: THE STORY OF THE CENTRAL VALLEY PROJECT (Stanford University Press, 1948) at p. 3.

13

Instream Rights and Pacific Salmon

When Canada and the United States entered into the Pacific Salmon Treaty in 1985, a primary mutual concern was to curtail overfishing at sea to avoid depletion of salmon stocks originating in Canadian and US freshwater streams. To further the conservation of such salmon stocks, the Pacific Salmon Treaty contains provisions to encourage and reward Canada and the United States for increasing the "production" of salmon originating in their respective streams.

To increase the production of salmon, Canada and the United States often focused on artificial propagation in hatcheries rather than preserving spawning grounds and natural habitat for wild salmon. This focus on hatcheries to produce salmon coincided with a period of more intensive onstream dam building, more intensive logging of slopes adjacent to and upland of salmon spawning grounds, and more intensive diversion of water out-of-stream for farms and cities that reduced instream flow. The artificially propagated salmon from hatcheries were intended to replace the wild salmon runs displaced because of habitat loss due to dams, logging, and diversions.

In terms of implementation of the Pacific Salmon Treaty, the interplay between increased hatchery salmon production and the conservation objective of preventing overfishing occurs through the Pacific Salmon Commission's "abundance forecasts," which serve as the basis to establish the total joint catch limits for the Canadian and US fishing fleets. Under the current methodology used by the Pacific Salmon Commission, the volume of salmon released by hatcheries is a key input in forecasting future abundance of salmon. Pursuant to this conservation methodology, an increase in hatchery salmon production translates into higher abundance forecasts, which in turn justifies higher limits for the total joint catch of salmon at sea.

The aforementioned conservation model for the Pacific Salmon Treaty might have initially made some sense in the abstract, but it has worked poorly in practice. This is because the Pacific Salmon Commission's abundance forecasts, which are based in considerable part on data regarding the volume of salmon produced in hatcheries, have generally *over-estimated* abundance as compared with actually documented abundance. The result is that the Pacific Salmon Commission has often set total joint catch limits too high given actual (as opposed to forecast) abundance of salmon stocks.

This chapter provides a critical analysis of the frequent discrepancy between actual abundance of Pacific salmon stocks and the Pacific Salmon Commission's abundance forecasts, and posits that this discrepancy may be the result of a fundamental faulty assumption in the Pacific Salmon Treaty's conservation model. This faulty assumption is that of continuing to treat wild salmon and artificially propagated hatchery salmon as similar in terms of anticipated survival and reproduction rates, and also the failure to take account of scientific studies documenting that salmon released from hatcheries tend to outcompete wild salmon stocks as the "mixed stocks" move downstream together to the ocean. This research indicates that hatchery salmon are not supplementing wild salmon stocks so much as directly contributing to the decline of wild salmon stocks. In this sense, hatcheries may more accurately be understood as a cause of salmon stock declines rather than a solution to such declines.

The identification of these faulty assumptions and missing elements in the Pacific Salmon Commission's conservation model suggests that the restoration of Pacific salmon stocks, and of achieving actual improvement in abundance, may ultimately depend on the restoration of wild salmon stocks. The restoration of Pacific wild salmon stocks may therefore hinge more on improving instream conditions and habitat, which in practical terms means facilitating the upstream and downstream passage of salmon, reducing logging on slopes adjacent to and upland of streams where salmon spawn, and curtailing out-of-stream diversions to ensure there is adequate instream flow to maintain cooler instream temperatures.

Beyond the Pacific Salmon Treaty between Canada and the United States, Japan and Russia have also developed bilateral arrangements for the conservation and management of salmon that spawn in their respective inland rivers. In terms of the bilateral salmon regime between Japan and Russia, the appropriate role of hatcheries and habitat protection has also been the subject of debate and discussion. The evolution and mistaken original assumptions of the Pacific Salmon Treaty may therefore also hold lessons for the Japan–Russia bilateral salmon regime.

LIFE CYCLE AND HABITAT NEEDS OF PACIFIC SALMON SPECIES

Pacific salmon are anadromous, which means they spawn and spend the first phase of their life in freshwater rivers, stream, creeks, or lakes. The juvenile salmon then migrate downstream to the Pacific Ocean where they spend a period of time in salt water, ultimately returning back upstream to their natal freshwater river, stream, creek, or lake. Some of the following are the major watersheds in the United States and Canada where Pacific salmon spawn and migrate through are (moving from north to south): the Yukon River watershed in Alaska; the Fraser River watershed in British Columbia; the Columbia River–Snake River watershed in Washington, Oregon and Idaho; the Klamath River–Trinity River watershed in Oregon and California; and the Sacramento River–San Joaquin River watershed in California. Beyond the need for downstream and upstream passage between the ocean and freshwater spawning grounds, Pacific salmon have other fundamental habitat needs. Salmon are cold-water fish with limited tolerance for higher water temperatures. Salmon prefer water temperatures below 55 degrees (Fahrenheit), suffer reduced growth and survival rates as water temperatures get close to 60 degrees (Fahrenheit) and are generally unable to survive in water warmer than 60 degrees (Fahrenheit).[1] Instream water temperatures can rise when instream flow is reduced either because water is retained in reservoirs behind dams or when significant amounts of water are diverted out of stream.

In terms of spawning, salmon require shallow clear water to lay their eggs, which is often found in the smaller tributaries rather than in the mainstem of larger rivers. When logging takes place on slopes upland and adjacent to natural salmon spawning grounds, this can result in erosion in which rain washes exposed soils downhill and into such grounds causing them either to fill in completely or suffer siltation adversely affecting water clarity.

Although all Pacific salmon species are anadromous, have similar general habitat parameters, and undertake the roundtrip journey from freshwater to ocean and back to freshwater, there are some important differences between pink salmon and other salmon species such as Chinook, coho, and sockeye. According to a 2010 report by the Yale Center for Environmental Law and Policy, titled *Hatch 22: The Problem with the Pacific Salmon Resurgence*:

> When young salmon from around the Pacific Rim leave their rivers, they enter a fierce competition for finite food resources in the great mixing chamber that

is the North Pacific ... there are winners and losers out there – and those results may have profound implications for hatchery management, international fisheries agreements and the future of Pacific Salmon ... The winners? Pink salmon ... Much of their success lies in the pinks' two-year life cycle. Young pink salmon hatch in early spring of an even-numbered year, overwinter in the ocean and then return to spawn – usually in the lower reaches of coastal rivers – in the autumn of the following odd-numbered year.

...

Other species [Chinook, coho and sockeye] have longer, more complicated life cycles. Sockeye salmon typically spawn in or near lakes. They live in freshwater for their first two years, then spend two years in the ocean before making the journey back to the spawning lake. Their journey to and from the lake can be epic. One run of sockeye spawns in Redfish Lake, Idaho – 900 miles from the Pacific. Chinook and coho also spend a lot of their lives in rivers, where they're susceptible to the wear and tear of dams, industrial pollution, high temperatures, low oxygen and a sketchier food supply caused by loss of habitat. It's no coincidence that a majority of federally listed threatened or endangered

Pacific salmon species [under the United States Endangered Species Act] are Chinook, coho and sockeye that spend at least part of their lives in two of the West's most industrialized water systems, Puget Sound and the Columbia River ... Pinks, by contrast, are built for 21st century reproductive success. Dash to the ocean, avoid the human-based threats in the river, eat like a fiend, then make a short-spring home to spawn. Pink salmon are conspicuous by their absence from the endangered species list.[2]

In addition to the fact that pink salmon tend to spawn in the lower reaches of coastal rivers while Chinook, coho, and sockeye tend to spawn in the higher reaches of watersheds, pinks tend to return to the natal spawning grounds after just two years while Chinook, coho, and sockeye salmon usually take about five years to complete their anadromous journey. The differences in the life cycles and migratory patterns of pink salmon versus other species of salmon are relevant in the context of the Pacific Salmon Treaty for at least two reasons.

First, pink salmon tend to be of lower commercial value while Chinook, coho, and sockeye salmon tend to be of higher commercial value. As a result, from the economic perspective of Canadian and Japanese fishermen, a decline in the abundance of high value Chinook, coho, and sockeye salmon stocks is not compensated for by an increase in the abundance of low value pink salmon.

Second, as mentioned briefly in this study's introduction and discussed more later, in the period from the 1920s to the 1970s, numerous onstream dams were constructed on many salmon-bearing rivers in the Pacific northwest, particularly in the United States in the Columbia River–Snake River watershed, Klamath River–Trinity River watershed and the Sacramento River–San Joaquin River watershed. The construction of these dams impeded salmon migration to the upper portions of these watersheds, which had a more pronounced adverse impact on wild Chinook, coho, and sockeye salmon stocks than on pink salmon stocks. This is because the natural spawning grounds of Chinook, coho, and sockeye salmon are often located above these dams while the natural spawning grounds of pink salmon are often located below these dams.

PRINCIPLES, STRUCTURE, AND TERMS OF THE PACIFIC SALMON TREATY

The original Pacific Salmon Treaty between Canada and the United States was signed in 1995. Since 1995, Canada and the United States have agreed to amendments to the Pacific Salmon Treaty in 1999, 2002, and most recently in 2018.

In terms of objectives, there are three core principles that underlie the Pacific Salmon Treaty: the conservation principle, the equity principle, and the existing fishing principle. The conservation principle, which is the focus of this chapter, calls for Canadian and US fishermen collectively to prevent overfishing to avoid reducing the overall abundance of Pacific salmon. The equity principle calls for a fair allocation of the economic benefits of salmon fishing between Canada and the United States based on a comparison of the volume of salmon that originate (or are produced), respectively, in the Canadian and United States inland waters. The existing fishing principle provides that, to the extent possible, implementation of the Pacific Salmon Treaty should seek to avoid interfering with or requiring a reduction of existing fishing levels by Canadian and US salmon fishermen. The equity principle and the existing fishing principle are important components of the Pacific Salmon Treaty regime but are generally outside the scope of this chapter.

In regard to implementation of the conservation principles, there are certain key provisions and terms set forth in the Pacific Salmon Treaty. Article III of the treaty provides "Each party shall conduct its fisheries and its salmon enhancement programs so as to: (a) prevent overfishing and provide for optimum production; (b) provide for each party to received benefits equivalent to the production of salmon originating in its waters."[3]

Article I of the Pacific Salmon Treaty then provides certain definitions to clarify aspects of the Article III conservation principle. First, Article I clarifies that the "stocks subject to this Treaty" refer to Pacific salmon stocks that "originate in the water of one party."[4] Of particular significance, the definition of "stocks subject to the treaty" does not distinguish between wild salmon and salmon artificially propagated in hatcheries. Second, Article I defines "enhancement" to mean "man-made improvements to natural habitat or application of artificial fish culture technology that will lead to an increase in salmon stocks."[5] The explicit reference to "artificial fish culture technology" in the definition of "enhancement" evidences that the drafters of the Pacific Salmon Treaty anticipated and expected that hatchery-produced salmon would be factored into assessments of the volume of salmon "produced" in and "originating" in Canada and the United States. It should also be noted that Article I of the treaty does not provide a definition of what constitutes "optimum production" as that term is used in Article III.

Structurally, primary authority for implementing the Pacific Salmon Treaty is vested in the Pacific Salmon Commission. Article II(3) of the treaty provides that the Pacific Salmon Commission shall consist of eight Commissioners, with four Commissioners appointed by Canada and four Commissioners appointed by the United States. To assist the Pacific Salmon Commission in its work, Articles II(18) and (19) provide that "The Commission shall establish Panels as specified in Annex I [of the treaty]" and that "The Panels shall provide information and make recommendation to the Commission with respect to the functions of the Commission and carry out such other functions as the Treaty may specify or as the Commission may direct."

Article III 3(a) and (b) of the Pacific Salmon Treaty provides that each year, the State of origin (Canada or the United States) shall submit preliminary information for the ensuring year to the other Party, and to the Commission, including "the estimated size of the run" and "the interrelationship between stocks." Based on this information from the parties, the Pacific Salmon Commission then prepares abundance forecasts for different Pacific salmon stocks in different regions and then develops total joint catch limits for fishing based on these abundance forecasts.

The definition of "enhancement" in Article I includes "improvements to natural habitat," but the remainder of the Pacific Salmon Treaty provides little guidance on how such habitat improvements should be factored into abundance forecasts or determinations of the volume of salmon "produced" in or "originating" in the respective inland waters of Canada and the United States.[6] The exception here is Chapter 8 of the treaty which specifically deals with salmon stocks originating in the Yukon River in Alaska. For Yukon River salmon stocks, Section 29(a) of Chapter 8 of the treaty provides that "salmon should be afforded unobstructed access to and from, and use of, existing migration, spawning and rearing habitats." Sections 37 and 38 of Chapter 8 establish a Restoration and Enhancement Fund for Yukon River salmon stocks and direct that "Artificial propagation shall not be used as a substitute for effective fishery regulation, stock and habitat management or protection" and that "The priorities for implementing projects with the Fund shall be in this order: (a) restoring habitat and wild stocks; (b) enhancing habitat; and (c) enhancing wild stocks." Chapter 8 further provides that, in terms of salmon stocks originating in the Yukon River, the term "restoration" of such stocks means "returning wild salmon stock to its natural production level."

Although Chapter 8 contains provisions to protect habitat and migratory passage for Yukon River salmon stocks and although Chapter 8 provides that restoration of Yukon River salmon should focus on wild salmon rather than artificial propagation of salmon in hatcheries, these Yukon River-specific provisions related to habitat protection, migratory passage, and wild stocks were not made generally applicable to other salmon stocks covered by the Pacific Salmon Treaty. This is perhaps explained by the fact that, unlike in the other major Pacific watersheds where salmon are present, there are no significant onstream dams located in the Yukon River watershed.

The absence of provisions in the Pacific Salmon Treaty to establish general obligations to protect and enhance habitat and migratory passage for wild salmon stocks was noted by fisheries law scholar Brent R.H. Johnson in his 1998 article *Swimming Against a Legal Current: A Critical Analysis of the Pacific Salmon Treaty*, published in the Dalhousie Journal of Legal Studies (at Dalhousie University School of Law in Halifax, Nova Scotia in Canada). In this 1998 article, Johnson writes: "The dependence of salmon on fresh water requires protected inland habitats and unobstructed water routes from the ocean to inland spawning grounds. Clearly, this can only be effectively provided for by the state in which the habitats and water routes are located ... It is somewhat curious that while the parties have specifically encouraged salmon enhancement, there is no particular obligation to ensure the preservation of salmon habitats." Johnson further notes: "[T]he failure to include habitat protection obligations appears to undermine the principle of conservation contained in article III, paragraph 1(a). Although this provision requires the parties in principle to ensure the 'optimum production' of stocks, the parties are not made directly responsible under the Treaty for the protection of salmon environments within their boundaries."[7]

ABUNDANCE FORECASTS PURSUANT TO THE PACIFIC SALMON TREATY

As noted previously, the total catch limits for different Pacific salmon stocks in different regions are derived from "abundance forecasts" for the coming season, and the data and information upon which such abundance forecasts rely tends to come from the parties to the Pacific Salmon Treaty, Canada, and the United States. An April 2018 publication by the State of Alaska, titled *Pacific Salmon Treaty Transparency*, explains the relationship between the Preseason Abundance Index ("Preseason AI") and the Postseason Abundance Index ("Postseason AI") as used by the Pacific Salmon Commission in setting harvest limits: "Preseason AI, the metrics upon which harvest limits are set by the Pacific Salmon Commission, is based on forecasts of driver stocks and projected maturation rates, while Postseason AI is based on observed survival and observed maturation rates."[8] In short, higher abundance forecasts allow for and justify higher harvest/fishing levels.

As author Kathleen A. Miller noted in her report *North American Pacific Salmon: A Case of Fragile Cooperation*, abundance forecasting is not a simple or easy task: "A particular weakness [of the Pacific Salmon Treaty] is the fact that effective implementation of abundance-based management requires that the parties agree on the indices of abundance that will be used to set their harvest targets. Abundance, however, is very difficult to forecast in advance of the arrival of the runs. Forecasting models are imperfect, and data inadequacies and the uncertain and uneven impacts of variable marine and river conditions impair the accuracy of the forecasts."[9]

In recent decades, fishery biologists began expressing concern about the reliability and accuracy of salmon abundance forecasting due to the tendency of such forecasting to not distinguish between salmon originating from natural spawning grounds and salmon originating from hatcheries. A 2010 article titled *Magnitude and Trends in Abundance of Hatchery and Wild Pink Salmon, Chum Salmon, and Sockeye Salmon in the North Pacific Ocean*, published by the American Fisheries Society, concluded as follows:

> Hatchery salmon may reduce variability in harvests but this benefit to fishermen may come with a cost to wild salmon productivity. Additionally, there can be substantial straying of hatchery fish into natural spawning areas, which can degrade the fitness and biological diversity of the wild populations ... Resource agencies often do not separately estimate and report hatchery and wild salmon in the catch, let alone the spawn counts. The presence of numerous hatchery salmon can reduce the accuracy of wild salmon abundance and productivity estimates, which are important for setting goals for harvest rates and spawning abundances.[10]

As implementation of the Pacific Salmon Treaty's abundance-based conservation model unfolded, consistent with the concerns noted in the 2010 article published by the American Fisheries Society, a reoccurring pattern began to emerge. The Pacific Salmon Commission's abundance forecasts (or Preseason Abundance Index) tended to significantly *overestimate* the abundance of many salmon stocks as compared with actually observed abundance (or Postseason AI). The pattern led the Pacific Salmon Commission to organize a conference in Portland, Oregon in early 2016 to consider the matter as it is related to declining Pacific Chinook salmon stocks, and to appoint a three-person Independent Technical Panel (ITP) to issue a report on the findings of the conference. In November 2016, the members of the ITP – Randall M. Peterman, Ray Beamshelf, and Brian Blue – submitted a report to the Pacific Salmon Commission titled *Review of Methods for Forecasting Chinook Salmon Abundance in the Pacific Salmon Treaty Areas* ("*2016 ITP Abundance Forecasting Report*").

The *2016 ITP Abundance Forecasting Report* begins by noting some of the assumptions that go into developing Preseason AI. According to the ITP, a "chief assumption" for abundance forecasting is that there is no difference between the marine survival rates of wild Chinook and hatchery Chinook salmon.[11] The *2016 ITP Abundance Forecasting Report* also notes that, under the Pacific Salmon Commission's existing Chinook model, hatchery stocks are treated as "surrogates for wild stocks."[12] These statements reflect that, under the current conservation model used pursuant to the Pacific Salmon Treaty, it does not appear that differences between wild salmon stocks and hatchery stocks or interactions between wild salmon stocks and hatchery salmon stocks are part of the core assumptions or methodology that goes into abundance forecasting under the Pacific Salmon Treaty.

The *2016 ITP Abundance Forecasting Report* then went on to document several instances of significant discrepancies between Preseason AI and Postseason AI. For example, the ITP reported that for the Columbia Upriver Summer Chinook stocks, the Pacific Salmon Commission abundance forecast overestimated the actual abundance by a mean absolute percent error of 22 percent. As another example, the ITP reported that for the North Oregon Coast Chinook stocks, the Pacific Salmon Commission abundance forecast overestimated the actual abundance by a mean absolute percent error of 31 percent.[13]

In terms of identifying the particular flaws or shortcomings in the Pacific Salmon Treaty conservation model that accounted for these overestimates and discrepancies, the *2016 ITP Abundance Forecasting Report* was less than specific, concluding: "Causes of the recent large discrepancies between the pre- and post-season AIs are unclear. However, the strong positive correlation in discrepancies across AABM [Aggregate Abundance Based Management] areas, along with other evidence, suggests that both the PSC [Pacific Salmon Commission] model and the agencies' stock-specific forecasting methods do not properly represent changes in key factors such as time-varying maturation rates, marine survival rates, or exploitation rates."[14] The *2016 ITP Abundance Forecasting Report* did not provide further guidance as to whether the failure of the current conservation model to properly "represent changes" in factors such as "time-varying maturation rates" and "marine survival rates" might relate to differences and interactions between wild salmon stocks and hatchery stocks, or might relate to interactions between different species of Pacific salmon (such as pink salmon interactions with Chinook, coho, and sockeye salmon).

As the following section of this chapter discusses, these differences and interactions between wild salmon stocks and hatchery salmon stocks (which are in turn related to differences and interactions between different species of Pacific salmon) may be the missing element in the Pacific Salmon Treaty conservation model that accounts for and explains the pattern of overestimates in abundance forecasting.

THE REPLACEMENT ASSUMPTION AND HATCHERY EFFECTS ON WILD SALMON

In the United States and Canada, many of the larger onstream dams in the Pacific Northwest were built in the period from 1930 to 1970. At the time these onstream dams were constructed, for both hydropower generation and water storage/water supply purposes, the proponents of such dams were aware that the structures would impede upstream and downstream migration of certain existing wild salmon runs. At the time, the strategy to mitigate the anticipated adverse impacts of dams on salmon stocks was to construct and operate salmon hatcheries below the dams. Under this strategy, the hatcheries would release large volumes of juvenile salmon in the lower reaches of rivers and these salmon would then return to spawn in these lower reaches, thereby "replacing" the wild salmon runs lost due to the dams' blockage of downstream and upstream passage from traditional spawning grounds in the higher reaches of the watershed. Thus was born the "replacement assumption," which maintained that dams and robust salmon stocks were compatible because lost wild salmon stocks could be replaced by operating hatcheries to artificially propagate salmon below the dams.

In his 1999 book *Salmon Without Rivers: A History of the Pacific Salmon Crisis*, fisheries biologist Jim Lichatowich explains as follows:

> Fundamentally, the salmon's decline has been the consequence of a vision based on flawed assumptions and unchallenged myths – a vision that has guided the relationship between salmon and humans for the past 150 years. We assumed we could control the biological productivity of salmon and improve upon natural processes we didn't even try to understand. We assumed we could have salmon without rivers ... Placing misguided confidence in technological solutions, salmon managers accepted the myth that controlling salmon production in hatcheries would ultimately lead to increased productivity. Despite the best of intentions, these hard-working people produced disaster because their efforts were based on false assumptions.[15]
>
> ...
>
> The plans to relocate upriver stocks to the lower river using artificial propagation was a straw that politicians readily grasped to promote the belief that power and salmon were compatible.[16]

In *Salmon Without Rivers*, Lichatowich continues:

> Today, as proof of their success, hatchery advocates note that artificially propagated salmon make up 80 percent or more of the total number of salmon in the Columbia [River Basin], but they fail to mention that the total run has crashed to less than 5 percent of its historical abundance. Measuring success by the percentage of hatchery fish in a shrinking production base was not only scientifically invalid but also insidiously enhanced the

illusion of hatchery success. At the same time the percentage of hatchery fish increased, hatcheries were contributing to the decline of wild salmon.[17]

Lichatowich further observes:

> One of the most troubling consequence of this flawed vision was that it diverted salmon managers' attention from the root cause of the salmon's decline. As a result, significant problems such as habitat destruction and overharvest were consistently ignored. Agency budgets and staff energy were devoted to artificial propagation instead of habitat protection.[18]

The analysis and conclusions of Lichatowich have been confirmed and echoed by many other studies that have assessed the effect of salmon hatcheries on wild salmon stocks and overall salmon abundancy. For example, in 2014, the Hatchery Scientific Review Group submitted a report to the United States Congress titled *On the Science of Hatcheries: An Updated Perspective on the Role of Hatcheries in Salmon and Steelhead Management in the Pacific Northwest*. The Hatchery Scientific Review Group was created as part of the Hatchery Reform Project established by the US Congress in 2000. In its 2014 report *On the Science of Hatcheries*, the Hatcheries Scientific Review Group found as follows:

> The traditional policy of replacing wild populations with hatchery fish is not consistent with today's conservation goals, environmental values, and scientific theories. Hatcheries cannot replace lost fish habitat and the natural populations that rely on it. It is now clear that the widespread use of hatchery programs has actually contributed to the overall decline of wild populations.[19]

Similarly, in its report *The Effects of Hatchery Production on Wild Salmon and Trout*, the group Wild Fish Conservancy determined the following in terms of the survival and reproduction rates of hatchery salmon: "The domestication selection by hatchery practices derails the 'survival of the fittest' concept. Those with the greatest fitness in a captive environment produce offspring that perform the worst in the wild." In its report, Wild Fish Conservancy went on to find that after 130 years of hatchery production, "Management continues to rely on hatchery production to mitigate for losses of wild fish abundance and habitat" despite clear evidence that "Artificial propagation contributes to declines in the survival and reproductive capacity of endangered wild fish."[20]

As a final example, in her 2004 article *The Salmon Hatchery Myth: When Bad Policy Happens to Good Science*, Melanie Kleiss reports:

[W]e have blindly depended upon hatcheries to compensate for overfishing and habitat destruction, even though science and historical trends indicate that hatcheries fail to meet this intended function. Despite widespread hatchery development, over 100 major Pacific salmon runs have gone extinct and many of the remaining 200-plus runs are at risk of disappearing. Even though studies indicate that hatchery fish may accelerate the extinction of salmon runs, faith in hatcheries continues.[21]

Kleiss notes:

The scientific literature as a whole provides a stunningly consistent message: hatchery fish could drive salmon populations closer to extinction ... Many studies find that juvenile hatchery salmon show more aggression and exhibit different predator behaviors than their wild counterparts[22] ... The scientific literature show almost without exception that hatchery salmon have lower overall survival rates and significantly lower breeding success rates[23] ... Therefore, while hatchery juveniles released into natural streams have a competitive advantage over wild fish due to increased aggression, size, or sheer number, their impaired ability to survive to adulthood and breed successfully can translate into an overall reduction in salmon population size.[24]

Kleiss goes on to conclude, "Hatcheries cannot replace wild populations and must remain secondary to habitat conservation as a recovery strategy for salmon populations. Nature simply does the job better."[25]

These studies all suggest that the replacement assumption – which for more than a century has served as the basis for Pacific salmon management and the foundation for claims that onstream dams and salmon conservation are compatible – has now been shown to be flawed and incorrect. The continuation of misplaced reliance on the replacement assumption, in turn, helps to explain the pattern of inaccuracies and overestimates with abundance forecasts under the Pacific Salmon Treaty. If more hatchery salmon are not the answer to declining Pacific salmon stocks, and are in fact contributing to such decline, then where does the answer lie?

HABITAT INSTEAD OF HATCHERIES – REORIENTING THE PACIFIC SALMON TREATY

With an enhanced understanding of the ways that hatcheries are adversely affecting wild Pacific salmon and contributing to declines in the overall abundance of Pacific salmon stocks, there is emerging consensus that expansion of salmon hatchery production will not solve the problem of Pacific salmon decline. There is also emerging consensus that the more viable strategy to restore declining Pacific salmon stocks is to improve natural habitat conditions (such as reducing out of stream diversions to maintain cooler instream temperatures and avoiding logging on slopes upland/adjacent to salmon spawning grounds) and to avoid or remove obstacles (such as dams) that impede downstream and upstream fish passage.

In his 1998 article, *Swimming Against a Legal Current: A Critical Analysis of the Pacific Salmon Treaty*, Brent Johnston suggests: "The parties [to the Pacific Salmon Treaty] need to reevaluate the manner in which the Treaty gives practical expression to the principle of conservation. This may include providing the PSC [Pacific Salmon Commission] with the responsibility for overseeing designated salmon habitat areas or including an annex to the Treaty which outlines obligations to ensure against habitat degradation."[26]

Similarly, in their article *Pacific Salmon at the Crossroads: Stocks at Risks from California, Oregon, Idaho and Washington*, fisheries biologists Willa Nehlsen, Jack E. Williams and James A. Lichatowich found:

> The decline in native salmon, steelhead, and sea-run cutthroat populations has resulted from habitat loss and damage, and inadequate passage and flows caused by hydropower, agriculture, logging and other developments; overfishing, primarily of weaker stocks in mixed-stock fisheries; and negative interaction with other fishes, including nonnative hatchery salmon and steelhead. While some attempts at remedying these threats have been made, they have not been enough to prevent the broad decline of stocks along the West Coast. A new paradigm that advances habitat restoration and ecosystem function rather than hatchery production is needed for many of these stocks to survive and prosper into the next century.[27]

The prospects for the Pacific Salmon Treaty to focus more on instream habitat conditions and removal of obstacles to downstream and upstream passage may be improved by recent amendments to the treaty at the end of 2018 that went into effect from January 1, 2019 (hereafter the "2019 Treaty Amendments"). While these recent amendments to the Pacific Salmon Treaty do not specifically address changes to the model and methodology used for abundance forecasts, they do suggest an increased recognition of differences between wild salmon stocks and hatchery stocks and highlight the need to strengthen habitat protection.

Attachment E to the 2019 Treaty Amendments, titled *Habitat and Restoration*, provides in its preamble as follows:

> Considering the agreements between the Parties to implement abundance-based management regimes designed to prevent overfishing ... Taking into

account the decline in the abundance and productivity of important naturally spawning stocks of Pacific salmon subject to this Treaty ... Recognizing
that **it is vital to protect and restore the salmon habitat** and to maintain
adequate water quality and quantity in order to improve spawning, the **safe
passage** of adult and juvenile salmon, and therefore, to optimize the production of important **naturally spawning stocks** ....Recognizing that **the Parties
can achieve the principles and objectives of this Treaty only if they maintain and increase the production of natural stocks** ... Recognizing that
a carefully designed enhancement program would contribute significantly to
the restoration of depressed **natural stocks** and help the Parties optimize
production (bold added).

Attachment E to the 2019 Treaty Amendments further states:

The parties agree: 1. To use their best efforts, consistent with applicable
law, to (a) **protect and restore the habitat to promote the safe passage** of
adult and juvenile salmon and to achieve high levels of **natural
production** ... (b) maintain and, as needed, **improve safe passage of
salmon to and from their natal streams**; and ... (c) maintain adequate
water quality and quantity.
      ...
      The parties agree to ... promote these objectives by requesting that the
[Pacific Salmon] Commission ... (b) periodically review and discuss information on the **habitat of naturally spawning stocks** subject to this Treaty
that cannot be restored through harvest controls alone and non-fishing
factors that affect the **safe passage** or survival of salmon, options for addressing non-fishing constraints and restoring optimum production, and progress
of the Parties to achieve the objectives for the stocks under the Treaty (bold
added).

The 2019 Treaty Amendments also include new language in Chapter 3
on Chinook Salmon that states: "The parties agree that ... while fishing
has contributed to the decline of some Chinook stocks, **the continued
status of Chinook stocks that are considered depressed generally reflects
the long-term cumulative effects of other factors, particularly chronic
habitat degradation**" and "deleterious **hatchery** practices." (bold added).[28]
The 2019 Treaty Amendments to Chapter 3 also added: "The parties
shall ... report annually on **naturally spawning Chinook stocks** in relation to agreed MSY [Maximum Sustainable Yield] or other biologically-
based escapement objectives, rebuilding exploitation rate objectives, or
other metrics, and evaluate trends in the status of stocks and report on
progress in **the rebuilding of naturally spawning Chinook stocks**" (bold
added).

In addition to the new habitat-focused and passage-focused provisions in Attachment E and Chapter 3, the 2019 Treaty Amendments also added Appendix A to Annex IV of the Pacific Salmon Treaty. The new Appendix A to Annex IV concerns the work of the Chinook Technical Committee (CTC) that reports to the Pacific Salmon Commission, and provides: "The CTC shall … report annually on **naturally spawning Chinook stocks** in relation to the agreed MSY of other biologically-based escapement objectives, rebuilding exploitation rate objectives, or other metrics, and evaluate trends in the status of stocks and **report on progress in the rebuilding of naturally spawning Chinook stocks**" (bold added). Pursuant to Appendix A, going forward it therefore appears that in addition to receiving annual data from Canada and the United States about the volume of fish propagated in and released from hatcheries, the Pacific Salmon Commission will also receive annual reports from the CTC focused specifically on wild Chinook salmon stocks and efforts to rebuild such stocks.

The changes reflected in the 2019 Treaty Amendments provide a potential foundation and opportunity for the Pacific Salmon Treaty to develop a more scientifically credible and robust model for assessing the overall health of Pacific salmon stocks. In terms of how this more scientifically credible and robust model might affect and how the Pacific Salmon Treaty operates in practice, it is important to keep in mind what the Pacific Salmon Commission cannot and can do.

Of particular significance, what the Pacific Salmon Commission cannot do is order the Canadian and United States governments to remove particular dams, install fish passage on particular dams, prohibit logging in areas upland of streams where salmon spawn, release water from upstream reservoirs, or reduce out-of-stream diversions to maintain instream water temperatures. These measures may be critical to providing safe passage and preserving habitat for wild salmon, but these are not measures that the Pacific Salmon Treaty authorizes the Pacific Salmon Commission to directly take. Given the current structure of the Pacific Salmon Treaty, such measures can only be ordered and enforced by the national governments (or perhaps the provincial/ state governments) of Canada and the United States.

Although the Pacific Salmon Commission may lack the authority to directly order the fish habitat and fish passage measures noted earlier, the Pacific Salmon Commission is nonetheless still positioned to play an important role in shifting the focus of salmon management from a reliance on hatcheries to a focus on improving habitat protection and passage. There are at least two ways in which the Pacific Salmon Commission can play this role, and neither requires substantive changes to the Pacific Salmon Treaty.

First, in terms of its abundance forecasting, the model used by the Pacific Salmon Commission (and the committees that provide guidance to the Pacific Salmon Commission) can be recalibrated so that it recognizes that reliance on hatcheries to produce salmon is in fact detrimental to the long-term abundance of Pacific salmon, and that investment in improving passage and habitat enhances the long-term abundance of Pacific salmon. With this recalibration, expanded reliance on hatcheries to produce salmon would result in a downward adjustment (rather than an upward adjustment) of the total joint catch and fishing limits for Canadian and US fishermen.

Second, in relation to the equity principle in the Pacific Salmon Treaty, and the "fair allocation" of fishing rights between Canadian and US fishermen, this recalibration would impact how fishing rights are allocated between the two countries. For example, if the United States is relying more on hatcheries to artificially produce salmon instead of maintaining passage and habitat for the production of wild salmon, then consistent with current science, the Pacific Salmon Commission should correspondingly reduce the United States allocation of fishing rights. Conversely, for example, if Canada is improving the production of wild salmon by maintaining and enhancing passage and habitat, then consistent with the current science the Pacific Salmon Commission should correspondingly increase Canada's allocation of fishing rights. At present, the Pacific Salmon Commission's allocation of fishing rights between Canada and the United States is based largely on the volume of salmon that "originate" in each respective country but little if any attention is paid to whether these "originations" are hatchery salmon or wild salmon. This is something the Pacific Salmon Commission can change.

Building on the 2019 Treaty Amendments, these are tangible changes that the Pacific Salmon Commission can make to help rebuild declining Pacific salmon stocks – to achieve "optimum production" per Article III of the Pacific Salmon Treaty. Moreover, these changes by the Pacific Salmon Commission, which would penalize reliance on hatchery-produced salmon and reward reliance on wild salmon stocks, may help prompt the Canadian and US governments to make similar changes in terms of domestic policy assumptions and priorities.

SALMON HATCHERIES AND CLIMATE CHANGE

As noted in the Introduction to this chapter, Japan and Russia have also developed bilateral arrangements for the conservation and management of salmon that originate in their respective inland waters. Although a review of these bilateral arrangements between Japan and Russia is outside the scope of this chapter, recent scientific studies on salmon stocks in the Japan–Russia region have raised an additional concern regarding reliance on hatchery salmon to maintain overall salmon abundance – the ability of hatchery salmon to adapt to rising water temperatures resulting from climate change-induced global warming.

In January 2020, Japanese fishery biologists, Shuichi Kitada and Hirohisa Kishino, released a preprint version of their article *Fitness Decline in Hatchery-Enhanced Salmon Populations is Manifested by Global Warming*. In this paper, Kitada and Kishino report as follows:

> Despite historical maximum hatchery releases and biomass of chum salmon in the North Pacific, chum salmon returning to Japan, where the world's largest chum salmon hatchery programme runs, have declined substantially for two decades … We argue that the long-term hatchery releases have reduced the athletic ability of hatchery fish, resulting in a continuous decline in the fitness of whole populations. A genetic mechanism of fitness decline in hatchery-enhanced salmon population is first manifested by global warming at the southern margin of the species.[29]

Kitada and Kishino go on to explain:

> Repeated hatchery operations substantially altered gene frequencies of thermally adapted LDH-A1 and LDH-B2 in Japanese chum salmon populations, which could be reflected in the reduced performance of skeletal and cardiac muscles. This may be a causal mechanism for fitness decline in Japan chum salmon populations.

Kitada and Kishino found:

> Evidence for reduced fitness of hatchery-reared fish in the wild and altered age and size at maturation is a serious cause for caution in hatchery stocking … The results suggest that artificial selection in hatcheries might drive maladaptation to climate change and act to opposite directions of natural selection.[30]

The data and preliminary findings in this paper suggest that the shortcomings of hatchery-reliant salmon management are likely to become more pronounced as global warming continues and water temperatures rise. This tendency will be as relevant to salmon conservation and management efforts in the Canada–United States region, and as serious a "cause for caution in hatchery stocking," as it will be in the Japan–Russia region.

WILD SALMON AND HATCHERY SALMON ARE NOT THE SAME

In considering the relationship between salmon habitat and salmon hatcheries, and the relationship between wild salmon stocks and hatchery-produced salmon, it is useful to return to the definition of "enhancement" set forth in

Article I of the Pacific Salmon Treaty. In Article I, "enhancement" is defined as "man-made improvements to natural habitat or application of artificial fish culture technology that will lead to an **increase** in salmon stocks" (bold added).[31] This definition suggests that Pacific salmon artificially propagated in hatcheries are only consistent with the Pacific Salmon Treaty to the extent that the production of such hatchery salmon result in an "increase in salmon stocks." It would follow, then, that salmon hatchery activities and practices that are shown to result in a long-term *decrease* in salmon stocks (e.g. due to the low survival and reproductive rates of hatchery salmon and the adverse effects on wild salmon stocks of interactions with hatchery salmon) would be inconsistent with the Pacific Salmon Treaty's notion of "enhancement" as well as the Pacific Salmon Treaty's objective of "optimum production." It is difficult to see how a hatchery-reliant system of producing salmon that results in the long-term decrease of salmon stocks could be considered "optimum."

To return to this chapter's starting point, of explaining and correcting the Pacific Salmon Commission pattern of overestimates in its abundance forecasting for Pacific salmon, it appears the Pacific Salmon Treaty finds itself at a crossroads. The Pacific Salmon Treaty's approach to setting fishing levels was premised in considerable part on the replacement assumption – that high levels of abundance (and therefore high levels of fishing) could be maintained through hatchery production even if dams, logging, and out-of-stream diversions of water continued to degrade the natural habitat for wild salmon stocks. Now that the replacement assumption has been shown to be faulty, there is a fundamental disconnect between science and policy. That is, the methodology underlying the Pacific Salmon Treaty's conservation model still relies extensively on hatcheries to maintain salmon abundance even through it is now understood that such hatcheries are contributing to the long-term decline of such abundance.

The 2019 Treaty Amendments, discussed in this chapter, reveal an emerging recognition of this disconnect between science and policy, and of the need to refocus on what can be done to improve instream habitat conditions (cooler water temperatures, protecting spawning grounds from siltation caused by logging) and downstream/upstream passage for wild salmon stocks. By recalibrating its abundance forecasts and its allocation of fishing rights to better reflect this science, there are meaningful changes the Pacific Salmon Commission can make to help shift this focus. The direct actions to improve passage and habitat for salmon, however, will need to be undertaken at the domestic level – by the federal and provincial/state governments of Canada and the United States.

As we look to the prospect of action at the domestic level by Canada and the United States, in closing some examples of how this might work in relation to dams can be noted. In the United States, Golden Ray Dam on the Rogue River in Oregon,[32] San Clemente Dam on the Carmel River in California[33] and two dams on the Elwha River in Washington state were recently removed,[34] and plans are underway to remove four dams in the Oregon–California Klamath River basin.[35] The calls for removal of dams on the Rogue River, the Carmel River, the Elwha River, and the Klamath River were prompted in part by salmon-related considerations, of the prospect of removing the dams to allow salmon passage and access to traditional spawning grounds in the higher reaches of these watersheds.[36]

As the Oregon-based conservation group WaterWatch reported in regard to the removal of Golden Ray Dam on the Rogue River: "The dam was a significant barrier to fish and its removal allows better access to 333 miles of salmon and steelhead spawning habitat upstream of the former dam. Gold Ray removal also reclaimed approximately 1.5 miles of salmon spawning habitat that was buried beneath the dam's impounded waters. Since removal, spawning surveys upstream of the former dam site show that use of this now-viable spawning ground has risen exponentially."[37]

And in Canada, there is the example of Moran Dam on the Fraser River in British Columbia. Moran Dam was a 720-foot-high structure proposed in the 1950s that would have been constructed on the mainstem of the Fraser River, 200 miles from the river's mouth.[38] The proponents of Moran Dam conceded that the structure would have significant adverse effects on Fraser River sockeye salmon, but consistent with the replacement assumption, proposed hatcheries below the dam to offset the anticipated damage to wild stocks. In 1960, as the controversy over Moran Dam unfolded, the International Pacific Salmon Fisheries Commission (IPSFC) based in British Columbia published a report titled *Sockeye and Pink Salmon Production in Relation to Proposed Dams in the Fraser River System*. This 1960 report concluded: "At the present time, artificial propagation is not a proven method of maintaining even small localized stocks of Fraser River sockeye and pink salmon."[39] As a consequence of the 1960 IPSFC report, Moran Dam was not built and wild stocks in the Fraser River watershed today remain generally healthier and more abundant than in watersheds (such as the Columbia River) where onstream dams were built in the lower reaches.[40]

The experience in the United States with dam removal on the Rogue River, the Carmel River, the Elwha River, and the Klamath River, and the experience in Canada with the decision to forego construction of Moran Dam on the Fraser River, provide examples of what it can mean in practice to restore and maintain the habitat conditions and passage needed for healthy abundant salmon stocks. Such examples give a sense of the types of actions Canada and the United States can undertake (or refrain from undertaking) going forward to give substance to the provisions of Attachment E to the 2019 amendments to the Pacific Salmon Treaty requiring the parties to "protect and restore the habitat to promote the safe passage of adult and juvenile salmon and to achieve high levels of natural production" and to maintain and improve "safe passage of salmon to and from their natal streams."

By bringing its abundance forecasting model and fishing limits more in line with current science – which recognizes that ultimately salmon hatcheries cannot replace wild salmon stocks – the Pacific Salmon Commission can highlight that "enhancement" and maintenance of "optimum production" of Pacific salmon stocks depend on the extent to which Canada and the United States maintain habitat conditions and passage for wild salmon.

Notes

1. Trout Unlimited, *Healing Troubled Waters: Preparing Trout and Salmon Habitat for a Changing Climate* (2007 Report).
2. Bruce Barcott, *Hatch-22: The Problem with the Pacific Salmon Resurgence*, Yale Environment 360 Report, November 2010.
3. Article III, Pacific Salmon Treaty.
4. Article I, Pacific Salmon Treaty.
5. Article I, Pacific Salmon Treaty.
6. Article I, Pacific Salmon Treaty.
7. Brent Johnston, *Swimming Against a Legal Current: A Critical Analysis of the Pacific Salmon Treaty*, 7 Dalhousie Journal of Legal Studies 125 (1998), pp. 141, 129.
8. *Pacific Salmon Treaty Transparency*, April 2018 publication by State of Alaska p. 20.
9. Kathleen A. Miller, *North American Pacific Salmon: A Case of Fragile Cooperation*, Report by Environmental and Societal Impacts Group, National Center for Atmospheric Research.
10. Gregory T. Ruggerone, Randall M. Peterman, Brigitte Dorner, and Katherine W. Myers, *Magnitude and Trends in Abundance of Hatchery and Wild Pink Salmon, Chum Salmon, and Sockeye Salmon in the North Pacific Ocean*, in Marine and Coastal Fisheries: Dynamics, Management, and Ecosystem Science, pp. 306–328 (American Fisheries Society, 2010).
11. Randall M. Peterman, Ray Beamshelf & Brian Blue, *Review of Methods for Forecasting Chinook Salmon Abundance in the Pacific Salmon Treaty*

Areas, November 2016. submission of Independent Technical Panel [ITP] to the Pacific Salmon Commission, pp. 45–46.

12. Randall M. Peterman, Ray Beamshelf & Brian Blue, *Review of Methods for Forecasting Chinook Salmon Abundance in the Pacific Salmon Treaty Areas*, November 2016 submission of Independent Technical Panel [ITP] to the Pacific Salmon Commission, p. 19.

13. Randall M. Peterman, Ray Beamshelf & Brian Blue, *Review of Methods for Forecasting Chinook Salmon Abundance in the Pacific Salmon Treaty Areas*, November 2016 submission of Independent Technical Panel [ITP] to the Pacific Salmon Commission, p. 6.

14. Randall M. Peterman, Ray Beamshelf & Brian Blue, *Review of Methods for Forecasting Chinook Salmon Abundance in the Pacific Salmon Treaty Areas*, November 2016 submission of Independent Technical Panel [ITP] to the Pacific Salmon Commission, p. 11.

15. Jim Lichatowich, SALMON WITHOUT RIVERS: A HISTORY OF THE PACIFIC SALMON CRISIS (Island Press, 1999) pp. 7–8.

16. Jim Lichatowich, SALMON WITHOUT RIVERS: A HISTORY OF THE PACIFIC SALMON CRISIS (Island Press, 1999) pp. 188–189.

17. Jim Lichatowich, SALMON WITHOUT RIVERS: A HISTORY OF THE PACIFIC SALMON CRISIS (Island Press, 1999) p. 198.

18. Jim Lichatowich, SALMON WITHOUT RIVERS: A HISTORY OF THE PACIFIC SALMON CRISIS (Island Press, 1999) p. 130.

19. Hatchery Scientific Review Group, *On the Science of Hatcheries: An Updated Perspective on the Role of Hatcheries in Salmon and Steelhead Management in the Pacific Northwest* (2014 Report to the United States Congress) p. 1.

20. *The Effects of Hatchery Production on Wild Salmon and Trout* (Report by Wild Fish Conservancy Northwest).

21. Melanie Kleiss, *The Salmon Hatchery Myth: When Bad Policy Happens to Good Science*, 6 MINNESOTA JOURNAL OF LAW, SCIENCE AND TECHNOLOGY 433 (2004), p. 433.

22. Melanie Kleiss, *The Salmon Hatchery Myth: When Bad Policy Happens to Good Science*, 6 MINNESOTA JOURNAL OF LAW, SCIENCE AND TECHNOLOGY 433 (2004), pp. 437–438.

23. Melanie Kleiss, *The Salmon Hatchery Myth: When Bad Policy Happens to Good Science*, 6 MINNESOTA JOURNAL OF LAW, SCIENCE AND TECHNOLOGY 433 (2004), p. 429.

24. Melanie Kleiss, *The Salmon Hatchery Myth: When Bad Policy Happens to Good Science*, 6 MINNESOTA JOURNAL OF LAW, SCIENCE AND TECHNOLOGY 433 (2004), p. 440.

25. Melanie Kleiss, *The Salmon Hatchery Myth: When Bad Policy Happens to Good Science*, 6 MINNESOTA JOURNAL OF LAW, SCIENCE AND TECHNOLOGY 433 (2004), p. 442.

26. Brent Johnston, *Swimming Against a Legal Current: A Critical Analysis of the Pacific Salmon Treaty*, 7 DALHOUSIE JOURNAL OF LEGAL STUDIES 125 (1998), p. 158.

27. Willa Nehlsen, Jack E. Williams and James A. Lichatowich, *Pacific Salmon at the Crossroads: Stocks at Risks from California, Oregon, Idaho and Washington*, FISHERIES 16 (2) (1991).

28. Amendments to Pacific Salmon Treaty, Appendix A to Annex IV, Chapter 3: Understanding Regarding Chinook Technical Committee Assignments Relating to Implementation of Chapter 3 of Annex IV.

29. Shuichi Kitada & Hiroshisa Kishino, *Fitness Decline in Hatchery-Enhanced Salmon Populations is Manifested by Global Warming*, BIORXIV (January 2020).

30. Shuichi Kitada & Hiroshisa Kishino, *Fitness Decline in Hatchery-Enhanced Salmon Populations is Manifested by Global Warming*, BIORXIV (January 2020).

31. Article I, Pacific Salmon Treaty.

32. WaterWatch, *Gold Ray Dam Comes Down* (2019).

33. Teresa L. Carey, *With San Clements Dam Gone, Are Steelhead Trout About to Make Comeback on the Carmel River?*, SAN JOSE MERCURY NEWS (July 7, 2017).

34. Kate Schimel, *After Its Dams Come Down, A River is Reborn – A Look at the Elwha Unleashed*, HIGH COUNTRY NEW (September 4, 2017).

35. Jacques Leslie, *Four Dams in the West Are Coming Down – A Victory Wrapped in Defeat for Smart Water Policy*, LOS ANGELES TIMES (November 2, 2017).

36. Kate Schimel, *After Its Dams Come Down, A River is Reborn – A Look at the Elwha Unleashed*, HIGH COUNTRY NEWS (September 4, 2017); Jacques Leslie, *Four Dams in the West Are Coming Down – A Victory Wrapped in Defeat for Smart Water Policy*, Los Angeles Times (November 2, 2017).

37. WaterWatch, *Gold Ray Dam Comes Down* (2019).

38. Jim Lichatowich, SALMON WITHOUT RIVERS: A HISTORY OF THE PACIFIC SALMON CRISIS (Island Press, 1999) pp. 195–196.

39. F. Andre and G. Green, *Sockeye and Pink Salmon Production in Relation to Proposed Dams in the Fraser River System*, Bulletin No. 11, International Pacific Salmon Fisheries Commission, New Westminister, British Columbia, 1960.

40. Jim Lichatowich, SALMON WITHOUT RIVERS: A HISTORY OF THE PACIFIC SALMON CRISIS (Island Press, 1999) pp. 195–196.

14

Instream Rights and Hatchery Fish

Globally, over the past century there has been an increasing trend to seek to reverse declines in wild fish stocks through the artificial rearing of fish in hatcheries, which are then released into the wild. As the use of fish hatcheries worldwide has increased, however, scientists have noted a troubling trend: increased reliance on hatcheries has often tended to result in further declines in wild fish stocks rather than the replenishment of such wild stocks. As was reported in a 2002 article titled *The Future of Stock Enhancement: Lessons for Hatchery Practice from Conservation Biology*:

> The world's fish species are under threat from habitat degradation and over-exploitation. In many instances, attempts to bolster stocks have been made by rearing fish in hatcheries and releasing them into the wild ... [A} substantial number of endangered species recovery programmes rely on the release of hatchery-reared individuals to ensure long-term population viability. Fisheries scientists have known about the behavioural deficits displayed by hatchery-reared fish and the resultant poor survival rates in the wild for over a century.[1]

Another global trend in the fisheries sector is the threat to saline-intolerant fish in rivers from seawater intrusion. This seawater intrusion is often caused by excessive upstream diversions and impoundment, which leave insufficient freshwater flow downstream to push back salt water coming in from the ocean. For instance, the Shatt Al-Arab River in Iraq is now experiencing increased seawater intrusion due to upstream diversions by Turkey in the Tigris River–Euphrates River watershed. Recent studies indicate that native freshwater fish species in the Shatt Al-Arab River are in decline as a result of the rising salinity levels caused by Turkey's upstream diversions and dams.[2]

The confluence of increased upstream diversions, reduced freshwater instream flow, rising salinity levels and expanding reliance on fish hatcheries has come together in a controversial new plan to restore an endangered fish species in California.

HATCHING A NEW CONSERVATION MODEL

Pursuant to the Endangered Species Act, in October 2019 the United States Fish and Wildlife Service (USFWS) of the Trump Administration issued a new Biological Opinion for coordinated operations of the Central Valley Project and the State Water Project (2019 Biological Opinion).[3] The Central Valley Project is operated by the United States Bureau of Reclamation (Reclamation), and the State Water Project is operated by the California Department of Water Resources.

The Central Valley Project and the State Water Project both divert fresh water from the Sacramento River and the San Joaquin River watersheds, and the reduced freshwater flow resulting from these diversions allows in additional ocean water, raising salinity levels.

The 2019 Biological Opinion issued by the Trump Administration found that anticipated water project operations would not jeopardize the survival of the endangered delta smelt, a fish species dependent on low-salinity conditions and found only in the brackish estuary where the fresh water of the Sacramento and San Joaquin Rivers mix with the seawater of the San Francisco Bay. The "no jeopardy" determination in the 2019 Biological Opinion contrasted with the previous 2008 Biological Opinion by the USFWS, which found that anticipated water project operations would likely push the endangered delta smelt into extinction due to elevated salinity levels.[4]

In comparing the 2008 Biological Opinion to the 2019 Biological Opinion, two key differences stand out. The 2008 Biological Opinion identified seawater intrusion and rising salinity as a primary driver of delta smelt decline and did not propose reliance on hatcheries to replace declining wild delta smelt populations.[5] In contrast, the 2019 Biological Opinion downplayed seawater intrusion and rising salinity as a primary driver of delta smelt declines and instead focused on the potential role that delta smelt artificially propagated in hatcheries might play in increasing delta smelt populations.[6]

This shift to greater reliance on hatcheries to maintain delta smelt is revealed in the following text in the 2019 Biological Opinion under the heading *Cultured Smelt Production from Fish Conservation and Culture Laboratory (FCCL)*:

> [T]he delta smelt faces a high risk of continued declines if the population is not supplemented. Reclamation proposes to fund a two-phase process that

would lead to annual supplementation of the wild delta smelt population with propagated fish within 3–5 years from issuance of the biological opinion. The first step in this process will be the development of a supplementation strategy within one year of the issuance of the BiOp that will describe the capacity needed at the hatchery facilities to accommodate the delta smelt production needed to meet genetic and other hatchery considerations with the goal of increasing production to a number and the life stages necessary to effectively augment the population.[7]

[USFWS] will work with partners to use this expanded delta smelt production at the FCCL to determine how a successful reintroduction program can be developed. This work will focus on production from FCCL in the near term, but [USFWS] recognizes that the expansion of the refugial population of the refugial populations and propagation of additional fish for supplementation will require a new facility. [USFWS], with support from Reclamation, has been pursuing and will continue to pursue a Delta Fish Technology Center, which could house the Delta Fish Species Conservation Hatchery discussed below to address these needs.[8]

. . .

Supplementation through the FCCL will increase the likelihood that the population of delta smelt will be sustained in the wild by achieving a robust, genetically diverse captive population.[9]

The increased production at FCCL and near-term population supplementation will help conserve diversity and increase resilience, and begin to augment the reproduction of delta smelt in the wild. Great numbers of successfully reproducing delta smelt will bolster the resilience of the population in poor recruitment years and allow the population to withstand conditions such as drought. Eventually, production and supplementation will be substantially increased through the Delta Fish Species Conservation Hatchery, providing additional benefits to delta smelt.[10]

For those of us that have studied the experience with reliance on hatcheries to try to maintain west coast salmon populations, the 2019 Biological Opinion's proposal to refocus delta smelt conservation efforts on hatchery production has an eerily familiar ring and theme. The familiar ring and theme are what can be called the "replacement assumption" – the premise that serious efforts to maintain the natural habitat that wild fisheries require to survive are not needed because the wild fish can be replaced with fish artificially propagated in hatcheries.[11]

As discussed later, in the case of west coast salmon, the scientific evidence is clear that the replacement assumption has proven faulty as the total abundance of salmon declined at the same time the propagation and release of hatchery salmon has expanded. Given this experience, fishery biologists working on west coast salmon are increasingly now rejecting the replacement assumption and calling for conservation efforts to refocus on natural habitat to restore wild salmon population.[12]

Before embarking on the proposed new hatchery-reliant conservation strategy for delta smelt laid out in the 2019 Biological Opinion, we would be wise to first more carefully study the documented failures of the previous hatchery-reliant conservation strategy for west coast salmon.

THE REPLACEMENT ASSUMPTION AND WEST COAST SALMON

As discussed in more detail in Chapter 13 of this book, in the United States many of the larger onstream dams on the west coast were built in the period from 1930 to 1970.[13] At the time these onstream dams were constructed, for both hydropower generation and water supply purposes, the proponents of such dams were aware that the structures would impede upstream and downstream migration of wild salmon runs.

At the time, the strategy to mitigate the anticipated adverse impacts of dams on salmon stocks was to construct and operate salmon hatcheries below the dams. Under this strategy, the hatcheries would release large volumes of juvenile salmon in the lower reaches of rivers and these salmon would then return to spawn in these lower reaches, thereby "replacing" the wild salmon runs lost due to the dams' blockage of traditional spawning grounds in the higher reaches of the watershed.[14]

In his 1999 book *Salmon Without Rivers: A History of the Pacific Salmon Crisis*, Jim Lichatowich (a fishery biologist with the USFWS) explains:

> Placing misguided confidence in technological solutions, salmon managers accepted the myth that controlling salmon production in hatcheries would ultimately lead to increased productivity. Despite the best of intentions, these hard-working people produced disaster because their efforts were based on false assumptions.

In *Salmon Without Rivers*, Lichatowich continues:

> Today, as proof of their success, hatchery advocates note that artificially propagated salmon make up 80 percent or more of the total number of salmon in the Columbia [River Basin], but they fail to mention that the total run has crashed to less than 5 percent of its historical abundance. Measuring success by the percentage of hatchery fish in a shrinking production base was not only scientifically invalid but also insidiously enhanced the

illusion of hatchery success. At the same time the percentage of hatchery fish increased, hatcheries were contributing to the decline of wild salmon.[15]

Lichatowich further observes:

One of the most troubling consequence of this flawed vision was that it diverted salmon managers' attention from the root cause of the salmon's decline. As a result, significant problems such as habitat destruction [] were consistently ignored. Agency budgets and staff energy were devoted to artificial propagation instead of habitat protection.[16]

The analysis and conclusions of Lichatowich have been confirmed and echoed by other studies that have assessed the effect of salmon hatcheries on wild salmon stocks and overall salmon abundancy.

For example, in 2014 the Hatchery Scientific Review Group submitted a report to the United States Congress titled *On the Science of Hatcheries: An Updated Perspective on the Role of Hatcheries in Salmon and Steelhead Management in the Pacific Northwest.*[17] The Hatchery Scientific Review Group was created as part of the Hatchery Reform Project established by the United States Congress in 2000. In its 2014 report *On the Science of Hatcheries*, the Hatcheries Scientific Review Group found:

The traditional policy of replacing wild populations with hatchery fish is not consistent with today's conservation goals, environmental values, and scientific theories. Hatcheries cannot replace lost fish habitat and the natural populations that rely on it. It is now clear that the widespread use of hatchery programs has actually contributed to the overall decline of wild populations.[18]

Similarly, in its report *The Effects of Hatchery Production on Wild Salmon and Trout*, the group Wild Fish Conservancy determined the following in terms of the survival and reproduction rates of hatchery salmon: "The domestication selection by hatchery practices derails the 'survival of the fittest' concept. Those with the greatest fitness in a captive environment produce offspring that perform the worst in the wild."[19] In its report, Wild Fish Conservancy went on to find that after more than a century of hatchery production, "management continues to rely on hatchery production to mitigate for losses of wild fish abundance and habitat" despite clear evidence that "artificial propagation contributes to declines in the survival and reproductive capacity of endangered wild fish."[20]

These studies all document the ways that the replacement assumption has failed west coast salmon. Yet, notwithstanding the failure of hatchery-reliant management for west coast salmon, the 2019 Biological Opinion now proposes hatchery-reliant management for the delta smelt.

FINDINGS OF FISHERY BIOLOGISTS AT FCCL DELTA SMELT HATCHERY

As discussed earlier, the 2019 Biological Opinion issued by the Trump Administration proposes to increase artificial propagation of delta smelt at the Fish Culture and Conservation Laboratory (FCCL), which is operated by the University of California at Davis. As set forth in the 2019 Biological Opinion, the plan is to then release the FCCL hatchery delta smelt into the wild where it is claimed these hatchery-produced fish will help supplement wild delta smelt populations.

Yet, in 2018, fishery biologists working at the FCCL published a scientific paper indicating that the release of hatchery delta smelt into the wild could adversely impact and actually reduce wild delta smelt populations. In their 2018 article titled, "A Conservation Hatchery Population of Delta Smelt Shows Evidence of Genetic Adaptation to Captivity After 9 Generations," published in the *Journal of Heredity*, these FCCL fishery biologists reported as follows:

> Selective pressures at the FCCL and in the wild differ considerably: the FCCL is a tightly controlled, predator-free environment with *ad libidum* food availability, whereas the Delta is an estuary with tidal changes in turbidity and temperature, and with larger seasonal and annual changes in temperature and salinity. Adaptation to captivity could cause rapid phenotypic and genetic divergence between wild and hatchery stocks ... hatcheries might induce epigenetic reprogramming, which may lower the fitness of hatchery-origin fish in the wild.[21]
>
> [I]t is questionable whether the release of [hatchery] fish would result in an overall benefit to the wild delta smelt population given that selection pressures between the field and hatchery differ substantially ... To date, there is no research on survival of FCCL-produced delta smelt in the wild because no fish have been released, as the release of FCCL delta smelt is not permitted.[22]

Similar concerns were identified in a 2018 article in the journal *San Francisco Estuary & Watershed Science*, titled *Considerations for the Use of Captive-Reared Delta Smelt for Species Recovery and Research*.[23] This article reported:

> Concerns have been raised about the potential risk to the wild Delta Smelt population from releasing hatchery-adapted fish that could introgress (interbreed) with the wild population. Such risks include reduced genetic diversity of the species, reduced fitness of the wild population, and/or unintentionally spreading pathogens from hatcheries.[24]

The 2018 article in the journal *San Francisco Estuary & Watershed Science* further found as follows:

> [E]ven with strong consensus on the dire status of wild Delta Smelt, experts will have significant concerns about supplementation. These concerns are primarily based on two, somewhat related issues: (1) supplementation will not be a useful action if the stressors that cause decline are not resolved, and so could lead to increased stress on the wild population; and (2) supplementation will be expensive and time-intensive, potentially reducing resources available for large-scape habitat restoration.[25]

The findings by FCCL fishery biologists, echoed in the article in *San Francisco Estuary & Watershed Science*, are difficult if not impossible to reconcile with the wishful claims in the 2019 Biological Opinion issued by the Trump Administration. The fishery biologists confirm that genetic adaptations among delta smelt raised in the FCCL may lower the survival of such hatchery fish in the wild, and that the crossing of hatchery delta smelt and wild delta smelt may reduce the overall populations of delta smelt in the wild. This 2018 article by the FCCL fishery biologists confirms that at present there is no research on how FCCL-produced delta smelt survive in the wild, because the release of such FCCL delta smelt into the wild is not now allowed (because of concerns about how the release of FCCL smelt into the wild might lead to further declines in wild delta smelt abundance).[26]

More to the point, the 2018 article by FCCL fishery biologists and the 2018 article in *San Francisco Estuary & Watershed Science* reveal that there is in fact no data or research to support the claims in the 2019 Biological Opinion that "supplementation through the FCCL will increase the likelihood that the population of delta smelt will be sustained in the wild"[27] or that "the increased production at FCCL and near-term population supplementation will help conserve diversity and increase resilience, and begin to augment the reproduction of delta smelt in the wild."[28]

Lastly, it should be noted that the 2019 Biological Opinion fails to explain why hatchery delta smelt will be able to survive in conditions that are unsuitable for wild delta smelt. The habitat analysis in the 2019 USFWS Biological Opinion admits that the current habitat conditions for wild delta smelt are so degraded that it is difficult for delta smelt to survive in such conditions. The degraded quality of such delta smelt habitat would be particularly acute in drought years, the same years that the 2019 Biological Opinion suggests that hatchery-produced delta smelt could be released into the wild to supplement declining wild stocks. But why would hatchery delta smelt produced at the FCCL fare any better than wild delta smelt once they are released into this degraded habitat? The 2019 Biological Opinion prepared by the Trump Administration offers no explanation for this disconnect.

HATCHERIES AND THE NO JEOPARDY DETERMINATION

Given the low numbers of delta smelt in the wild, there may be sound scientific reasons for the FCCL laboratory to capture and study delta smelt. The better we understand the biology of delta smelt, perhaps the better we will be able to ensure that we maintain the habitat conditions so that wild delta smelt can recover and improve.

However, as the 2018 article by the FCCL biologists makes plain, current science does not support the claim that the release of FCCL-produced delta smelt into the wild would supplement wild delta smelt stocks (in fact the science indicates such releases are likely to damage such wild stocks) and that for this reason it is unlikely that FCCL will be allowed by the USFWS to release such hatchery delta smelt into the wild.

This means that, in reality, the FCCL (and the new Delta Fish Technology Center/Delta Fish Species Conservation Hatchery proposed in the 2019 Biological Opinion) will likely continue to operate as closed captive breeding facilities. Such closed captive breeding facilities may serve as independent scientific research purpose, but they will not contribute to sustaining or restoring delta smelt populations in the wild as the 2019 Biological Opinion claims. Rather, such closed captive breeding facilities will simply be laboratories to preserve genetic specimens of a delta smelt population that was allowed to go extinct by our failing to maintain the habitat conditions the species needed to survive in the wild.

This approach to dealing with endangered species – by preserving species in laboratories rather than maintaining the habitat in which such species need to survive – is antithetical to the basic structure and purpose of the Endangered Species Act.[29] More specifically, the Endangered Species Act provides for the designation and protection of "critical habitat" to maintain and restore all listed species.[30] The focus on "critical habitat" evidences that the Endangered Species Act is concerned first and foremost with preserving species in the wild. The concept of "critical habitat" becomes nonsensical when applied to a species that only exists in a laboratory.

In sum, as we evaluate the credibility and coherence of the hatchery-dependent strategy for delta smelt conservation set forth in the 2019 Biological Opinion prepared by the Trump Administration, and whether (from a legal standpoint) there is substantial evidence to justify reliance on this strategy, there are two key considerations and questions to keep in mind.

First, if reliance on hatcheries to replace and supplement wild stocks has proven such a failure in regard to west coast salmon, why is the 2019 Biological Opinion justified in its claims that such hatcheries will be effective in replacing and supplementing wild delta smelt stocks?

Second, if the focus of the Endangered Species Act is on maintaining habitat conditions for species to survive in the wild rather than preserving specimens of species in laboratories, and if the FCCL fishery biologists are correct that there is little chance hatchery delta smelt will ever be released into the wild, then how do the hatchery-components of the 2019 Biological Opinion support the no jeopardy determination in regard to the impacts of water project operations on the delta smelt?

These issues and considerations may soon be addressed by the courts. More specifically, on December 2, 2019, the 2019 Biological Opinion was challenged in a lawsuit filed in federal district court by the Pacific Coast Federation of Fishermen's Associations, the Institute for Fisheries Resources, Golden State Salmon Association, Natural Resources Defense Council, Defenders of Wildlife and the Bay Institute.[31] The initial complaint filed in this lawsuit did not make specific reference to the hatchery components of the 2019 Biological Opinion but did allege the following:

> By increasing diversions and exports, the proposed plan will allow salt water to intrude further upstream into the Delta, infiltrating the Delta Smelt's habitat. Upstream movement of the low salinity zone is likely to constrict and further degrade the habitat of Delta Smelt, reduce survival and geographic distribution, and increase the risk of extinction.[32]
>
> . . .
>
> The Fish and Wildlife Service Biological Opinion improperly relied on uncertain mitigation measures without adequate evidence that the mitigation measures are reasonably certain to occur and will be effective to address the adverse impacts that have already been identified to ensure protection of the Delta Smelt and its critical habitat. In relying on these uncertain mitigation measures, the Fish and Wildlife Service Biological Opinion violates Section 7(a)(2) of the Endangered Species Act and is arbitrary, capricious, an abuse of discretion, and not in accordance with law, in violation of the Administrative Procedures Act, 5 U.S.C. §702(2).[33]

The "uncertain mitigation measures" challenged in the lawsuit filed by conservation/fishery groups may well include the hatchery components of the 2019 Biological Opinion. This litigation may therefore provide an opportunity for the federal courts to rule on the question of whether or not there is substantial evidence to support the Trump Administration's reliance on hatcheries to prevent the endangered delta smelt from going extinct.

As we look to the question of seawater intrusion and increased reliance on fish hatcheries outside California, the recent developments with the delta smelt reveal again the disconnect that often occurs between science and policy. That is despite the strong scientific evidence that what the delta smelt needs is increased fresh water flows to bring down salinity levels, and despite the lack of scientific evidence suggesting that hatchery-produced delta smelt will help restore dwindling wild delta smelt stocks, the government nonetheless appears set to embark on a policy that forgoes increased instream flow and habitat restoration in favor of a hatchery-reliant strategy. This scientifically unjustified outcome is the result of the powerful economic interest and political clout of those stakeholders who wish to continue the high levels of diversion and impoundment of water upstream.

This unfortunate dynamic is not limited to California. Globally, hatcheries are often looked to as the way to mitigate the effects of insufficient instream flow even though the science indicates that this hatchery mitigation strategy will fail and may in fact worsen conditions for fish species already at risk.

There may also be considerations involved that arguably go beyond economics and science, as fishery biologists Colum Brown and Rachel L. Ray noted in their 2002 article *The Future of Stock Enhancement: Lessons for Hatchery Practice from Conservation Biology*, "[R]eleasing fish in the wild knowing they are totally unprepared for survival and the majority will die, presents a considerable ethical conundrum that ought to be addressed."[34] Some final food for thought.

Notes

1. Colum Brown & Rachel L. Day, *The Future of Stock Enhancement: Lessons for Hatchery Practices from Conservation Biology* (Animal Science Repository, The Humane Society Institute for Science and Policy, 2002).

2. Abdul-Razak Mohamed & Entiser K. Hameed, *Impacts of Saltwater Intrusion on Fish Assemblage in the Middle Part of the Shatt Al-Arab River, Iraq,* Asian Journal of Applied Sciences (2019).

3. Biological Opinion – For the Reinitiation of Consultation on the Coordinated Operations of the Central Valley Project and the State Water Project (issued October 21, 2019 by the United States Fish and Wildlife Service).

4. Formal Endangered Species Act Consultation on the Coordinated Operations of the Central Valley Project and State Water Project (issued by United States Fish and Wildlife Service on December 15, 2008).

5. Formal Endangered Species Act Consultation on the Coordinated Operations of the Central Valley Project and State Water Project (issued by United States Fish and Wildlife Service on December 15, 2008); Biological Opinion – For the Reinitiation of Consultation on the Coordinated Operations of the Central Valley Project and the State Water Project (issued October 21, 2019 by the United States Fish and Wildlife Service).

6. Formal Endangered Species Act Consultation on the Coordinated Operations of the Central Valley Project and State Water Project (issued by United States Fish and Wildlife Service on December 15, 2008); Biological Opinion – For the Reinitiation of Consultation on the Coordinated Operations of the Central Valley Project and the State Water Project (issued October 21, 2019 by the United States Fish and Wildlife Service).

7. Biological Opinion – For the Reinitiation of Consultation on the Coordinated Operations of the Central Valley Project and the State Water Project (issued October 21, 2019 by the United States Fish and Wildlife Service) at 171.

8. Biological Opinion – For the Reinitiation of Consultation on the Coordinated Operations of the Central Valley Project and the State Water Project (issued October 21, 2019 by the United States Fish and Wildlife Service) at 171.

9. Biological Opinion – For the Reinitiation of Consultation on the Coordinated Operations of the Central Valley Project and the State Water Project (issued October 21, 2019 by the United States Fish and Wildlife Service) at 172.

10. Biological Opinion – For the Reinitiation of Consultation on the Coordinated Operations of the Central Valley Project and the State Water Project (issued October 21, 2019 by the United States Fish and Wildlife Service) at 212.

11. Paul Stanton Kibel, *Of Habitat and Hatcheries: Old and New Conservation Assumptions in the Pacific Salmon Treaty*, WASHINGTON JOURNAL OF ENVIRONMENTAL LAW AND POLICY (publication forthcoming in 2020).

12. Paul Stanton Kibel, *Of Habitat and Hatcheries: Old and New Conservation Assumptions in the Pacific Salmon Treaty*, WASHINGTON JOURNAL OF ENVIRONMENTAL LAW AND POLICY (publication forthcoming in 2020). [13]

13. Jim Lichatowich, SALMON WITHOUT RIVERS: A HISTORY OF THE PACIFIC SALMON CRISIS (Island Press 1999).

14. Jim Lichatowich, SALMON WITHOUT RIVERS: A HISTORY OF THE PACIFIC SALMON CRISIS (Island Press 1999). [15]
15. Jim Lichatowich, SALMON WITHOUT RIVERS: A HISTORY OF THE PACIFIC SALMON CRISIS (Island Press 1999). [15]
16. Jim Lichatowich, SALMON WITHOUT RIVERS: A HISTORY OF THE PACIFIC SALMON CRISIS (Island Press 1999). [15]
17. Hatchery Scientific Review Group, *On the Science of Hatcheries: An Updated Perspective on the Role of Hatcheries in Salmon and Steelhead Management in the Pacific Northwest* (2014 Report to the United States Congress).
18. Hatchery Scientific Review Group, *On the Science of Hatcheries: An Updated Perspective on the Role of Hatcheries in Salmon and Steelhead Management in the Pacific Northwest* (2014 Report to the United States Congress), p. 1. [22]
19. *The Effects of Hatchery Production on Wild Salmon and Trout* (Report by Wild Fish Conservancy Northwest).
20. *The Effects of Hatchery Production on Wild Salmon and Trout* (Report by Wild Fish Conservancy Northwest). [25]
21. Finger, Mahardja, Fisch, Benjamin, Lindberg, Ellison, Ghebremarian, Hung & May, *A Conservation Hatchery Population of Delta Smelt Shows Evidence of Genetic Adaptation to Captivity After 9 Generations*, 109 JOURNAL OF HEREDITY 6 (2018) pages 689–699.
22. Finger, Mahardja, Fisch, Benjamin, Lindberg, Ellison, Ghebremarian, Hung & May, *A Conservation Hatchery Population of Delta Smelt Shows Evidence of Genetic Adaptation to Captivity After 9 Generations*, 109 JOURNAL OF HEREDITY 6 (2018) pages 689–699.
23. Joanna Lessard et al., *Considerations for the Use of Captive-Reared Delta Smelt for Species Recovery and Research*, San Francisco Estuary and Watershed Science (October 2018), p. 1.
24. Joanna Lessard et al., *Considerations for the Use of Captive-Reared Delta Smelt for Species Recovery and Research*, San Francisco Estuary and Watershed Science (October 2018), p. 7.
25. Joanna Lessard et al., *Considerations for the Use of Captive-Reared Delta Smelt for Species Recovery and Research*, San Francisco Estuary and Watershed Science (October 2018), p. 3.
26. Finger, Mahardja, Fisch, Benjamin, Lindberg, Ellison, Ghebremarian, Hung & May, *A Conservation Hatchery Population of Delta Smelt Shows Evidence of Genetic Adaptation to Captivity After 9 Generations*, 109 JOURNAL OF HEREDITY 6 (2018) pages 689–699.
27. Biological Opinion – For the Preinitiation of Consultation on the Coordinated Operations of the Central Valley Project and the State Water Project (issued October 21, 2019 by the United States Fish and Wildlife Service) at 171.

28. Biological Opinion – For the Reinitiation of Consultation on the Coordinated Operations of the Central Valley Project and the State Water Project (issued October 21, 2019 by the United States Fish and Wildlife Service) at 172.

29. Critical Habit: What Is It? (United States Fish and Wildlife Service) https://www.fws.gov/endangered/esa-library/pdf/critical_habitat.pdf.

30. Critical Habit: What Is It? (United States Fish and Wildlife Service) www.fws.gov/endangered/esa-library/pdf/critical_habitat.pdf.

31. *Pacific Coast Federation of Fishermen's Associations et al.* v. *U.S. Fish and Wildlife Service et al.*, Complaint for Declaratory and Injunctive Relief (Case No. 19-7897, United States District Court for the Northern District of California, filed December 2, 2019).

32. *Pacific Coast Federation of Fishermen's Associations et al.* v. *U.S. Fish and Wildlife Service et al.*, Complaint for Declaratory and Injunctive Relief (Case No. 19-7897, United States District Court for the Northern District of California, filed December 2, 2019), p. 33.

33. *Pacific Coast Federation of Fishermen's Associations et al.* v. *U.S. Fish and Wildlife Service et al.*, Complaint for Declaratory and Injunctive Relief (Case No. 19-7897, United States District Court for the Northern District of California, filed December 2, 2019), p. 45.

34. Colum Brown & Rachel L. Day, *The Future of Stock Enhancement: Lessons for Hatchery Practices from Conservation Biology* (Animal Science Repository, The Humane Society Institute for Science and Policy, 2002).

15

Instream Rights as Indigenous Rights

SACRED SALMON

In the preceding chapters of this book, we have reviewed multiple sources of state, federal, and international law that establish a right to keep water instream. The sources of law reviewed in the preceding chapters, however, have generally not framed this right as a fundamental human right. When viewed in the context of the broader field of indigenous rights, we can discern the basis for framing the right to keep water instream as a traditional established human right.

Throughout the world, there are many indigenous cultures in which salmon is central and essential to tribal identity. For instance, in Siberia and the Russian Far East, the Itelmen ethnic group on the Kamchatka Peninsula petitioned the Governor of Kamchatka and the federal fishing agency to protect indigenous fishing rights.[1] As another example, in British Columbia in Canada, First Nations on the west coast of Vancouver Island have banded together to form the Nuuchahnulth Salmon Alliance to press the provincial and federal Canadian governments to strengthen protection of salmon stocks from logging operations that degrade spawning waters.[2]

In this chapter, we examine three case studies of how indigenous communities have attempted to use state, federal, and international law to ensure that there is adequate flowing water to sustain the salmon stocks upon which their tribal cultures depend. Two of these case studies come from the United States – from the Columbia River basin in the Pacific Northwest and from the Klamath River basin in California – and the other comes from the Saru River in Japan. In these case studies, we see both the past shortcomings of efforts to ground the right to fish and water in indigenous rights, as well as the potential of such efforts going forward.

YAKIMA FISHING RIGHTS AND CELILO FALLS ON THE COLUMBIA RIVER

Celilo Falls was located on the Oregon side of the Columbia River near the town The Dalles, east of the city of Portland. According to author Katrine Barber in her 2005 book *Death of Celilo Falls*:

> Rapid currents and exposed rocks created a navigational nightmare. The rapids' backwaters and eddies also constituted what many considered the best nine-mile stretch of fishing sites on the continent.[3]
>
> . . .
>
> When salmon migrated, fishers waited on scaffolds that hung from cliffs above the roaring water of the falls or on platforms that reached out over the river like pointed fingers. From these cantilevers, Indians lowered mobile and stationary nets deep into the water where millions of salmon forced their way up the river. The rushing current pushed the fish backward, stunning them and allowing the Indians to skillfully scoop up the fish.[4]

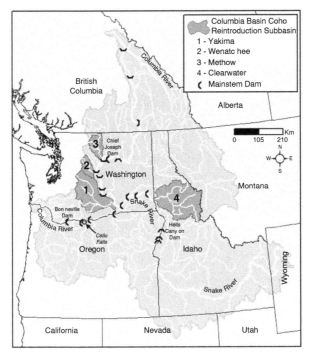

MAP 15.1 Map of Celilo Falls and the Columbia River Basin

The Native American (Indian) tribes that traditionally fished at Celilo Falls included the Yakima, Umatilla, Warm Springs, Wasco, and Wishram. For these tribes, salmon represented the essential connection between human cultures and the natural world. This connection was evidenced by the First Salmon Ceremony common among the salmon-dependent Columbia River basin tribes, when the return of spring salmon runs marked the end of winter and meals of dried foods.[5]

In 1855, the United States entered into a series of treaties with Pacific Northwest tribes, including the Yakima and the Umatilla in the Columbia River Basin. These treaties became known as the Stevens Treaties, after Isaac Stevens who negotiated them on behalf of the United States. The 1855 Stevens Treaties with the Yakima and the Umatilla provided that the tribes retained "the right of taking fish at all usual and accustomed places, in common with all citizens of the Territory."[6] The term "Territory" referred to the Oregon Territory, because in 1855, Oregon, Washington, and Idaho had not yet been admitted as new states of the United States.

Over the course of the century that followed the 1855 Stevens Treaties, the Yakima were often successful in defending their fishing rights in the courts. Often represented by the US Bureau of Indian Affairs (BIA), which acted in a trustee capacity in such litigation, the Yakima were able to preserve their treaty fishing rights against claims by non-Indian fishers in two important federal court cases.

In the first case, *Seufert Brothers Company* v. *United States* (*Seufert*), a fishing company in Oregon attempted to oust the Yakima from access to Celilo Falls on the southern shore of the Columbia River and restrict the tribe's fishing to the northern shore (Washington) of the river. In its 1919 decision in *Seufert*, the United States Supreme Court upheld the right of the Yakima to salmon fish at Celilo Falls and other spots on the Oregon side of the Columbia River, relying on the "usual and accustomed sites" language in the 1955 treaty.[7]

In the second case, *United States* v. *Earnest Cramer and E.R. Cramer* (*Cramer*), the BIA filed suit in federal district court in Portland, Oregon, on behalf of the Yakima in response to non-Indian fishermen that had constructed fishing scaffolds at Celilo Falls and other traditional Yakima fishing spots along the Columbia River. In his 1946 decision in *Cramer*, again relying on the provisions in the 1855 treaty, federal district udge, James Alger Fee, found in favor of the Yakima, granting temporary restraining orders against the Cramers prohibiting them from fishing at Celilo Falls and ordering the Cramers to remove their fishing scaffolds at that location.[8]

The Yakimas' court victories in the *Seufert* and *Cramer* cases, however, would soon be erased by the plans of the US Army Corps of Engineers to build a new The Dalles Dam on the Columbia River. The reservoir behind The Dalles Dam, to be named Lake Celilo (strangely to commemorate the spot the dam would flood and bury), would inundate Celilo Falls and cover it with slack water. Moreover, the dam itself would block the upstream passage of returning salmon to the spot where Celilo Falls had been located. The economic justifications given for The Dalles Dam were hydro-electric power, flood control, and improved river navigation. In an effort to give some recognition to the terms in the 1855 Stevens Treaties, the US Army Corps of Engineers offered the Yakima and other tribes' monetary settlements for their lost fishing rights and lost fishing income resulting from the inundation of Celilo Falls.

At the 1951 Appropriations Committee Hearing for the United States House of Representatives, Thomas Yallup (attorney for the Yakima) presented testimony emphasizing the religious importance of Celilo Falls to the tribe, explaining: "Fishing in the falls water is held to be sacred to the Indians" and who described Celilo Falls as a site where Indians caught "sacred fish" for their "customary religious practices, which have been practiced for centuries and are protected now." During the hearing, when a congressman asked Yallup if another site on the Columbia River could provide the Yakima with a substitute for Celilo Falls, Yallup responded that an alternate site "would not be a substitute to our beliefs."[9]

When the United States House of Representatives and the US Senate approved the funds to construct The Dalles Dam in 1953, the Yakima (in a final attempt to save Celilo Falls) requested that Congress consider relocating the dam thirteen miles upriver from its proposed location. In support of the relocation alternative, Thomas Yallup argued that the dam should be built "at some other place rather than destroy the place which we have held sacred."[10] The proposal for an alternative dam location, however, was never given serious consideration by the Army Corps of Engineers and Congress. The Dalles Dam was constructed in its originally proposed location and Celilo Falls was drowned by the rising waters of Lake Celilo.

As author Katrine Barber observed:

> Although the federal government defended local Indians when the states of Oregon and Washington threatened their rights, it was the federal government itself that struck the crucial blow against Native fishing in the region. Through the authorization of the dams, Congress decided that the Indians did not have a superior right to fish the Columbia when that right competed

with economic progress . . . What did it matter if Indians retained the right to fish in 'usual and accustomed' places if those places (and the fish themselves) could not survive regional progress?"[11]

In her book, Barber offers this account of the how local Native Americans experienced the following celebrations that accompanied the completion of The Dallas Dam in 1957:

> Celebrations and commemorations reveal what people consider important. As these celebrations suggest, most non-Indian people hailed The Dalles Dam as progress. The ceremonies that accompanied the various phases of construction celebrated a remade river, a "highway" upon which goods transported to and from The Dalles would be accompanied by the hum of electrical generators. In contrast, the region's Indians mourned the loss of fishing sites and a core way of life. Rosita Wellsey remembered that as a child she watched the floodwaters behind the dam inundate Celilo: "As the little islands disappeared, I could see my grandmother trembling, like something was hitting her . . . she just put out her hand and she started to cry."[12]

In the *Seufert* and *Cramer* cases, the BIA and the federal courts both stepped in to honor the federal government's trustee obligations to the Yakima and preserve the tribe's fishing rights from encroachment by third parties. When it came to federal dam building, however, the federal government was all too ready to set aside its trustee obligations to tribes for what it perceived as more paramount economic and political interests.

THE AINU HUMAN RIGHTS AND NIBUTANI DAM ON THE SARU RIVER IN JAPAN

The Saru River is located in the Hokkaido District in northern Japan. The capital of the Hokkaido District is the city of Sapporo. The Ainu ethnic people that live along and near the Saru River consider themselves ethnically and culturally distinct from the Japanese. In the area near the town of Nibutani, just south of the Saru River, a study conducted in 1995 indicated that 70 percent of residents were Ainu.[13]

In the traditional Ainu language, the word for salmon is *shiepe*, which also means staple food. Salmon is a critical source of food for the Ainu people, and a critical part of Ainu culture in terms of harvest and preparation methods and dining rituals.[14] The historical treatment of the Ainu by the Japanese has been brutal, with particular efforts by the Japanese to break the Ainu people's connection to salmon and salmon fishing.

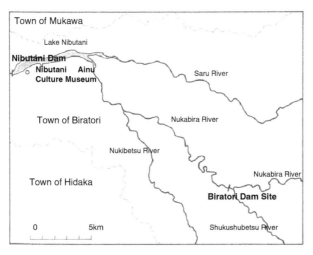

MAP 15.2 Map of the Saru River and Nibutani Dam

In a 1997 decision by the Sapporo District Court (discussed in more detail later), the following findings were made:

> In 1873 ... the use of *uray* nets (e.g. catching fish by placing stakes across a river to bar fish from travelling up except at a single open space where sets are set), one of the traditional Ainu fishing method, was prohibited for salmon fishing at the Toyohira, Hassamu, Kotani and Shinoro Rivers ... In 1878, fishing for salmon and trout was banned entirely for all rivers around Sapporo ... Thereafter, poaching salmon in the rivers of the Chitose area was prohibited. And after the traditional Ainu fishing method by *tesu* nets was prohibited, salmon and trout fishing even for personal household consumption was prohibited in 1897 ... Putting the above-recognized facts together with the overall purport of the arguments submitted, we further find as follows: Because their livelihood has been sustained principally by fishing, the above-described prohibitions of fisheries, etc. plunged the Ainu people into destitution ... To say that those policies failed to consider the Ainu people's unique dietary customs, manners and customs, language is unavoidable. And the deterioration of the Ainu people's unique manners and customs, language, etc. was a direct consequence thereof.[15]
>
> ...
>
> The fundamental characteristics of Ainu culture are focused around hunting, gathering and fishing, spending their lives together with nature. Because this culture was born from worshipping the bounty of nature together with their gods, the culture's notion of nature bonds together an area's culture with

the land cherished by that culture in a connection so extraordinarily close that it can never be severed.[16]

In 1986, the Hokkaido Development Bureau approved the construction of a Nibutani Dam on the Saru River. The proposed new dam did not provide for upstream or downstream passage of salmon, and the reservoir behind the dam (Lake Nibutani) would result in the inundation of several sacred Ainu sites including *Poromoy Chashi*, situated on a flat riverside terrace.[17] The Hokkaido Development Bureau approved Nibutani Dam without consultations with the Ainu.

In an effort to preserve salmon runs on the Saru River as well as sacred sites such as *Poromoy Chashi*, in 1993, a lawsuit was filed in Sapporo District Court against the Hokkaido Appropriations Committee by two Ainu residents – Kiazawa Tadashi and Kayano Shigeru – whose property had been confiscated to make way for Nibutani Dam and the reservoir behind it. Plaintiffs Kiazawa and Kayano relied on two main legal sources in support of their claim that the approval and construction of the dam violated the rights of the Ainu.

First, Kiazawa and Kayano alleged the approval and construction of Nibutani Dam violated Article 13 of the Japanese Constitution. Article 13 provides that "All of the people shall be respected as individuals. Their right to life, liberty and the pursuit of happiness shall, to the extent that it does not interfere with the public welfare, be the supreme consideration in legislation and in other governmental affairs."[18]

Second, Kiazawa and Kayano further alleged the approval and construction of Nibutani Dam had violated the 1966 United Nations International Covenant on Civil and Political Rights (ICCPR), which the Japanese Parliament ratified in 1979. Article 27 of the ICCPR provides "In those states in which ethnic, religious or linguistic minorities exist, persons belonging to such minorities shall not be denied the right, in community with other members of their group, to enjoy their own culture, to profess and practice their own religion, or to use their own language."[19]

Thus, unlike with the salmon-related claims of the Yakima in the United States, the Ainu claims to preserve salmon were not grounded in treaties with the national government that recognized fishing rights. Rather, the legal claims of the Ainu (in terms of the lawsuit filed by Kiazawa and Kayano) were grounded in human rights/indigenous rights law set forth in a domestic constitution and an international treaty.

In a statement submitted to the court, plaintiff Kayano Shigeru recounted his own experiences and those of his father in regard to the Saru River and salmon:

My father was detained on a charge of fishing salmon by the Japanese police when I was a little child. A Japanese rule prohibiting salmon fishing by the Ainu, who had relied upon salmon as their staple, meant death to the Ainu ... Hokkaido was inhabited by Ainu people before the Japanese invasion. Every stream and swamp, in addition to the mountains and rivers, is named using the Ainu language ... The Ainu have 15 ways of fishing salmon and more than 30 ways of cooking it. I wish the Japanese Government would let the Ainu have the right to fish salmon again.[20]

In terms of the claims under Article 13 of the Japanese Constitution, the Sapporo District Court found as follows:

Diversity exists in an unmistakable fashion as the respective differences in the particulars faced by each individual ... Premised upon this diversity and these differences, Article 13 demands meaningful, not superficial, respect for individuals and the differences between them ... If we look at these points in terms of the relationship between a dominant majority and minority who do not belong to the majority, it often happens that the majority people, being a majority, consequently tend to ignore or forget the interests of the minority ... The minority's distinct ethnic culture is an essential commodity to sustain its ethnicity without being assimilated into the majority. And thus, it must be said that for the individuals who belong to an ethnic group, the right to enjoy their distinct ethnic culture is a right that is needed for their self-survival as a person ... Accordingly, we agree that Constitution Art. 13 guarantees the plaintiffs' the right to enjoy the distinct ethnic culture of the Ainu people, which is the minority to which the plaintiffs belong.[21]

In terms of the claims under Article 27 of the ICCPR, the Sapporo District Court determined:

It is proper to understand that the ICCPR, as set out above, guarantees to individuals belonging to a minority the right to enjoy that minority's distinct culture. Together with this, there is an obligation imposed upon all contracting parties to exercise due care with regard to this guarantee when deciding upon, or executing, national policies which have the risk of adversely affecting a minority's culture, etc. Thus, the Ainu people, as a minority which has preserved the uniqueness of its culture, are guaranteed the right to enjoy their culture by ICCPR Article 27, and accordingly, it must be said that our nation has a duty to faithfully observe this guarantee ... Indeed, the rights arising under the ICCPR Art. 27 are not unlimited ... But in light of the aims of ICCPR Art. 27, any limits on the guarantee of rights must be kept to the narrowest degree necessary.[22]

Building on these interpretations of Article 13 of the Japanese Constitution and Article 27 of the ICCPR, the Sapporo District Court went on to hold as follows:

> Of course, it is conceivable that these various values may be compromised for the public interest. But in cases where such concessions are to be sought, there must also be the greatest degree of consideration that a sense of remorse concerning matters such as that described above of the historical background of the coerced deterioration of the Ainu people's unique ethnic culture caused by assimilationist policies ... Absent such remorseful consideration, what results is the thoughtless theft of nature, including land in an indigenous region that is deeply connected to a distinct ethnic culture ... Of course, there is absolutely no bar on using land originally issued pursuant to the Hokkaido Former Aboriginals Protection Act for the public interest, but here too, the greatest degree of consideration seems warranted. If such consideration is lacking, it reflects the majority's careless and selfish policymaking and our judgment finding illegality cannot be avoided.[23]
>
> ...
>
> Taking all that has been written above together, we find that the Minister of Construction, who was the authorizing agency and the agent for the enterprise authority in the instant matter, neglected the investigative and research procedures that were necessary to judge the priority of the competing interests accompanying the accomplishment of the Project Plan. He unreasonably made little of and ignored various factors and values that should have been given the highest regard ... Therefore, we conclude that the instant Project Authorization was in violation of the Land Expropriation Law Article 20(3) and that such illegality succeeded to the Confiscatory Administrative Rulings.[24]

When it came time to fashioning a remedy, however, notwithstanding that it found the approval of Nibutani Dam to be unlawful, the Sapporo District Court was unwilling to halt construction or order the dam's removal. In its ruling, the Court stated: "With the Nibutani Dam already compete and filling with water, we are forced to recognize the extraordinary harm to the public interest that would arise from reversing the Confiscatory Administrative Rulings."[25] The plaintiffs Kiazawa and Kayano, and the Ainu people, were left with a strong proclamation of illegality but were provided no injunctive relief.

As author Georgia Stevens reflected in her 2004 article titled *More than Paper: Protecting Ainu Culture and Influencing Japanese Dam Development*:

> The ultimate outcome of the case rendered the legal content of Article 27 and the constitutional protection as mere rhetoric. While the court held that the

administrative decisions to expropriate Ainu land and approve the dam project were illegal, it would not reverse the all-but-complete dam construction ... Instead the plaintiffs were denied substantive relief on the basis that considerations of 'public interest' dictated that the dam should be completed. And so the dam remains.[26]

Yet the completion of Nibutani Dam and the 1997 Sapporo District Court decision are not the end of the story. In part as a result of international media coverage of the Ainu-Nibutani Dam controversy and other indigenous-natural resource conflicts around the world, in 2007, the UN General Assembly adopted the Declaration on the Rights of Indigenous Peoples. This declaration included provisions that speak to situations where indigenous groups have deep cultural ties to fishery resources and the instream flows such that fishery resources need. Article 25 of the United Nations Declaration provides: "Indigenous peoples have the right to maintain and strengthen their distinctive spiritual relationship with their traditionally owned or otherwise occupied and used lands, territories, waters and coastal seas and other resources and to uphold their responsibilities to future generations in this regard."[27] Article 26 of the United Nations Declaration provides:

(1) Indigenous peoples have the right to the lands, territories and resources which they have traditionally owned, occupied or otherwise used or acquired. (2) Indigenous peoples have the right to own, use, develop and control the lands, territories and resources that they possess by reason of traditional ownership or other traditional occupation or use, as well as those which they have otherwise acquired. (3) States shall give legal recognition and protection to these lands, territories and resources. Such recognition shall be conducted with due respect to the customs, traditions and land tenure systems of the indigenous peoples concerned.[28]

In June 2008, a year after the United Nations General Assembly adopted the Declaration on the Right of Indigenous Peoples, the Japanese Diet officially designated the Ainu as an indigenous people of the northern part of Japan and in particular of Hokkaido. Based on this designation, the Japanese Government established a high-level panel of experts on Ainu affairs that resulted in funding for local investigations and research to document and preserve Ainu culture and language.[29] Therefore, although the Ainu were unable to stop the construction of Nibutani Dam, the litigation the Ainu brought concerning the dam set political events in motion that may help to better secure the legal status of the Ainu people.

KARUK FISHING RIGHTS AND DIVERSIONS ON STANSHAW CREEK IN CALIFORNIA

In Northern California, Stanshaw Creek is a tributary to the Klamath River and traditionally served as an important spawning ground for salmon and steelhead. However, as a result of upstream diversions by Marble Mountain Ranch, the instream flow in Stanshaw Creek was so depleted that the creek often lost its connectivity with the downstream Klamath River.

To address the impacts of these diversions, the enforcement unit of the California State Water Resources Control Board (State Water Board) brought an administrative action against Marble Mountain Ranch alleging violations of California public trust law and California reasonable use law. This enforcement action, which sought to reduce diversions to provide sufficient instream flows to sustain salmon and steelhead populations in Stanshaw Creek and restore connectivity between Stanshaw Creek and the Klamath River, culminated in several days of hearings in November 2017 before the State Water Board.

Among the parties that participated in the 2017 State Water Board hearings on the Stanshaw Creek diversions were the National Marine Fisheries Service (NMFS), the California Department of Fish and Wildlife (CDFW), the Karuk Tribe and Klamath Riverkeeper. The Karuk Tribe's reservation is located along the Klamath River (downstream of the confluence of Stanshaw Creek and the Klamath River). Klamath Riverkeeper is a nonprofit conservation organization focused on protecting and restoring the fisheries and ecosystems in the Klamath River watershed.

In addition to presenting live testimony at the 2017 State Water Board hearings, the Karuk Tribe and Klamath Riverkeeper jointly prepared and submitted a Post-Hearing Closing Brief in March 2018. The decision of the Karuk Tribe and Klamath Riverkeeper to work together to file a joint Post-Hearing Closing Brief, rather than filing separate briefs, came out of the mutual realization that there was important interplay between the indigenous claims asserted by the Karuk Tribe and the more traditional environmental claims asserted by Klamath Riverkeeper. As the respective legal counsel for the Karuk Tribe and Klamath Riverkeeper discussed this interplay following the hearings before the State Water Board, it seemed like the connections between these different claims might be more effectively laid out in a joint brief rather than in separate briefs. My understanding of these discussions comes from my direct involvement, as I served as Klamath Riverkeeper's legal counsel for the Stanshaw Creek State Water Board hearings.

To provide a sense of this interplay, it is worth quoting at length from the joint Post-Hearing Closing Brief filed by the Karuk Tribe and Klamath Riverkeeper. The brief began by describing the Karuk Tribe and its connection to Klamath River salmon that traditionally spawned in Stanshaw Creek as follows:

> With over 3,600 members, the Karuk Tribe is the second largest federally recognized Indian Tribe in California. The Klamath River is the lifeblood of the Karuk people. Salmonids, including Chinook salmon, federally-protected Coho salmon, and steelhead, are essential to the health and well-being of the Karuk Tribe. As Leaf Hillman, Director of the Karuk Department of Natural Resources and cultural leader stated: 'We consider ourselves as salmon people, as salmon has been one of our primary subsistence foods for countless generations in the place where we have our aboriginal roots, so we say from time immemorial. The importance of salmon to the Karuk people continues today, even though the resource is in decline and is nearly decimated by over 165 years of resource extraction and dams and diversions since the Klamath gold rush era.'

According to Mr. Hillman:

> 'The salmon, not only do we rely on and have relied on the past, but we continue to rely on to the extent that salmon still persist in the Basin. We continue to rely on salmon for not only our subsistence use, but also salmon have been used in our ceremonies as well as our basic identity is tied very closely to the salmon. And we consider salmon to be a very close relative of ours and therefore are obliged to take care of them much as we are obliged to take care of our relations; human relations as well as our nonhuman relations. The decline of salmon has immeasurable negative impacts on the Karuk people.'[30]

After laying out the tribal perspective on restoring Klamath River basin salmon and restoring Stanshaw Creek instream flows, the joint Post-Hearing Closing Brief then provided more detail regarding alleged violations of California public trust law and what remedy was needed to correct these violations:

> The public trust doctrine establishes that the waters and wildlife of the state belong to the people, and that the state acts as a trustee to manage and protect these resources and their associated public uses for its peoples' benefit. (*Nat'l Audubon Soc'y v. Superior Court* (1983) 33 Cal. 3d 419, 441–49; *see also* Cal. Const., art. X, § 5; Cal. Const., art. I, § 25.) The purpose of the public trust "evolve[s] in tandem with the changing public perception of the values and uses of waterways." (*Audubon*, 33 Cal.3d at 434) The public trust doctrine applies to constrain the extraction of water from navigable waters that impacts

navigation and other public interests, such as the right to fish, bathe, swim, and use for recreation.

(*Id.* at 434–37.)

Ecological values are among those values protected by the public trust. (*Id.* at 435.)

As the state agencies responsible for administering California's water resources, including allocation of recycled water, the public trust doctrine imposes on the State Board an *affirmative* duty to take the public trust into account in the planning and allocation of those resources, and to protect impacted public trust uses whenever feasible. (*Id.* at 441, 445–47.) This is a continuing duty, and includes the obligation to *reconsider* terms and conditions of past orders, decisions, or water allocations to protect public trust resources.

In terms of the particular conditions on Stanshaw Creek, and a proposed remedy to address these alleged public trust law violations, the joint Post-Hearing Closing Brief stated as follows:

The Karuk Tribe, the NMFS, CDFW, and the Regional Board agree that the Marble Mountain Ranch diversion has significant deleterious impacts on Stanshaw Creek and the salmon and steelhead that depend on it. There are no other diversions that cause the severe negative impacts on public trust beneficial uses the creek provides. Mr. Soto, biologist for the Karuk Tribe, confirmed that dewatering of Stanshaw Creek in summer months resulted in killing of juvenile Coho salmon. As a result of the Marble Mountain Ranch diversion in spring, summer and fall, Stanshaw Creek is nearly dewatered, and the cold-water pool adjacent to the Klamath River loses its ecological functionality. According to Mr. Soto, as well as fishery experts from NMFS and CDFW, the most significant problems created by the Stanshaw Creek diversion are two-fold:

First, fish are excluded from Stanshaw Creek's thermal refuge when low flows fail to connect the creek to the river. As a result, these salmon are forced to seek refuge in other locations further upstream or downstream which extends their exposure to lethally warm conditions. Second, the fish residing in the refuge pool are trapped and unable to migrate away from harmful conditions or predators. Fish require regular connectivity between the pond and the Klamath River to ensure they are able to avoid these problems, which occur at different points in time. Mr. Soto, as well as experts from NMFS and CDFW, testified that limiting the Marble Mountain Ranch diversions to ensure that 90% of the flow was permitted to bypass the diversion structure, and maintaining a minimum flow of at least 2 cfs below the diversion.

In their March 2018 joint brief, the Karuk Tribe and Klamath Riverkeeper then offered the following account of the ways that tribes' fishing rights and California public trust law dovetail and inform each other:

> Protecting public trust beneficial uses in the Klamath River Basin will protect and preserve the Karuk Tribe's culture and spiritual and physical health. The Klamath River salmon, including those that use Stanshaw Creek, are both a public trust resource and a tribal trust resource, which means the United States government has an obligation to protect these resources for the benefit of the Karuk Tribe.[31]

As of the writing of this book, the State Water Board has not yet rendered its decision in the Stanshaw Creek diversion hearing. It therefore remains to be seen whether the arguments raised in the Post-Hearing Closing Brief, about the ways tribal fishing rights can inform the interpretation and enforcement of California public trust law, will be accepted and relied upon by the State Water Board.

THE INDIGENOUS RIGHT TO FISH AND WATER

The experiences with the Yakima people at Celilo Falls, the Ainu people on the Saru River, and the Karuk people in the Klamath River basin have practical implications for efforts to establish and build the foundations of an enforceable right to keep water instream. In addition to revealing the ways that instream rights can be grounded directly in indigenous fishing rights, these experiences also suggest how the indigenous relationship to fish and water can affect the ways we understand and implement other sources of law.

For example, under environmental impact assessment laws, such as California's Environmental Quality Act (CEQA) and the federal National Environmental Policy Act (NEPA), agencies are required to consider alternatives to avoid or reduce significant adverse environmental impacts. When injury to the cultural heritage of indigenous salmon-dependent people is understood as an "environmental impact" separate and distinct from the biological impact of projects on salmon stocks, we see how the indigenous right to fish and water can factor into traditional environmental impact assessment laws. Had NEPA been in force at the time The Dalles Dam was being considered, perhaps the US Army Corps of Engineers might have been required to give more serious consideration to the Yakima proposal to relocate the dam a few miles upstream to avoid the significant adverse cultural tribal impacts that would be caused by the loss of Celilo Falls.

As another example, in Chapter 7 of this book, we explored how provisions of the Federal Power Act provide authority for the Federal Energy Regulatory Commission (FERC) to impose salmon-protection measures as part of the relicensing process for hydro-electric dams. Given that Native American fishing rights (and related Native American instream flow rights) are protected by federal law and apply to all federal agencies, FERC therefore appears to have an obligation to take proper account of these indigenous rights in decisions about whether to relicense hydro-electric dams and how such hydro-electric dams should operate. The experience with federal construction of The Dalles Dam on the Columbia River, which destroyed Celilo Falls, provides a cautionary tale from which FERC can learn.

In regard to indigenous rights recognized under international law, the experience of the Ainu people on the Saru River in Japan suggests that when the cultural heritage and sacred religious ceremonies of indigenous people are on the line, providing monetary compensation for riverside lands taken and lost fishing income may not be sufficient. To provide meaningful protection of such indigenous rights to fish and water, international law may need to be interpreted or amended to provide for a right to injunctive relief to preserve the underlying resources from destruction.

As a final illustration, in Chapter 1 of this book, we discussed salmon's status as a "public trust" resource and noncommercial fishing's status as a "public trust" use, and examined how California public trust law can be deployed to better protect salmon and noncommercial salmon fishing. The experience of the Karuk Tribe's efforts to reduce diversions on California's Stanshaw Creek reveal the ways that indigenous rights to fish and water can overlay and inform public trust law. That is, when the public trust resources and public trust uses involved also happen to be indigenous resources and uses, then perhaps such public trust resources and uses are properly entitled to a heightened level of protection under public trust law.

Perhaps the greatest value of framing instream rights as indigenous rights is that it puts a distinctly human face on the need for adequate instream flows. It reminds us that such instream flows are not just about preserving fish stocks and ecosystems. At times they are also about preserving cultures and civilizations.

Notes

1. David Quammen, *Where the Salmon Rule*, NATIONAL GEOGRAPHIC (August 2009).

2. Judith Lavoie, *Bringing Back the Trees to Bring Back the Salmon*, THE NARWHAL (March 14, 2019); Megan Thomas, *Old-Growth Logging Threatens Culture, Says Nuu-chah-nulth Tribal Council*, CBC NEWS (November 10, 2018).
3. Katrine Barber, DEATH OF CELILO FALLS (University of Washington Press, 2005) p. 19.
4. Katrine Barber, DEATH OF CELILO FALLS (University of Washington Press, 2005) p. 23.
5. Katrine Barber, DEATH OF CELILO FALLS (University of Washington Press, 2005) pp. 24, 38.
6. Katrine Barber, DEATH OF CELILO FALLS (University of Washington Press, 2005) p. 51.
7. *Seufert Brothers Company* v. *United States*, 249 U.S. 194 (1919).
8. *United States* v. *Ernest Cramer and E.R. Cramer*, in United States District Court of Oregon at Portland, Civil and Criminal Case files, 1922–1947, National Archives – Pacific Northwest Region.
9. Katrine Barber, DEATH OF CELILO FALLS (University of Washington Press, 2005) p. 83.
10. Katrine Barber, DEATH OF CELILO FALLS (University of Washington Press, 2005) p. 89.
11. Katrine Barber, DEATH OF CELILO FALLS (University of Washington Press, 2005) p. 63.
12. Katrine Barber, DEATH OF CELILO FALLS (University of Washington Press, 2005) pp. 5–6.
13. *Kayano et al.* v. *Hokkaido Expropriation Committee*: The Nibutani Dam Decision (translated by Mark A. Levin, available in Volume 38 of INTERNATIONAL LEGAL MATERIALS) pp. 17–18.
14. *Kayano et al.* v. *Hokkaido Expropriation Committee*: The Nibutani Dam Decision (translated by Mark A. Levin, available in Volume 38 of INTERNATIONAL LEGAL MATERIALS) p. 19.
15. *Kayano et al.* v. *Hokkaido Expropriation Committee*: The Nibutani Dam Decision (translated by Mark A. Levin, available in Volume 38 of INTERNATIONAL LEGAL MATERIALS) pp. 27–28.
16. *Kayano et al.* v. *Hokkaido Expropriation Committee*: The Nibutani Dam Decision (translated by Mark A. Levin, available in Volume 38 of INTERNATIONAL LEGAL MATERIALS) p. 34.
17. *Kayano et al.* v. *Hokkaido Expropriation Committee*: The Nibutani Dam Decision (translated by Mark A. Levin, available in Volume 38 of INTERNATIONAL LEGAL MATERIALS) p. 20.
18. Japanese Constitution, Article 13.
19. Article 27 of International Covenant on Civil and Political Rights (Adopted by the General Assembly of the United Nations on December 19, 1966).

20. Hiroshi Maruyama, *Ainu Landowners' Struggle for Justice and the Illegitimacy of the Nibutani Dam Project in Hokkaido Japan*, INTERNATIONAL COMMUNITY LAW REVIEW (2012) p. 71.

21. *Kayano et al.* v. *Hokkaido Expropriation Committee*: The Nibutani Dam Decision (translated by Mark A. Levin, available in Volume 38 of INTERNATIONAL LEGAL MATERIALS) pp. 27–28.

22. *Kayano et al.* v. *Hokkaido Expropriation Committee*: The Nibutani Dam Decision (translated by Mark A. Levin, available in Volume 38 of INTERNATIONAL LEGAL MATERIALS) p. 27.

23. *Kayano et al.* v. *Hokkaido Expropriation Committee*: The Nibutani Dam Decision (translated by Mark A. Levin, available in Volume 38 of INTERNATIONAL LEGAL MATERIALS) p. 36.

24. *Kayano et al.* v. *Hokkaido Expropriation Committee*: The Nibutani Dam Decision (translated by Mark A. Levin, available in Volume 38 of INTERNATIONAL LEGAL MATERIALS) p. 38.

25. *Kayano et al.* v. *Hokkaido Expropriation Committee*: The Nibutani Dam Decision (translated by Mark A. Levin, available in Volume 38 of INTERNATIONAL LEGAL MATERIALS) p. 38.

26. Georgia Stevens, *More Than Paper: Protecting Ainu Culture and Influencing Japanese Dam Development*, CULTURAL SURVIVAL (December 2004).

27. Article 25, Declaration on the Rights of Indigenous Peoples (Resolution Adopted by the General Assembly of the United Nations on December 13, 2007).

28. Article 26, Declaration on the Rights of Indigenous Peoples (Resolution Adopted by the General Assembly of the United Nations on December 13, 2007).

29. Hiroshi Maruyama, *Ainu Landowners' Struggle for Justice and the Illegitimacy of the Nibutani Dam Project in Hokkaido Japan*, International Community Law Review (2012) p. 63.

30. Karuk Tribe and Klamath Riverkeeper, *March 2018 Joint Post-Hearing Closing Brief* (Douglas and Heidi Cole and Marble Mountain Ranch – Waste and Unreasonable Use Hearing, California State Water Resources Control Board).

31. Karuk Tribe and Klamath Riverkeeper, *March 2018 Joint Post-Hearing Closing Brief* (Douglas and Heidi Cole and Marble Mountain Ranch – Waste and Unreasonable Use Hearing, California State Water Resources Control Board).

Conclusion

Policy Disconnected from Science

In Chapter 13 on *Instream Rights and Pacific Salmon*, we saw how lingering adherence to the "replacement assumption" has resulted in a reoccurring tendency of the Pacific Salmon Commission to issue inaccurate abundance forecasts. That is, notwithstanding the scientific consensus that salmon hatcheries are contributing to the decline of salmon stocks, the Pacific Salmon Commission has continued to look to the volume of hatchery releases as a predictor of salmon abundance. And in Chapter 14, on *Instream Rights and Fish Hatcheries*, we saw how there are now proposals to apply the "replacement assumption" to delta smelt stocks despite scientific consensus that supplementation with hatchery fish is likely to damage rather than restore wild delta smelt stocks.

The reasons for this disconnect in abundance forecasting with salmon can most likely be explained by the influence of those whose economic self-interest is most at risk by acknowledging the replacement assumption is incorrect – those who rely on hydropower and diverted water from the onstream dams located upriver of the salmon hatcheries, and those employed by the salmon hatcheries. An admission that the restoration of salmon stocks requires more fish passage and instream flows, rather than more hatcheries, would challenge existing policies regarding dams, high levels of out-of-stream diversions, and hatchery operations. So those resisting this challenge call for more study before any policy changes are made. And the policy status quo staggers forward, increasingly detached from established science.

The same goes for delta smelt. The proposal to focus on delta smelt hatchery production rather than habitat restoration enables current or expanded levels of out-of-stream diversion of water, notwithstanding the science showing this hatchery strategy is almost certain to fail. And again, the policy status quo staggers forward and the gap between policy and science widens.

Unfortunately, the examples of salmon hatcheries impact on salmon abundance, and the proposals to expand delta smelt hatcheries are not isolated situations where policy is disconnected from science. This dynamic scenario is

pervasive throughout the water policy sector. Consider the following additional examples, all drawn from the chapters of this book.

In Chapter 2, on *Instream Rights and Unreasonable Use*, we examined the
high rates of evapotranspiration for irrigation water applied in the summer and
early fall in California's San Joaquin Valley. Such evapotranspired water is
of no benefit to the crops being irrigated, and such evapotranspired water is
permanently lost to the local basin, because it neither percolates down into the
groundwater nor flows back into local surface waters. The waste and unreasonable use associated with such high levels of evapotranspiration is well
documented, and the needed policy changes that flow from this recognition
are clear enough – to enact regulatory programs that discourage or prohibit
irrigation in places and in a manner that permits such high levels of evapotranspiration. Yet this has not happened. The policy status quo continues to
tolerate and facilitate high levels of evapotranspiration by agricultural irrigators in San Joaquin Valley.

As another illustration, in Chapter 4, on *Instream Rights and Watershed
Governance*, we confronted the hydrologic reality that the only way to secure
adequate instream flow in the mainstems of larger rivers is to also secure
adequate instream flow from the tributaries that feed into the mainstems of
such larger rivers. This is not a theory in dispute, it is basic watershed science.
Yet, despite the fact there is broad scientific consensus that additional instream
flows from California's San Joaquin River into the Bay Delta are needed to
restore endangered fisheries, there remains strong resistance to establishing
instream flow requirements for the San Joaquin River's three main tributaries –
the Merced River, the Tuolumne River, and the Stanislaus River. Efforts by
well-financed agribusiness interests are hard at work pressing their claims in
court and before agencies and the legislatures that the link between instream
flows and fisheries is still yet to be established or (in the alternative) that before
imposing instream flow requirements on the San Joaquin River's tributaries
we should first study and explore whether there might be other ways to
increase the San Joaquin River's inflow into the Bay Delta.

And then in Chapter 6 on *Instream Rights as Water Temperatures Rise* and
Chapter 7 on *Instream Rights as Sea Levels Rise*, we were faced with two
aspects of climate change's impact on fisheries. The first climate change
impact is that as air temperatures rise so will instream water temperatures.
The second climate change impact is that as sea levels rise seawater will push
further into coastal estuaries and drive up salinity levels in coastal rivers.
Neither of these impacts is subject to credible scientific debate at this point,
and the policy changes needed to respond to how these impacts will affect
fisheries have been identified – more passage to allow fish to reach higher-

elevation spawning grounds, less out-of-stream diversions and more releases from upriver dams, and more instream freshwater flows to push the seawater back. Yet, we see that so far there has been little progress on implementing these policy changes. It is easier to simply downplay the science and continue with the status quo by ignoring instream temperatures and salinity levels that are rising.

As we think about how to overcome this tendency for policy to remain disconnected from science in the water policy sector, three strategies come to mind.

The first strategy is to consider whether it is fair or politically feasible that particular stakeholders bear the lion's share of the economic loss associated with the policy changes that flow from the science. We may need to remove certain dams or install improved fish passage on existing dams to restore declining salmon stocks, but does this necessarily mean that dam operators or those reliant on the hydropower and water from dams should shoulder all of the costs associated with this change? If we want to improve water efficiency and water conservation in the agricultural sector, should the public assist farmers with financial support to help upgrade irrigation systems rather than requiring farmers to bears all of these costs? If there are broader societal and environmental benefits resulting from these changes, then might it be appropriate for the public to share in absorbing some of these costs and in helping those stakeholders acutely reliant on the status quo to transition to a new paradigm? By reducing the acute and severe ways certain stakeholders are likely to be economically impacted by acknowledging good science, we might lessen their resistance to such good science. Therefore, it is not simply a question of fairness; it is a question of what may be politically feasible.

Consider the recent experience with dam removal efforts on the Klamath River, which flows through Southern Oregon and Northern California. There are four dams on the Klamath River – Iron Gate Dam, Copco 1 Dam, Copco 2 Dam, and J.C. Boyle Dam – that were constructed in the early 1900s without any passage for salmon. The removal of these four dams would open up hundreds of miles of prime spawning habitat for salmon, habitat at cooler higher elevations that may enable salmon to better adapt to climate change.[1] In the context of the relicensing proceedings before the Federal Energy Regulatory Commission (FERC), tribal and conservation groups initially proposed that the agency order the dam's owner, Pacific Corporation, to decommission and remove the dams, with this decommissioning and removal to be paid for entirely by Pacific Corporation.

The 2010 settlement that ultimately emerged, however, provided for cost-sharing by the dam operator, state government, and the ratepayers for the electricity provided by the dams. The total estimated costs for removal of the four dams came to around $400 million.[2] Pacific Corporation agreed to provide approximately $200 million toward the removal and decommissioning costs, but this was a cap, with California (through funds made available through a state water bond) agreeing to cover excess costs. Under the settlement, the states of California and Oregon also allowed Pacific Corporation to seek adjustments in electrical utility rates, to recoup some of the costs of removal and decommissioning from ratepayers.[3] With this cost-sharing framework in place, Pacific Corporation agreed to voluntarily surrender its FERC licenses and abandon efforts to relicense its four Klamath River dams.

Although most conservation groups and tribes were pleased with the end result of the settlement, the four dams on the Klamath River were coming down; the cost-sharing elements of the settlement were controversial. Some groups believed that it was inappropriate to allow Pacific Corporation's shareholders to shift much of the costs associated with the dam removal to taxpayers and utility ratepayers. Yet, if all of the costs of removal had fallen on Pacific Corporation's shareholders, it is uncertain whether the company would have voluntarily agreed to removal, and the company might have pressed for FERC to relicense its Klamath River dams. The controversial cost-sharing elements are what lessened Pacific Corporation's opposition to dam removal, and made it possible for the company to justify the decision to abandon FERC relicensing to its shareholders. It is also true that there was a broad and diverse constituency that might benefit from removal of the dams, including commercial and sport fishermen and including tribes that were culturally and economically dependent on salmon. Under these circumstances, there is a credible argument that cost-sharing was not only the most feasible option for dam removal but perhaps a relatively fair option as well.

Does the Klamath River dam removal cost-sharing model work in all situations? No, it does not. But what this cost-sharing model suggests is that, when it comes to steps needed to improve how we manage water resources to improve instream flow, sometimes there may be a more feasible middle course between (on the one extreme) insisting that the current beneficiaries of the status quo pay for *all* the costs to achieve this objective and (on the other extreme) shielding current beneficiaries of the status quo from *any* of these costs to achieve this objective. The cost-sharing approach, in some but not all situations, can help shift the conversation from whether to make the changes to better align policy with science to what is an equitable and feasible way to pay for making these changes.

The second strategy is to develop regulatory programs that are better able to isolate the underlying science from political pressures. An example of this might be the public trust Bay Delta flow criteria developed by California's State Water Board, discussed in Chapter 1 on *Instream Rights and the Public Trust*. In Chapter 1, we saw how California adopted legislation to decouple the first phase and the second phase of its public trust methodology. Although the second phase of this methodology inherently involves political and economic balancing, the first phase of this methodology (which considers what actions are needed to fully protect public resources and uses) is essentially a scientific inquiry. The government's formal and clear embrace of scientific findings makes it more difficult to ignore such findings when it comes to policy making.

Another example of this is the provisions of California's Sustainable Groundwater Management Act (SGMA) that focus on the effects of groundwater pumping on interconnected surface waters. As detailed in Chapter 8, on *Instream Rights and Groundwater Extraction*, SGMA requires the development of hydrologic models and water budgets that account for the interactions between groundwater pumping and surface instream flows, and also requires the development of quantitative thresholds and monitoring to prevent such pumping from adversely affecting fish species dependent on such surface water flows. These SGMA provisions represent an effort to establish a more credible and robust scientific foundation for water policy.

The third strategy brings us back full circle to where this book began, with the discussion in the introduction of the public right to keep water instream. The clearer the recognition of a public right to keep water stream – a public right that acts as an enforceable source of law to counter private claims to divert water out of stream or impound water behind dams – the more regulatory agencies and courts and legislatures will be compelled to bridge the gaps that exist between science and policy. Because so long as we lack laws and policies that reflect the scientific evidence of what instream flows are needed to maintain river ecosystems, fisheries and water quality, the public's right to keep water instream will remain a legal theory rather than the law itself. In this sense, science and the law will either succeed together, or fail together.

Notes

1. Tara Lohan, *Here's How the Largest Dam Removal Project in the U.S. Would Work*, KQED Environment (July 20, 2018).
2. Tara Lohan, *Here's How the Largest Dam Removal Project in the U.S. Would Work*, KQED Environment (July 20, 2018).
3. 2010 Klamath Hydroelectric Settlement Agreement.

About the Author

Paul Stanton Kibel is Professor at Golden Gate University (GGU), School of Law in San Francisco, California, where he teaches *Water Law*, directs the GGU Center on Urban Environmental Law (CUEL) and serves as Faculty Editor for the GGU ENVIRONMENTAL LAW JOURNAL. He has also taught *Water Law* at the University of California–Berkeley Boalt Hall School of Law and *Water Policy in the West* at the Goldman School of Public Policy at the University of California–Berkeley. Kibel holds an LLM from the University of California–Berkeley Boalt Hall School of Law and a BA from Colgate University in New York. He is also natural resource counsel to the Water and Power Law Group. Kibel previously published two books, *The Earth on Trial: Environmental Law on the International Stage* (Routledge) and *Rivertown: Rethinking Urban Rivers* (MIT Press), and his articles have appeared in such journals as the STANFORD ENVIRONMENTAL LAW JOURNAL, GEORGETOWN INTERNATIONAL ENVIRONMENTAL LAW REVIEW, COLUMBIA JOURNAL OF TRANSNATIONAL LAW, BERKELEY JOURNAL OF INTERNATIONAL LAW, ECOLOGY LAW QUARTERLY, NYU ENVIRONMENTAL LAW JOURNAL, VIRGINIA ENVIRONMENTAL LAW JOURNAL, UCLA JOURNAL OF INTERNATIONAL LAW & FOREIGN AFFAIRS, and the WILLIAM AND MARY ENVIRONMENTAL LAW & POLICY REVIEW.

Index

CPSIA information can be obtained
at www.ICGtesting.com
Printed in the USA
LVHW050431130122
708310LV00021B/2800